KING ARTHUR: KING OF KINGS

ABOUT THE BOOK

Markale has written the definitive work on King Arthur. By means of masterly historical, geographical and literary deduction he recreates the real three-dimensional King Arthur, the Celtic warrior-hero who organized the resistance to the Saxon onslaught in fifth-century England. His unsurpassed knowledge of Celtic history has enabled him to reconstruct precisely for us the world in which King Arthur lived, its heroes and its values and to define the place which Arthur occupied in such a world.

In the Arthurian legends which subsequently rose around his person, he and the Round Table represent all our ideals of knightly virtue, chivalry and Christianity. These Arthurian ideals are at the very heart of Western literature and thought, its inspiration and lodestar. They continue to exert a unique formative power on our personal and moral concepts.

Markale demonstrates that these powerful values and ideals belong to the Celtic heritage. The values implicit in the Round Table, where all men are equal and justice is flexible and benign, where individual reason prevails over institutional and political fanaticism—these were the values with which the Celtic world opposed Imperial Rome. They belong to the world which produced King Arthur and which he championed.

ABOUT THE AUTHOR

Jean Markale is the greatest living authority on the Celtic past. He is Professor of Celtic History at the Sorbonne in Paris. His studies of Celtic law, religion, literature and society are recognized as the definitive works in their field. His *Women of the Celts* published by Gordon & Cremonesi won universal esteem as a classic study of Celtic society.

KING ARTHUR:
KING OF KINGS

Jean Markale

Translated by Christine Hauch

GORDON & CREMONESI

© Payot, Paris 1976
© Translation Gordon Cremonesi Ltd 1977

First published as *Le Roi Arthur et La Société Celtique*
by Payot, Paris 1976.

Designed by Heather Gordon

Set in 10 on 11pt Baskerville
by Preface Ltd., Salisbury, Wilts.
and printed in Great Britain
by The Anchor Press Ltd, Tiptree, Essex

British Library / Library of Congress
Cataloguing in Publication Data
Markale, Jean
King Arthur, King of Kings
1. Arthur, King
I. Title   II. Hauch, Christine
398 .352   PN57.A6   77-30054

ISBN   0-86033-044-3

Gordon & Cremonesi Publishers
London and New York
New River House
34 Seymour Road
London N8 0BE

Dedication to KING ARTHUR

Etre an heol hag ar glao,
D'ar mare ma ren ar seiz burzud . . .

Between the sunshine and the rain,
In the royal days of the seven wonders . . .

Per-Jakez HELIAS

Contents

INTRODUCTION: Epic and History   9

PART I. King Arthur in the Medieval World

1. Arthurian Literature   23
2. The Political Background   48
   The Plantagenets   49
   John of Salisbury   54
   Glastonbury Abbey   64
   Arthurian Chivalry   70

PART II. King Arthur in the Celtic World

3. Britain in the Dark Ages   77
   Roman Britain   78
   Celtic Britain   80
   The New Kings of Britain   90
4. King Arthur in History   97
5. The Arthurian Myth   111
   The Political Aspect   113
   The Theme of Sovereignty   121
   The Unfaithful Queen   129
   Arthur's Companions   133
   Similar Legends   137
   Arthur the God   144

6. The Early Saga of Arthur   148

Part III. Waiting for Arthur

7. The Specific Qualities of the Celts   177
    Roman Society and Celtic Society   178
    The Contribution of the Celts   193
8. Arthur's Legacy   202

Notes   221
Select Bibliography   232
Index   234

Epic and History

OW that science is no longer encumbered by the restrictive shackles of theology, it has become general practice to pour scorn on any form of historical writing thought to have pre-dated scientific method. Just as alchemy and astrology tend to be regarded as the muddle-headed precursors of chemistry and astronomy, so the myths and epics of world civilizations are dismissed as less important than documented evidence. We have become so conditioned into thinking history a more valuable discipline than the study of epic that we even laud the serious approach of particular modern historians over the laughable credulity of those whom linguistic hairsplitting terms historiographers or collectors of stories.

This belief in the superiority of history is not merely a false one; it is also, in the last analysis, not strictly scientific. Modern historians rely on an endless number of unverifiable traditions, truisms and scraps of evidence which, taken on their own, are no more than subjective interpretations of some moment in the past. The image of Louis the Pious administering justice under an oak tree at Vincennes, for example, necessarily excludes any reference to the genocide he committed in Southern France. Similarly, the portrayal of Louis XIV as the Sun King, a symbol of French greatness against the sumptuous backdrop of Versailles, wilfully overlooks the way in which he rejected Colbert's brilliant economic policies for the lavish ideas of Louvais. The resulting burden of taxation upon his people to produce funds which were immediately squandered is well documented by Saint-Simon. But Saint-Simon is considered too biased to be a real historian. He is merely a writer of memoirs; though why prejudice, disloyalty and court gossip should be any further from historical truth than the intellectual masturbation of academic nitpickers, it is hard to tell.

The concept of objectivity which underlies the division between historian and historiographer is an undemonstrable one. Objectivity has nothing to do with the pursuit of pure intellect. It is simply a device used to sway men's minds towards specific ideologies or to promote the delusion that language makes things unchangeable. But words are subject to infinite nuances of meaning and interpretation which make any verbal utterance both ephemeral and subjective. Language can be unchangeable in its form of expression, but then only in some dead idiom which has ceased to evolve. The Fathers of the Church realized this when they chose Latin as a vehicle for perpetuating their form of the truth, although the need to translate the Vulgate for people who could not understand it raised the old problem of objectivity again. So, practically speaking, objectivity is impossible to achieve. When we feel the need to recount something, we are bound to express our own view of it, to elaborate or, almost unconsciously, to omit details which for all their importance we consider trivial or irrelevant.

Even an exact science like mathematics depends ultimately on the man who makes the formulae and who is subject to the same vagaries of interpretation as the historian. The totally objective computer is useless without the programming and input of ordinary mortals. Science has no greater, real claim to an objective understanding of man and the world around him than any other discipline. We are all eternal subjects stumbling across eternal objects. Our understanding of the outside world comes both from our subjective perception of things and from their objective effect on us. The only way we could hope to achieve a balance between them would be by shutting off the outside world entirely and then we might just as well not exist at all.

If it is impossible to achieve total objectivity, then we have to look at history and its relations with other human sciences in a much wider perspective than is generally accepted. There must be no attempts to stress the importance of historical science over and above that of the oral tradition or to neglect sources of information which are all too readily classified as useless or fictitious.

For once we accept history as a scientific discipline, we come face to face with a glaring paradox. The scientific historian has no sense of evolution, but confines himself to seeking out the causes of events according to deductive principles which enable separate facts to be linked together, and then tries to formulate laws to be compulsorily applied to his body of knowledge, however relative they may be. The basis of true science, however, is the scientific fact which can be observed, recreated under similar conditions and subjected to experiment; while historical fact, although observable, cannot be subjected to experiment or recreated totally as it was. "History repeating itself" refers to analogous situations, not identical ones. In any case, the human factor in this human science is too unpredictable, too open to the flights of free will to be discounted. The methods employed by modern historians would be better described as para-scientific, since the kinds of evidence on which they rely belong only in appearance to the world of science.

Only the doctrine of dialectical materialism has offered any coherent method of resolving the internal contradictions inherent in historical science. Marxism rejects any claim to objectivity as one of the oppressive fetishes of the human mind and, put at its simplest, attempts to by-pass the internal contradictions of history and make it the approachable story of human evolution in which reality shifts from one moment to the next. This explains why Marxist historians are frequently accused of bias and opportunism, although their critics reveal their own prejudices in their accusations. And their criticism takes no account of the fundamental reality that history cannot be comprehensible unless it speaks the language of its audience. Language, being as fluid as the thought it expresses, must be transitory, relative and circumstantial in form. The same argument applies to all cultural manifestations, as the various rebirths of non-written, popular tradition in ever changing social contexts makes only too clear.[1]

Indeed, recent research in the field of linguistics has led to increasing acceptance of the view of history as a living thing which reacts to external stimuli according to predeterminable laws in the same way as language does. The history of events which restores the past and present to us in literary form is apparently giving way to a structuralist history far more concerned with statistics and with the relations between the basic facts. If the structuralist approach succeeds where the history of events has failed, we may well be on our way to a much better understanding of the evolution of mankind and to more accurate projections about it.

The one major drawback of structural history is that it tends towards abstraction of a specialist kind, and in so doing loses touch with the concrete facts of life which give any historical research its value. Besides, history is powerless to predict the future. Even the most advanced mathematical methods will never give it that scientific certainty which many people consider so desirable. For, unless the technicians of our new seminaries of the intellect decide to create a new world in which some huge robot masterminds our every activity, we shall always retain our fundamental freedom to alter the course of history.

Meanwhile, by trying too hard to be objective, scientific and truthful, we are allowing the real to escape us.[2] There is now a widespread confusion between what is true and what is real, resulting from the ever widening gap between man and nature. The real is what exists. The truth is our judgment about what exists. But truth varies according to circumstances and the immediate criteria which form the basis of any particular civilization. So, to lay claim to the truth is merely to suspend judgment almost arbitrarily at a specific moment in the shifting of human thought, ignoring the fact that the real is by its very nature beyond judgment. Marxist method requires history to be neither true nor false, but to get as close as possible to the real in all its complexity. The historical process is then a natural one in which man can emerge from his struggle against the contradictions and crises of life a more forceful and conscious being. And it is up to the historian to reveal the man-made world as clearly as possible, leaving questions of truth and falsehood aside. Only by examining the way mankind has acted upon its environment can history hope to grasp the reality of human development.

Another drawback of the structuralist method, however scrupulous its deductive process may be, lies in its tendency to fragment reality. History then becomes a series of marginal comments which are increasingly difficult to weld together into a synchronous whole; whereas our observation of the phases of movement or of the facets of a single object tells us that nothing in reality is isolated. Marxist method, on the other hand, reasons by synthesis. Facts and ideas are analysed in isolation and then drawn together in the hope of discovering relationships between them. The Marxist historian thereby attempts to follow the underlying progression of human development and to resolve the inherent contradictions of the synthetical process. His ultimate aim is to attain some reality or some thought which is at the same time more comprehensive and more complex in its uniqueness.

Man finds it hard to view himself and his environment *in toto*. Since the only way he can begin to understand the delicate mechanics of reality is by breaking it down into its constituent parts, he is often faced with a mass of mutually exclusive contradictions. Manicheism and, through its Manicheism, Christianity solved the problem in a practical manner by dividing the world into for and against, day and night, good and evil. The concepts of truth and falsehood, the real and the imaginary came from the same source. This kind of polarization, however attractive an answer it may have seemed to the apparently infinite progress of thought, is unacceptable now, except perhaps to the mentally retarded inheritors of Greek thinking. It has been said, with some justification, that philosophy died with Socrates and was born again with Descartes. We can see inklings of this in the paralysing syllogistic reasoning practised in the intervening years. And since history is bound up with the systems of thought which form it, we could equally well say that history died with Herodotus and was born again with Michelet, the first man to approach the tales of the past scientifically.

Yet pre-Socratic philosophy had opened the way to a conception of history as a continual evolution, ever shaken by the fluctuations of its internal movement. Even Pascal, who was very much a thinker in the Greek tradition, abandoned what he considered the futile seeking after truth for the pursuit of sanctity. And as sanctity, for Pascal, represented all that was most real in himself, we might conclude that he was the first thinker to stress the search for the real over and above the search for the true.

The elliptical course he followed through the *Pensées* reflects the tentative intellectual gropings of mankind across the quagmire of contradictions, transitions and superficial differences with which reality presents us, towards some awareness of the underlying motion of progress. The same human difficulties can be seen in the peripatetic course of history and in the wanderings and the constant warfare undertaken by the warrior heroes of the Celtic Arthurian epic.

There are two possible means of dealing with these contradictions, whatever their symbolic form. We can reject them all as failures on the part of the human mind to grasp some eternal and unchanging truth. But this Manichean solution tends to deny the actual conditions in which man strives after knowledge, since the search for objectivity in the form of pure truth is ultimately concerned to shut off the outside world.

Alternatively we can adopt the dialectical approach. While accepting that the human mind is seeking after the truth which lies beyond all its apparent contradictions, we have also to accept that these very contradictions are themselves facets of reality with an objective significance of their own. Man need no longer look for objectivity in himself, but can concentrate on his subjective search for the real considering each contradictory aspect in turn before reintegrating it into the whole picture.

I have already established elsewhere[3] that those systems of thought which escaped the influence of Greece reasoned in this dialectical way, though we can hardly label the Welsh and Irish authors of Celtic epic as Marxists. But, at a time when history and epic were fused together, the so-called barbarian thinkers did recognise the futility of seeking after the truth and neglecting reality. One of the best known Celtic legends concerns the crossing of a river, a metaphor for the way men's minds move from one aspect of reality to its opposite, from one river bank to the other, in order to encompass the whole. The links between the various aspects are there to be seen: the river continues to flow. But the current sweeps the water away bringing fresh manifestations of reality continually before men's eyes. And the thoughts of the observers themselves are constantly changing. Reality lies in this all-embracing complexity of movement. The basic principle of the dialectic method is, therefore, the belief that the reality attained by a process of analysis and synthesis is always reality in movement.

History, or what we understand by history, is the archetype of reality in movement. Its complexity is evident in the way historians use the allied disciplines of sociology, ethnology, anthropology, geography, mathematics, linguistics and archaeology. But there is one drawback in bringing all these specialist fields to bear on historical study, and that is the possibility that history will become so much more comprehensive in its scope, that the examination of human evolution at a specific point in time ceases to be the historian's primary objective.

In his book *Structural Anthropology*, Claude Levi-Strauss compares history and ethnography, and he comes to the conclusion that "both study societies which are other than the one we live in." Then, having asked "To what end are these two disciplines working?" he again asks "Can it be an exact reconstruction of what has happened or is happening in the society under examination?" This, however, "would be to forget that in both cases, we are dealing with systems of representation which differ for each member of the group and which, taken as a whole, differ from the representation of the researcher. The best ethnographic study will never turn the reader into a native. The French Revolution of 1789 experienced by an aristocrat is not the same phenomenon as the French Revolution of 1789 experienced by a sans-culotte, and neither would coincide with the French Revolution of 1789 seen by a Michelet or a Taine." These comments perfectly encapsulate the impossibility of making truth the aim of history. The experiences of the aristocrat and the sans-culotte, the ideas of Michelet are all subjective facets of the same reality and cannot be discussed in terms of truth or falsehood. The concrete, changing experience of reality is far removed from the intellectuals' fanatical abstractions from life. Levi-Strauss continues, "All we can hope for from the historian and the ethnographer is that they succeed in widening some particular experience which them becomes accessible *as an experience* to men of other countries or other eras."

But there is one field of study which historians obstinately refuse to recognize as a science, and therefore disdain to use. This we shall call the study of myth. The more generally used word mythology implies a containment of the inherent nature of myth within the *logos* or word. And while it is the word which gives a myth permanence, it also forces the speaker to use a coded language which cannot convey all the nuances of the original mythical idea. Mythology in any case follows the ideology of the moment which usually serves the immediate, practical interests of the ruling class, and has nothing to do with ideal truth, far less concrete reality.[4] Research into myths, then, should enable us to attain far greater historical precision than those who follow the school of classical rationalism would like to admit.

For when we examine history, and especially the history of events, more closely, we find that in many cases it is merely myth made concrete. There may have been a tendency to deify historical characters, but the converse is also true. In Roman history, for example, the great one-eyed god of the Indo-Europeans has become Horatio Cocles who defended the Pontus Sublicius against the Etruscans, and the one-armed god appears as Mucius Scaevola, the tricky lawyer. On the other hand, there have been many instances of historical characters being regarded as personifications of myths. Vercingetorix is an incarnation of the king who ruled over that other world which the Celts found almost more real than their own. Alexander the Great consciously played his part of a god descended to earth. We could find any number of people who consciously or unconsciously assumed the physical or moral attributes of a divinity, or of some existing myth. Jesus of Nazareth was only one of a number of Christs hailed in his day. The myth of the Messiah so dominated the Jewish people at the time that it was bound to take on human form in one way or another.

It seems strange that, given the undeniable mythical element in history, historians should find it so difficult to accept that epic or the tales of popular oral traditions (both of which express myth) contain historical elements. Like history, epic need not be examined for truth or falsehood. Either it exists or it does not. The work of Herodotus is as much epic as history, but his evidence might well be passed over today. His description of the arrival of the Persians at Delphi and their terrified panic at the sight of the Greek gods seems almost ludicrously incredible. But the fact that Pausanias and Diodorus of Sicily have the same tale to tell about the Gauls of Brennus suggests that all three historians were expressing different aspects of reality.

The only true difference between epic, which conveys reality through myth, and history, which conveys the same reality through events, is an epistemological one: history is epic presented in a supposedly objective way, while epic is history presented in a subjective way, In practice, however, history and epic are much closer even than this, because it is impossible to express any historical event in a totally objective way. The Napoleonic epic is a fine example of confusion between the two.

So if we want to understand something of the great story of mankind, our first task must be to demystify history and to restore it to its rightful place amongst the human sciences. And whether we look for evidence in history or epic matters little, for both will give us clues to the reality we seek.

The one criticism which might be levelled at the dialectical approach is that our grasp of reality depends on our subjective perceptions and must therefore be imperfect. This phenomenological argument, like Kant's theory of *noumena,* expresses the current scepticism as to whether it is possible to apprehend reality *in toto.* Our knowledge of things relies entirely on the phenomena they stimulate in us. We as subjective observers can never get inside the basic reality of external objects. The subject — object dichotomy then becomes an insurmountable obstacle to real knowledge; and all we can do is shut ourselves away in Plato's allegorical cave, admit our human weakness in this regard and stop asking questions to which we cannot provide the answers. But the human mind is never happy to down tools in this way. Once moving, thought drives ever onwards, reaching for the impossible.

And thought provides us with a counter argument to the phenomenologists. The question of our inability to really know an object does not arise, because its very existence depends on our perception of it and reactions to it. If we were not there it would not exist any more than we should. The sole means of proving the existence of anything is by the dialectical argument which runs: I exist only in relation to the outside world, and the outside world exists only in relation to me or people like me. The being in isolation cannot know it exists and is therefore nothing. But the being in relation to other beings can lay claim to existence and therefore to reality. The complex phenomenon of interaction between the perceiver and the perceived constitutes the only true reality. No one, for example, can see or touch electricity, but equally no one doubts its existence. We

even talk about electrical phenomena. We do not, however, become aware of electrical current until we plug something into a socket. Only then can we perceive
its reality, and this reality is simply the movement resulting from the interaction
of contradictory forces. This, the dialectical materialist definition of reality, is
the only plausible one. It enables us to leave the realm of metaphysical explanations and chart the real through measurable movements of energy. With a new
scale of values we can go beyond the perceptions of a fragmented and ill-defined
existence to a conception of the whole.

In this light, the differentiation between objective history and subjective epic
is patently absurd. The problem we ought to be discussing here has not yet been
raised. And that is the difference between the real and the imaginary.

Here, too, any system of logic which relies on two opposites only imposes an
absolute contradiction. If the real is defined as everything that is, the unreal
must necessarily be what is not. But we cannot think of the unreal in terms of an
absolute, since it is merely the result of a mental process opposing what is and
what is not. The concept of the unreal, which belongs only to the domain of
thought, and then only in strict opposition to the real, then becomes confused
with the imaginary, also a product of human thought which has no objective
material existence in relation to the subject. This comes close to the problem of
the difference between sleeping and waking which many philosophers have
examined, and which only arises from "the recognition of the real as a solid sub-
stance, the otherness of things, objective, positive and present" (Jean-Marie
Benoist, *Marx est mort*). Engels described the real as a "nature without anything
added from elsewhere," which is a re-application of Bacon's comment that art,
in the dual sense of art and technology, is nature with the addition of man.

It may well be that there is no problem here at all. In his *Materialism and
Empiriocriticism*, Lenin said that the opposition of matter and consciousness
had no meaning except within the bounds of the fundamental gnoseological
question: what is of primary and what of secondary importance? Beyond these
bounds this opposition remains unquestionably relative. This applies to
history as a science and to epic in which history took its first, and arguably its
perfect, form. The imaginary is built on perfectly real foundations from a relative objectivity which turns it into matter. This *hyle*, as Sartre calls it, is homo-
geneous, like nature without anything added from elsewhere, and becomes an
analogon within human thought. The analogon establishes a tenuous bridge
between pure reality and whatever is imagined. Poetic creation, artistic creation
of all kinds and, indeed, any form of human activity are the result of this fundamental process. So it appears difficult to make formal distinctions between what
is real and what is imagined without leading the argument into irrelevancies.

If we regard history as a pure science of the real, a product of materialism, we
are bound to reject epic and anything imagined as vague and totally indefinable
idealism. As Jean-Marie Benoist points out in *Marx est mort*, the dichotomy
between matter and idea establishes a dialectical relationship between two
contradictory terms and therefore operates within a narrow field of logic where
the *logos* of metaphysical discussion has no part to play. Whereas the establishment of metaphysical discussion enables us to make deductions about the nature
of things and their existence, to make the same hypotheses about identity as Parmenides did.

For the whole problem revolves round Parmenides' hypothesis of identity.
The principle of absolutes formulated by Aristotle, but already latent in Plato,
which attempts to throw off the rigid embrace of Parmenidean thinking, has

poisoned all subsequent efforts to explain the world, and history in particular. When Parmenides says "It was not in the past and it will not be in the future, since it is now, entire in its existence, one and indivisible," he is only expressing the basic idea that the now, the present reabsorbs all the contradictions of history, and gives epic its ability to gather everything into itself. For the peculiar property of epic is that it systematically confuses times and places. It fuses characters who were different in a distant reality and brings them to life in a present which is open only to the kind of critical consciousness which will lead to original and conceptual theorizing.

Anything which is imagined is real in the sense that the man who thinks it believes in its reality at the time his mind conceives it. While reality is a continual shift in men's minds, the imaginary is a personal, subjective shift in one man's mind which he can transmit to others in the separate form of a story. Whether his audience regards it as real or imaginary, it will still provoke a new shift of thought in their minds, another element of reality. Epic and all popular traditions of the epic kind are constant shifts of thought, creating a continuous present time in which all contradictions can be absorbed.

History, like epic, however, is never the work of a single individual but requires a continual collective effort. "It is the masses who make history," says Althusser (*La Pensée*, no. 138). And this applies as much to epic and the experiences of history as to written or recorded history. Engels wrote, "Thus it is that up until now history has followed the same course as any natural process and has remained subject to the same laws of movement as nature" (quoted by Althusser in *Pour Marx*). Epic, however, has one advantage over history. The very subjectivity of its approach allows it to record more real facts than any history influenced by ideologies intent on eliminating counter-ideologies.

These ideologies, which Marxists would call fetishes, make history as unscientific as epic. In the areas of religion or ethics they all too often take on an independent life and come to be regarded as fact, even as models for future events. They cut across the movement of individuals and classes to crystallize one moment of development. The hero of history and the hero of epic are both fetishes, given the human form which circumstances require. But they are no more true, false, real or imaginary than the events they are assumed to set in motion. They fulfil a function and that is all. History and epic are merely two facets of a single reality.

With every political upheaval, whether it results from external aggression or internal revolution, there has been an attempt to make a clean sweep, to wipe out whole peoples or their culture. When the Romans subjugated Gaul they made every effort to drain the lifeblood of the country by outlawing druidism and making Latin the official language. And it was not for want of effort on their part that they did not achieve the same ends in Britain. "Saint" Louis' decision to pacify the Occitanian South of France resulted in concerted efforts to destroy the cultural patrimony which gave the South its originality and its dominance over the northern regions, to their loss. The Normans who colonized England virtually eliminated Saxon culture over a period of centuries; although admittedly the Saxons had previously done much the same thing to the Britons while the papacy turned a blind eye. When Roman Catholic Spain and France or Protestant Holland and England fixed their sights on the rich virgin lands of Africa and America they almost totally destroyed the cultures of the indigenous populations there. The successful revolutionists in 1789 claimed to have no more need of scholars, poets or intellectuals. The 1968 Cultural Revolution in

Maoist China swept away anything, good, bad or indifferent, which resembled the former culture of the Celestial Empire. There are any number of examples of this kind, and not all of them belong to areas over which we have no control.

But it is not part of our brief to analyse the causes of this process, nor to deplore it as the French left-wing political successors of its 19th-century practitioners tend to do now. Suffice it to say that any dominant ideology reshapes history to suit itself.

But the more misshapen history becomes in the service of ideology, the more flourishing the popular tradition which questions it. During the German occupation of France from 1940 to 1944 the subversive, oral tradition gained new vigour and literature abounded in double meanings and half-tone backgrounds. Similarly the medieval epics which were totally pagan in spirit continued to flourish in the face of the Roman Apostolic Church. Even the *chansons de geste,* despite their propagandizing for the Crusades, contain clear traces of much older traditions. The Church, and more especially the Cistercians, were apparently responsible for the initial diffusion of the Round Table romances in Western Europe, hoping as they did to spread the good word through the myth of the Grail. And yet the Arthurian tales retain all kinds of non-Christian themes.

And it is in this respect that further study of King Arthur and the Round Table romances takes on a fuller significance. We must search for the deep-seated reality of the man and his society through the many faces in which he has come down to us.

It was long believed that the Celtic Arthurian writings were mere adaptations of 12th and 13th-century French originals. And even now some scholars are reluctant to admit that the Round Table romances originated among the Celts, though linguistic research has shown that the Celtic texts pre-dated the French. But there can be no doubt that the greater part of these romances was Celtic in origin. At a time when the Celtic nations were disappearing from the political map of Europe, their language bowing before the pressure of English and French, there seems to have been a sort of compensatory drive of Celtic traditions into Europe.

But these traditions were resurrected into a world totally different from the true universe of the Celts. And we cannot hope to study Arthur and the literature he inspired without examining the atmosphere in which the "matter of Britain" developed. For history has never been closer to epic, nor epic so widely portrayed as history. The *Historia Regum Britanniae,* which sparked off a great deal of the interest in the Arthurian world, has been the subject of much scholarly discussion as to its legendary content. But ultimately this changes nothing. Before history began to lay claim to scientific accuracy, historians were quite content to record legend and myth alongside events, as Herodotus, Livy, Xenophon, Tacitus and Suetonius show all too clearly.

We must cease first of all to look upon epic as a primitive, inferior and undisciplined form of history. We do not regard the cave paintings of prehistoric Europe as rough sketches for Classical art. They are the finished portrayals of the feelings of the men who made them. In the same way epic, as a form, closely matches the needs of its original audience.

What characterizes the bulk of epic writing is the way in which it blows up insignificant events which have caught the imagination for some reason into full-scale adventures of their own. The *Chanson de Roland,* for example, in which Charlemagne's rearguard faces a horde of Saracens, was based on a minor clash between Charlemagne's booty-hunting rearguard and the mountain people of the Basque country. There is a similar tendency to exaggerate the most easily comprehensible elements of any given situation. So, if we return to *Roland*, the defeat of the Frankish forces was to be explained in terms of a huge army of Saracens battling against a handful of exceptionally valiant Franks. We also find that character and plot become simplified. but the reason for such exaggerations and simplifications is clear. Epic, even when written down, was intended for a live audience. And just as the main characters and action of a stage play need to retain a clear line throughout a drama, so the outline of the myth on which any epic was based had to stand out against the mass of descriptive detail demanded by its audience.

The heroes of epic are carefully chosen to match some moral, political or social ideal. But although we could rightfully label them as ideological fetishes in the Marxist sense, their role is accepted and acknowledged. The struggle between good and evil which they embody symbolizes the contradictory patterns of human thought. If we look behind the heroes' struggles, to the social background against which they take place and scientifically examine the many facets of life we find there, we may well discover a natural process. Clearly this process will not be biological, chemical or physical, but by bringing the various disciplines of the human sciences to bear on it, we should be able to trace those laws which govern the formation, development and decay of human societies and the way one society replaces another.

Even economic developments play their part in the creation of epic. Underlying the *Iliad* is the rivalry between the Asian Greeks and the European Greeks for commercial control of the Eastern Mediterranean. The fact that the actual narrative starts with a trite little tale of marital infidelity should not blind us to the practical reasons for war between Greeks and Trojans. Indeed, the more exaggeratedly disinterested the dominant ideologies may appear, the stronger their latent interests usually are. The very subjectivity of epic allows us to examine the almost subconscious phenomena behind actions too often condemned as imaginary rather than authentic.

In fact, if we refuse to accept the dichotomy between history, and epic, to disassociate the real and the imaginary, the study of any civilization becomes much more interesting and comprehensive. We can look at the thoughts and actions which shaped it together. There is no need for the separation between thoughts and events which strict historical discipline requires. In this respect, the epic of the Celts will teach us far more about their civilization and their society than the incomplete historical evidence that they or their other contemporaries have left us.[5]

Neither the Gauls, the Britons nor the Irish ever tried to record their own histories in writing. Such pursuits held no interest for them. They passed the account of their development from one generation to the next in the form of stories. But their lack of interest in historical writing as such means that we can look at them through the total if confused picture which their own complex mass of traditions paints for us.

It was their refusal to disassociate the real and the imaginary which won the Celts their place in history and much of the suspicion levelled against them. It was hard for societies raised on dualistic dichotomy to understand the unitarian Celtic approach, especially as there were no proven facts to cling to. Classical and medieval histories of the Celts are obviously much closer to extravagant epic than to a simple narration of events. For the Celtic mind, continual digressions into the fanciful and the supernatural did not interrupt the flow of reality. But the Celtic peoples must have appeared completely unfathomable to any observer imbued with the principles of classical humanism. And it is this same classical humanism that we must leave behind if we are to analyse the winding course of Celtic civilization through its epic traditions.

Paradoxes abound. The various Celtic peoples were never able to achieve political unity; and yet no civilization has even spoken so much of the principle of supreme royalty. But they did maintain a common language and religion from Northern Italy to Ireland and from Spain to the North West banks of the Rhine. The Celts spent much of their time fighting both in wars against external aggressors and in fierce domestic quarrels; and yet they greatly valued the pleasures of the peaceful life.

In fact, many of the epic tales of war in the British and Irish tradition refer to symbolic conflicts. The symbols take various forms. We find brother fighting brother, hero against hero, gods against men and gods against fairy people. There are expeditions to the Other World, which may lie just around the corner or far over the water; and quests for mysterious objects which must be found for the hero to keep his strength or his honour. But all of them represent a concerted attempt to reconcile the contradictions inherent in social life and man's resultant sense of alienation in its most profound diversity. This alienation is essentially practical, that is economic, social and political rather than ideological. Celtic epic portrays the great inner struggles of man and his conflicts with his environment through real battles against hostile forces.

To understand this alienation and through it the workings of Celtic society, we must take each object, hero or event as one element of a shifting reality and explore its own inherent contradictions, its own internal movement, it own immutability. For the factional conflicts of Celtic society are merely another aspect of what Marxists call class conflict, a form of struggle reinforced in our day by the divisions of developed industrial societies.

For Hegel the concept of the "nation" was at the root of historical, political self-awareness. And these nations form the basic framework of Celtic history and epic. The division of peoples into many small social groups like the *tuatha* of Ireland fostered the internal contradictions of society by establishing a real struggle, either for dominance or for survival. If we substitute the word *tuath*, or tribe, for class in the Marxist argument, we can see that each social sphere in Marx's words "begins to acquire an awareness of itself as separate from the others not when it is itself oppressed, but when circumstances which it has done nothing to bring about create a new social sphere which it can oppress in its turn" *(Oeuvres philosophiques)*.

We can usefully approach any examination of Celtic society from this angle, especially now when the concept of the nation, even in the more limited sense of a region, a country or an ethnic group, is beginning to supersede the concept of class. When confronted by what he regards as aggression from the workers of another state, the modern working man will side more readily with his own bosses than with his foreign brothers. Prejudice against immigrant labour and the pattern of recent wars makes this only too clear. It seems unlikely that the workers of many nations will unite against capitalism for many years to come. But recognizing this does not mean that we should condone the aggressive face of nationalism. Rather we should reiterate Marx's condemnation of Hegel's worship of the state as a "mystique degenerating into mystification."

And it is vital that we reject the Hegelian idea of the state as far as the Celts are concerned. The Celtic king was no *rex* embodying active force in the Germano-

Roman mould, but a moral leader of the Indian type whose authority operated only through the existing social context. The kingdom of the Celtic king extended only as far as his eyes could see. He could not enslave his people or impose his own will upon them unchallenged.

We can find no better personification of the Celtic king than Arthur, the celebrated medieval European hero and one of the great unknown quantities of history. Historical or legendary, true or false, real or imaginary, none of these distinctions applies. The reality of King Arthur lies in all the evidence we can muster concerning him, the romances, the histories, his changing face over the years. And through him we shall be able to trace the broad outlines of the Celtic king, the nucleus of an hierarchial society now neglected despite its useful lessons for the modern world.

The aim of this study of King Arthur and Celtic society, then, is to examine a character without deciding *a priori* whether he is real or imaginary, and with him the main currents of thought behind his creation. As the great epic fresco surrounding Arthur unfolds before us, we shall find the society our forebears yearned for, whose only chance of life lay in the great Celtic dream of freedom regained.

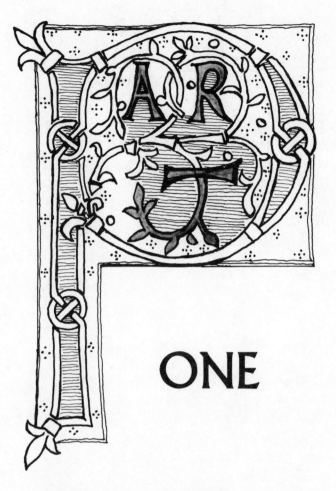

PART ONE

King Arthur in the Medieval World

CHAPTER ONE

Arthurian Literature

T was in the 12th century that the first written manifestations of Arthurian legend appeared. These can be described as literary works, though they also include elements of historical writing. Indeed, the text which has long been regarded as the springboard for all Arthurian literature is the *Historia Regum Britanniae*. This "history" was written in Latin by the Welsh Geoffrey of Monmouth and dates from 1132. Purporting to be a part of the vast, national epic of the Britons from their mythical origins onwards, Geoffrey's work was translated into Welsh under the title *Brut y Brenhinedd* (Brut of the Kings) and adapted into French by the Anglo-Norman Robert Wace in his *Roman du Brut* in about 1155.[1] This French version had most influence on the continental writers and was to lead to a crystallization of the various epic traditions taking Arthur as their central character.

Until then Arthur had only figured as one character among many in the tales of British history. But from the second half of the 12th century Arthurian material became far more epic in nature and even provided fuel for the writers of romances. This transformation, together with the subsequent literary fortunes of Arthur and his knights, can be laid at the door of Chrétien de Troyes, the romance writer from Champagne who originated the genre.

For it was Chrétien de Troyes' *Érec et Énide* which brought the "matter of Britain" into European literature. Admittedly Arthur is only a peripheral character as far as the main action of this romance is concerned, but his presence in the tale is essential. The other characters revolve around him; their sole justification for existence lies in their support for him and his attempts to civilize the world. The original theme of the tale was probably as old as the hills, but Chrétien introduced a new emphasis on psychological motivation which reflected interests prevalent at the court of Champagne. The chief of these was the concept of "courtly love" or *fine amor,* which grew from the cult of the Virgin Mary and the code of the Southern French troubadours. In fact *Érec et Énide* retains elements of both courtly and more fatalistic Celtic attitudes since it ultimately rejects *fine amor* in favour of conjugal love. But what makes the work interesting is its typically Arthurian backcloth and its introduction of the characters who were to people Arthurian romances over the years to come.

Érec et Énide: Chrétien de Troyes

One Easter Day, King Arthur was holding court at Cardigan when he decided to revive the custom of the White Stag. This meant that whoever managed to hunt down the White Stag could kiss the most beautiful maiden at court. Gawain, the king's nephew, was convinced that irreparable quarrels were almost bound to ensue and tried to deter him. But the king was unmoved and the hunt began. Queen Guinevere was riding at the rear with a lady-in-waiting and Érec, son of Lac, when an unknown knight and his dwarf squire appeared and insulted her. While Érec set off in pursuit of them, the hunt drew to a close and King Arthur asked for the trial of the kiss to start. Gawain tried again to dissuade him. So the king sought the advice of his knights, Yder, Kai and Girflet, only to agree with the queen that they should wait until Érec had returned. Érec, however, became involved in all kinds of adventures. Rescued by a poor vassal he fell in love with the man's beautiful daughter, Énide. He finally triumphed over the unknown knight, who turned out, strangely enough, to be Yder, son of Nut, one of the knights with Arthur a few pages earlier. Érec sent him as a prisoner to Guinevere, then himself returned to court with Énide where there was universal agreement that her beauty entitled her to receive the customary kiss. Érec and Énide were married at Pentecost amidst great rejoicing; and many famous people, including Maheloas and Guigomar, attended the celebrations. After the feasting and tournaments Érec took Énide back to his own country where he forgot his duty as a knight in the pleasures of conjugal love. But when Énide repeated some remarks she had heard his men make about him Érec was furious and dragged her through a series of adventures to prove that he was still just as brave and valiant as before. Finally, when his father had died, Érec was crowned king at Nantes in the presence of Arthur and all his knights.

There is much to interest us in *Érec et Énide.* First, we see that the court of King Arthur is continually on the move, although it keeps the great religious festivals. Secondly, the king has a duty to maintain certain traditions of magical origin whatever the consequences. Thirdly, it is clear that the king, even when inactive, remains the nucleus of a society formed by kings of other countries, of this or the Other World. Finally, and perhaps most significantly, Chrétien has borrowed a large number of characters directly from Celtic mythology. Yder, Kai and Girflet are Welsh in origin. Yder is Edern, son of Nut, one of the first of the Celtic Guinevere's lovers, who became "saint" Edern in Brittany. Kai is Arthur's foster brother and traditionally one of his earliest companions. While Girflet is Gilvaethwy, son of Don, who appears in the fourth branch of the *Mabinogion* with his brother Gwyddyon the magician. Maheloas is Maelwas, a god of the Other World, described in *Érec et Énide* as Lord of the Isle of Glass. And Guigomar is said to be the lover of Arthur's sister, Morgan. Even place names have been adapted from British originals. For Nantes must surely be based on the Welsh *nant*, a valley.

Chrétien's *Érec* was adapted into German by Hartmann von Aue towards the end of the 12th century. The Welsh *Gereint and Enid* dating from the same period also appears to be an adaption, possibly even a translation of the same work, although there are significant differences in the details. It is more likely, in fact, that the Welsh author and Chrétien used some common but unknown source.[2]

Chrétien's second Arthurian romance, *Cligès ou la Fausse Morte*, is of comparatively little interest since the author merely uses the setting as an excuse to ride his personal hobby-horse, a condemnation of the adulterous love of Tristan and Iseult.

But the third romance, *Lancelot or Le Chevalier à la Charrette*, is of paramount importance. The totally separate Breton legend concerning Lancelot has been consciously introduced into the Arthurian world. And underlying the whole story is the ancient theme concerning Arthur and Guinevere.

Le Chevalier á la Charrétte: Chrétien de Troyes

King Arthur was holding court at some unspecified place during the feast of Ascension, when an unknown knight (later identified as Meleagant) arrived. The stranger announced that he could take the queen away with him unless a knight chosen by Arthur himself successfully fought him for her, in which case he would also release all Arthur's warriors held captive in his kingdom. Arthur made no reply, whereupon Kai claimed as the obligatory gift of Celtic custom the right to fight the unknown knight. Arthur had no choice but to let him go, although Kai soon returned, defeated by the stranger, who had taken Guinevere to his own country. Gawain, secretly in love with the queen perhaps, obtained his uncle's permission to pursue the abductor. On his way he met a knight (later identified as Lancelot du Lac) who had gone after the queen independently. During the course of various adventures which befell the two heroes, Lancelot was forced after a moment's hesitation to mount the cart of infamy reserved for condemned criminals in order to find out which direction the queen and her abductor had taken. He then fought and overcame a knight who tried to stop his crossing a ford. Lancelot was about to spare the loser's life when a young woman asked for his head and promised her help should Lancelot ever need it. Finally Lancelot reached the Outskirts of the Kingdom of Gorre, or Voirre (Glass) whence no strangers ever returned. A stretch of turbulent water barring the way could only be crossed by the equally dangerous Bridge of the Sword or Bridge Under the Water. Lancelot took the Bridge of the Sword, crawling laboriously along a huge sword which cut his flesh to ribbons, while Gawain narrowly escaped drowning on the Bridge Under the Water. Then Lancelot fought Meleagant and easily defeated him. Good King Baudemagu begged Lancelot to spare his son's life. So Lancelot was declared the winner and another fight arranged for one year later. Lancelot was taken to the queen, who refused to be reconciled with him because he had put reason before his love for her in hesitating to mount the cart, and demanded a series of humiliating proofs of his continued passion. Meleagant then trapped Lancelot and imprisoned him in a lonely tower. So Gawain took the queen back to court. A year later Meleagant was waiting at the appointed spot, confident that Lancelot would not appear and therefore be branded as a coward, when Meleagant's sister, the young woman at the ford, freed the captive knight. Lancelot then killed Meleagant, to the great satisfaction of Gawain and King Arthur, who was thereby avenged of the wrong done to his wife and through her to himself.

The basic plot of this story is based on the universal theme of a divine or fairy queen, married to a mortal, who is then reclaimed by her own people. So much is evident from Chrétien's description of the Kingdom of Gorre, which identifies it with the Celtic Other World. Also Baudemagu, Meleagant's father, has a name which may easily be a corruption of Bran-Magu, or Bran of the Plain, the plain being synonymous with the Other World in ancient Celtic terminology. The oldest Celtic version of the story is probably the Irish *Tale of Etaine*. Etaine, wife of Eochaid Aireainn, is the reincarnation of a former Etaine, wife of Mider, king of the Other World and, incidentally, one of the faces of Maelwas-Meleagant. Mider manages by subtle use of the custom of the obligatory gift to recover Etaine and take her off into his Other World. The old Norse saga of Tristan and Gottfried von Strassburg's version of the legend contain a similar episode in which Mark loses Iseult to an Irish harpist who has claimed the obligatory gift before agreeing to play for the king.[3]

There are many other examples of this kind in Celtic literature. The Ulster hero Cú Chulainn fights Curoi, a god of the Other World, to recover Blathnait. Blathnait's Welsh counterpart Blodeuwedd appears in the fourth branch of the *Mabinogion* where Gronw Pebyr kills her husband Lleu Llaw Gyffes, though here the story branches out into different mythical themes and Blodeuwedd is ultimately punished for her infidelity by Lleu's father. There are clear links in all these stories with the Greek myth of Kore or Persephone, the daughter of Demeter, who was taken down to the Underworld by the god Hades. Indeed, as R. S. Loomis shows in his book *Celtic Myth*, a later French romance entitled *Arthur of Britain* has a character called Florence (like Blathnait and Blodeuwedd, "born of flowers") who is compared to Proserpine, the Roman version of Persephone.

Ulrich von Zatzikhoven's late 12th-century work *Lanzelet* tells how Queen Guinevere is held prisoner in a magic castle by Falerin. Only Madruc, or Malduc, another magician, is able with Tristan's help to free her. *Lanzelet* is a translation from a French tale which was, in its turn, a translation from a Breton original; and it is interesting to see how the Arthurian episodes have been artifically introduced into a different legendary setting. Here Lancelot is not in love with the queen at all.[4] Another German romance, *Die Crone*, which is attributed to Heinrich von dem Turlin tells how Queen Guinevere was abducted by Gasozein who claimed to have prior rights to her;[5] and in *Durmart the Welshman* Queen Fenice is taken by the fearful Brun of Morrois.[6] Then there is the final act in the Arthurian epic, where Queen Guinevere's loyalty to Arthur after her abduction by the traitor Mordret seems more than suspect, whatever version of the story we choose to read.

Obviously it is hard to say exactly where Chrétien found his subject matter for the *Chevalier à la Charrette*, though there is evidence from two sources to suggest that this particular Arthurian theme was well known throughout Europe at the beginning of the 12th century.

The first of these, Caradoc of Llancarvan's *Vita Gildae*, written at the beginning of the 12th century, links the story to the Abbey of Glastonbury. Gildas goes to settle in Glastonbury which is known as the Urbs Vitrea (Town of Glass), which is obviously no ordinary monastery. Here Maelwas is holding

Guennevar, wife of King Arthur, prisoner. Arthur, who is described as *tyrannus* (a translation of the Welsh *tiern*, or tribal chief), lays siege to the Urbs Vitrea, reclaiming Guennevar as "uxorem suam violatam et raptam a praedicto iniquo rege." But the town is protected by the surrounding marshland; and Maelwas can count on the support of the local inhabitants in Somerset. So Arthur appeals to the armies of Dumnonia and the war continues. Gildas then performs the role of peacemaker. The queen returns to Arthur and the monastery benefits by substantial gifts.

The other piece of evidence is carved in stone on the architrave of Modena Cathedral in Italy. Here there is both a pictorial representation of the episode and the names of the characters involved. *Artus de Bretania, Isdermus, Che, Galvagnus, Galvariun, Burmaltus, Mardoc and Winlogee,* or Arthur, Yder, Kai, Gawain, Gauvarien, Burmald, Mardoc and Guinevere, are all clearly labelled.

The sculpture shows the queen being held in a fortress defended by the warrior Mardoc. A knight stands fighting Gawain, Gauvarien and Kai on the battlements. In front of Arthur is a servant armed with a horned stick, who is Yder.[7] The scenes obviously illustrate the story of the *Chevalier à la Charrette* though many of the details differ. And, curiously, since the names are rough attempts to Latinise Breton originals, there is no sign of Lancelot.

All those texts which describe the abduction of Guinevere concur on certain points. Except in the sculpture at Modena where he joins in the fighting, Arthur appears always to submit passively to the situation. He even tries to prevent Kai defending the queen and only allows Gawain to go after Maelwas because he has no choice. Clearly the king has far less authority than we would expect to find in a leader of all the Britons.

There is also the whole question of the obligatory gift. A visitor to the court, whoever he is and wherever he comes from, can in certain circumstances ask the king for a gift without revealing what it is; and the king must grant it. In many of the Welsh and Irish tales this leads to disaster, although in *Kulwch and Olwen* Arthur adds the cautious qualification "excepting only my ship, my mantle, my sword Caledvwlch, my spear Rhongomynyad, my shield Wynebgwrthucher, my knife Carnwennan and my wife Gwenhwyvar."[8]

Finally the unwelcome intruder is in every case a magician or a person from the Other World. This suggests that the king is in conflict with supernatural powers which appear as divinities like Maelwas, Curoi or Mider or as Druidic magicians. We might learn something here from the tale of Finn, one of the Irish models for Arthur. When Finn meets his first wife, Sadv, she is a doe. When she becomes a woman again, she explains that the Black Druid had changed her into an animal partly to prove his power over her and partly as an act of vengeance. As long as she lives in Finn's fortress she is out of reach of the Druid's influence, but he tricks her into coming out and turns her into a doe for ever. She then gives birth to a child, Oisin, who escapes the curse but whose name, which means fawn, is a permanent reminder of his origins.[9] Behind this story loom traces of a struggle for precedence between king and Druid which is reflected in the early Celtic custom forbidding a king to speak in public before his Druid.

Chrétien's third Arthurian work, *Yvain*, or the *Chevalier au Lion*, which dates from about 1170, consigns Arthur to an even smaller role in the main narrative thread than the story of Lancelot.

Le Chevalier au Lion: Chrétien de Troyes
King Arthur was holding his Pentecostal court at Carduel [Carlisle]. During

the day he expressed a wish to go and rest which the members of the court opposed. But Queen Guinevere sent him to lie down and soon after he went to sleep. Meanwhile a quarrel erupted between Kai and the knight Calogrenant who was ordered to describe his adventures in the forest of Broceliande. He told how he had poured water on the steps of a fountain there, unleashing a terrible storm. After the storm had passed, he had heard magical birds singing on a pine tree nearby and had been attacked by a knight in black who accused him of having ruined part of his lands by bringing about the storm. The black knight had beaten and humiliated him. When the king woke, he asked what they had been talking about. On hearing the story, Arthur vowed to go to Broceliande within a fortnight with any of his knights who wished to come. However, Yvain, son of King Uryen,[10] left the court in secret and went to look for the fountain of Barenton on his own.[11] His adventures followed the course already described by Calogrenant, but Yvain managed to mortally wound the black knight who fled into his fortress. When Yvain followed he was taken prisoner, but set free by the fairy servant Luned who gave him a magic ring to make him invisible. In this way he managed to escape the vassals of the black knight who were intent on avenging their seigneur's death. Yvain fell in love with the black knight's widow, Laudine, and with the help of Luned's magic married her. He then became the defender of the fountain. When Arthur reached the fountain and unleashed the storm, neither he nor any of his knights recognized the strange knight who appeared as Yvain. With the king's permission Kai went to fight him but was unhorsed by his opponent. Yvain then revealed his identity and welcomed the whole company to the domain of Laudine.[12] Before leaving, Gawain persuaded Yvain to go with Arthur and the other knights. Laudine gave her permission, but only on condition that he return after a specific time or be banished from her sight for ever. When the appointed day had passed and Yvain had still not returned, a girl arrived at court one day. She called on all the members of the court to witness that Yvain had broken his promise and told him that Laudine released him. Half crazed Yvain fled into the forest where fairies brought him back to sanity. He then saved the life of a lion which became his faithful companion, freed Luned who had been wrongfully condemned, and managed, again with Luned's help, to win back his former place in Laundine's affections.

The Welsh version of Yvain, which is entitled *Owein* or the *Lady of the Fountain*, was long thought to be a translation of the French romance. But recent studies have shown that Chrétien de Troyes and the anonymous Welsh author used the same source; and if we compare the two works we find obvious differences in the two writers' attitudes to and use of their material. At the end of the story Chrétien's hero settles into a life of comfort with Laudine, while Owein continues living at court where the king refers to him as a *penteulu*, or very important person, almost a viceroy. The Welsh tale ends by saying that Owein stayed with Arthur "until he went to his own land with the three hundred swords of Kynverchin and his flight of ravens, and they were victorious wherever they went."[13]

At the time when Chrétien de Troyes was writing his *Yvain*, the Anglo-Normans, Beroul and Thomas, and the Germans, Eilhart von Oberg and Gott-fried von Strassburg were producing their versions of the Tristan legend. The story of Tristan and Iseult originated in Ireland and moved to Cornwall, where it is clearly located before ending in Brittany.[14] But Arthurian material was proving so successful that the authors of Tristan showed no hesitation in artificially incorporating their tale into the Arthurian tradition. Béroul makes his Queen Iseult swear the solemn oath which will clear her of all suspicion of adultery in the presence of King Arthur and all the Round Table knights. Thomas includes the anecdote about the giant who cuts off kings' beards, already mentioned in the *Historia Regum Britanniae*, and uses it to praise Arthur "who of all the kings of the land, showed such honour, such fortitude and such valour that he was never beaten in single combat."[15] The 13th-century prose *Tristan* links Tristan even more closely to Arthur, and by the 15th century, when Thomas Malory wrote his *Morte d'Arthur*, the Tristan legend has become an integral part of Arthurian tradition.

At this same time, the poetess Marie de France who probably lived at the court of Henry II was writing *lais*, or verse stories, based on legends originating in Britain or Brittany. Marie's only lay to be closely connected with the Arthurian tradition, however, is the *Lai de Lanval*. Here Queen Guinevere is trying to arrange the death of a young knight whom she loves but who has rebuffed her advances. It seems quite probable that Marie chose arbitrarily to attach the tale to Guinevere, since the basic theme occurs in other, anonymous Breton lays of roughly the same period, notably *Graelent-Meur* and *La Chasse au Blanc Porc*.[16] One of these anonymous lays, however, the *Lai de Tyrolet*, is specifically Arthurian in setting and the central character appears to be a model for Perceval.

Le Lai de Tyrolet: anonymous Breton
Tyrolet had spent his childhood in the woods on his mother's land hunting wild animals. He knew the language of animals and could summon them when he wished. He heard of the marvels of Arthur's court and decided to go there. The day he arrived, a beautiful girl appeared and offered marriage and her throne to whichever of the knights could bring back the white foot of a particular stag. This stag was guarded by lions which made it very difficult to approach. But the girl promised to give the daring knight a small white dog to guide him. Bedivere, one of Arthur's oldest companions, decided to try. The dog led him to a wider river and swam across it. But Bedivere took fright and returned to court, saying that a sudden illness had prevented him from going any further. Tyrolet then asked to go. Led by the dog, he crossed the river, found the stag and whistled it to him. Hearing the screams of the stag as Tyrolet cut off its foot the lions ran to the rescue. Tyrolet killed them all, but then fell exhausted to the ground. A knight appeared and Tyrolet asked him to take the stag's foot to the girl for him. But the knight, thinking Tyrolet dead, pretended that he had cut off the foot and claimed the reward for himself. The girl did not believe him and stalled for time. Meanwhile the dog had returned and an anxious Gawain went to look for Tyrolet. He found him unconscious and left him in the care of a girl, probably a fairy, who was to take him to a doctor. Gawain then rushed back to court to denounce the traitor. The knight declared himself ready to fight for his cause but when Tyrolet appeared and reproached him for his infamous conduct he fell at the young man's feet and begged for mercy. Tyrolet married the girl who took him back to her own country.[17]

The trials undergone by a naive simpleton who becomes a wise knight are the subject of Chrétien's fourth and last Arthurian romance, *Perceval* or *Le Conte du Graal.* This unfinished work was the most successful of all his romances, perhaps because nobody knew how he intended to finish it. A number of authors wrote sequels to it or adapted it, often without much reference to the original.

Perceval: Chrétian de Troyes

Perceval did not know who he really was. He lived a solitary life on his mother's land because she was determined that he should not die as his father had done, in a tournament. When out hunting in the forest, one day, Perceval met three knights whom he took at first to be angels. But when they explained what being a knight meant, Perceval immediately determined to go to Arthur's court so that he could become one too. His mother agreed against her better judgment, but lavished a great deal of advice on him, which he later followed to the letter thereby incurring various trials and tribulations. When Perceval arrived at Carduel [Carlisle] where Arthur was holding court, he found the king brooding. A red knight had just taken the queen's cup and insulted Arthur. Perceval spoke to the king but received no reply, so he mounted his horse again to ride away. But in the process he knocked against a piece of Arthur's armour and disturbed the king. When Perceval asked for the red knight's weapons Kai ironically told him to get them for himself. So off he set. On his way he saluted a girl who had not laughed for years, and she then began prophesying Perceval's future exploits. Kai was furious, hit the girl and threw Arthur's jester who had also foretold glory for Perceval into the fire. Arthur reproached Kai for his brutality, but the jester said that Kai would be punished for it with a broken arm. While Arthur worried about his fate, Perceval found the red knight and with an astonishing combination of bravery and naivety succeeded in killing him. He then embarked on a series of successful adventures, sending all his prisoners back to Arthur. He freed the beautiful Blanchefleur with whom he fell in love, and made his way to the Castle of the Grail where he saw a strange procession. A girl then told him, much to his distress, that if he had asked a question about the procession, he would have cured his host, the Fisher King, and restored prosperity to the kingdom. On his subsequent travels he saw a crow drinking drops of blood on the snow and was reminded of Blanchefleur whose hair was black like the crow, lips red like the blood and whose skin was white like snow. Two of Arthur's knights, Sagremor and Kai, found him, but he ignored their greeting and fought against them. He broke Kai's arm, as the jester had prophesied, but finally allowed Gawain to take him to Arthur who was then at Carlion [Caerleon on Usk]. A hideous maiden arrived on a mule and began to curse Perceval for not asking the question which would have cured the Fisher King. She then announced that there was to be a quest to find the mysterious castle. Perceval swore never to stay in one place for more than a night until he had discovered the reasons for the Grail procession. He then travelled aimlessly across a waste land for five years. Meanwhile Gawain performed various brave exploits, notably in Cornwall where he found Arthur's mother. He freed the prisoners confined in a fortress surrounded by a river, but refused to stay there. As he crossed back over the river, the boatman announced that the spell on the land had been broken.

This is where Chrétien's narrative ends. Such a break in the story, generally attributed to the author's death, was bound to excite other writers to take up the thread of the tale, or to try and explain the existing romance. An *Elucidation* and four *Continuations*, therefore, followed soon after. The increasingly Christian flavour of the continuations suggests that the Church was unhappy with the Celtic paganism of Chrétien's themes. Only the *Elucidation* retains the spirit of the ancient British traditions.

L'Elucidation

When Arthur was holding a plenary court, a knight named Blihis Bliheris[18] came to tell the assembled company how the mysterious castle ruled by the Fisher King had disappeared. Once this castle had been visible to everybody and travellers were received by maidens who gave them food and drink from golden dishes. But a king called Amangon had assaulted one of the maidens and snatched the golden cup which she was offering to her guests. The maidens had immediately disappeared, the king had come to a bad end, the land grown sterile, wells dried up and the road leading to the castle had disappeared. Blihis added that it was up to Arthur's knights to find it somewhere among the marshes and forests. For when the castle was found again, life would be joyful and the land prosperous once more. They had also to find the Fisher King who was a great magician. The tale ends by declaring that it would be Gawain who found the Fisher King.

Neither this fabricated introduction nor Chrétien's *Perceval* contain anything to suggest that the mysterious object in the Fisher King's castle was meant to represent the sacred vessel containing the blood of Christ; that particular medieval confidence trick was perpetrated by the authors of the *Continuations* who were probably influenced by the Cistercians.

The first continuation is primarily concerned with the adventures of Gawain and his fight with Bran de Lis whose sister Gawain has raped. But the second and third continuations do follow convincingly on from Chrétien's work to complete the story against a classical Arthurian background. Briefly, Perceval finds the Fisher King's castle, asks the relevant questions and returns, after various further adventures, to Arthur's court. There a messenger arrives to proclaim Perceval the successor to his dying uncle, the Fisher King, and Arthur crowns him king at Corbenic, the Grail Castle. When Perceval dies seven years later, the Grail and the processional objects disappear with him.

Despite the later Christian veneer, the guiding line of all these works is the Celtic theme of a quest for magical objects belonging to the Other World. These the hero had to bring back in order to expiate some crime or to justify his claims to kingship. Perceval's crime is his simple-mindedness. But he is also pre-destined to become the Fisher King's successor. So his adventures are both a form of atonement and a kind of initiation test for the acquisition of sovereignty. The other knights who venture forth on the quest are not destined for the same goal. The French versions of the Perceval legend clearly illustrate the path towards a sovereign authority which is both temporal and spiritual. Many of the popular tales of Brittany follow similar themes.[19] A young man leaves his family to seek his fortune and somehow acquires objects or secret knowledge belonging to the Other World. Over the course of his many adventures he grows more wise and eventually becomes king, either by marrying a king's daughter or fiancée, or by getting rid of the reigning king. In many of the Irish epics, on the other hand, the hero or heroes have committed some offence and set off on their extraordinary adventures in obedience to the laws of private vengeance. *The Adven-*

tures of Art Son of Conn and *The Fate of the Children of Tuiren* are typical.[20] *The Adventures of Art* is actually about the acquisition of sovereign power after the king of Ireland has sinned by contracting a misalliance with a woman banished from the Other World. In this respect Conn is like the Fisher-King for Conn's kingdom also becomes barren as a result of his fault; and both are portrayed as sexually and politically impotent figures. There has to be a young man to carry on after him (in this case his sister's son); but the successor must first prove his capability to rule.

The same theme governs the narrative of the Welsh Arthurian tale *Kulwch and Olwen*. Here sovereignty is represented by the daughter of a king whom the hero has to satisfy by bringing him magical objects from the Other World. He then kills the king. The strange tale of *Peredur* can be taken as the Welsh version of Perceval. In fact the similarities between *Peredur, Perceval* and the *Lai de Tyrolet*, and between *Peredur* and the continuations of Chrétien's work show that the authors of all these works drew upon some common store of Celtic legends for their subject matter.

The German version, Wolfram von Eschenbach's *Parzifal*, is far more directly influenced by Chrétien's *Perceval*. Indeed Wolfram acknowledges as much and translates many of Chrétien's scenes in their entirety. But he also claims to have used other sources, especially Kyot the Provençal. And while *Parzifal* as a whole is distinctly Christian, even mystical in tone, with the Arthurian elements played down, it does contain references to a story of vengeance which bring it much closer to *Peredur* than to *Perceval*. The Fisher King has become Amfortas (probably from the Latin word *infirmitas*), the guardians of the Grail are Templars, the maiden on the mule is Kundry, the Grail itself is a stone. But the hero is still a young simpleton who achieves kingship with the help of a woman. Wolfram's *Parzifal* is a major work which should be studied in detail for the light it sheds not only on the significance of the Grail but also on the significance of the Arthurian adventure as a form of initiation to some higher destiny.[21]

All the versions of the story we have discussed so far remain essentially similar despite their shift towards a Christian interpretation of the legend. But the *Fourth Continuation* of Chrétian's *Perceval*, which was attributed to Gerbet de Montreuil, lays the legend open to the introduction of a whole new range of characters. For the author ignores the other continuations and goes back to where Chrétien left off. And his Perceval, although he finds the Fisher King, is told that the king can only be cured by a pious knight seeking the Grail. This leads one to suppose that the knight in question is not Perceval at all.

There were yet more versions of the Perceval story. One writer who played an important part in the development of the legend was Robert de Boron. We know that Robert was born some time in the latter half of the 12th century because he dedicated his work to his friend Gautier de Montbeliard who went on the crusade in 1199 never to return. As far as we can determine, Robert lived in Britain and had links of some kind with the Abbey of Glastonbury where the tombs of Arthur and Guinevere were "discovered" in 1191. Robert de Boron elaborated on the origins of the Grail. According to him it was the dish from which Christ ate the Last Supper, which Joseph of Arimathea then kept and brought with him to England. Robert also reworked the myth of Merlin which was originally part of the northern British tradition. Unfortunately almost all we have left of Robert's work are some fragments of his *Joseph* and a few lines from the beginning of the *Histoire de Merlin*. But his spirit has survived in the works of others. A prose adaptation of his *Merlin* was included in the *Lancelot in Prose*. And a rather obscure work known as the *Didot-Perceval* follows in Robert's footsteps by making a legend once suspected of heresy into a highly Christian tale.

Didot-Perceval

Before his death Alain, Perceval's father, was told by the Holy Ghost that his son would become the Grail King. He therefore advised him to go and become a knight at Arthur's court. So Perceval went to be knighted by Arthur and took part in the Pentecost festivities when the Round Table was to be reinstituted on the suggestion of Merlin the Wizard. Perceval was very successful in the ceremonial tournaments and claimed the right to sit in the Perilous Seat. This was one of the seats at the Round Table which Merlin had said must be kept empty until the man chosen by God appeared to take his place in it. Any man incautious enough to sit there unsanctioned would be destroyed. After initially refusing Perceval's request, Arthur reluctantly agreed to it on Gawain's insistence. But as soon as Perceval sat down the stone opened beneath his feet, a voice cried out of the earth and darkness fell. Then a mysterious voice criticized Arthur for having allowed the offence to be committed and said that as a consequence Perceval's grandfather, Bron the Fisher King, had collapsed. The only hope of Bron's recovery and the stone's being rejoined lay in whichever of the Round Table knights proved most brave, made his way to the Fisher King's castle and there asked the right questions about the Grail. All the knights wanted to go in quest of the Grail, and Perceval swore never to stay two nights in the same place until he found the marvellous castle. During the course of his subsequent adventures Perceval learnt from his sister of his mother's death. He also met Merlin disguised as a woodcutter, who reminded him to ask the questions about the Grail promptly. But when Perceval found the Fisher King's castle and witnessed the Grail procession he remembered only his mother's advice to be humble and did not dare ask any questions. When he woke the next day the castle was empty. For seven years he wandered desperately round the forests not knowing what to do next. Meanwhile the other knights had reached the Fisher King's castle, but, to their shame, they could not pass the test. Perceval met his uncle, the hermit, who told of his sister's death, which Perceval mourned for two months. Then Merlin, again disguised as a woodcutter, set him on the road back to the Fisher King's castle. This time Perceval asked the questions. The king was immediately cured, but died three days later having named Perceval as his successor. That same day the knights who had returned from the Quest were assembled at court when they heard a terrible noise and saw the stone of the Perilous Seat join together again. Merlin went to the Grail castle with his friend and master, Blaise. Arthur's troubles were not over, however. He had to journey to France and then to Italy to fight the would-be invaders of Britain. But despite his military successes abroad, his nephew Mordret, whom he had left as regent in his absence, had spread false rumours of his death and taken power. Arthur returned hastily to Britain and won a first battle against Mordret who took shelter with a king of Ireland. Many of the knights of the Round Table had died in combat, including Kai, Gawain, Bedivere and Sagremor. But Arthur pursued Mordret to Ireland where he killed him and the king who had given him shelter. Arthur was wounded himself, however, and taken to the Isle of Avalon by his sister Morgan la Fée. There he was to be taken off so that he could one day return to rule Britain again. Meanwhile Perceval, now Grail King, mourned his dead companions and spent his days praying for them. Merlin built a house not far from the Grail castle where he continued to prophesy all that God commanded him and dictated the above tale to Blaise.

The *Didot-Perceval* obviously had a great influence on the way the pagan Celtic legend developed into a courtly Christian one. It laid the way open for sub-sequent writers to embroider on the theme of Arthurian chivalry. Many of the Celtic elements are still evident. The stone which splits in two is borrowed from two Irish traditions, the first concerning two blocks of stone at Tara which separated to indicate that the future king was present, and the second concerning the stone of Fal which cried out for the same reason. King Bron is referred to as the "rich" King Bron, presumably as an allusion to the treasures of the Other World. But these elements are only used to pad out the basic panegyic of chivalrous ideas which the 13th-century Church was so anxious to promote. Perceval, the perfect knight, has become so much the central character of the tale that he is even made responsible for the Fisher King's troubles.

So there appeared the huge collection of stories known as the *Lancelot in Prose* or the *Corpus Lancelot-Grail*.[22] Notwithstanding the large number of authors responsible for its creation, the whole work follows a strict pattern and claims to cover the entire history of Arthur and his knights. The clerks involved in this literary experiment were clearly motivated by political and moral concerns, but also by a nostalgia for the great Celtic civilization which had never been revealed in all its glory.

Lancelot in Prose. Part 1, The Story of the Holy Grail

Joseph of Arimathea had collected the blood of Christ in the dish used during the Last Supper and set off on a journey round the world with his son Josephus to find a safe place for the precious relic. On his travels he converted the pagan kings Evallach (Owein's grandfather) and Seraphe who took the christian names Nascien and Mordrain and prophesied about the future line of the Holy Grail. Joseph and his companions then settled somewhere in Britain. King Mordrain became blind when he tried to get too close to the Grail. After Joseph and Josephus had died, their descendents built the castle of Corbenic to house the Grail. After various conflicts the land around Corbenic was bound by spells to become barren. Only the Good Knight who was to come to Corbenic would be able to restore fertility to the land and cure Mordrain of his blindness.

Part 2, The Story of Merlin

Merlin was the son of a nun and a devil and was therefore a man of extra-ordinary gifts who could talk even as a baby. He was a prophet first for King Vortigern and then for Uther Pendragon who made him his close friend and adviser also. When Uther was holding court at Carduel in Wales [actually Carlisle], he fell in love with the beautiful Ygern, wife of Duke Hoel of Tintagel. She repelled Uther's advances and the furious duke took her back to Tintagel. Uther then laid siege to Tintagel, nominally to punish the duke for insulting him by leaving the court, but in fact because he still loved

Ygern. Merlin cast a spell on Uther so that he would look like Hoel and could spend a night with Ygern in Tintagel castle. Soon after, Hoel was killed and Uther married Ygern. But when she had a son Uther could not admit to being the child's father and gave the newly born infant into Merlin's care. Merlin arranged for the future Arthur to be brought up by Sir Antor who already had a son the same age called Kai. When Uther Pendragon died sixteen years later, two years after his wife, all the barons in the kingdom gathered in London [historically in Saxon hands by this time] to elect a new king and seek Merlin's advice about their choice. On Christmas morning when the congregation came out into the church square they saw a huge piece of dressed stone and on top of it an iron anvil. A sword was embedded up to the hilt in the anvil and underneath was written "Whoever removes this sword will be the king chosen by Jesus Christ."[23] Naturally all the high-ranking barons tried to remove the sword but without success. On New Year's Day when everybody was attending the customary tournament, Kai asked Arthur to fetch the sword he had forgotten. On his way through the deserted square Arthur noticed the sword in the anvil. He pulled it out quite easily and took it to Kai, saying that he had not had time to find his, but was giving him the one from the anvil. Kai was very upset, but took the sword to his father Antor and said that he himself had drawn it from the anvil.[24] Antor did not believe him and, when he finally discovered the truth, had the sword returned. He then asked the archbishop if his younger son, who was not yet a knight, could try to draw it out. The archbishop agreed and Arthur again removed the sword without any difficulty. Even so, the barons refused to believe that an obscure youth could have achieved such a miracle and demanded that the sword be returned to the anvil until Candlemas [the Celtic festival of Imbolc] when they should have another opportunity to try and pull it out. Again none of them succeeded and again, on the day of Candlemas, Arthur drew out the sword Escalibur.[25] Although the barons prevaricated, Arthur was crowned king at Pentecost. But when he held his first court at Caerleon soon after, the chief barons, who included Loth of Orkney, Urien of Gorre, Ydier of Cornwall and Carodos Biebras,[26] rose in revolt against him. Merlin then revealed Arthur's true parentage, but to no avail. With Merlin's help, however, Arthur succeeded in putting the rebels to flight. He then went to the aid of his continental vassals, King Ban of Benoic (Lancelot's father) and King Bohort of Gaunes (Bohort's father). With the help of King Leodagan, he managed to save them and to force a coalition of Gauls, Romans and Germans led by Duke Frolle into retreat. Arthur fell in love with Leodagan's daughter, Guinevere,[27] but on Merlin's advice returned to Britain to help the rebel barons who were now fighting the Saxons. On the way he joined company with Gawain and the sons of King Loth who, together with Yvain, son of Urien, and Sagremor became his knights. The great battle against the Saxons took place on Salisbury Plain and the Britons' valour carried the day. With peace restored. Arthur married Guinevere at Carohaise (probably Carhays in Cornwall), amid great celebrations. Merlin magically arranged for King Ban of Benoic and Agravadain's beautiful daughter, Elaine, to sleep together and that night Lancelot was conceived. Merlin then went back to the forest of Broceliande[28] because he had fallen in love with Vivienne[29] and hoped to win her over with brilliant displays of magic. Soon after, Arthur was holding court in London when a knight arrived and challenged Arthur on behalf of the giant Rion.

Rion had been making a cloak from the beards of all the kings he had beaten and wanted Arthur's beard to complete it. Arthur agreed to fight the giant. Then Merlin who had returned to court in disguise told Arthur and the assembled knights that God had decided that a fellowship should be instituted around Arthur. It was to be symbolized by a round table "to show that none of those who sit there has precedence over any other," and would bring "great good and great marvels to the kingdom." But the seat to the right of the king was to remain empty "in memory of Our Lord Jesus Christ," and anybody who sat there would be risking death, unless he was "the best knight in the world who will find the Holy Grail and know its truth and its meaning." The king agreed and immediately a round table appeared in the middle of the hall. Around the table stood 150 wooden seats, most of them bearing the names of the knights who were to sit there, in gold lettering. The knights took their places all swearing to respect the oath uttered by Gawain that anyone coming to the court to ask for help should receive it. It was also agreed that if one of the knights should disappear, the others should go one by one to look for him, each searching for a year and a day. On that day Sir Guyomard fell in love with Arthur's sister, Morgan, and she with him.[30] From then on Guinevere and Morgan shared a mutual hatred and jealousy of each other. Arthur and his fellow knights then went out to fight Rion, whom Arthur himself succeeded in killing. A little later when Arthur was holding court at Camaalot (Cadbury), he heard tell of a giant who was terrorizing the region between Mont-Saint-Michel and the Peril de la Mer. So he crossed the channel and with help of his fellow knights killed the giant. When he returned to Camaalot Merlin told him that he was leaving him for ever and disappeared. But Gawain decided to go and search for him for a year and a day as the rule of the Round Table demanded. After various adventures he reached a forest where he heard Merlin's voice telling him that Vivienne had cast a spell on him while he was asleep and had shut him up in an invisible castle. But Merlin had no complaints for he had known what would happen and was happy to be living with his love. So Gawain returned to King Arthur at Carduel and told his story.

Part 3, The Book of Lancelot

Hard pressed by Claudas of the Waste Land, King Ban of Benoic[31] fled with his wife and his son Lancelot, only to die of his wounds. A fairy of the waters took the child and arranged for him to be brought up by the Lady of the Lake (Vivienne). Claudas had also invaded the lands of Bohort of Gaunes whom he had killed. Bohort's two sons, Lionel and Bohort, were deeply shocked. They were brought up with their cousin Lancelot. When Lancelot reached the age of eighteen the Lady of the Lake took him to the court of King Arthur. He was made a knight at Camaalot during the Feast of Saint John. Then, when the Lady of Nohant asked Arthur for help, Lancelot was given permission to act as her champion and left with Kai. This mission accomplished he travelled on until he arrived at the castle of the Dolourous Guard which lay under a spell. There he found empty tombs bearing the names of knights of the Round Table who were still alive. On one of them was written "This tomb stone will never be lifted by any man except he who conquers the Dolorous Guard." Lancelot lifted the slab to see other letters which read "Here will lie Lancelot, son of King Ban of Benoic" so telling Lancelot who he was. He then went to rescue Gawain and various other knights from a trap and returned to find that Arthur and Guinevere had come to the Dolorous Guard but could not make their way in. Lancelot took them into the castle, then almost drowned when he swooned in ecstasy before Guinevere, whom he had loved from the first moment he saw her. Galehaut, Lord of the Far Islands, challenged Arthur to combat and invaded the kingdom. Lancelot, who was a prisoner of the Lady of Malehaut, obtained leave to go and fight for Arthur. He used Galehaut's admiration for him to make peace and Galehaut became a knight of the Round Table. Galehaut then fell in love with the Lady of Malehaut, to whom Lancelot had returned, and acted as go-between for him and Guinevere. Sent by Vivienne, Lionel and Bohort arrived at Arthur's court to find that Lancelot had disappeared, much to the queen's anxiety. Gawain went to look for him and eventually found him. Meanwhile Arthur's army had gone to do battle with the Saxons and the Irish [probably at the historic battle of Trwyrwyd in the British kingdom of Strathclyde]. Lancelot and Galehaut joined in the battle in disguise. King Arthur succumbed to the charms of the enchantress Camille who kept him prisoner. That night Lancelot went to Guinevere's bed. Camille then captured Lancelot, Galehaut and Gawain, but King Yder saved the British army. Lancelot became temporarily insane, but was cured by Vivienne.[32] He freed Arthur and his fellow knights from captivity and Camille killed herself. Lancelot and Galehaut then left court for a short stay in Sorelais. While they were away a maiden came to Camaalot and accused Guinevere of having taken the real queen's place on her wedding day. Arthur dedided to delay hearing the case until the next court at Candlemas. But before the hearing the false Guinevere arrived, lured Arthur into the forest and had him taken to Carmelide where he fell totally under her spell. During Arthur's absence Gawain was named regent. After Easter Arthur sent a message summoning all his barons to a court at Carmelide. There the true Guinevere was condemned to be dethroned, banished and have her hands cut. Lancelot, who had heard of Guinevere's troubles, offered to defend her, but Arthur refused to reinstate his wife and would only allow her to go and live with Lancelot in Sorelais. The pope then issued an interdict on the kingdom of Britain. Arthur fell ill and repented his injustice. The false Guinevere also fell ill and confessed the truth before she died. Lancelot persuaded Guinevere to return to Arthur and was himself persuaded to resume his place at the Round Table. After the king had held court at London where he made Lionel knight, the knights set off on their adventures again. Yvain tried to storm the Dolorous Tower. Galessin, duke of Clarence, found himself a prisoner in the Valley of No Return, which Morgana had spellbound so that any knight fickle to his lady had to stay there. Lancelot's perfect love for Guinevere enabled him to break the spell and free 130 knights. But Morgan caught Lancelot and tried unsuccessfully to get the queen's ring which he wore on his finger. She allowed him to try and free Gawain who was a prisoner in the Dolorous Tower, Caradoc's castle. When Arthur's army attacked the tower Yvain and Galessin were taken prisoner, but Lancelot killed Caradoc, freed Gawain, Galessin and Yvain and returned to Morgan. She then exchanged the queen's ring for a copy and sent a messenger to Arthur's court to say that Lancelot, now mortally wounded, had confessed his sin with the queen and was asking for forgiveness. The messenger also brought the queen's ring which Lancelot was supposedly returning. Guinevere skilfully defended herself to the suspicious Arthur, and Galehaut, Lionel, Gawain and Yvain left

to look for Lancelot. Under the influence of a magic potion which Morgan
had made him drink Lancelot imagined that the queen was betraying him.
Morgan then let him go, on condition that he never return to Arthur's court
and speak to no knight or lady before Christmas. So when Gawain and Yvain
found him he would not speak to them, but went crazy again and spent the
whole winter roaming round the forest. Again Vivienne cured him.
During the Ascension celebrations at Camaalot Meleagant insulted the
king and took the queen away with him. Gawain and Lancelot rushed after
him and after many adventures Gawain returned the queen to court while
Lancelot remained Meleagant's prisoner. But freed by Meleagant's sister,
Lancelot killed him in a tournament. He then returned to court where
Arthur had his adventures recorded in writing. Lancelot's cousin Bohort
then went off adventuring. He was received at King Brangore's court and fell
in love with his daughter. Lancelot learned that his friend Galehaut had died
and had him buried at his castle, now known as the Joyous Guard. He
rescued Meleagant's sister, who had been sentenced to death, and returned to
Arthur's court. At Pentecost Arthur went to hunt in the forest of Camaalot
with Guinevere, escorted by Kai, Dodinel, Sagremor and Lancelot. An
unknown knight tried to seize the queen, but when Lancelot went to her aid
an old woman appeared and reminded him that he had once promised to
help her. While Lancelot followed the old woman into a series of adventures,
the king and queen returned to court and were told that he had died. Gawain
resolved to go and find Lancelot, alive or dead, and knights went with him.
Queen Guinevere sent one of her cousins to Brittany to beg Vivienne for
help. Meanwhile the sick Lancelot was being cared for by a maiden who sent
word to Arthur and Guinevere that he was alive but that his illness had made
him bald. Lionel and the queen persuaded Arthur to hold a great tournament at Camaalot convinced that Lancelot would come to take part. But he
was having some difficulty throwing off the maiden who had fallen in love
with him. Rescued from the clutches of three enchantresses who had
captured him while he was asleep, Lancelot then went to stay with stay with
a lady admirer who took him to Corbenic, the Fisher King's castle. After
successfully taking a girl from a burning bowl and killing a snake, Lancelot
was warmly welcomed by the Fisher King, Pelles. His daughter Elaine, the
bearer of the Grail, fell for Lancelot and helped by the spells of her governess,
Brisane, she arranged that he should come to her bed under the impression
that she was Guinevere. That night Galahad was conceived. When he woke
Lancelot was furious with Elaine, but finally forgave her the deception. He
then learnt that Sir Hector was the natural son of Ban and his own half
brother. Lancelot made his way into the Lost Forest from which no one ever
returned and there found a group of knights and ladies engaged in a kind of
perpetual dance. When Lancelot joined in the dance he forgot everything.[33]
Towards the evening he was sat in a chair and a crown was put on his head.
Immediately a statue of the king fell from a tower and broke. The spell was
also broken and the dancers regained their memory. Meanwhile, at
Camaalot, Arthur, Guinevere and Gawain awaited Lancelot's return, still
hoping that he would take part in the tournament. When he did finally
arrive, he fought incognito, although the queen recognized him. Yder, too,
had guessed Lancelot's identity and asked for a new tourney although
Lancelot had won the first. This time Lancelot chased the knights partici-
pating in the tournament right back to Camaalot and, on Arthur's request,

revealed his identity. Although Gawain had been seriously wounded, and all the knights humiliated, the whole court rejoiced and Arthur called for his clerks to record the exploits of his errant knights. Guinevere told Lancelot that she was sorry that the sins he had committed with her had prevented his being successful at the Grail castle; to which he replied that all his valour came from his love for her. When Lancelot set off on his adventures again, he was captured by Morgan and shut in her castle. Seeing a mural depicting the story of Aeneas, he thought to paint the walls of his room with the story of his adventures and his love for Guinevere. Morgan agreed, hoping that he would produce some incriminating evidence she could use against him later. Lancelot spent two winters and a summer in his prison, then broke the bars on his windows and escaped, much to Morgan's fury. Meanwhile the messenger from Guinevere to Vivienne had been mistreated by Claudas of the Waste Land. Claudas then used Lancelot's absence as an opportunity to insult Arthur. One of Claudas' vassals even went so far as to sit on the Perilous Seat but was immediately destroyed. An exhausted Lancelot then returned to Camaalot where, hearing of Claudas' activities, he decided to go and avenge his fellow countrymen. Arthur pledged his support. But Claudas made an alliance with the Romans and although Arthur's expeditionary force to the continent began by winning all their battles, they were soon under a great deal of pressure. Lancelot, who had remained in Britain during this time, asked Arthur for further help. So together they crossed the Channel and saved the day. Duke Frolle of Germany who had made claims to the land was killed and Claudas admitted defeat and gave Arthur back the keys of the kingdom of Gaunes. Arthur wished to make Lancelot King of Gaul but he refused, suggesting instead that his brother Hector should become King of Benoic, Bohort King of Gaunes and Lionel King of Gaul. All three refused, however, preferring the life of the errant knight. When Arthur and the British army returned to Camaalot, Elaine appeared at court with Brisane. Rejected by Guinevere, who believed that he had deceived her, Lancelot left Camaalot and became insane again, this time for several years. When Guinevere found out what had really happened she was grief stricken. Bohort, Hector and Lionel went to look for Lancelot, together with Perceval who had recently come to court to be made a knight. Lancelot finally arrived at Corbenic where Elaine recognized him and cured him of his madness with the Holy Grail. There Perceval and Hector found him and told him that the queen knew the truth and wanted him to return. So Lancelot took his son Galahad to be educated at an abbey near Camaalot, then went back to Arthur's court where Guinevere accorded him a passionate greeting and Arthur rejoiced that the best knight in the world had returned.

Part 4, The Quest for the Holy Grail
King Arthur was holding court at Camaalot on the day of Pentecost. But custom demanded that the festivities should not begin until some adventure or marvel had occurred. Then the knights saw these words appear on the Perilous Seat: "454 years after the passion of Jesus Christ, on the day of Pentecost, this seat will know its master." A squire arrived to announce that a piece of red marble with a marvellous sword stuck in it had just appeared floating on the river. The stone bore an inscription to the effect that the sword could only be removed by the best knight in the world. But Lancelot refused, and Gawain who agreed to try next, albeit reluctantly, failed to remove it.[34] A

wise man then arrived with the young Galahad. The windows and doors
closed of their own accord and Galahad sat unscathed on the Perilous Seat.
During the festivities the Holy Grail appeared, hidden behind a veil, to
provide food and drink for everybody. Galahad easily drew the sword from
the stone and was recognized as Lancelot's son. Guinevere felt both proud
and jealous at the same time. The knights of the Round Table then decided,
to Arthur's grief, to go and look for the Grail castle and discover its secrets.
The queen bade a tender farewell to Lancelot. Galahad was successful in a
series of adventures, but Perceval went mad and was tempted by the devil in
the form of a woman. When Perceval did reach the Fisher King's castle, he
failed to utter the right words. Bohort and Lancelot had repented their past
sins, but while Bohort came through his adventures successfully, Lancelot
only just managed to gain admittance to the Grail castle where he was well
treated. Through a half-open door he caught sight of a light coming from
the Grail, but when he tried to cross the threshold, a voice forbad him to
enter. Finally Galahad, Perceval and Bohort cured the Fisher King and
restored prosperity to the land. Then they came to the walls of a mysterious
city. Galahad was allowed in to see what the sacred vessel contained, but the
heavenly vision was too much for him and he died. Perceval turned hermit
and died some time later. Bohort, the only survivor of the successful quest,
retuned to Arthur's court, where the king had the tale of his adventures
written down.

Part 5, *The Death of King Arthur*
All those who had survived the quest for the Holy Grail had returned to
court. Arthur was grief-stricken because twenty-two of his best knights had
killed each other in single combat without knowing whom they were fighting. Gawain bore much of the responsibility for this. Lancelot and the
queen, however, continued their love affair as incautiously as ever, even
when discovered by Agravain, one of Gawain's brothers. King Arthur
decided to hold a great tournament on Winchester Plain to toughen his
remaining knights. Determined to take part in the jousting incognito,
Lancelot feigned illness. Agravain, who had been waiting to use his knowledge against Lancelot, assumed that this illness was being used as an excuse
for Lancelot to remain with the queen, and told the king about their love. He
even suggested that he and Arthur should catch them in the act, to which
Arthur very reluctantly agreed.[35] But Lancelot left and went to Winchester
where he lodged with the vassal of Escalot whose daughter fell in love with
him. Rather than hurt her feelings Lancelot promised to wear her colours in
the tournament. Then when he was wounded she nursed him back to health.
Later Arthur and Gawain stayed in the same house, and when the incorri-
gible Gawain made advances to the Maiden of Escalot she showed him
Lancelot's shield, saying that she would only ever love the man who had won
the tournament. So Arthur and Gawain learnt not only that Lancelot had
been the unidentified victor of the tournament, but also that he was
apparently in love. Arthur was greatly relieved, but when she heard the news
Guinevere was racked by jealousy. As members of the Breton clan, Bohort,
Lionel and Hector also fell foul of the queen, and began to consider leaving
court. Later, however, a little boat floated down to the walls of Camaalot. It
contained the dead body of the Maiden of Escalot and a message saying that
she had died for love of Lancelot who had rejected her. Although Queen

Guinevere regretted her hardness towards him, his enemies began gossiping about the lovers again. When the queen was accused of having given a poisoned fruit to one of the knights of the Round Table, nobody was prepared to champion her until Lancelot arrived and successfully defended her cause.[36] Later Arthur and some of his knights lost their way in the forest and came to Morgan's castle. She welcomed her brother warmly and showed him the room where Lancelot had illustrated his relationship with the queen on the wall. Although very disturbed Arthur refused to believe his sister completely. But Lancelot and Guinevere continued to be as foolhardy as ever, and Agravain again went to Arthur. Mordret advised the king to pretend that he was going hunting so that Guinevere and Lancelot would be left alone. Sure enough, the lovers were caught in *flagrante delicto*, but although Agravain and Mordret seized hold of Guinevere, Lancelot escaped. Guinevere was condemned to the stake and was about to be executed when Lancelot and the Breton knights descended on the knights guarding her. In the terrible massacre that followed Gawain's brothers Agravain and Guerrehes were killed. Arthur laid siege to the Joyous Guard, where Lancelot, Bohort, Lionel, Hector and Guinevere had taken shelter. But after a fierce battle the bishop of Rochester came on the orders of the pope to make peace. The queen was to be returned to Arthur and the Bretons were to return to their own country. So Lancelot and his fellow knights went home and fortified their cities in case of attack. Gawain, who had previously tried to dissuade Agravain from betraying the lovers,[37] was now full of hatred for his former friend and urged Arthur to mount an expedition to the continent to punish Lancelot. The king, anxious not to offend his nephew and his barons, agreed to go, leaving the kingdom in Mordret's hands. To avoid a full-scale war it was agreed that Gawain and Lancelot should fight a duel to the death. Then if Gawain were to be killed Arthur would return to Britain. Although Lancelot gained the upper hand in the duel he would not kill Gawain despite Bohort's insistence that he should. While Arthur was having Gawain taken care of, he learnt that Mordret had spread a rumour that the king was dead, formed an alliance with the Saxons and the Irish and taken full control in Britain. On his death bed Gawain warned his uncle not to fight Mordret himself and, regretting his quarrel with Lancelot, bemoaned the fact that such a model of chivalry should not be there to defend the kingdom. Arthur returned to Britain nevertheless and prepared to meet Mordret's army on Salisbury Plain (at the battle of Camlaan, according to the Welsh tradition). Despite the most sinister omens, Arthur would not withdraw; and as the battle raged the last of the Round Table knights were killed. Finally Arthur and Mordret came face to face. Arthur killed Mordret but, mortally wounded himself, he left the battle field with Girflet, son of Do. Rather than see his sword Escalibur fall into any hands but Lancelot's, Arthur then asked Girflet to go and throw it into a lake. But Girflet wanted to keep it and twice returned to the king saying that he had obeyed him. Arthur would not believe him because Girflet could report no marvels having occurred when he threw the sword into the water. And finally the reluctant knight did throw the sword into the lake whereupon a hand rose from the water to take it. Then Arthur asked Girflet to leave him on the sea shore and go. Girflet obeyed but hid behind a rock to see a group of women appear from a boat and take Arthur aboard. Obviously the king had been taken to the Isle of Avalon by his sister Morgan and her servants. Girflet then took refuge with some monks but died eighteen days later. Guinevere, who had fled to a tower to escape Mordret, then went to live in an abbey. When Lancelot learnt what had happened, he formed an army and crossed the Channel with Bohort and Lionel to avenge Arthur's death by killing Mordret's sons. Then the Breton heroes also retired to an abbey. Lancelot died soon after. Only Bohort survived, to become the last of the knights of the Round Table.[38]

Despite its inherent contradictions, this vast epic work has a remarkably clear and cohesive thread running through it. Obviously many episodes have been omitted from the summary above, which concentrates on the purely Arthurian material, leaving the sections devoted to Tristan, Merlin and the Grail aside. But behind the battles of its god-like heroes. whether against the powers of darkness or each other, behind the curious mixture of Christian miracle and pagan marvel, the *Lancelot in Prose* remains a single, if strangely anomalous work.

It was very successful throughout the Middle Ages and Thomas Malory used it as a foundation for his *Morte d'Arthur* more than two centuries after the *Lancelot* was originally compiled. Altogether it provided Western Europe with its own epic, which owed nothing to the Greek and Roman traditions, and which produced a real literary renaissance among European writers.

For the *Lancelot in Prose* is only one version of the Arthurian story among many others written at the same time or later. Some of these borrowed from the *Lancelot,* some used all kinds of disparate sources. That is certainly the impression we get from *Perlesvaux,* a strange composite tale written between 1191 and 1212 under the influence of the Abbey of Glastonbury.

Perlesvaux
Perlesvaux received his name [Lose the Valleys or *Perd-les-vaux*] when his mother's enemies took his inheritance from him. When he had gone to the castle of the Fisher King, he had not dared ask the right questions although the Fisher King was dying and the whole country under a curse. King Arthur himself lost his power to give and his court was abandoned. On Guinevere's advice Arthur made a pilgrimage to the Chapel of St Augustine in Wales. He could not go into the chapel, but hearing the mass from outside he had a vision. On his return he won a fight against the Knight of the Flaming Spear and grew aware that his power to give had returned. So he held court at Penzance where three messengers came from the Fisher King to tell of their master's condition and to leave a shield which had belonged to Joseph of Arimathea for Perceval. The knights set off on the Quest for the Grail. Gawain learned that he had to obtain the sword which had beheaded John the Baptist. This he did by killing a giant who had taken the son of King Gurgalan, but he was unable to prevent the giant from killing the young man. However, the king was grateful to Gawain and he and his people were converted to Christianity, although they still carried out the pagan ritual of cutting the victim's body into strips, which they put into a cauldron to stew, and then drinking the brew. Gawain crossed the Perilous Bridge into the Grail castle and was received by the Fisher King. He witnessed the procession of the Grail, but he too omitted to ask the vital question. The following morning the place was deserted. Gawain found his horse ready saddled and rode off into a storm. Lancelot, meanwhile, had made his way into a ruined city (the city of Souls) where invisible creatures could be heard wailing. A

knight holding a large axe appeared and asked Lancelot to cut off his head. Lancelot was then to return a year later and undergo the same treatment. Lancelot agreed but when he left, the body and the head had disappeared. He then went to the Fisher King's castle where he was warmly welcomed, but where his sins prevented him from seeing the Grail and the spear. Perlesvaux had also pursued a series of adventures, changing his armour and his weapons as he went along. Coming to Penzance by night, he took the shield left there for him and a sword brought back by Gawain. He then saved Lancelot from mortal danger and killed the enemies who had taken his mother's land. One of them he strung up by the feet so that his head fell into a bowl full of the blood of the other twelve men Perlesvaux had decapitated. He then returned to Arthur's court and celebrations were held in his honour. Meanwhile Lancelot had returned to the city of Souls to lay his own head on the block, but had only to undergo a mock execution. Perlesvaux forced his way into the Turning Castle, killed the devilish Knight of the Dragon and then entered the Copper Tower which melted before his eyes. Perlesvaux's triumphs broke the spells laid on the countryside and the Grail reappeared at the Fisher King's castle. The Fisher King had died and was buried in a chapel which became miraculously illuminated every night. Arthur, then at Carduel (Carlisle), learned of Perlesvaux's success. Two suns appeared on the horizon. Kai fled when it was discovered that he had murdered Arthur's son. Just as Arthur decided to make a pilgrimage to the Grail castle, Guinevere died and was buried at Avalon (here identified with Glastonbury). On his journey towards the Grail castle Arthur stayed in a deserted house haunted by devilish phantoms, where he found the decapitated heads of 200 men. Arthur, Lancelot and Gawain put the spirits to flight. Then, after a journey to Tintagel where an old priest told him who his parents were, Arthur arrived at the Grail castle and was received by Perlesvaux. An inconsolable Lancelot visited Guinevere's grave. After accomplishing further marvels Perlesvaux left to follow the ship containing the body of the Fisher King and the sacred objects on its voyage to the Other World. Only a hermit remained in the Grail castle and when he died the place became a ruin.

Perlesvaux is a rhapsody on Celtic themes. We find in it the royal custom of the obligatory gift, the strange ritual of execution which forms the basis of the English Sir Gawain and the Green Knight and occurs in the Irish Feast of Briciu, and, of course, the decapitated heads which appear throughout the various Celtic traditions. It was obviously written by a clerk attached in some way to the Abbey of Glastonbury who was familiar with Celtic legends and was therefore presumably intended to spiritually uplift the Christian flock. But the inclusion of distinctly pagan material, such as the ritual hanging by the feet practised by the Celts in honour of Teutates, and the cannibalistic meal which dates back to pre-Celtic times, brings Perlesvaux much closer to the Welsh Peredur than to other versions of the Grail story influenced by the 13th-century monastic orders. It is far more a glorification of the Plantagenet monarchy and the monasticism of the Island Church than a deliberate exhortation to the faithful to combat the forces of evil. And unlike the Cistercian versions of the story, Perlesvaux leaves its hero on the way to further adventures in the Outer World. Just as Arthur lies waiting for the right moment to reunite Britain and Brittany, so the Grail lies waiting for the daring or the faithful to find it again.

Throughout the 13th and 14th centuries, European writers continued to exploit the "matter of Britain" in prose and verse works. Their literary value varies a great deal, but all of them are linked in some way to King Arthur, even if very tenuously. Many of them fall outside the usual literary classifications, but they remain an interesting mixture of their authors' imagination and written or oral traditional tales. The 13th-century *Romance of Jauffre,* for example, combines Celtic ideas and the spirit of the Troubadours.

Romance of Jauffre

After Jauffre had been made a knight at Arthur's Pentecostal court, an armed but unknown knight rode into the hall and struck the knight standing next to Guinevere dead at her feet.[39] He then told the assembled company that his name was Taulat de Ruginon and that he would return the next year to commit the same crime unless one of the knights stopped him. Jauffre immediately obtained Arthur's permission to go after him. But when, three days later, exhausted from a fight with a giant along the way, Jauffre had still not found Taulat, he fell into a doze and his horse took him to the gates of a marvellous garden. The garden belonged to Brunissen, a young orphan who had mourned continually for the last seven years, and whose only joy was to listen to the song of the magical birds in her orchard.[40] Jauffre entered the garden and fell asleep, but his intrusion stopped the birds singing and Brunissen sent her servants to find out what had happened. After fighting them off Jauffre went back to sleep again only to be seized by a hundred knights. He was then condemned to death, but managed to escape much to the sorrow of Brunissen who had by now fallen in love with him. Jauffre was then cared for by a cowherd who told him who Brunissen was but angrily refused to explain the general lamentations Jauffre had witnessed in the castle, and attacked him with an axe. Jauffre ran away and found himself in another castle where a king was lying wounded on a bed. An old woman appeared and told Jauffre that this king and Brunissen had both suffered at the hands of Taulat, and that it was out of respect for the king's sufferings that the people sighed and lamented. Jauffre lay in wait for Taulat who had been coming once a month to strike the wounded king. When Taulat arrived Jauffre beat him and sent him wounded to Arthur's court. He then went to fetch Brunissen and married her at Carduel.

Unlike the *Lancelot en Prose* or the various versions of the Perceval story, romances of this kind were biographical poems, centred round a single hero. Then there were romances based on some single event which set a series of adventures in motion. The 14th century saw a wealth of poems of both these types, still firmly lodged within the Arthurian tradition but no longer written for political or ecclesiastical reasons. A romance like *Meriadeuc* fits into both categories.

Meriadeuc

Meriadeuc was also known as the Knight with Two Swords and acquired his nickname after a strange series of adventures. A knight named Brien de la Gastine arrived at Arthur's court to ask the king for a gift. Bound to agree to this, Arthur learnt that Brien wished Gawain to act as his champion in a duel against his enemy Bleheri. Gawain mortally wounded Bleheri who, before he died, asked that he should be buried in the Ruined Chapel with his sword by his side. He added that whoever girded on the sword would lose it only to a knight as valiant as himself. As the result of an extra-ordinary adventure Lore, the beautiful young Queen of Cardigan, put on the sword and went to Arthur's court to find a knight who would take it from her and whom she could then marry. Various knights tried unsuccessfully. But the young Meriadeuc, then Gawain's squire, asked to be made a knight so that he could try. He succeeded, but immediately left court, much to Lore's grief. He now had two swords, hence the nickname. Arthur promised Lore that he would find Meriadeuc and set off to look for him. Meanwhile Meriadeuc had learnt that the Bleheri Gawain had killed was his father. Full of hatred for his father's murderer, Meriadeuc went to fight Gawain, but his mother stopped the fight and made peace between them. During Arthur's absence, a disloyal vassal had invaded the land and taken many prisoners. Meriadeuc then encountered the treacherous Roux of the Perilous Valley, killed him and freed the prisoners. Arthur welcomed Meriadeuc at court and there the Knight with Two Swords married Lore. It was he who overcame King Ris of Outre Hombre who demanded Arthur's beard for the border of a cloak.

In most of these episodic poems Gawain is either the leading character or one of several central figures. He totally eclipses the other Round Table knights, Lancelot included, both by the variety of his adventures and by his skill in dealing with difficult situations. Gawain belongs to an area of Celtic myth which is also part of the structure of Celtic society itself. For the son of the reigning king's sister is invariably the heir apparent and in most cases the queen's lover as well.

Arthurian legend continued to develop right into the 15th century. None of the 15th-century authors, however, was as detailed and precise as Thomas Malory. His *Morte d'Arthur* is a masterpiece of English literature and a vital piece of documentary evidence since it covers the whole of the Arthurian legend, including various episodes unrecorded in the continental and Welsh traditions.

The fourth book of the *Morte d'Arthur* especially contains some extraordinary anecdotes concerning the relationship between King Arthur and his sister Morgan la Fée which are found nowhere else. Where these anecdotes come from we have no way of knowing. They totally contradict the version of the legend found in the *Lancelot in Prose* and in Geoffrey of Monmouth's *Vita Merlini*. They do, however, form an integral part of Arthurian literature.

The Story of Morgan and Arthur: Thomas Malory
When stag hunting with Uryen and Accolon of Gaul, who was Morgan's lover, Arthur and his companions found themselves on the seashore where they saw a boat with silken sails beached on the sand. There appeared to be nobody on board, so Arthur persuaded his knights to look inside. The whole interior was magnificently decorated with silk. Suddenly darkness fell and a hundred torches appeared to light the scene. Twelve beautiful maidens came to greet Arthur and took him and his two companions into a room where a sumptuous meal lay ready for them. After Arthur, Uryen and Accolon had eaten and drunk their fill, they were taken to three separate rooms where they slept deeply. but the next day Uryen woke to find himself in bed with his wife Morgan at Camaalot, while Arthur woke in a dark prison among a score of other knights. They told the king that they had been taken prisoner by Damas, the master of the castle who was the most treacherous knight in the world but also the most cowardly. A girl came to Arthur to suggest that he fight a knight to win freedom for himself and the other captives. To this the

king readily agreed. Accolon meanwhile had woken by a fountain where a hideous dwarf came to tell him that Morgan wished him to fight a knight for her and would send him Arthur's sword to make him invincible. Another messenger from Morgan then went to Arthur with a perfect imitation of Escalibur for him to use in the fight. So Accolon and Arthur rode out to fight each other without knowing who their opponent was. Luckily the Lady of the Lake[41] had discovered Morgan's treachery and just when Accolon was gaining the upper hand she arrived and magicked the real Escalibur out of his hands. Arthur then picked it up and won the fight. Seriously wounded, Accolon confessed that he was Morgan's lover and that she had asked him to kill Arthur. She would then have been free to kill her husband King Uryen and marry Accolon. Arthur was astounded by these revelations, but spared Accolon's life and demanded that Damas release his fellow captives. Four days later Accolon died. Meanwhile, assuming that Arthur had been killed, Morgan decided to go ahead with her plan. While Uryen was still asleep she called for her servant and asked her to fetch her master's sword. But the terrified servant went to Yvain, Uryen's son, and told him everything. Yvain told her to do as her mistress had bid her. Then just as Morgan was holding the sword poised over Uryen's head, Yvain burst into the room and took it from her. Morgan pretended that she had had a momentary fit of madness. She then learnt how Accolon had died and was totally grief stricken. Furious with Arthur, she sent him a magnificent, magic cloak which would burn the skin of whoever put it on. Arthur took it as a gesture of reconciliation from Morgan and was about to put it on when the Lady of the Lake appeared and warned him of the danger. Arthur angrily banished his sister from court. Then he pardoned Uryen who had been no more than a victim, but for some reason banished Yvain, who left the court with Gawain. (*Morte d'Arthur*, translated into modern English by Janet Cowen, Penguin Books)

This selection of Arthurian literature would not be complete without a mention of an extraordinary 16th-century work, which is probably one of the last works based on the Arthurian legends to show any real originality. The exact title of the work is "the great and inestimable Chronicles of the great and enormous giant Gargantua, containing his genealogy, the size and strength of his body and the marvellous feats of arms he performed for King Arthur, as shown hereafter." Attributed to Rabelais, it was published in 1532 at Lyon, at the same time as Rabelais' *Pantagruel* and the anonymous *Great Chronicles of Gargantua*. Its interest lies in the way the author has linked the Arthurian legends and popular folklore in the shape of Gargantua.

The story starts with a half magical, half ribald account of Gargantua's conception. Knowing that he will sooner or later become Vivienne's captive, Merlin promises Arthur to provide help against his enemies. He fashions a man named Grandgousier from the bones of a male whale and a phial of Lancelot's blood, and a woman named Gargamelle from the bones of a female whale and ten pounds of Guinevere's nail clippings. These two larger than life characters then produce the giant Gargantua. When his parents die, Merlin arrives to take him to Arthur. The king is very impressed by his size and agrees to have a sixty foot iron club made for him. With this formidable weapon Gargantua then destroys the entire army of Gog and Magog[42] and kills 100,210 soldiers of the rebellious Dutch and Irish armies. After remaining in Arthur's service for two hundred years, three months and four days exactly, he is transported to fairyland by Gain,

Melusine and various others.

It seems unlikely that Rabelais was actually responsible for this work, though he would undoubtedly have been capable of writing it. Its comic nature should not blind us to the power of the traditional basis which underlies it. Clearly Arthurian legend was still very much alive in the 16th century or there would have been no need to include it in the then fashionable cycle of Gargantua stories which were actually part of Gallic and French folklore.

Obviously there is far too much Arthurian literary material for us to examine and analyse it all in a work of this kind. And we have left some of the works written in Welsh, Latin, French and English to be discussed in a later chapter on the historical figure of Arthur. But it is hoped this chapter has given some indication of the size and scope of the literature, so that we can go on to examine the reasons behind its existence and development.

For although the Arthurian romances are now acknowledged to be Celtic in origin, the question of how Celtic legends passed into French and German literary writings still remains. Perhaps the Britons and later the Anglo-Normans handed them on. Perhaps it was the Bretons, or the devoted habitues of the court of Poitiers where Eleanor of Aquitaine, one of the great influences on the 12th-century European intelligentsia, held sway. There are also questions to be asked about the politics behind the romances. They did, after all, reach the height of their popularity at a time when the Anglo-Angevin Plantagenet dynasty was becoming increasingly powerful in its opposition to the continental Capétian monarchy. And as the Capetians claimed to be the descendants of Charlemagne, so Henry II claimed his descent from Arthur.

There are other areas for discussion as well. We have to examine the historical evidence for Arthur, the 6th-century Briton, and his political position in a Britain which had just found independence from the Romans, only to have it threatened by the Saxon invaders. And finally, we have to look at the mythology behind the man. His Roman sounding name suggests connexions with the bear; and all the ancient gods of the Celtic pantheon have contributed something to his legend. It may well be that we reach no definite conclusions in any of these areas. But there can be little doubt that they add a great deal of interest to any study of the Arthurian tradition.

CHAPTER TWO

The Political Background

UR view of the Arthurian epic is a medieval one, as full of misleading clichés as the Romantics' fervid images of the Middle Ages. It is all fortified castles surrounded by high walls walls and deep moats, richly decorated pavilions and magnificent clothes. The knights we see are actually a perfect reflection of the "courtly" aristocrats who peopled the palaces of the 12th and 13th century Europe. The classical Arthurian romances take their readers into the courts of Southern France which have been clearly described by the chroniclers of the time and which have nothing to do with Celtic society. Indeed, the Frenchness of the manners portrayed by Chrétien de Troyes or the anonymous authors of the *Lancelot in Prose* has led a good number of scholars to suppose that the Arthurian romances were not based upon Celtic legends at all, but the original works of French minds.

Before going any further, there are two basic comments to be made about such suppositions. Firstly, the scope of French civilization or, to be more accurate, Occitanian French civilization in the 12th and 13th centuries embraced the aristocratic culture of both Great Britain and France. Since the time of William the Conqueror, the kings of England had been French in language and education and had scattered nobles and churchmen of French origin all over the country. Furthermore, the marriage of Eleanor of Aquitaine to an Angevin prince, who subsequently became king of England, had brought more than one third of the area of France under the political thrall of the English monarch, himself a vassal of the Capetian king. Clearly, therefore, there was little distinction in cultural terms between France and Britain, between Carlisle, London or Canterbury and Poitiers, Paris or Troyes.

Secondly, there was a long gap between the writing of the romances and the events they purported to describe. The kinds of distortion time imposes are evident in the *chansons de geste* which were written at the end of the 11th and beginning of the 12th centuries about events which happened round the year 800 during the Carolingian era. There is a gap of three centuries between the historical Charlemagne and the character who bears his name in the *chansons de geste*, and the whole decor of the tales, the people and their behaviour belong to the year 1100, to a society governed by feudal laws which did not exist at the time of Charlemagne. As far as the Arthurian romances are concerned, there is an even greater time lag. Written in the 12th century, the events they relate are assumed to have taken place around the 6th. Six centuries have changed men and manners from those of Merovingian or post-Roman-imperial times into their "courtly" counterparts. So it is hardly surprising that the King Arthur of the Round Table romances behaves more like a refined, English or French, 12th-century king, than a 6th-century confederate chief of the Celtic peoples. Six centuries have obscured the Arthur who led the Britons in their final onslaught against the Germanic invaders who were to change Britain into an England essentially different both in culture and language.

Meanwhile, however, the 12th and 13th-century French Arthurian romances are as they are; and it is through them that we have to examine the Arthurian phenomenon in full awareness of the political background which they betray. Only then can we hope to assemble a real picture of the 6th-century Arthur, who lived in an entirely different social context. In his *L'Aventure Chevaleresque*, Erich Köhler does not claim to be retrieving the Celtic sources, but merely seeks to define the various social relationships existing at the time when the romances were written. And he comments that "the Celtic national hero, Arthur, owes his success on French soil to the fact that he exactly matches the aspirations of the higher nobility, then court nobility."[1] He adds that the courtly romance was "encouraged by the princely houses of Blois, Champagne and Flanders who still opposed the monarchy, while the Capetian kings remained deliberately aloof from the literature of their time which was shaped by the political situation." In fact "Arthur is never a sovereign, a true king; he is always the symbol of an ideal feudal state constructed to maintain the perfect human order it represents." The most important vassal of the Capetian king, with whom the French monarchy was to have most difficulties despite the strength of its legal rights to suzerainty was the count of Anjou, duke of Normandy, owner of Aquitane and Brittany, and also incidentally king of England, So while the Capetian king could not see anything of himself in Arthur, the Plantagenet king found it easier to accept the image of a flexible and aristocratic monarchy presented in the Arthurian romances. The Plantagenets, therefore, encouraged, if not actively began, the diffusion of the Arthurian legend.

The Plantagenets

There has been fierce debate on this subject. Some scholars have maintained that the proliferation of Arthurian romances was due to the activities of three men who worked for the count of Anjou and other Anglo-Norman dignitaries. "Geoffrey of Monmouth, Gautier of Oxford and Caradoc of Llancarvan composed a worthy trio. The two former set out to hoodwink their royal patron Count Robert of Gloucester (the natural son of Henry I of England), who, like the other Anglo-Normans of the day, was curious about the ancient history of his new country. Geoffrey was also motivated by Welsh patriotism, his jealousy of the success of the Chronicles of William of Malmesbury and Henry of Huntingdon, who were also protected by Count Robert and Alexander, bishop of Lincoln, and perhaps most of all by the desire to make his way in the world."[2] These early 12th-century writers are therefore said to have invented the Arthurian legend in order to flatter the Anglo-Norman monarchy by tracing it back to noble forebears as Virgil had his protector Augustus by proving that the *gens Julia* could be traced back to the goddess Venus.

Admittedly the Anglo-Norman dynasty, which became the Anglo-Angevin dynasty with the succession of Henry II, had reasons enough to suffer from a guilty conscience. Their forefathers had kept the throne purely by force. Virtually the only links between the 12th-century kings of England and the traditional Saxon monarchy lay in a few marriages arranged for that specific purpose. The Normans felt like usurpers in a country which was not theirs. They had kept their continental way of thought, spent most of their time on the continent and spoke French. They felt the need to justify their presence in Great Britain. In that sense it is quite likely that the kings of England and their followers did indeed encourage the clerks who worked so hard to trace their descent from mythical or historical antecedents like Arthur. This was certainly the case with the *Historia Regum Britanniae* in which much is made of the links between Britain and Brittany, both of which Arthur is supposed to have governed. There is a certain amount of historical evidence for the connexion, but it took a mind of some cunning to use it to make Arthur a continental king who defended Britain from the unwelcome Saxon invaders and Brittany from Frankish invaders on the continent. For once the Anglo-Norman or Anglo-Angevin kings could be seen as inheritors of the Celtic kingdom of Britain and Brittany, the Capetian dynasty was bound to assume the role of the aggressor.

To take steps of this kind, however, required a certain amount of man-handling of history and support from traditional Celtic epic which was already regarded by the Celtic peoples as historical writing because of their peculiar ability to dream up their national history. Geoffrey of Monmouth invented nothing. He has too long been held responsible for the Arthurian romances. Admittedly he was one of the first men to spread this epic tale of the kingdom of Britain, to create a cycle of adventures around the character of Arthur. But in the *Vita Merlini* and the *Prophecies of Merlin*, which he wrote before the *Historia*, it is the Scots bard Myrddin Merlin who comes to the rescue of the Britons. Geoffrey merely transferred some of the magical and prophetic aspects of these works to the *Historia*, and other writers were quick to exploit them for the greater glory of a monarchy now regarded as successors to the Celtic kings. Moreover, Geoffrey says at the beginning of his *Historia* that his book owes much to Gautier of Oxford who supposedly gave him "an old book written in the British language" with a request that he should translate it into Latin. There is no reason to doubt Geoffrey's words. The British book certainly existed, but it may well have been written by Gautier himself who was as anxious as Geoffrey to please the Norman monarchy. And it is significant that the third member of the trio, Caradoc of Llancarvan, took up the story of the kingdom of Britain from the point where Geoffrey left off. But while Geoffrey translated British into Latin to make it intelligible to the European reader, Caradoc translated old Latin chronicles into Welsh.[3]

We now know for certain that Geoffrey did not invent the Arthurian cycle; and, what is more, he was by no means the sole propagator of it. The Arthurian legend existed in perfectly structured and developed form before his time and was known not only in England and the Celtic countries, but also in France and Italy where the sculptures on Modena cathedral date from the early years of the 12th century before the *Historia* was written. Basically Geoffrey, Gautier and Caradoc were using the actual situation to their own advantage, and it is that situation which interests us. We can argue that the Anglo-Norman kings needed to prove the nobility of their descent and relied on Celtic tradition to legalize their claim to the English throne. But since these kings had usurped the Saxon throne, it would surely have been more rational to establish links with Edward the Confessor's line, especially as he was a recognized saint of the Church. What sense could there be in tracing connexions with a people conquered and assimilated by the Saxons long before, when a solid Anglo-Saxon royal line existed and was by then firmly lodged in popular tradition?

There are several answers to this question. First, there was a wide gap between what it is convenient to call the intellectual elite of England, which was wholly French in outlook and converted to Norman law, and the mass of the people. The large majority of the English were still Saxon, with the exception of the inhabitants of Cornwall and Cumberland who were still basically Celtic. Not only were there misunderstandings between the Normans and Saxons, but also positive opposition. Walter Scott illustrates this hostility in his novel *Ivanhoe*. The Norman conquest was too fresh in men's memories for any real reconciliation to take place until the 15th-century, when the Plantagenets were replaced by the Tudors who came from Celtic Wales.

Secondly, the Normans and the Celts were united by a common enmity towards the Saxons. Despite their differences they had felt bound to join forces as early as 1066 when William the Conqueror invaded England bringing with him a large contingent of Breton nobles who wanted revenge on the Saxons and to regain the lands of their forefathers. William had rewarded them by allotting them areas of Saxon land. To take one example, the count of Richmond could trace his descent straight back to the duke of Brittany. So, since the Norman monarchy had settled in England there had been a kind of complicity between the two peoples who conquered the Saxons. Indeed in Brittany the Saxons are still called the *Saozon ruzh*, or red Saxons, a term used both for English tourists and for those ancient enemies who forced the early Britons to settle in Brittany.

The third answer is also political in nature. The Anglo-Norman monarchy and, more especially, the Anglo-Angevin kings were continental rulers. A king of England who relied solely on his Saxon heritage would be hard put to justify his claims to large areas of the continent. And since this area included Celtic Brittany, a common denominator had to be found. Pan-Celticism answered the need perfectly. The dream of both the Arthurian legends and the Plantagenet kings was to unite the British Isles with the area once known as Gaul and thus eliminate the dangerous competition of the Capetian monarchy which was firmly implanted in the Ile de France but whose suzerainty over the provinces was merely a matter of form. It was in pursuit of this dream that Henry II had himself elected High King of Ireland and married his son Geoffrey to the daughter of the duke of Brittany. Plantagenet policy is also readily observable in the way the English sovereigns ignored Salic law and pressed their claim to the French crown through Isabella, wife of Edward II of England and daughter of Philip of France. Indeed the Hundred Years War was a direct result of this policy, the desire to realize the Arthurian dream of a great empire reuniting all the countries previously under Celtic domination.

These comments about the political background against which the Arthurian romances were developed may seem like gross generalizations, but they offer the only explanation as to why Celtic legends which had been in existence for centuries should suddenly become the chief concern of European romance writers. These writers were under the direct or indirect influence of the Plantagenets or their allies. The authors of the various versions of the Tristan legend were Anglo-Norman. Chrétien de Troyes lived at the court of Champagne which was suffused with Celtic and Southern French culture and linked to Eleanor of Aquitaine and the "English" nobility. The authors of the *Lancelot in Prose* who made Arthur the central figure of their epic were playing along with the Anglo-Angevin dynasty, whether consciously or not. While the Breton or Welsh authors clearly had every interest in developing their own traditions and grasped the opportunity with both hands.

Besides, both Capetians and Plantagenets were prepared to use any weapons, literature included, to further their own cause in a struggle where the Capetians enjoyed greater legal claims to power and the Plantagenets greater physical force.

As successors to the Carolingians, the Capetians featured in the legend of Charlemagne narrated in the *chansons de geste*. Whether these were the works of clerks, as Joseph Bedier suggests, or came from Germanic ballads, as Gaston Paris proposes, makes little difference. The fact remains that the Charlemagne they portray is not a Carolingian king but a Capetian monarch. Their central theme is that of an empire under the temporal rule of an emperor and the spiritual rule of the Pope. The papacy had fallen out with the German Holy Roman Emperor and turned readily to the less threatening king of France. This explains the deeply Christian nature of the Frankish epics: they bear witness to a constant struggle betweeen Christianity as represented by Charlemagne, king of France (justifiably regarded as a German in the German principalities since he never spoke a word of Early French), and Islam or any other non-Roman Catholic religion as represented by the Infidel. The *chansons de geste* set out to glorify the French monarchy at a time when there was a growing tendency to justify the present through the past. It was also the time of the Crusades; and these epics provided excellent propaganda with their insistence on the exploits of feudal warriors in the service of their king, but more especially in the service of God. Their ideological goal was the conversion of the world to Christianity and as such countered the theories of a holy war preached by the Moslems. Finally they offered the partisans of Capetian rule an opportunity to underline the value of a monarchy firmly settled on the continent which spent its time defending the Christian faith.

The Round Table romances are in many ways very like the *chansons de geste*. Obviously manners had developed. The fierce feudal society described in the *Chanson de Roland* or the *Chanson de Guillaume* has gone. But the warriors' conduct remains very similar. The Arthurian hero fights for his king, but also for God, not very well perhaps, but the intention is there. The Quest for the Holy Grail is like the Conquest of Jerusalem. Just as the heroes of the *chansons de geste* had to defend a Christianity constantly beleaguered by Infidels of all kinds, so the heroes of the Round Table romances had to defend the Christian kingdom of Arthur. In a number of texts the frontiers of Arthur's kingdom are marked by crosses. Beyond lie heathen lands, haunted by the devils and fairies of Celtic mythology which Christianity has failed to win over to the side of right. We have an example in Edern and Gwynn, the two sons of Nudd. Edern became a saint in Brittany, whereas Gwynn remained the Welsh guardian of the Underworld. In all the 13th-century literature, particularly the *Lancelot.in Prose* which came directly from Anglo-Angevin and Cistercian influences, the character of Arthur becomes the symbol of Christianity. His defeat at Camlaan is the defeat of Christianity as a whole by the forces of darkness in the shape of Arthur's nephew, Mordret, the ally of the heathen Saxons and Irish. However, since Arthur is to return to unite Britain and Brittany once more, hope remains secure and the flavour of messianism continues.

For Arthur did not die. He will return. There was a similar legend at about the same time concerning Frederick Barbarossa, emperor of Germany, who supposedly lies sleeping somewhere in the mountains of the Black Forest and will one day return for the greater glory of the German peoples. Baldr, son of Wotan or Odin in old Germanic mythology, was also to return to start a new golden age after the world had suffered much war and turmoil. The myth of Baldr's return was unhappily personified in Hitler who came to make the German people absolute masters of the world. Mythology played a considerable part in the Nazi phenomenon, drawing as it did on the subconscious culture of the German peoples. The belief in Arthur's return is not a literary invention but a myth deeply rooted among Celtic peoples. In Richard Barber's book, *Arthur of Albion*, he quotes from an account written by a monk from Laon who was travelling in South West England in 1113: "From there (Exeter) we went to the province called Devon where we were shown the Chair and the Oven of King Arthur, famous in the history of the Britons, and we were told that this had been his country. In the town called Bodmin . . . a certain man . . . kept watch in the presence of the relic . . . But, just as the Bretons are wont to quarrel with the French about King Arthur, the same man began to argue with one of our companions, Haganellus . . . saying that Arthur was still alive." This document, which has no literary pretensions, proves that Celtic peoples on both sides of the Channel were familiar with the legend and could sink all their hopes and their desire for revenge in the anticipation of Arthur's return.

So, having established the political background to the creation of the Arthurian romances, we can safely conclude that the image of the sleeping King Arthur, a king who would return to reunite Great Britain and Brittany and to win back Gaul, was bound to be identified with the Anglo-Norman dynasty.

There had been a well thought out attempt to rework the Arthurian myth for the advancement of the Anglo-Normans before Henry II acceded to the English throne. This was during the period of strife between the Saxons and the Normans on the one hand and between the Saxons and the Celts on the other, when Stephen of Blois and Mathilda were quarrelling over the English throne. So that when Henry appeared, with his hands on the continent and his impressive and politically active queen, Eleanor of Aquitaine, it was logical that the court writers should exploit existing legends still further. They had only to give them form, to build a body of literature round them. Then the exploits of Arthur and his knights could stand as symbols of Angevin attempts to realize the Celtic dream, in the same way as the *chansons de geste* represented the continental authority of the Capetians.

However far-fetched this line of reasoning may appear at first glance, it is one which has been seriously debated for some time. Discussion on the subject has been side-tracked into arguments as to whether the Arthurian legends reached the romance writers through the Bretons or the British, which need not concern us here. For the fact remains that any courtier wishing to benefit from Henry's acknowledged munificence had an interest in representing this important political figure as the inheritor of a King Arthur who ruled over a great empire both in Britain and on the continent. A desire to please Henry II must surely have been one of the most important causes, if not *the* most important, of the rapid dissemination of Arthurian legends throughout 12th and 13th-century Europe.

There is further evidence to support this argument. We have scarcely touched upon the Anglo-Angevins' method of government. The geographical position of their lands set them apart from other European sovereigns straight away. And they were also in a delicate political position because the society in which they lived was still theoretically a feudal one. So their freedom was restricted to a certain extent by the will of their suzerain king, although his authority was limited to the moral sphere. Interestingly, the political theorists of the 12th century were Anglo-Normans. One of them, John of Salisbury, deserves fairly detailed examination, since his writings hold the key to any discussion of Plantagenet desires to rebuild Arthur's empire, legendary or no.

John Of Salisbury

John of Salisbury was the author of a political treatise entitled *Policraticus* which he completed after many years' work in 1159. So he is representative of the attitudes of clerks associated with the Anglo-Norman court at the end of the purely feudal era. For it was then that the first signs of urban emancipation and the creation of an independent class of knights began to threaten the existing structures. The interest of John's work lies in the fact that it appears to be a theologically based consideration of the political institutions of the Early Middle Ages, from which he draws his own conclusions. This means that the *Policraticus* is totally independent from the continental schools of thought which were later to give rise to Thomism. The remarkable lack of Aristotelian influence in the treatise places it closer to the Barbarian pragmatism of early medieval Europe than to the still far-reaching and all-powerful Roman dogmatism of continental Church doctrine. This probably resulted from a tendency to reach back to the Bible and the writings of the early Church Fathers, but also from a resurgence of the singular attitudes of the early Celtic Church which were linked to memories of Druidism. So the ideas we find in John of Salisbury's writings shed a great deal of light on the aspirations of the 12th-century Anglo-Norman kings, on the demands of those nobles opposed to monarchical power and, finally, on some of the customs revealed in the Arthurian romances.

In summarizing John's beliefs, we should first stress the fact that they form a feudal doctine basically concerned with the transmission of office and property through heredity. The oath of fealty remains as important as ever, since it defines all the relationships between a prince and his subjects. However, it is no longer a mere formality but a true commitment on both sides, rather in the way a contract might be entered into under Celtic legislation by two parties swearing an oath in the presence of those supernatural powers who were to monitor its application. So significant does John consider the oath that he totally denies even the right of tyrannicide, which he considers justifiable in some cases, to those who have sworn an oath of fealty to the tyrant. In fact he inclines towards a form of government like that supported by the Jewish people under the Judges, before the establishment of the throne of Israel.

The basis of John's ideas is the mooted existence of some prior, transcendental Law. From here he moves logically, if surprisingly, to the conclusion that any people who would follow this Law and accept its basic demands needs no king.

Here, in the middle of the 12th century, was the expression of a doctrine which was to reach full development at the end of the 19th and beginning of the 20th centuries with libertarian theorists like Élisée Reclus or Kropotkin. But even before John, various Celtic peoples in Britain and Ireland appear to have tried a similar system of anarchical existence.

However, a society which relies on the mutual trust of its members needs an administrator, as Rousseau was later to stress. And here John turns to biblical sources to suggest that the ideal administrator would be a judge, like Samuel. (We might note, in passing, that in Celtic societies the Druid's role as priest and judge was practically one and the same.) Seeing that most peoples have finally opted for monarchy or some other form of government, John suggests that the establishment of such governments marks a neglect of the Law and is, in fact, a punishment from God on men who cannot obey. This kind of argument sounds more like Montesquieu or even Rousseau: "The first patriarchs followed nature, the best guide in life. They were succeeded by a line of leaders starting with Moses, who followed the Law, then by judges who ruled the people through the authority of the Law. And we see that the latter were priests. In the end, because of the anger of the Lord, they had kings, some of them good, most of them wicked." This tallies with St Augustine's comment in the *De Civitate Dei* that the just men of early times were more like shepherds of their flocks than kings of men. But the fact remains: men do have kings. It is difficult to reconcile John's theory of initial anarchy with the actual existence of a king, since the code of intelligible laws backed by divine authority which he suggests virtually eliminates the need for any other than an administrative government. If men are basically good they will obey the Law without being forced to. John's notions of egalitarianism are close to those of Rousseau and Diderot. In his work Western individualism emerges against a curiously collectivist background: "Men will only be able to communicate and live harmoniously with each other if they are grouped together, or group themselves together, according to the dispassionate reasoning of divine law. And it is better to form a group of one's own accord, than to be organized by the authority of government."

But this is pure theory and must be the ultimate aim of every human society. Until the long awaited Utopia is here the people need a king. So John of Salisbury defines the role of the king in a society which is only partly feudal because based on an oath of fealty which people are free to reject if they do not wish to utter it.

The king is first and foremost a prince in the sense of the Latin words *princeps*, the first head, and as such he is the representative of the community and minister of the common interest. He supports the public *persona* and must look upon himself as the servant of the people. It is not an honour or a privilege to be king, but a duty which imposes further obligations as the needs of the people increase. The king is an officer, but his acts are those of the *universitas*, or organised community which he heads. This might look like a democratic form of government, but it is not. For the king's authority comes not from the people but from the Law. The king can only be judged by God who is ultimately responsible for ensuring that the Law is observed. In fact "the community (*universitas*) stands in the same position vis à vis the prince as does a pupil with his tutor" (*Policraticus*, v, 7). The prince is responsible for the community but he is not answerable to it, nor even to his own conscience, but to the watchful eye of his external, personalized god. "The prince is the servant of the Lord, but he fulfils his duty by faithfully serving his fellow servants (of God and the Law), otherwise called his subjects" (*Policraticus*, IV, 7).

We now come to the problem of choosing a king. John appears to be questioning the notion of the hereditary monarchy when he says "The power of the king does not come to him through flesh or blood" (IV, 3). But in fact the monarchy was not theoretically hereditary in either England or France at this time. The son of the reigning king had to be legally elected during the lifetime of his father. This practice continued until the time of Philip Augustus in France and Edward I in England. The king had also to be enthroned in the sight of the people, since it was through this act that their basic relationship was established. Neither Richard the Lionheart nor Henry III became king until they were actually crowned; while Edward I, who was absent when his father died, did not accede to the throne until the nobles proclaimed him king four days later. John, however, appears to be going further than this. His work even contains hints of the Thomist formula *a deo per populum* (from god, through the people). He writes "While ordinary public office may pass from the man who holds it to his heir, the government of the people is not passed on in the same way as a matter of right: it is accorded to the individual who has in him the spirit of God and a knowledge of the Law" (v, 6). We should note, however, that for John there is a fundamental difference between the *populus*, which is the people taken as a whole, and the *universitas*, which is the structured body. Indeed, at the coronation of King John, Bishop Hubert made a speech to the effect that the *universitas*, as well as the clerks and the people, had to agree to the choice of king. The *populus*, as an unorganized body, has no *persona* and cannot act in concert. The *universitas*, on the other hand, is an active unity, not subject to limitations from the prince, which can act and speak on its own account even against the prince if needs be. Clearly the men who drew up the Magna Carta which was to become the basis of English constitutional monarchy took their inspiration from John of Salisbury.

So the king is confronted with a series of obligations which he is bound to respect because they represent a force superior to his own. "There are the laws of the state, the rights of the community. These the king must respect. If he violates them loyalty is no longer expected of the subjects, who have the right to rebel." Ancient Celtic tradition also placed the king under a number of strict obligations, many of them magical in origin as might be expected in a society where Druidism promoted the idea of continual contact between the mortal and the supernatural.[4] John of Salisbury thought in terms of moral imperatives, but the basic idea remains the same. The king's duties are to the wise as to the foolish, to the young as to the old. His shield protects the weak and he must keep the innocent safe from the cunning of the wicked. The authors of the Arthurian romances often modelled Arthur on John's ideal king. Arthur may be a leader accepted by the people and by the nobles who form the *universitas*, he may have been chosen by God (or supernatural powers), but he stands first and foremost as the guardian of justice and protector of the weak and oppressed.

There remains the problem of administration. John scarcely goes into detail here, presumably wishing to leave decision-making to the king to suit the situation. This is the kind of Anglo-Saxon pragmatism encapsulated in the phrase "Wait and see." In fact, within John's theoretical state there can be no defined administrative organization. In a feudal society every landowner is a prince, on whatever scale. And as the idea of community interest continues to remain predominant, the prince, as the representative of this community, is in some sense the owner of all the goods of his subjects. His subjects are only tenants, more the guardians than the owners of their property. Here the sacred cow of Roman law, the idea of private property, is thrown to the wind. The *Policraticus* is very much in the Celtic and Germanic tradition. The feudal contracts of Teutonic Europe and the *cheptel* contracts of the Celtic countries both ensure that the real owner of land is the community as represented by its leader. But human frailty makes abuses of the system inevitable and John of Salisbury takes care to state that "the prince will not regard as his own the wealth of others which he is administering on their account, nor will he treat as private any property of the treasury which is recognized as being public" (IV, 5).

If the king ceases to fulfil his duties he becomes a tyrant and tyranny is clearly a punishment from God. But even well-deserved punishment can be mitigated and the people still have the right to revolt. Indeed, since tyranny implies government by force, flouting of the Law and enslavement of the people, active resistance to the despot becomes a positive duty. "It is better to take the crown from a prince's head than to allow order and the best part of the community to be destroyed for his pleasure" (VIII, 7). This is tantamount to making revolution and tyrannicide legal.

John of Salisbury takes his examples from ancient and ecclesiastical history and from the Bible. He solemnly declares, "It is as legal to kill a tyrant as it is to kill a sworn enemy" (VIII, 20). Tyrannicide, however, is not an isolated act of retaliation but rather an act of collective responsibility on the part of the *populus*. Although, normally, any legal action requires the involvement of the *universitas*, the change from prince to tyrant temporarily suspends the usual legal requirements. So whether tyrannicide is committed by one or many members of the *populus* they are all individually concerned in the act.[5]

It would be an overstatement to say that the theories of the *Policraticus* were ever put into effect. It left its mark on the Magna Carta and the Plantagenets often used it, but only as a weapon against their Capetian suzerain. In fact Henry II and his sons were more like tyrants than princes. So, like all liberal works of this kind, the *Policraticus* remains a kind of pious hope, proof of the underlying tendencies of an age when feudalism was edging towards an aristocratic system of government corrupted by the influence of the urban middle-classes.[6]

Even so, the authors of the Arthurian romances must certainly have read John's work or at least heard about it. An extremely subtle dialectic of power can be seen in the events at the Arthurian court. The Arthur of most 12th and 13th-century romances has no personal authority except insofar as he respects the higher Law which is formed neither by him nor by any of the knights seated at the Round Table. The knights of the Round Table constitute a real *universitas*. When Arthur removes the sword from the stone and is declared king by supernatural powers, the people or *populus* immediately acclaim him. But the nobles of the *universitas* do not recognize his authority straight away and even join forces against him. According to the author of *Merlin*, Arthur is not legally king until the assembly of barons accept him as one of their own. (The Law which demands agreement between *universitas* and *populus* must be respected.) But even then Arthur is not an absolute ruler. He is often seen to be weak and defenceless, not only against his own more powerful vassals, but also against the enemies who come to mock him in his own court. It is because the whole fellowship of knights is under attack in the person of the king that one of the knights offers, in the name of that fellowship, to avenge the insult or remove any danger to the established order.

The members of the *universitas* must act in concert. If King Arthur chooses to disregard the Law, he is severely recalled to order by one of the members of the fellowship, usually Kai or Gawain. At the beginning of *Érec et Énide*, for example, Arthur has to take part in the trial of the white stag; and at the beginning of the *Chevalier à la Charrette*, Kai threatens to leave unless Arthur obeys the law of the obligatory gift. Arthur's authority, therefore, lasts only as long as he continues to fulfil his office as executor of the Law. He seems more imposed upon than imposing, more passive than active. So, if someone comes to asked for. As a trustee for the goods of the community he cannot look upon them as his own property, but must dispose of them as his own property, but must dispose of them according to established law. There is a gross contradiction between his theoretical omnipotence and his actual position as servant of his subjects.

However, membership of the *universitas* has its advantages for the knight who has sworn the oath of fealty; and in this Arthur is no different from the rest, as the lack of precedence at the Round Table proves. A single, isolated knight is nothing; but his attachment to the group makes him a person who gains his identity within the social body he helps to form. In him the antitheses of individual and group are dialectically resolved. And when he sets out on his adventures, it is never for strictly individual motives but for communal reasons, that is as a person. As Erich Köhler comments "man no longer feels like a separate entity, but like the meetingpoint of two opposing forces" (*L'Aventure chevaleresque*, p. 184).

"The triumph of the Arthurian hero is the result of his exemplary efforts to overcome the rift between the individual and society. Psychologically this is possible because the tension between the inner man and the world outside is resolved in the first instance by an adaptation on the part of the individual to the alienating structures of society" (*L'Aventure chevaleresque*, p. 287). But there were compensations for the individual who alienated his freedom of action for the sake of the Arthurian community. As a social animal, man can only hope to achieve true identity within a society. The community is always the result of a moral compromise between the opposing needs of the individual and of society. And having made this compromise, the knight finds a new freedom of action within the community. Erich Köhler adds "the [courtly] romance comes down on the side of the knightly individual by showing that in the end society needs the redemption which the individual brings it" (*L'Aventure chevaleresque*, p. 287).

In this sense the legend of Tristan is the antithesis of most Arthurian romances and should not really be included in the cycle. It owes its place there to those 12th-century writers who wanted to ennoble the tale. Tristan adopts a decidedly antisocial and revolutionary attitude towards the courtly society in which an author like Thomas chooses to place him. For in Tristan's case, "the aim is not to overcome the rift in harmony, but to support the claim of the individual by accepting it" (*L'Aventure chevaleresque*, p. 285). All those writers who took the Tristan legend as their subject set the story in a far more clearly Celtic background than that of the other Arthurian romances. The love of Chrétien's Lancelot for Guinevere has a social function since it leads him to undertake deeds of valour in the service of the community. It is "courtly love" or *fine amor*, an oath of love and service to the *domina* (who is usually the suzerain's wife which reinforces the previous oath of fealty to the suzerain himself. Through it the individual's links with society are tightened, especially as the *domina* is a symbol of sovereignty and thereby of the whole social body.

But although the love of Lancelot and Guinevere initially conforms to the theories of *fine amor,* it eventually degenerates. "In the cycle of Lancelot and the Grail cycle the doomladen aspect of Tristan's love casts a shadow over the love between Lancelot and Guinevere. Arthur begins to look more and more like King Mark. The characters at Arthur's court who weave intrigues against the lovers seem like Tristan's enemies. In the *Mort du roi Arthur* the individualism of Tristan's love has already so affected the courtly order that the whole kingdom falls" (*L'Aventure chevaleresque,* pp. 3-9). Robert Bresson brings out this same idea in his film *Lancelot du Lac* in which the individualistic love of Lancelot and Guinevere leads to fatal rivalries among the knights of the Round Table. A society such as theirs which relies on mutual trust is then doomed to fail.

But there are other more important reasons for the disintegration of Arthurian society which Erich Köhler also brings to light. He shows Arthur's court to be an ideal society of the *Policraticus* type, founded on peace and generosity and forming a closed world, a kind of microcosm. Confronting it there is an equally idealized but much larger anti-world which is hostile and dangerous, devilish in appearance. So the Arthurian world has to maintain a balance between the anti-world and itself. Within the Arthurian world, as within the ideal early Celtic kingdom, the community is held together by some form of internal stability. That is why the knights turn outwards to what is clearly a memory of the Celtic Other World to combat the forces of disruption there. But theirs are individual adventures through which the knights can establish an identity not available to them inside the group, while proving the power of the group by the exploits of its members. "The adventures of the chosen knight, which he is so quick to undertake, is part of a continually renewed effort to counteract a spell and re-establish an order constantly threatened from outside" (*L'Aventure chevaler-esque,* p. 90). So by the time we reach the last act of the great Arthurian drama in the *Mort du roi Arthur,* there are no more deeds to be done, no more stability to be maintained between the Arthurian world and the anti-world. Lacking a goal the knights of the Round Table sink into an inertia which will ultimately destroy their society by reviving its internal instability.

Furthermore, any society based on fellowship runs the risk of collapsing as its members disappear. It becomes very difficult for King Arthur to replace the knights he has lost and who, significantly, have killed each other during the quest for the Grail. The Arthurian society operates in a vacuum, and unable to draw fresh blood from outside it finally exhausts its own internal reserves. It is an aloof society of aristocrats highly conscious of their prerogatives and disdainful of the lower classes, a *universitas* which becomes increasingly distant from the *populus* it has ceased to represent. It no longer serves any purpose. Mordret's seizure of power is like a revolution in which the *populus* takes the place of the *universitas.*

And yet Mordret as Arthur's nephew (and illegitimate son) is himself a member of the *universitas.* Although he is not the king's favourite nephew, he could legally lay claim to the throne without resorting to open revolt. But without knowing that Gawain, his brother and rival for the succession, is mortally wounded, he spreads the rumour that Arthur is dead, declares himself king and relies on the support of men outside Arthurian society in his fight. Despite dire predictions of his own downfall Arthur has to destroy the tyrant in the name of the Law he represents. But it is too late. The total disintegration of Arthurian society has already taken place and the final duel to the death produces no victor. Although the Bretons come to avenge him, Arthur's kingdom is exposed to the destructive forces of the anti-world. When Arthur dies, a grandiose dream of unity and harmony dies with him. The Celts' shortlived chance of reconciling the individual and society in a relationship based on mutual trust has gone.

We should note, too, that Mordret tries to take Guinevere, though there is confusion between the various authors as to whether she connives with him. Geoffrey of Monmouth seems to believe that she did, which would tally with the Celtic image of the queen disposing of her favours as she pleases. In the *Mort du roi Arthur*, with its heavy overtones of Christian morality, Guinevere escapes from Mordret and barricades herself in a tower. What is really interesting about this episode is that Mordret wants to marry Guinevere in order to legitimize his position. She, after all, as the king's wife, is the symbol of the *universitas*; and for the Celts she would have been the embodiment of sovereignty itself.

This leads us to an examination of the role of Guinevere, politically and mythologically speaking, and of women in general as portrayed in the Arthurian romances. Many of the knights' adventures follow from the abduction of the queen or some insult to her. In Chrétien's *Perceval*, an arrogant knight takes the queen's cup and challenges the assembled company to get it back from him. In the *Lancelot*, Meleagant abducts the queen herself. And because the queen represents the *universitas*, such acts are felt to be an intolerable affront to the sovereignty of the king and to the knights themselves.

In all the Arthurian romances there are maidens and ladies who influence the course of the action: Vivienne, Lady of the Lake, the daughter of the Fisher King, the Maiden of the Mule, Meleagant's sister, all those fairy-like châtelaines who draw the knights into the most complicated adventures because service of a lady is as important as the service of the feudal lord. But the paradigm is clearly Guinevere, the core of a whole circle of exceptional knighthood.

There is a mythological background to this in the Celtic Arthurian legends which gave their subject matter to the romances. All of them reflect the privileged position of women in an Indo-European society which had assimilated the customs of the aboriginal peoples originally living in Western Europe.[7] The ladies of Arthurian romances are reincarnations of ancient goddesses who had power of life and death, and more especially of the sun goddesses worshipped by civilizations submerged by the tidal wave of Indo-European patriarchy. These goddesses lived on, however, in the form of myths, protected from total annihilation by the inherent qualities of the mythical form.[8]

The feudal society of 12th-century Europe was undergoing a transformation from a totally male-oriented society which relied exclusively on masculine strength to one in which greater recognition was accorded to women. Having previously been regarded as inferior and evil, often for religious reasons, women, at least among the nobility, owed their re-evaluation to yet more religious causes. For in the 12th century the cult of the Virgin Mary grew at an astonishing rate. She was seen not only as the redeemer of womankind from the sins of Eve, but also as the *dame* or *domina*, who from her position just below the lord or *dominus* could intercede with him for mankind as a whole. The fact that she was also the mother of God, and as such the paradigm of motherhood, also made her the mother of all men who, as sons of a single mother, became brothers in the Christian fellowship.

The idea of the great Christian brotherhood is behind all the philosophical theories of the time and underlies the concept of the libertarian family suggested by John of Salisbury's ideal society. Through it, the wife of the seigneur, whether queen or baroness, becomes not only the mother but also the ideal mistress of the knights who undertake to serve her, and though her the community she represents. Behind the idea of *fine amor*, which is an ethical and practical code for optimum relations between lover and mistress, lies the conception of the woman as a symbol of society. Any questions which arise from the idea of courtly love come from differences in interpretation of the bond between the lover knight and his lady. The bond might take the form of a carefully controlled sexual relationship, an emotional attachment in which sexual drives were sublimated, an inspirational influence on the knight to perform great feats for his lady, or a mother-son relationship both on the religious and social levels. *Fine amor* remains the original contribution of the troubadours to the whole argument of conflict between the individual and social groups. It influenced all the courtly romances. But the Celtic background of the Arthurian romances, where individualistic love like Tristan's carried some weight, dealt a death blow to *fine amor*. In any case, the romance writers came mainly from the North and were less susceptible to the subtle reasoning of the Mediterranean troubadours. So the love of Lancelot and Guinevere finally turns sour. In the beginning, however, as we can see from Chrétien's *Lancelot*, courtly love motivated all the knight's adventures.

It is clear that Eleanor of Aquitaine had something to do with this. Her very nature, her decided taste for the arts and letters, her Southern French upbringing, the fact that she was in her own right heiress to a third of French territory, all these things meant that she had a determining influence on the spirit of her age and its Arthurian literature. She was queen for seventy years, first of France and then of England, but she was in no way content to play second fiddle to her royal husbands. Even when Henry II eventually imprisoned her, she continued to leave her mark on the political life of the time.

The section of Geoffrey of Monmouth's *Historia* usually known as the Prophecies of Merlin is said to contain allusions to Eleanor. "Next after the Boar shall come the Ram of the Castle of Venus, with golden horns and a beard of silver. It will breathe such a fog from its nostrils that the entire surface of the island will be overshadowed by it ... Women shall become snake-like in their gait and every step they take will be full of arrogance. The Castle of Venus will be restored and Cupid's arrows will continue to wound. The source of the river Amne shall turn to blood; and two kings will fight each other at the Ford of the Staff for the sake of a Lioness" (*Historia Regum Britanniae*, VII, 2, trans. Lewis Thorpe). It is tempting to take the Lioness to be Eleanor, since it was her land that the kings of France and England disputed. The Castle of Venus could easily be a reference to the courts of love which she held. Obviously this kind of prophecy can be interpreted any way one wishes, but the mere fact that the clerks of the time should have considered connecting Eleanor with prognostications about the future of Britain reveals their interest in her.

We can be almost certain that she was used as a model for the Queen Guinevere of many of the Arthurian romances. The two women match each other in beauty and authority, in political awareness and amorous adventures. Both are surrounded by a conspiratorial atmosphere, both reigned for a long time.

In fact Eleanor's own life is so inextricably mixed up with legends about her, that it is almost impossible to distinguish between them. First, there were three, but not necessarily three contradictory, reasons given for her joining her husband Louis VII on the Second Crusade. The first concerned her love of adventure, the second her sense of excitement at being amongst fighting men, and the third her husband's fears that she would be unfaithful during his absence. All these reasons would also be in character with the Guinevere portrayed in the French romances. Then there are fanciful accounts of Eleanor's behaviour in the Middle East. She is said to have gone into battle in armour at the head of a troop of Amazon-like women who had also accompanied their husbands.

A chronicler known as the Minstrel of Rheims describes how during this same crusade, Eleanor fell in love with the Sultan Saladin, without having met him, through tales of his virtues. They corresponded, he confessing a similar passion for her, and planned to run away together to his country. Eleanor left the palace at Tyre where she was staying and was about to join her Saracen lover on his boat when one of her maids told Louis that she was nowhere to be found and he caught her just in time. When ordered to explain herself Eleanor is then supposed to have replied "In the name of God because of your wickedness, because you are not worth a rotten apple. And I have heard so much good about Saladin whom I love more than you. And you should know that you cannot keep me for ever." We should perhaps point out that Saladin was only ten years old at the time. But there is no reason why Eleanor should not have fallen in love with some man of almost legendary wealth and boldness whom she did not actually know. This was something which Celtic heroes and heroines often did. In any case, whether factual or fictitious, this anecdote places Eleanor in the same league as the Guinevere of the earliest traditions who was abducted by other knights than Meleagant and Lancelot.

There were other amorous adventures attributed to Eleanor. When Louis VII needed help in the Second Crusade he sent for Raymond of Toulouse, Eleanor's uncle, who was holding Antioch. But, according to William of Tyre and John of Salisbury, Louis' request came to nothing partly because Raymond himself needed help and partly because the two men were supposed to have quarrelled over Eleanor. It was easy enough to assume from this account that Eleanor had an incestuous affection for her uncle. There even exists an English ballad purporting to be her confession of guilt.

Then there was the story of Eleanor and Bernard of Ventadour, the Southern French troubadour. After being hounded out of Ventadour by a jealous husband, he was said to have taken refuge with Eleanor, either shortly after Louis divorced her or just after her marriage to Henry II, according to which version of the story one reads. Bernard's passionate love poetry is supposed to be evidence of their affairs. Either way, Eleanor's reputation had been made, and her separation from the king of France did nothing to improve it, although their marriage was officially annulled on grounds of consanguinity. Giraldus Cambrensis, the Welsh chronicler, who was usually well informed about what went on in the Plantagenet empire, claims that while still married to Louis, Eleanor had amorous relations with Henry Plantagenet's father, Geoffrey, then seneschal of France. And it was widely rumoured in the princely courts that Eleanor had been Henry's mistress well before her separation from Louis. Such, stories, coupled with her attendance at the "courts of love" where noble ladies discussed the casuistry of *fine amor*, left little doubt in the minds of her contemporaries that Eleanor was indeed a passionate lover.

She also engaged in various conspiracies at court and had frequent quarrels with Henry II, even going so far as to help her sons when they rebelled against their father. And it seems clear that she was exceedingly jealous of Henry's mistresses, especially one named Rosamund whom she is supposed to have poisoned. All these aspects of Eleanor's character make comparisons with Guinevere almost inevitable.

Apart from the stories about her, true or untrue, Eleanor's position at the centre of the cultured society of 12th-century Western Europe supports such comparisons. She spent much of her time at Poitiers which had become a melting pot for all the great minds of the age; and it seems likely that French-speaking writers may have heard the Celtic legends from Breton or British story tellers there. Indeed, the Welsh *fabulator* Bledhri was said to have lived at Poitiers under Eleanor's patronage. There was a link between Eleanor and Chrétien de Troyes, through Marie de Champagne, Eleanor's daughter and Chrétien's patroness. And apart from the possibility that Chrétien was trying to flatter his patroness by making his Guinevere ressemble her mother, there was a further suggestion that Chrétien was actually related to the English royal house as nephew to Stephen of Blois, Henry's predecessor on the English throne.

However we approach the question of the spread of the Arthurian romances, we seem always to come up against the Plantagenets and their political aspirations. Their influence even affected the geographical settings of the French romances. Geoffrey of Monmouth had established links between England and Normandy by making Kai the founder of Caen, and Bedwyr (Bedivere) the founder of Bayeux. But the French writers went further. The Arthur of Welsh legend had been king of Wales, Dumnonia (Devon and Cornwall) and Strathclyde (NW England / SW Scotland), the rest of Britain being collectively known as *Lloegr* or *Lloegyr*, a name used specifically to denote the areas occupied by the Saxon enemy. In the French romances, Logres becomes the name of Arthur's kingdom and covers both Great Britain and Brittany, presumably so that Brittany can be included in the Plantagenet sphere of influence.

This argument is upheld by the sad tale of Arthur I of Brittany. Konan IV of Brittany was already closely connected with the Anglo-Angevins in their struggle against Capetian authority. But when he abdicated and retired to the county of Richmond, a gift to the Bretons in 1066, Henry II took the opportunity to marry his third son, Geoffrey, to Konan's heiress Constance. Geoffrey, however, showed a certain amount of opposition to Henry's plan for Brittany and when he died in 1186 Henry himself took over the administration of the duchy. Then in 1187 Constance gave birth to Geoffrey's son, who was given the name Arthur. Clearly both the Bretons and the Plantagenets had their own reasons for this choice of name. For the Bretons, who were becoming increasingly well acquainted with the Arthurian legends, the symbolism of the name Arthur was obvious. For Henry II the name meant even more. He had succeeded in giving Brittany an heir who was both the legitimate descendant of the Breton ruling house and the grandson of the English king, and as a crowning achievement, this heir was called Arthur.

The Capetians were not amused. Philip Augustus, as Arthur's suzerain, arranged to have the child educated under his supervision and ensured that Arthur felt little love for his father's family. He even sent the young prince to lay siege to his grand-mother Eleanor in Mirebeau in Poitou. But Henry obviously had more long term plans for Arthur, which might well have changed the course of history had not the jealous John, aware that his father had no such plans for him, gone to Eleanor's rescue, captured Arthur and murdered him in 1203.

John had cause to feel aggrieved. As the youngest of Henry and Eleanor's four sons, he was born some distance from the throne. But Henry, the eldest son, died prematurely in 1183 without issue, and Richard the Lionheart, the second son and heir apparent, was a homosexual and would obviously not have a child. Henry II's plans to bring Brittany under Plantagenet rule through Arthur were confirmed when Richard recognized the young duke of Brittany as his sole heir after his father's death. John could have laid claim to be regent until Arthur's majority but he could never hope to be king while the boy was alive. So he killed him, according to some stories with his own hands, lost any hope of retaining control over Brittany and foiled Henry's machinations once and for all.

We come now to 1190, a year after Henry II's death, when an event occurred which lends support to the suggestion that Henry was empire-building and that the Plantagenets had their own reasons for reworking the Arthurian legends. For it was then that the graves of Arthur and Guinevere were "discovered" at Glastonbury.

Glastonbury Abbey

Let us start by examining the existing documents concerning the "discovery," which are fairly precise if contradictory in some particulars. First there is the evidence of Giraldus Cambrensis, one of the more reliable sources for the history of this period, whose knowledge of the main regions of the British Isles and their respective traditions makes him a valuable aid to any study of the Celts and the Arthurian phenomenon. In 1192, two years after the event, he wrote:

Arthur, the famous British king, is still remembered, nor will this memory die out, for he is much praised in the history of the excellent monastery of Glastonbury, of which he himself was in his time a distinguished patron and a generous endower and supporter . . . His body, for which popular stories have invented a fantastic ending, saying that it had been carried to a remote place, and was not subject to death, was found in recent times at Glastonbury between two stone pyramids standing in the burial ground. It was deep in the earth, enclosed in a hollow oak, and the discovery was accompanied by wonderful and almost miraculous signs. It was reverently transferred to the church and placed in a marble tomb. And a leaden cross was found laid under the stone, not above, as is the custom today, but rather fastened on beneath it. We saw this, and traced the inscription which was not showing, but turned in towards the stone: "Here lies buried the famous king Arthur with Guinevere his second wife in the isle of Avalon." In this there are several remarkable things: he had two wives, of which the last was buried at the same time as him, and indeed her bones were discovered with those of her husband: however, they were separate, since two parts of the coffin, at the head, were divided off, to contain the bones of a man, while the remaining third at the foot contained the bones of a woman set apart. There was also uncovered a golden tress of hair that had belonged to a beautiful woman in its pristine condition and colour, which, when a certain monk eagerly snatched it up, suddenly dissolved into dust. Signs that the body had been buried here were found in the records of the place, in the letters inscribed on the pyramids, although these were almost obliterated by age, and in the visions and revelations seen by holy men and clerks: *but chiefly through Henry II King of England who had heard from an aged British singer that his (Arthur's) body would be found at least sixteen feet deep in the earth, not in a stone tomb, but in a hollow oak.*[9] This Henry had told the monks;[10] and the body was at the depth stated and almost concealed, lest, in the event of the Saxons occupying the island, against whom he had fought with so much energy in his lifetime, it should be brought to light, and for that reason, the inscription on the cross which would have revealed the truth was turned inwards to the stone, to conceal at that time what the coffin contained, and yet inform other centuries. What is now called Glastonbury was in former times called the Isle of Avalon, for it is almost an island, being entirely surrounded by marshes, whence it is named in British Inis Avallon, that is the apple-bearing island, because apples (in British, aval) used to abound in that place. Whence Morgan, a noblewoman who was ruler of that region and closely related to Arthur, after the Battle of Camlann carried him away to the island now called Glastonbury to be healed of his wounds. It used also to be called in British Inis Gutrin, that is, the isle of glass: hence the Saxons called it Glastingeburi. For in their tongue glas means glass, and a camp or town is called buri. We know that the bones of Arthur's body that were discovered were so large that in this we might see the fulfilment of the poet's words:

Grandisque effossis mirabitur ossa sepulchris

(When the graves are opened, they shall marvel at the great size of the bones) [Virgil, *Georgics* I, 497]

The thighbone, when placed next to the tallest man present, as the abbot showed us, and fastened to the ground by his foot, reached three inches above his knee. And the skull was of a great, indeed prodigious, capacity, to the extent that the space between the brows and between the eyes was a palm's breadth. But in the skull there were ten or more wounds, which had all healed into scars with the exception of one, which made a great cleft, and seemed to have been the sole cause of death. (Quoted by Richard Barber, *Arthur of Albion*, London, 1961, pp. 55-7.)

It appears from the detail included in this account that Giraldus obtained much of his information on the spot. He may even have seen the unusual size of the thigh bone for himself. But despite his slightly derogatory remarks about the popular traditions concerning Arthur's removal to the Isle of Avalon, he is not himself always entirely accurate in his comments on Glastonbury and the nature of the graves. To start with, it is out of the question that Arthur was a patron of the abbey, since those archaeological finds relating to the Arthurian period which have been made in the area all come from Glastonbury Tor rather than from the abbey itself, and suggest that there was a fortress rather than a monastery there in the Dark Ages. The two pyramids of stone do suggest that the graves belonged to Britons of the post-Roman era, since it was Celtic custom at the time to erect a raised stone over a grave in this way. But the reference to the Isle of Avalon in the inscription on the cross dates it as coming from the second half of the 12th century, since all the early 12th-century writers call Glastonbury Inis Gutrin. Any identification of Glastonbury with the Isle of Avalon may have been inspired by the Plantagenets and encouraged by the monks who hoped to make their abbey a centre of pilgrimage. The monks may also have forged the archives for the same purpose, since they were not above writing and aging other documents to improve their standing. Certainly Giraldus misunderstood the etymology of the name Glastonbury which really meant "the settlement of the race of Glas" and was Saxon in origin. The translation of Glastingeburi into Inis Gutrin probably reflected the influence of Celtic legends about the Tower of Glass.

The inscription, too, presents a real problem, since a markedly different version of it appears in Ralph of Coggeshall's *Chronicum Anglicanum*, written in about 1200.

> 1191: This year were found at Glastonbury, the bones of the most renowned Arthur, formerly king of Britain, buried in a very ancient coffin, over which two stone pyramids had been built: on the sides of these was an inscription, illegible on account of the rudeness of the script and its worn condition. The bones were discovered as follows: as they were digging up this ground to bury a monk who had urgently desired in his lifetime to be interred there, they discovered a certain coffin, on which a leaden cross had been placed, bearing the inscription, "Here lies the famous King Arthur, buried in the isle of Avalon." For this place, which surrounded by marshes, was formerly called the isle of Avalon, that is, the isle of apples. (*Arthur of Albion*, pp. 57-8).

Giraldus Cambrensis' version of the inscription might seem the more accurate since he saw it for himself, but Ralph's version does tally with that on an engraving of the cross published in 1610 in Camden's *Britannia*. In any case, there are other differences between the two accounts. The date of the discovery itself varies, though 1190 is now regarded by historians as the correct one. Guinevere has disappeared from Ralph's inscription, though he gives no indication as to whether her body was in the coffin. The coffin itself is an innovation; and the letters on the stone pyramids have become totally illegible (perhaps because they were written in Irish oghamic script?). Henry II has vanished from the story, but this may be because with the years the monks had become disenchanted with the Plantagenets and wanted the credit for discovering the grave to remain theirs alone. There is no way of knowing which of the two accounts is nearer the truth. Besides, there is yet another version, written by Adam of Domerham: roughly a century after the discovery:

> The King [Richard I] . . . elevated as Abbot, Henry de Sully, Prior of Bermondsey, a man born of royal stock . . . He, frequently urged to dispose more fittingly of the famous king Arthur (for he had lain for 643 years near the old Church between two pyramids, once magnificently carved), one day surrounded the place with curtains and ordered that digging should be carried out . . . The abbot and convent, raising up the remains, joyfully translated them into the great church, placing them in a double tomb, magnificently carved. The King's body was set by itself at the head of the tomb, that of the queen at the foot or the eastern part, and there they remain to the present day. (Quoted by Geoffrey Ashe, *The Quest for Arthur's Britain*, p. 99.)

This tells us the exact spot where the supposed corpse of Arthur was found (the old church being the Lady Chapel) and that there were indeed two bodies. The 648 years during which the bodies had lain in the ground take us back to the battle of Camlaan where Arthur was fatally wounded, variously dated as 537 or 541, according to the *Annales Cambriae* and the *Annals of Tigernach* respectively. Richard the Lionheart's desire to see Arthur's body more gloriously entombed betrays his father's preoccupation with the Celtic king. Indeed in 1191 Richard tried to pass himself off as Arthur's distant successor by giving King

Tancredi of Sicily a sword which he claimed was Escalibur.

Attempts to trace the origins of the house of Anjou back to a mysterious, fairy-like woman were also current at the courts of both Henry II and Richard. Giraldus Cambrensis has some delightful stories to tell on the subject: whenever this beautiful she-demon went to mass she tried to leave the church after the gospel, he says, and if forcibly restrained she would disappear into thin air. This character clearly belonged to the same tradition as Morgan and Melusine.

Such stories might also explain why King John had his marriage to Hadwita of Gloucester annulled (as her cousin, he could claim consanguinity), and was remarried to Isabel of Angoulême, then only twelve years old, in 1200. John was forced to fight a war against Hugues of Lusignan who had been betrothed to Isabel, but could at least pretend to have as great a claim to be descended from fairy people as the Lusignans, the supposed descendants of Melusine.

The other Plantagenets were equally interested in the Arthurian tradition. According to the *Annals of Waverly,* Edward I himself witnessed the exhumation of Arthur's bones and their removal to the treasure of the church at Glastonbury in 1278. Adam of Domerham also records the event:

> The lord Edward . . . with his consort, the lady Eleanor, came to Glastonbury . . . to celebrate Easter . . . That following Tuesday at dusk, the lord king had the tomb of the famous King Arthur opened. Wherein, in two caskets painted with their pictures and arms, were found separately the bones of the said king, which were of great size, and those of Queen Guinevere, which were of marvellous beauty. . . On the following day . . . the lord king replaced the bones of the king and those of the queen, each in their own casket, having wrapped them in costly silks. When they had been sealed they ordered the tomb to be placed forthwith in front of the high altar, [11] after the removal of the skulls for the veneration of the people. (*The Quest for Arthur's Britain*, pp. 99-100).

Edward's interest in Arthur at that particular time was clearly not gratuitous. he had just won his first political victory over Llywelyn ap Gruffydd, the chief of North Wales and would-be successor to Arthur, who had had to renounce all his previous claims to being supreme king of the Welsh. A few days after Arthur's remains were moved, Edward proclaimed his son, the future Edward II, prince of Wales, thereby killing all hopes of Welsh independence and attaching the throne of Wales to the English monarchy, as it still is today. Later, Edward III lavished favours on the abbey of Glastonbury which he visited in 1331; he also planned to reinstitute the Round Table by gathering the great barons of the realm around him.

The Plantagenets were clearly anxious to use Arthurian material for political purposes in the same way as the Capetians had used the *chansons de geste*. They were also jealous of the papal protection accorded to the Capetians, their claims to miracle-working and the spiritual authority granted them by the ceremony of coronation. These two factors go a long way to explaining the importance of Glastonbury and Fontevrault abbeys, which the Anglo-Angevin kings hoped to place on a level with the abbey of St Denis which had played such a vital part in the development of the Charlemagne cycle.

Glastonbury is in Somerset, in a place occupied first by the Romans and then by the Celts of the Dark Ages. Its isolated position in the middle of marshland made it the subject of strange legends among the neighbouring population, and these the 12th-century monks were quick to use to attract sightseers and pilgrims. Probably founded by continental missionaries, the monastery at Glastonbury was supposed to have been the meeting place of the great saints of the Celtic church. St Patrick, the apostle of Ireland, was supposed to have lived and been buried there. St Bridget of Ireland was said to have visited the place. St Gildas, the apostle of the Britons, supposedly stayed there before travelling to Brittany where he founded the monastery in Rhuys which bears his name. There were even totally improbable claims that the abbey had been founded by the Welsh St David, though it is possible that his holy remains were brought there for safe-keeping during the Viking invasions. But, however unlikely some of the stories may have been, there is no doubt that Glastonbury was traditionally regarded as a pan-Celtic monastery. It was also a meeting place, if not for the saints of the legends, then at least for the zealots of the British Church which had broken away from the restrictions of Rome and remained determinedly independent in outlook and practice. The influence of the Briton Pelagius was widespread. And because of his teaching and the elements of Druidism it had adopted, Celtic Christianity bordered on the heretical.

We should point out that Glastonbury's geographical position made it a natural focal point for the Celtic world. It stood on the route from Cornwall to Wales, not far from the Roman settlement of Bath, the episcopal seat of Wells, the Celtic fortress of Cadbury (probably Arthur's Camelot) and Salisbury Plain with its megalithic monuments. It was near the Bristol Channel and the mouth of the Severn, both frequently visited by Irish pirates; and though basically within Celtic territory it was close to the area controlled by the Angles and Saxons.

The origins of Glastonbury remain shrouded in mystery, although William of Malmesbury comes up with an interesting account of them in his *De Antiquitate Glastoniensis ecclesiae*:

> The ancient chronicles of the Britons tell how twelve brothers came from the northern part of Britain into the West.[12] There they held several regions, Vendotia [Gwynedd, N.W. Wales], Demetia [Dyfed, S.W. Wales], Buthir, Kedwelli, which they were given by their uncle Cunedda.[13] [Among them]... Glasteing. It was this Glasteing who journeyed across the lands of the Southern Angles, from a town called Escabtiorne [Eastbourne], to near Wells in pursuit of one of his sows. From Wells he travelled on along a water-logged and pot-holed road called Sugewege or Sows Way, until he caught his sow under an apple tree near the church we speak of. From then until now the church has been called Eadcyrcenes Epple [Oldchurchen Apples] because of the apples from this tree. This is why the sow was called Eadcyrce Suge [Oldchurch Sow]. Unlike other sows, this one had eight legs, surprising to relate. When Glasteing saw that he had come to a good place he brought his family to live there and spent the rest of his days there. So this island which the Britons called Ynisgutrin [isle of glass] ... came to be known as Glastonbury or Glasteing's settlement when the Saxon's occupied the area. But it was also known as Insula Avalonia, and this name came about because Glasteing, as we have said, found his sow under an apple tree by an old church, and having found apples, a rare occurrence in that land, he called the place Avalonia, or the Island of Apples, (*Avalla* being the British word for poma in Latin[14]). The name was also said to have come from Avalloc[15] who went to live there with his daughters because of the solitude of the island.[16]

We know that one of William's sources was a 10th-century genealogy contained in one of the manuscripts of Nennius' *Historia Brittonum* (Harleian 3859). This lists the names of the sons of Cunedda, but they are called "sons of Glast and thence the Glastenic who had come from the region we call Loytcoyt [Lichfield]";[17] and according to the genealogy Glast is the supposed ancestor of a 10th-century Welsh king.

The significance of this detail might appear trifling were it not for the fact that the name of the founder of Glastonbury should actually be Glast rather than Glasteing, which is the result of an incorrect breakdown of the name Glastingaburi. So the tale of the hero pursuing a sow takes on a new light. Ferdinand Lot has commented that the story was altered by the monks to fit in with local topography, the marshy road from the abbey to the neighbouring bishopric of Wells being known as Sows Way; and he states that the legend is undeniably Celtic in flavour.[18]

In fact it seems very likely that it originated in Ireland. *The Book of Armagh*, of which the manuscript dates from about 807, contains a story about St Patrick bringing a swineherd named Cas mac Glais (Cas son of Glas) back to life. The same man also appears in the *Glossary of Cormac* at the beginning of the 10th century, though this time he is Glas son of Cas. Here the name Glas is used to explain the name Glassdimbir in Ireland[19], "the church on the shore of the sea of Icht. This is the place where Glass son of Cas, the swineherd of king Hiruath, stopped to let his swine graze on the fruit [of an apple tree]. It was he whom Patrick later brought back to life."[20]

The similarities between the two stories must surely be more than coincidental, especially when we remember that the Irish frequently visited the abbey of Glastonbury. We should not, however, fall into the trap of assuming that all British legends originated in Ireland, as if the British were incapable of inventing their own. Legends travelled in both directions. In any case, the provenance of legends is of comparatively little interest. The Greco-Latin contribution to Western civilization has been much overemphasized in this respect. What matters is that legends are the realizations and localizations of a myth and myths, if not universal, are at least common to a whole cultural group. The story of the swineherd may belong to an early Celtic store of such legends.

For there are similar tales in the British and Breton traditions. While hunting a magical white boar. Guingamor finds his way to fairyland where he falls in love with the queen. In the fourth branch of the Welsh *Mabinogion*, Gwyddyon manages to find his son Lleu by pursuing a sow to the tree where Lleu is perched in the form of an eagle. In Nennius' *Historia Brittonum*, Arthur himself goes out to hunt the *porcus troitus*, the magic wild boar which also appears as the *Twyrch Trywth* again pursued by Arthur in the Welsh tale of *Kulhwch and Olwen*. We shall return to the hunt of the magic boar in a later chapter. But in the meantime there is no denying the link between Glas(t), Guingamor, Gwyddyon and Arthur. And the fact that this particular legend should be used to explain the origins of Glastonbury, whatever its real ties with the isle of Avalon may have been, give it a special place in Arthurian legend. Obviously there is no way of proving whether the graves found there in 1190 were indeed those of Arthur and Guinevere; but stranger things have been known to happen. And equally, there is no way of proving that King Arthur did not exist, or that he was not linked in some way with Glastonbury, as the evidence tends to suggest. The history of Britain in the Dark Ages is itself an epic, and every epic must retain some element of mystery.

Arthurian Chivalry

So the Arthurian tradition made its entry into Europe, aided and abetted by local legends from Wales, Cornwall and Glastonbury, which were then disseminated by the bards and singers of Britain and Brittany and actively promoted by the Plantagenets and their allies as a propaganda weapon against the Capetians' Carolingian epics. But this tradition would never have achieved such rapid and fruitful growth had it not been sown in the fertile ground of 12th-century Western Europe.

Feudalism was gradually being eaten away by the contradictions inherent in its own system. The feudal system was originally based on Charlemagne's attempts to establish a form of obligatory support and protection between the various levels of the social hierarchy, and thus theoretically to maintain total balance between groups with opposing interests. The oath of fealty worked both ways: it entitled the seigneur to service from his vassal, and the vassal to the protection of his seigneur. The grants of lands and goods which followed the swearing of the oath were supposed to ensure that every member of society then received whatever his needs and his rank entitled him to. But although the feudal system as a whole appeared faultless in theory, in practice it could only work if the central structure held firm.

In the 12th century the rigid hierarchy of Western European feudalism was increasingly disregarded. The weak could no longer expect the protection of the strong as a matter of right. And so an apparently new social class of knights developed in opposition to the self-interested seigneurs and their powerful vassals.

In the beginning the knights were no more than self-seeking mercenary soldiers. Often the disinherited sons of the petty nobility whose only fortune lay in their horse and their weapons, they would hire out their services as warriors to any wealthier landowning noble who needed fighting men. Success in battle was rewarded by the granting of a fief, or a piece of land, from the noble to the knight, who could then employ poorer knights to serve him. Conflict between members of the nobility and attacks from the increasing numbers of brigands and highwaymen ensured a constant need for professional soldiers. Indeed some of the brigands were themselves knights fighting for noblemen who had no other source of income, in mountainous areas for example. Under the influence of the Church they gradually assumed the role of protector to merchants and travellers, exacting tolls for a safe passage rather than stealing their goods.

As an increasing number of knights settled on their own land and society became more stable, so the demand for knights grew. And eventually a number of commoners who had trailed after the knights as squires or ordinary servants managed to penetrate the knightly class. They had first, however, to satisfy the rigid conditions required for knighthood, which included proving their worth as warriors, having a certain amount of money, finding a sponsor and going through a complicated initiation ritual.

The knights were subject to feudal laws and supposed only to serve the man to whom they had sworn fealty. Difficulties arose when one knight swore loyalty to several seigneurs; so the position of liege lord was introduced to give one seigneur precedence over others of the same hierarchical level. Later the Church imposed moral and spiritual requirements on the knights, insisting that they should protect everybody's goods and help widows, orphans and anybody threatened by injustice, especially, of course, men of the Church. The knight was also to support the Church in its fight against the heathen. Here the crusades provided an important outlet for the increasing numbers of out-of-work knights who could be found no other occupation and were becoming a burden on the economy. The liberation of Christ's tomb in Jerusalem from Moslem hands provided the perfect religious justification for ensuring that a potentially dangerous group of professional soldiers was out of harm's way, wreaking destruction in non-Christian countries.

The acquisition of a divine mission gave knights considerable moral standing. Every 12th-century knight, whether he was a noble landowner of an impoverished commoner, enjoyed the reputation of almost supernatural power. Mysticism crept into the concept of chivalry, and religious orders like the Knights Templar and the Teutonic Knights were created. The church was trying every means possible to exert both temporal and spiritual authority over Western Europe so that colonies could be formed elsewhere in the name of triumphant Christianity. This meant that by the 12th century the knightly class was becoming increasingly conscious of its special position in the social hierarchy, not only in terms of its physical strength, but also in terms of the moral pressure it could bring to bear on political development.

It was then that the feudal pyramid began to crumble. Service to God made fealty to some distant suzerain in the shape of a king appear irrelevant to the knights. And the more powerful vassals in the hierarchy were losing respect for the structures of their society.

The French monarch, who had inherited the feudal system, naturally tried to remedy the situation, but he made the mistake of trying to bypass the nobility and establish direct contact between himself and the people to his own advantage. This particular policy of eliminating what Montesquieu later called the intermediary powers remained French royal policy for centuries. And as a result France became a strong, highly centralized kingdom until the Jacobins of 1789 imposed their own brand of centralist, technocratic government, which continues to fetter the country to this day.

The efforts of the 12th-century Capetian king to set up a unitarian system of government antagonized his great vassals, and, more especially, the class of knights which had enjoyed great freedom of action within the feudal hierarchy however shaky it had become. Their attitude is evident in the 12th and 13th-century Arthurian romances. As Erich Köhler says "The change from the *chansons de geste* to the courtly romances is marked by a shift in narrative motivation from external to internal events" (*L'Aventure chevaleresque*, p. 185).

The *chansons de geste* were written to promote the unity of the Capetian kingdom, the service of the suzerain king and of his suzerain, God. So although their creators were given to geographical flights of fancy, the world of these epics is very precisely defined. The world of the courtly romances, on the other hand, is a "non-temporal universe because it makes claims to universality" (*L'Aventure chevaleresque*, p. 46). For the feudal courtly society described in them "boasts of a universal law unrestricted by national boundaries." Whereas "the policies of the Capetians oppose the very idea of a hierarchy, a supranational organization of society" (*L'Aventure chevaleresque*, p. 43). "The Arthurian world can only be localized in the topography of its legendary matter and not in any real place" (*ibid.*).

Clearly the Plantagenets, as vassals of the Capetians, contributed to the spread of this point of view. They proclaimed themselves defenders of traditional feudalism, though they were quite prepared to adopt the centralist ideas of their political adversaries when it suited them to do so. Politically they were bound to support those vassals who were exploiting the existing system against any attempts to replace it with nationalism. And it is clear from the Arthurian texts written at this time that it was the knights who formed that group of rebellious vassals.

For the Arthurian knights have little in common with our ideas about Christian chivalry at the time of the crusades. To start with, their claims to be acting in the name of Christianity sent them questing after the Grail rather than battling against the Infidel. The supernatural forces they do have to contend with are not necessarily diabolic; they may be merely fairy-like in a non-perjorative sense. There is none of the fundamental dichotomy between the henchmen of Satan and the righteous sons of God seen in the *chansons de geste*. Indeed it is sometimes hard to make out what the Arthurian knight is actually fighting for: his king possibly, his lady, a rash promise made to someone along the way, a maiden in distress, any of these. The continual references to religion and the service of Christ in no way disguise the fact that the romances are essentially pagan in nature. Those hermits and monasteries which do make their appearance are always shrouded in a strong odour of sulphur.

When the knights go into battle it is seldom for their king, except to avenge an insult to the Arthurian community from some importunate outsider, or to free the king from imprisonment. For Arthur remains merely the focal point of the collective society. When the knights send their prisoners back to him, they may well be just as anxious to see their exploits acclaimed by the court as they are to see homage rendered to their king. The order of knights imposes its own law on Arthur. It is John of Salisbury's *universitas* which really holds sway.

Whether the anti-monarchist spirit of the Arthurian romances tallies with Celtic attitudes is a point to which we shall return when discussing the Celts themselves. But there is no doubt that it matches the prevailing spirit among the 12th and 13th-century knights. Arthurian chivalry is directed solely towards the satisfaction of honour and the self-interested acquisition of wealth or emotional gain. Love, which is the prime mover of many of the adventures undertaken by the errant knights of the romances has little to do with the generally accepted idea of chivalry. It is perhaps not too outrageous to suggest that the Arthurian knights fight for women rather than for ideas in the same way that the heroes of American Westerns value the speed of the draw over the law of the land. The spirit of chivalry has gone, along with notions of defending the innocent and punishing the guilty. Lancelot, Bohort, Gawain and the rest may claim to be ardent upholders of justice, indeed they do often come to the aid of those who ask for their services, but they actually spend more of their time in the kind of internecine conflict described in the *Quest for the Holy Grail* and the *Death of King Arthur*. Gone, too, is the selfless devotion expected of the knight who has sworn faithfully to serve his seigneur. Lancelot spends his time deceiving the king with a complicit Guinevere, aided and abetted by Bohort and Lionel. Agravain puts his jealousy of Lancelot before the interests of the knightly fellowship. Galahad is not really of this world, and is totally immersed in his predestined mission. Gawain thinks only about women. Mordret is motivated by the idea of wresting power from Arthur, whose inability to resolve the internal conflicts of his society has made him too weak to prevail. And these are the ''model'' knights who form the fellowship of the Round Table.

It is worth stressing the point that Arthurian knighthood represents a political attempt on the part of one social class to maintain a system of corrupt feudalism which is profitable to itself alone. In all the texts the peasants are despised as servants or outcasts. In the *Lancelot in Prose* the hero is even prepared to kill a villein who demands a toll from him. The mass of the people only appear in a sympathetic light when Arthur draws the sword from the stone to become king and when Tristan and Iseult are condemned to death; but these two episodes are purely Celtic in atmosphere. Only a romantic Western scholar could find the heroes of Arthurian romance attractive. They are self-centred brutes who arrogantly satisfy their basest instincts with no regard for the Christianity they are supposed to represent nor, indeed, for the most elementary humanity, let alone the spirit of democracy.[21] In this they accurately reflect the real lives of the Plantagenets, despite the stylistic veneer of elegance and refinement which Eleanor's hypocritical courtly society gave them. Henry, Eleanor and their sons spent much of their time making war or plotting murder. Geoffrey Plantagenet, who died horribly mutilated and trampled by his horse during a tournament, was even reputed to have declared "Do you not realize that it is in our own inherited natures to dislike one another, and that brother must always fight against brother and son against father."

Another facet of the Arthurian knights which makes them totally unlike the brave and honest warriors of the *chansons de geste* is their intelligence. The Carolingian knights are doltish in their stupidity, while the romance writers are careful to stress the intellectual capacities of their heroes.

This was a departure from the accepted standards of chivalry in earlier feudal times, and can be taken to represent the knightly society's claims to self-government. Until then knights had been schooled in the martial arts but left scholarship and literature to the clerks. Courtly society demanded that they acquire artistic accomplishments as well. The knights of the *chansons de geste* might be expected to be valiant like Roland or wise like Oliver, but the Arthurian knights are both valiant and wise, their wisdom enhanced by all the intellectual and artistic learning open to members of their social class. Gawain is a model of decorum, Lancelot the brilliant pupil of the Lady of the Lake. Tristan writes lays and plays the harp well. In fact, the only character to have missed out on the benefits of 12th-century courtly education is King Arthur himself, who cannot read or write. And it is possible that the emphasis laid on his illiteracy is intended to pinpoint the uselessness of the monarchy, or at least the king's separateness from the knightly class. There is, anyhow, too great a tendency to portray Arthur as a downtrodden but happy cuckold, quite unlike the Celtic king who is bound by his service to the community to give of his possessions, including his wife. The story of Lancelot and Guinevere's love, which a horrifyingly naive Arthur is always ready to help along, must be one of the silliest tales medieval literature has given us. The fact that people are prepared to interpret it as the triumph of love, or to make feature films about it, only proves that there will always be an audience sentimental enough to sigh over Guinevere's unhappiness or Lancelot's afflictions. As it turns out, the original Celtic Guinevere was a snarling bitch of a woman, but one who symbolized a specific concept of sovereignty; while the Breton Lancelot, artificially introduced into the Arthurian cycle by the courtly writers, was a man of quite a different mettle.[22]

Apart from Chrétien de Troyes, who was purely a romance writer, and the authors of Tristan, who wrote about a mythological subject beyond retrieval, all the authors of the Arthurian romances were ardent and undiscriminating propagandists of the courtly nobility. And since these nobles were claiming independence from royal authority, the power of their position in society had to be reflected in the romances. The heroic adventures contained in the traditional legends of Britain formed an ideal treasure store for the writers to misappropriate.

For misappropriate the "matter of Britain" is what they did. The Round Table romances may have given the world Celtic legends which would otherwise have been lost, but in the process they betrayed and ridiculed them. The 12th and 13th-century French parodies of Celtic epic are all too often rendered unreadable by their inflated style and their crushing pedantry. Their authors exploited adventures which they did not really understand because they happened to fit nicely into the decor. Their shameful sycophancy towards the knightly class was compounded by their nonsensical attempts to impose Christianity on essentially pagan myths.[23] The society of knights may be revealed in all its glory, but the absurd way in which the tales are abridged and distorted to fit the knightly cause must surely bring niggling doubts to those who still believe that the Round Table romances are the most dazzling expression of the Celtic spirit.

It is time we acknowledged once and for all that the Round Table romances are not Celtic, but merely the degenerate literary products of an equally degenerate knightly society which nevertheless hoped to rule the world. There may have been Celtic models for each of the Arthurian tales, but they must have passed through countless hands before becoming the barren dustheaps the French writers made them.

So it is important to decode the Arthurian romances, now that we have demystified them; and to penetrate the real society of our hypothetical King Arthur. Our examination of the medieval face of Arthur has shown it to be the joint product of an ambitious nobility and a hypocritical Catholic Church,[24] an image it may be necessary to reject. A study of the Dark Ages in Western Europe may well bring us closer to Arthur's true face, and to the mentality, customs and political concepts of the Celts.

PART TWO

King Arthur in the Celtic World

CHAPTER THREE

Britain in the Dark Ages

HE occupying Roman army which Julius Caesar led into Gaul marched under pretext of mediating between the different Gallic peoples and of protecting them from invading Teutonic tribes. But it soon became clear that occupation did not necessarily constitute conquest. The rebellion of the Veneti, who brought a powerful Breton confederation with them, was typical of the many uprisings he had to face, though possibly the most savage of such outbreaks. Caesar had spies and informers everywhere, however, and it was not long before he learnt that every uprising was encouraged and supported, if not actively directed, by the inhabitants of Britain.

So he sent a delegation to Britain headed by Volusenus, one of his lieutenants. The Britons in their turn sent ambassadors to Caesar, supposedly to offer him hostages, but actually to sound out the real intentions of the Romans. Caesar then ordered his rather unreliable ally Commius the Atrebatian to "visit as many tribes as possible, to urge them to entrust themselves to the protection of Rome and to announce his impending arrival" (*The Conquest of Gaul*, v , i transl. by Handford, Penguin). Whether Commius did as he was told we do not know, but when Caesar landed in Britain in 55 BC he was met by a hostile army. He did manage, however, to set up various fortified encampments and to observe the country and its peoples for himself. He then returned to the continent and made more careful preparations for a second expedition. This time he had the British chief Cassivellaunus to contend with, but he apparently succeeded in subduing some of the island tribes before returning to Gaul. There he sent news of his resounding victories to the Roman senate.

It was in AD 43 that the Roman conquest of Britain really began, on the decision of the emperor Claudius. There were two specific reasons for such a

step. First, the geographical location of the British Isles made them an ideal van-
tage point from which to watch over the invasion routes from the North and
thereby protect existing Roman colonies on the continent; and secondly, the
Druidism which had been stamped out in Gaul continued to flourish in Britain.
Its chief sanctuaries and schools were situated there. Obviously the only way to
ensure that Roman ideas remained secure in Gaul was by taking the island. The
conquest of Britain moved slowly. Changing their tactics from those used on the
continent, where whole kingdoms had been taken over, the Romans were content to play the tribes off against one another in a series of alliances. So the lands
of the Regni in the South East, the Iceni in the East and the Brigantes in the Yorkshire area became Roman protectorates. The difference between protection and
occupation may seem negligible, but what it meant was that the Romans left
the traditional social hierarchies of the British more or less intact, so that they
could call upon their support as allies even though they were unable to maintain a fullscale occupation force in the farther outposts of the Empire. This
explains why Britain remained essentially less Romanized than Gaul, and why
the use of the Celtic language was retained alongside the introduction of Latin
among the privileged classes.

Not all the Britons were prepared to accept the new situation, however. In
what is now Wales, skirmishes with the Ordovices and the Silures kept the
Roman forces continually on their toes. Caratacus, the king of the Silures, led an
organized rebellion, but was eventually betrayed to the Romans in the year 51 by
Cartismandua, queen of the Brigantes, with whom he had taken refuge. Another
rebellion broke out when the Romans refused to recognize the agreement they
had made to honour the political testament of Prasutagus, king of the Iceni. His
widow, Queen Boudicca, declared war against the Romans, and many tribes
which had been waiting for just such an opportunity to shake off the Roman
yoke joined forces with her. But she was defeated. So, too, in 61 were the
Ordovices. The Romans then invaded the island of Mona (Anglesey), massacred
the Druids who lived there and looted the most important Druidic sanctuary of
the Celtic world. Gradually Britain was forced to accept Roman rule, though the
more mountainous areas retained some independence. By 80 AD Agricola had
reached the South of Scotland and was planning an expedition to Ireland. Their
victory at Mount Grapius made the Romans masters of the Lowlands. After
then, however, the Romans and the Britons established a kind of truce. And
although rebellion continued, both sides became united in a common interest.

Roman Britain

For the people of Northern Britain, who were never Romanized, made fearsome
neighbours. These Picts were undoubtedly Celtic peoples but their origins
remain obscure and it is impossible to classify them more specifically. Like all
mountain peoples with poor natural resources, they made frequent forays on the
richer, better cultivated Lowlands. Even before the Roman conquest there were
many Pictish raids on the more peaceable tribes of the South. These essentially
sedentary, agricultural peoples, some of them immigrants from Belgium, feared
and resented the fierce men from the North. So when the Romans came and
offered them the *pax romana*, they accepted it partly because they hoped to form
a united front controlled by firm yet flexible Roman law, but more because they
hoped that the Roman legions would protect them from the Picts. This is one of

the more significant reasons why the British felt at home within the imperial framework, to the extent that they later considered themselves the last remaining members of the Roman Empire. We can see evidence of the cooperation between Romans and Islanders in the way the Emperor Hadrian himself, helped by British recruits, came to prevent the southward sweep of the Picts and the Low-landers in the second century. It was then that Hadrian built his wall from Carlisle to Newcastle, to defend the *pax romana* from the men of the North. In around 140, however, there were fresh disturbances and the fortresses along the wall were destroyed. Antoninus Pius, Hadrian's successor, had another, much simpler earth-wall constructed further North, between Glasgow and Edin-burgh, though this, the Antonine Wall, was not very effective.

In about 196 the raids started again. In 208 Septimus Severus succeeded in making the area relatively peaceful, but in 211 Caracalla withdrew the permanent Roman garrisons to Hadrian's Wall. And it was then that the policing of the frontier changed in a way which was to have considerable impor-tance as far as later British history was concerned.

For the Roman administration decided to create defensive outposts staffed en-tirely by non-regular troops or frontier patrols. And all the soldiers employed in this area were British. Naturally the Romans picked the fiercest of the British tribes for the job and in some cases whole tribes moved northwards to defend the frontiers. It was then that the Otadini settled in the area between the Clyde and the Tyne. This tribe, which gave its name to Aneurin's poem the *Gododdin*, was to play a decisive part in the breakdown of Roman power in Britain. But for the time being, the use of British troops worked perfectly. Britain in the 3rd and 4th centuries remained peaceful and prosperous. Scots (Irish) pirates raided the West Coast from time to time, chiefly in Wales; but, defended from the Picts and the Caledonians, the rest of Britain formed a united and subjugated whole.

Like other occupied territories which gradually acquired Roman citizenship, Britain was a province divided into "dioceses". There were four of these: the area round London, known as *Britannia Prima*, the western region around Caerwent (*Venta Silurum*) and the important town of Caerleon on Usk (*Isca Silurum*), known as *Britannia Secunda*, and the two northern dioceses, *Maxima Caesariensis* and *Flavia Caesariensis*. The great legionary fortresses were at *Eburacum* (York), on the frontiers of the land of the Parisi and of the Brigantes, *Deva* (Chester, or *Castra Legionum*, the City of the Legions) on the frontiers of the Ordovices and the Cornovi in central Britain, and *Isca Silurum*, also known as the City of the Legions. There were settlements of veterans at *Lindum* (Lin-coln) among the Coritani, at *Camulodunum* (Colchester) among the Trino-vantes and at *Glevum* (Gloucester) among the Silures and the Dobunni. But out-side these small concentrations of power, Roman control was fairly limited. The forests, the Welsh valleys and the Pennine dales were still very much in British hands.

In Britain, as throughout the Empire, the Romans improved and developed the existing network of native roads so that troops and heavy materials could be moved rapidly from place to place. The roads were also used as trade routes by the Greek and Latin merchants who followed in the wake of every Roman army of occupation. Roman roads in Britain were about seven metres wide and covered in gravel to provide an all-weather surface for cavalry, heavy chariots and for the lighter convoys which took officials on their special missions.

The actual administration mirrored the kind of imperial bureacracy imposed on all occupied territories. Initially Roman policy was directed towards the construction of towns in which large numbers of people could be gathered, partly so as to keep them under observation, and partly to speed up the process of Romanization. Although this particular policy was less successful in Britain than in Gaul, the idea that all local government should tend towards an urban structure remained basic to the administration. The citizens of a town or a colony, whether Roman or not, elected their own magistrates from a body called the *municipium*. These magistrates automatically became *decurions* after a strictly limited term of office and were then able to sit on the *ordo*, which was a sort of permanent town council, a miniature senate of non-elected members.

The population of Britain, generally put at about 1,000,000 for the most prosperous period of Roman occupation, was mostly grouped into regional *civitates*, or cantons, which disregarded the tribal groupings of early Celtic society. The government of the *civitates* fell to councils which theoretically resembled the town councils, but which actually enjoyed far fewer rights and privileges, because it was more difficult to retain control over rural people than over townspeople.

There were many towns, none of them very large. The area of London, for example, was about thirteen hectares, even though all the housing was detached. Public buildings were very grand and included *basilica*, or meeting halls, amphitheatres, arenas and baths. But after the 4th century, for some reason the towns began to decay. The only large settlements to survive were former fortresses like *Luguvallum* (Carlisle), *Pons Aelius* (Newcastle) *Durobrivae* (Rochester), *Dubris* (Dover) and *Isca Dumnoniorum* (Exeter); sanctuaries or spas like *Verulamium* (St Albans) or *Aquae Sulis* (Bath); and district capitals like *Moridunum* (Carmarthen), *Calleva Atrebatum* (Silchester), *Venta Belgarum* (Winchester) and *Durovernum* (Canterbury).

Life in the country, on the other hand, continued to develop. There were many *villas*, or large agricultural estates, but these were scattered around the country in isolated positions, rather than collected into villages of the medieval type. The numbers of villas were greater in those areas where towns were few. The land was put to various uses, often being ploughed into vast fields by heavy, wheeled ploughs, unlike the lighter versions used by the villagers on their smaller allotments. The villas were owned by Britons who were educated and looked like Romans. But apart from them, the Britons remained obstinately attached to the Celtic way of life throughout the period of Roman occupation. The Romans and converted Britons made great efforts to Romanize the rest of the people. But although Latin was used for admistrative purposes, commercial dealings, chronicles, and later for religious practice, the British language continued to develop alongside it, eventually fragmenting into Welsh, Cornish and Breton. Roman influence in Britain was essentially on the administrative level. It formed a kind of establishment held together by the common interests of the moment. But it was never the basis of a new civilization, as in Gaul.

Celtic Britain

"The Roman occupation of Britain can best be likened to a great flood tide, and the close came as the tide recedes, not by a sudden event, not even by a series of events, but by a gradual process, as the ebb-tide leaves the shore."[1] Obviously there were preliminary indications that the end was coming during the comparatively peaceful 4th century. The Irish stepped up their raids on the west coast.

They controlled the Irish Sea and could cross it in their small, leather-covered coracles (*curragh*) unmolested. Some of them even settled in Britain. In Wales, for example, they passed on traditions later found in the literature of Gwynedd, and in Dyfed they founded princely houses.

But the Irish were not the only people engaged in the migration of Europeans which accompanied the decline of the Empire. The Picts had begun their expeditions towards the South again. And a new force had appeared, in the shape of the Teutonic peoples from Frisia or the mouth of the Elbe. Usually grouped together under the collective name of Saxons, although actually a mixture of Jutes, Saxons, Angles and Frisians, they were moving determinedly westward, as so many of the Indo-European peoples had before them.

From all appearances the Saxons began by making minor forays along the coastlines nearest their countries of origin, and were initially employed by the Romans as mercenaries to reinforce their northern legions. According to the legends about King Vortigern, the Britons themselves made an alliance with Saxons specifically to defend them against the Picts and the Irish.

In 367, however, the Irish, Picts and Saxons attacked on three fronts at once. The northern defence line collapsed, although it was temporarily restored by Theodosius. In 395 the Gallo-Roman general Stilichon succeeded in pushing back and subduing the Picts, but he moved the outposts of the Empire further southward. He was helped by Maxentius, another general, later immortalized in Welsh legend as Macsen Wledig.[2] Maxentius also repelled the Picts and Scots, with some brutality according to contemporary chronicles. But in 383, the occupying army in Britain proclaimed him emperor and he left for Gaul taking the best of his troops, including the Seguntienses from Caernarvon, to set up court at Treves. Then in 407, Constantine, the governor of Britain, was forced by what remained of the Roman army to usurp the title of emperor and leave the island for Gaul with his troops. As the Byzantine historian Procopius remarked, "After that time the Romans were never able to reconquer Britain which continued to be governed by tyrants."[3] And in 410 the Emperor Honorius informed the *civitates* of Britain that they could no longer rely on the imperial armies to defend them. After fifty years of unacknowledged defencelessness, Britain had official independence.

It was then that the period known as the Dark Ages began. Despite the name, this was an era of considerable interest. Nora Chadwick has pointed out in her *Studies in Early British history* that most of the languages, ideals and traditions which still predominate in much of the British Isles first took shape during this time. It was also during this period that the Arthurian phenomenon was to appear, hesitantly at first, but developing over the centuries into the very symbol of the Dark Ages. The process by which traditions and events that had nothing to do with Arthur gradually crystallised around him can also be observed in the great continental figure of Charlemagne. For Charlemagne, however, there is unquestionable evidence of his actual existence, whereas Arthur's existence remained open to any number of conflicting hypotheses. As a contemporary English historian says, "The Arthurian legend turns out under scrutiny to be the visionary projection of Britain's experience as a Roman land that became independent."[4] This is surely one more reason why we should try to find acceptable answers to the questions concerning Arthur's existence, both on the purely historical level and on the level of myth. For we cannot disregard the presence of myth in history, even less in connexion with the Celts.

Recent archaeological discoveries have shed some light on Celtic settlements of the period and on the British way of life at a time when the newly independent Britons had undergone a fairly superficial Romanization and a far more profound conversion to Christianity. But apart from these, the scanty documented evidence is unreliable. There are three written works covering the period. *De Exidio Britanniae* is the chronicle of a 6th-century British monk, Gildas, who emigrated to Brittany to found a hermitage at Bieuzy-les-Eaux (Morbihan) and a monastery at Saint-Gildas de Rhuys (Morbihan). The author of this work appears far more anxious to inveigh against the vices of his countrymen than to write a history,[5] *The History of the English Church and People* is, as its name suggests, essentially an ecclesiastical chronicle. Its author, the Venerable Bede, an Anglo-Saxon priest, lived at the end of the 7th and beginning of the 8th centuries. His work had a profound influence on medieval writers, although Bede's anti-British attitudes lead him to omit many of the more interesting facets of Dark Age history. Finally, there is the curiously jumbled *Historia Brittonum* by Nennius. There are several extant manuscripts of this work but none of them dates from before the 10th century; and the work as a whole forms a kind of extravaganza based on British traditions of various periods.[6] These three documents form a basis for any study of the Dark Ages and the dawning of the Arthurian phenomenon.

However unreliable the documents may be, we do know for certain that Britain totally abandoned the administrative machinery of the Roman Empire in about 450, after fifty years or so of virtual independence. The new Britain continued its claim to be the last citizen state of the Empire, but was actually as Celtic in customs and language as it had ever been. The elected municipal magistrates of the Roman administration went and government reverted to the Celtic system of separate tribes ruled over by chiefs whom Gildas called *tyranni*. Typical of these leaders was the Vortigern described by Bede, who became the Gwrtheyrn Gwrteneu of Welsh epic. His name means great chief, from *vor* or *guor*, an augmentative prefix, and *tigerno*, which originally meant head of the household or family. The same term was used in various parts of the Celtic world to denote a chief. The Bretons called their leaders *machtiern*, and the foster-father of Pryderi in the Welsh *Mabinogion* is called Teyrnon.

It is important to define what Gildas and subsequent hisorians meant by the word *tyrannus*. It was not used censoriously, rather in recognition of the fact that chiefs of the Celts came to power through force or through elections within a princely family. In the various Celtic kingdoms, Ireland included, monarchy was not hereditary. The leader of the *tuath* or tribe was chosen from among the family of the reigning chief, and once elected held office for an unlimited period. The word *tyrannus* therefore denotes a transition from the Roman, magisterial system of limited office to the Celtic rule of the *tiern*.

The abandonment of Roman *civitates* for Celtic tribes suggests that the *tyranni* came from those sections of the British population least touched by the imperial administration. And it seems likely that they were among those northern Britons whom the Romans had employed to guard the Pictish frontiers. For towards the beginning of the 5th century these people began to migrate south-westwards, more particularly towards Wales.

When speaking of Maelgwyn Guynedd, a 6th-century king of North West Wales, Nennius mentions his ancestor Cunedda who "had come from the North, from the region called Manau Guotodin (the land of the Otadini), 146 years before Maelgwyn's reign, with his eight sons. And he had driven the Scots (the Irish Gaels) out of the area after terrible massacres so that they never returned" (*Historia Brittonum*, chap. 62). There is no reason to suppose that this was an isolated incident. Since the British allowed the Saxons to settle as *foederati* in heavily forested areas in the way the Romans had done, the northern Britons must have moved towards the South West. All that is, except the peoples of Rheged (Cumberland) and Strathclyde, who had long formed strong and homogenous groups and preferred to stay where they were.

A mass movement of Northern Britons would explain one aspect of the migration of Britons to Brittany which historians tend to underestimate. Nora Chadwick argues convincingly in her book *Early Brittany* that this migration actually took place a hundred years before the generally accepted date. She bases her argument on four observations. First, the majority of the British leaders came from Central Wales, where there was no pressure from the Saxons. Second, most of the founding saints are traditionally connected with the South and West Wales. Third, there are linguistic links between the Devon—Cornwall peninsula and Brittany. And finally, none of the migrants appear to have come from East, South East or East Central England. A logical conclusion would therefore be that the Western Britons could foresee a situation arising where they were being attacked not only by their existing enemies the Irish from the West, but also by the Saxons from the East, and that they accordingly took to their boats to look for a more peaceful life over the sea.

But Nora Chadwick appears to overlook a fifth, and equally valid argument. Wholesale migration from Wales and the Devon–Cornwall peninsula may just as easily have resulted from the overpopulation following an influx of Britons from the North and East. This would certainly prove that the peoples of South and West Britain formed a large, cohesive mass during the Dark Ages.

What is certain is that the Northern Britons exerted considerable influence on the literature of those areas in which they came to settle. Most of what is now classified as Welsh literature, especially the poetry, is actually 12th and 13th-century adaptions of much earlier oral traditions. And although these manuscripts are written in Welsh of the middle period, with traces of Old Welsh, the 6th-century authors who were supposed to have composed the works spoke a British language which had evolved from Gallic, the Welsh language being a later development. But it is the specific references they contain to the Northern Britons which give us unequivocal evidence as to the provenance of these writings. Aneurin's *Godaddin* is a panegyric of the Otadini and could only have been composed by a fellow countryman. The poetry of Taliesin sings the praises of the historical king Uryen of Rheged and his son Owein. The bard Myrddin, whom Geoffrey of Monmouth later turned into Merlin[7] wrote poetry in honour of the British chiefs of Strathclyde. Myrddin himself went mad after a battle and wandered round the forest of Kelyddon (*Silva Caldonia*). Indeed, the whole legend of the prophet Merlin is connected with the life of St Kentigern who came from the same area. Ifor Williams has shown that the poems of Llywarch-Hen are all that remains of a saga of Powys;[8] and Llywarch-Hen was a Northern British chief who emigrated to Wales after staying in the land of Uryen, whom he exalts in his work.[9] If the bards originally came from the North, so too must their masters have done. For the Celtic chiefs always took their personal bards on their travels to celebrate their exploits and those of the whole community in their chants.

Bardic poetry appears to have flourished during the 6th century. Nennius writes of the bards at the court of Maelgwyn, and mentions their names. "Then Talhaern Tataguen [Iron Forehead, Father of Inspiration] was famous for his poems, as was Nwirin [Aneurin], Taliesin, Bluchbardd and Cian who is called Gueinth Guaut. They also won renown for British poetry at that time" (*Historia Brittonum*, chap. 62). Bardic poetry developed from the ancient Celtic tradition of oral rather than written culture. This tradition is also evident in the Irish *fili*, who, like the British bards, inherited some practices of Druidism. Roman attempts to impose their own form of civilization had had little effect on the Britons, except in the religious sphere where the written word was accepted.

For the Britons, like all the citizens of the Empire, had been converted to Christianity, not that the Christian gospel had much influence outside the towns and the wealthy, Romanized villas. The bulk of the rural populations of both Gaul and Britain remained pagan, practising a degenerate form of Druidism. Some of the sanctuaries dedicated to Celtic gods date from the last years of the Empire. Nodens, who is the god Nuada of Irish epic, and the Nudd of Welsh epic, was worshipped at *Glevum* (Gloucester). His sons, Edern and Gwynn, were later brought into the Arthurian tradition. Some of the old Druidic sanctuaries were restored and others, like the fortress of Maiden Castle, were actually built during this period.[10]

The continuity of Celtic pagan beliefs in the cultural environment, which later produced the Arthurian legend, explains why so many of Arthur's companions are former gods or goddesses relegated to the rank of magicians, wizards or fairies. Apart from the sons of Nudd, we can also recognize the Irish god Mananann, one of the sons of the goddess Dana, in the form of Manawydan, the Gallic god Maponos in the form of Mabon, and the mother-goddess Matrona in the form of Modron. Other characters are the result of an amalgam between some historic hero and an ancient divinity. The way in which heroes acquired the attributes of gods can be seen in Arthur and his two original followers, Kai and Bedwyr, who together recreate the Indo-European triad known as Odin, Tyrr and Thor in Teutonic mythology and Mithras, Varuna and Indra in Indian mythology.

And yet the Britons were officially Christians. And what is more, they regarded themselves as orthodox members of the faith, unlike the Germanic invaders whom they considered to be either pagans or heretics. The British Church leaders of the 5th and 6th centuries were undoubtedly strong and active in their beliefs. They were responsible for the conversion of Ireland. And while the old Celtic sanctuaries were being rebuilt, the British Christians were building a church in honour of the British martyr Saint Alban at Verulamium. A whole series of native saints followed after Saint Patrick; there were Saint Ninian, Saint Kentigern, Saint Gildas, Saint Iltud and many others. The Celtic countries in fact produced more saints than almost any other, even though the Roman Church did not accord official recognition to all of them.

For the British Church had its peculiarities and clung to them. There were great quarrels with Rome over the ecclesiastical tonsure and the calculation of Easter Day. The ecclesiastical hierarchy also differed from the Roman mainstream. The Roman Church had instituted a system of episcopal dioceses closely based on the administrative divisions of the Empire; while the British Church preferred a system of abbot-bishops in which the whole accent of ecclesiastical administration was placed on monastic life. Any monk who founded a religious establishment became the spiritual leader and focal point of the surrounding area. An abbot was more important than a bishop. Unlike the strict, closed orders of the continent, the British monasteries grew up round churches. The communities which settled around them were composed of ordinary families as well as monks, and although the whole group shared a common religious life, it had far greater freedom in other respects. Eventually the small towns created by the collection of houses around the church proved successful rivals to the old towns which the Romans had tried and largely failed to build.[11]

Then there was Pelagianism. This doctrine, which was developed by the British monk Pelagius, found its first converts in Europe and North Africa, but was widely and well received in Britain. Pelagius' theory of the Free Will, his denial of the value of grace and his rejection of the concept of original sin were bound to appeal to peoples who had believed in Druidism. The pope never actually declared Pelagianism a heresy, but the emperor threatened to confiscate the goods of anyone who upheld it. It was probably to counteract the spread of Pelagianism that Saint Germanus of Auxerre came to Britain in 429 and again in 447. This would explain the various legendary accounts of dissension between Germanus and King Vortigern; for it is likely that Vortigern, who sought a return to early Celtic institutions, was a defender of Pelagianism, if not a total apostate.

If we take into consideration the religious quarrels, the resurgence of old Celtic mythology and the increasing poetic output of the bards, it becomes clear that the Dark Ages in Britain were a time of some cultural development. Certainly Britain suffered far less from the "barbarian" period which followed the breakdown of the Roman Empire and the impetus of the Teutonic hordes on the continent. Continental Europe underwent a series of invasions from the Ostrogoths, Visigoths, Vandals and Franks, while the various British peoples remained united in language, religion and culture. Even when the imperial structures had gone, the Britons still regarded themselves as citizens of the Empire. Although it was not a state in the sense we would give the word today, Britain did form a nation. And despite continuous domestic quarrels, there was that sense of belonging to one nation which enabled the British to form a united front against the Saxons, Pictish and Gaelic invaders.

A sense of belonging, however, was all it was. The various tribes continued to exercise self-government although they were also prepared to set up federations and alliances against their external enemies. The *tiern* headed the social hierarchy of each tribe. Theoretically his word was law, but in practice he was far more a moral symbol, his powers limited to demanding respect for ancient customs and traditions. What prestige he enjoyed he won for himself by brave deeds on the battlefield, by the extent of his generosity and by his choice of courtiers and bards. But as soon as he ceased to be what Taliesin called a "distributor," as soon as he proved incapable of leading his warriors to victory, some bolder or more self-important rival would appear to take his place.

The *tiern* was the nucleus of an undefined social group consisting chiefly of warriors, many of whom were prepared to fight for any cause which promised some material rewards. These warriors might be considered the nobility of the era. The way their interest in personal gain overrode any altruistic concern for the weak or unfortunate is reflected in the behaviour of some of the Round Table knights portrayed in the French romances. The feudal system did not exist. The notion of loyal service was limited to the relationship between each individual warrior and the man who offered him favours or the spoils of war. In such peace time as they enjoyed, these men presumably spent their days hunting or watching the herds which the *tiern* could assign to their charge on behalf of the community as a whole. *Cheptel* contracts, whereby livestock was leased out in this way, certainly existed in Ireland during this period and there is no reason why the Britons should not have adopted a similar system. The *tiern* remained the centre of tribal life, its living symbol. He was the spokesman for the rights of the community, but would only be obeyed if he lived up to the aspirations of those who had chosen him.

Theoretically every member of the tribe had a say in the choice of leader, but in practice only the warriors exercised this right. For there were social inequalities within the tribe. Social status, however, had nothing to do with the ownership of land. Celtic notions of property hovered somewhere between private and communal ownership. The Romans had based their system on the sacred principle of individual property, whereas the Britons, like all Celtic peoples, supported a system of communal, tribal property. The boundaries of communal land remained ill-defined, since its extent would depend on the ability of the tribe to maintain it. But to make the best use of it the *tiern* would entrust the management of the land to certain members of the tribe chosen for their abilities. The men who had worked the old agricultural estates formed round the Roman villas may well have remained there during the Dark Ages, but their claims to private ownership would probably have been contested. They would have been required to labour in the name of the whole community, even if they were allocated the bulk of their products in return. In this respect the Celtic system appears to have been fairly flexible.

But if wealth through land did not constitute a criterion for nobility, rank must have been measured in some other way. And it seems likely that social inequality was determined by degrees of skill in the martial arts. The warrior could always keep the upper hand over the weaker or more peaceable lower classes. There were servants who did the manual work of the tribe and were probably fairly well treated because the community relied on their efforts. But even when the introduction of Christianity put an end to actual slavery, the domestic servants, the agricultural workers and grooms, the unskilled workers if you like, had no recognised position in society and must have led miserable lives. The craftsmen and merchants probably kept the status they had been accorded under the Roman Empire. There were always jobs for them to do, and although they were not of the highest rank they probably carried some weight in the community.

Recent archaeological finds on the sites occupied by the Britons in the Dark Ages have given us a clearer picture of Arthur's contemporaries. Generally speaking, little had changed since the Empire. There was the same mixture of cultivation, stock-rearing and craftsmanship as before. The need for weapons kept the metal workers busy, and a demand for personal adornment supported a thriving jewellery and garment-making industry.

But the Britain of the Dark Ages was not merely a degenerate version of Roman or early Celtic Britain. The 5th and 6th-century Britons had developed and perfected the technical skills they inherited from their forebears. Their decision to abandon Roman civilization for that of their Celtic ancestors was a deliberate one. They wanted to become Celts again. The Dark Ages is a misnomer for this period. It would be far better termed the golden age of the Celtic renaissance in Britain. Of this the Arthurian phenomenon, with all its political and mythological implications, is startling proof.

Peacetime methods of transport had not changed. The heavy, horse-drawn chariots of the Empire continued to roll along prehistoric roads which the Romans had resurfaced. Agricultural workers used the ox carts that are now taken as a stereotypic image of Celtic civilization. The warriors, however, had abandoned the war chariot once favoured by the Gauls in the early battle against the Romans. These chariots were obviously used in Britain at one time, for Caesar describes them in his account of his first visit here. They were driven by charioteers who were capable of all kinds of acrobatics, even on the shafts, and were used mainly to carry spear-hurling warriors to the thickest parts of the battle. The charioteer would then carry on to a less congested area, wheel about and return to fetch the warrior. There are descriptions of chariot warfare in the works of classical antiquity and in the Irish epic, particularly as concerns Cú Chulainn and his charioteer Loeg. Indeed the use of chariots in Ireland continued throughout the Dark Ages. By Caesar's time, however, the Gauls were fighting as troops of *equites* or cavalrymen, a form of warfare which spread to Britain in the 5th and 6th centuries and later to Ireland. The bold horsemanship of the Britons in the Dark Ages will obviously be a point of interest when we come to examine the Arthurian fellowship in closer detail. For the knights were probably based on cavalrymen of the British type, moving swiftly about the country under the leadership of a single chief.

Domestic building at this period appears to have been fairly varied. Those areas unaffected by war still boasted villas in the Gallo-Roman style. Then solitary, new houses were built near some source of water, in forest clearings or on the edges of woodland. It was there that the chiefs lived, with their retinue of bodyguards and their warrior elite. These houses were constructed on dry-stone foundations with wattle and daub walls and thatched roofs. They were usually circular with a central hearth under a hole in the roof to let the smoke out. The chief and his men would gather round the fire, sitting in a circle on the straw-covered floor to eat from the cauldron held over the flames. As we shall see, it was this custom, and this custom alone, which gave rise to the legends of the Arthurian Round Table. No matter how many far-fetched comments people may choose to make, no matter how often the Round Table is interpreted as an esoteric symbol, it will remain just a memory of times when men sat round the hearth to eat and drink.

The poorer peasants lived in smaller, circular houses without foundations, and had to share their accomodation with their livestock. There are vivid records of these dirty, smoke-filled houses in the literature of Ireland and Wales.[12]

In time of war, however, and in those days this meant a large proportion of the time, the chief moved to a fortified camp on high ground. Many of the hill forts used date from the early Iron Age but had fallen into disuse during the Roman occupation to be restored in the Dark Ages. Typical of these are Tintagel and Castle Dore in Cornwall. Dinas Powys and Deganwy in Wales, Glastonbury Tor and Cadbury in Somerset and Maiden Castle in Dorset.

These forts play an important part in Arthurian epic. The writers of the 12th and 13th centuries transformed them into medieval strongholds which would comfortably have contained the great gatherings of knights who attended Arthur's court. But these castles are an anachronism. Celtic forts could not have been more different. Earth, timber and sometimes even metal were used in their construction as well as stone. Unlike the multi-storey castles of the 12th century on their rocky perches, the Celtic forts spread horizontally and comprised a series of small houses enclosed by a fortified wall. As far as the hill forts are concerned, archaeology and the Celtic story tellers agree. Even the medieval versions of the Tristan legend, especially Béroul's *Tristan*, give us a reasonable idea of what the fort at Tintagel must have been like before the construction of the 12th-century castle whose ruined walls still stand there.

The sites of Celtic forts have been found on hills, rocky outcrops or on artificial mounds of earth and stone constructed in some spot where there was a wide view of the surrounding area. The ramparts were obviously the most important part of the fort. On a steep slope only a bank and ditch might be necessary, or there might be a wooden palisade surrounding all or part of the hill top. As the weakest point in any form of construction the entrance was always heavily protected and often Z-shaped with a timber walk-way and small towers erected above the gate itself. The road leading to the gateway would be laid out so as to force the enemy to walk along the ramparts with his left shield-arm away from the fort, leaving his body exposed.

The ramparts took different forms, often dictated by the position of those ancient sites which the Britons decided to re-use. The most primitive of them were earth and stone banks, as wide as they were high, with a protective timber wall forming a circle at the top. In areas where stone was plentiful huge blocks of undressed rock would be piled up to form the defences. Elsewhere the Britons used the same methods which Caesar had observed in Gaul. "Balks of timber are laid on the ground at regular intervals of two feet along the whole line on which the wall is to be built, at right angles to it. These are made fast to one another by long beams running across them at their points, and are covered with a quantity of rubble; and the two-foot intervals between them are faced with large stones fitted tightly in. When this first course has been placed in position and fastened together, another course is laid on top. The same interval of two feet is kept between the balks of the second course, but they are not in contact with those of the first course, being separated from them by a course of stones two feet high; thus every balk is separated from each of its neighbours by one large stone, and so held firmly in position. By the addition of further courses, the fabric is raised to the required height" (*Gallic Wars* VII, 2). The ramparts of Avaricum (Bourges) were built in this way. It meant that the timbers were protected from fire by earth and stone.

Another strange system of fortification in use during the Dark Ages actually dated back to the end of the Bronze Age, i.e. about 800 BC. This process was known as vitrification. The core of the rampart was made of a hard, compact mass of stone which was heated until it looked like thick, rough glass. Obviously the heating process took place *in situ*. The builders must have piled up the stone and sand with wood and then set light to it. As archaeologists have pointed out, the process presented great technical difficulties, but the result was an impregnable wall. The fort of Peran near Saint-Brieuc (Côtes-du-Nord) is a model of this type of construction. The process of vitrification presumably gave rise to the names *Urbs Vitrea, Kaer Gutrin* and the *Royaume de Gorre*, or all those cities of glass mentioned in the Arthurian romances and in the Celtic tradition generally. Clearly any peculiarity of terrain or defensive system which struck the imagination might be translated into a symbol of a mythological place.

Inside the ramparts people carried on all kinds of activities. Some of the hillforts became permanent settlements and places of assembly in peacetime also. There is evidence that the metal workers continued their trade inside many forts. And there were stockpiles of raw materials and barns for the crops. Arthur held his plenary courts in forts of this kind to coincide with the great Celtic and Christian religious festivals. In Ireland, too, the grand assemblies always coincided with the important festivals of the Celtic calendar, especially the feast of Samain on November 1 when the celebrations lasted for three days and three nights.

The houses inside varied widely. There were huts for servants, circular mud-wall houses with thatched roofs, some of them with a corbelled arch. The various houses would stand detached if there was enough room, or huddled together in confined spaces. Irish literature suggests that the chief's houses had some modicum of comfort. There is certainly an impression in Béroul's *Tristan* that running water was available, for Tristan was able to arrange meetings with the queen by throwing wood shavings into a stream which carried them into the house where Iseult lived. So presumably small canals were built in some forts to take water from a natural source to the interiors of the houses. There was no furniture and the Britons, like the Gauls, ate, sat and slept on the straw-covered earth floor.[13] But they did have a great number of tools and implements: pots, bowls, metal cauldrons, spits and so on. So that, although modern comforts as we would understand them were sadly lacking, the practical essentials were there.

It is possible to discern the outlines of courtyards or *llys* between the houses. One of these, which the Welsh called the *cadlys* and the Irish the *airlis*, was a circular stockade used for keeping in the livestock which constituted the only real wealth of the community.

The chief's house was more spacious than the others, but it often served a dual purpose as dwelling place and meeting hall. A rectangular building with the hearth either in the middle or, as at Dinas Powys, slightly to one side, it was made of stone or wood with drystone foundations. According to *Kulhwch and Olwen*, Arthur's hall appears to have been wooden, but not on ground level. There were no steps, however, only a stone ramp which could easily be climbed by a horse. And "whereas everyone else dismounted outside at the mounting-block Kulhwch rode in on his steed" (*Mabinogion*). Neither were there any corridors. The adjacent rooms either opened directly onto the great hall or formed totally separate lodgings. The hall itself was richly decorated to show the magnificence of the chief and the wealth of his tribe. The grand assemblies at which important decisions were made were held there. On entering, the warriors would put their weapons down by the walls. They also hung their trophies on the walls, displaying them like museum pieces.

As we can see, the British way of life in the Arthurian era had nothing in common with life under the Empire. It was barbarian in the sense of being totally alien to Roman customs and practices, but not degenerate. For the British clung fiercely to the hope of resurrecting the old ways. Life may have been rough and ready; the almost continuous warfare made for a violent society. But for the ruling classes at least luxurious living was not totally out of the question. Descriptions of Celtic forts all emphasize the precious treasures displayed there, the beauty of the architecture, the delicacy of jewels and valuables, the splendour of the weapons and the lustrous colours of the clothes. Such sumptuousness and the huge poetic output of the bards attached to the tribal chiefs give us some idea of how vital the civilization of the Dark Ages really was. But, unhappily for the Britons, the promise of a brilliant future never matured. There was too little time. And if the Arthurian era is now referred to as the Dark Ages, the fault lies with the invaders who were eventually to turn Britain into England and to kill all British hopes of rebuilding an ideal Celtic society based on respect for ancient tradition.

The New Kings of Britain

After the year 410 the Britons were officially left to their own devices, for the Roman troops had left the island never to return. The Empire had overgrown its own strength and, when it collapsed, various independent kingdoms modelled on more "barbarian" lines were formed. Only the Eastern Empire remained cut off from the rest of Europe. Despite its internal conflicts, it was united by a form of Christianity less wide-spread in its sphere of influence than Roman Catholicism, but which ultimately produced Eastern Orthodoxy. The culture of the Eastern Empire was Greek in language and easily absorbed what remained of ancient Hellenistic thought, although the golden age of Greece itself had accompanied the formation of rival city-states. In the West, on the other hand, the centralist, unitarian aspirations of the Romans ran counter to the wide variety of different peoples who lived within the Roman sphere of influence. And the improbable and artificial bonds created by the Empire were powerless to resist the slow infiltration of Germanic barbarians and the claims of their new leaders to autonomy. Britain, as an island, had always escaped the worst rigours of Roman centralism and enjoyed a special status within the Empire. It was therefore able to return more easily to pre-Roman, Celtic ways. By 450 the Roman power structure had broken down completely and the country was divided into a number of small kingdoms based on the tribal system of the ancient Celts. Much of the impetus to re-adopt the old customs came from the northern tribes, which had retained Celtic traditions more successfully.

But the local *tyranni* mentioned by Gildas and Bede were in a precarious position. The push of Germanic peoples to the West threatened Britain as much as the continent. Clearly the local leaders had to form a united front against them. This, in any case, would explain why Vortigern, who was merely a local *tiern*, became so important. The Celtic tribes had obviously formed a confederation to fight the Picts, the Irish and the Saxons who held various key positions in the East and North East, and looked to Vortigen as their leader.

Gildas tells us how the Britons played the Saxons off against the Picts, although he does not name the leader responsible for this idea. (But then Gildas very rarely mentions peoples by name.) Bede, on the other hand, is much more specific. According to him, the Britons "consulted how they might obtain help to repel the frequent attacks of their northern neighbours, and all agreed with the advice of their king, Vortigen, to call on the assistance of the Saxon peoples across the sea" (Bede, I, chap. 14). Here Vortigern has become the supreme leader and policy maker for the British troops. This whole story is corroborated by Nennius' *Historia Brittonum* which adds further detail, some of it bordering on the fantastical.

> For years the Britons lived in fear. Vortigern was king of Britain and during his reign he was threatened both by the Picts and Scots and by the Romans, but not by Ambrosius.[14] Then three boatloads of men banished from Germany arrived. Among them were the brothers Hengist and Horsa, the son of Guietgils, the son of Guitta, the son of Wodin ... the son of Geta, which made him son of god, not the God of gods, amen, the God of armies, but one of the idols they worshipped. Vortigern welcomed them and gave them the island they called Thanet, which the Britons call Rudhim (Chap. 31) ... It was then that Saint Germanus came to preach in Britain (Chap. 32).

It would seem from this account that around the year 450 the Saxons were less of a threat to the Britons than their age-old enemies the Picts and the Irish. This would support the suggestion that British emigration to Brittany followed pressure from the Irish and indirectly from the Picts, who had been responsible for the movements of people towards the South West, rather than from the Saxons. But Nennius' view of these Saxons as exiles seeking refuge differs from Bede's account.

> In the year of our Lord 449, Martian became Emperor with Valentinian and forty-sixth successor to Augustus, ruling for seven years. In his time the Angles or Saxons came to Britain at the invitation of King Vortigern in three longships and were granted lands in the eastern part of the island on condition that they protected the country: nevertheless, their real intention was to attack it. At first they engaged the enemy advancing from the North and having defeated them, sent back news of their success to their homeland, adding that the country was fertile and the Britons cowardly. Whereupon a larger fleet came over with a great body of warriors, which, when joined to the original forces, constituted an invincible army. These also received grants of land and money from the Britons, on condition that they maintained the peace and security of the island against all enemies . . . These newcomers were from the three most formidable races of Germany, the Saxons, Angles and Jutes . . . Their first chieftains are said to have been Hengist and Horsa. The latter was subsequently killed in battle against the Britons and was buried in east Kent where a monument bearing his name still stands. They were sons of Victgilsus, whose father was Vecta, son of Woden . . . (Bede, *History of the English Church and People*, I, 15)

Gildas also suggests that the decision to invite the Saxons was taken by "*omnes conciliari cum superbo tyranno*" (all the councillors with their proud tyrant) because of continual harassment from the Picts who were attacking the British coastlines from their coracles (*De Excidio Britanniae*, chap. 23). Obviously the Britons intended to use the Saxons as mercenaries, just as the Romans had done before them. The *superbus tyrannus* Gildas refers to must be Vortigern.

Nennius goes on in his version to suggest that the Saxons whom Vortigern had summoned as reinforcements then used the British leader's desire for Hengist's daughter to obtain favours from him and were thus able to bring over more of their fellow countrymen without fear of retaliation. However fanciful this particular account of events may be, recent archaeological discoveries in Great Britain do show that the early Saxon invasions were peaceful and presumably followed a summons on behalf of the British. Vortigern probably did become an accomplice of the Saxons. Having once invited them, it would have been hard to ask them to leave. Certainly Bede, who does not mention Vortigern again, has no doubts as to the greed of the Saxons.

> It was not long before such hordes of these alien peoples crowded into the island that the natives who had invited them began to live in terror, for the Angles suddenly made an alliance with the Picts whom they had recently repelled, and prepared to turn their arms against their allies. They began by demanding a greater supply of provisions; then, seeking to provoke a quarrel, threatened that unless larger supplies were forthcoming, they would terminate their treaty and ravage the whole island. Nor were they slow

to carry out their threats. In short, the fires kindled by the pagans proved to be God's just punishment on the sins of the nation, just as the fires once kindled by the Chaldeans destroyed the walls and palaces of Jerusalem. For, as the just Judge ordained, these heathen conquerors devastated the surrounding cities and countryside, extended the conflagration from the eastern to the western shores without opposition, and established a stranglehold over nearly all the doomed island. Public and private buildings were razed; priests were slain at the altar; bishops and people alike, regardless of rank, were destroyed with fire and sword, and one remained to bury those who had suffered a cruel death. A few wretched survivors captured in the hills were butchered wholesale, and others, desperate with hunger, came out and surrendered to the enemy for food, although they were doomed to lifelong slavery even if they escaped instant massacre. Some fled overseas in their misery; others, clinging to their homeland, eked out a wretched and fearful existence among the mountains, forests and crags, ever on the alert for danger. (Bede, I, 15)

Bede's ominous picture of the situation is probably quite close to reality, though his insistence that the sufferings borne by the Britons were due to their sins can obviously be taken with a pinch of salt. Vortigern and the British chiefs had allowed the wolf into the fold, just as the Heduens had called on Julius Caesar and his legions to protect them from the Helvetii. According to Nennius, however, some of the Britons resisted. Guorthemir (Gwrthevyr), one of Vortigern's sons, apparently decided to expel the Saxons and accordingly rose against his father whom he banished.

The king invited his wise men and asked them what he should do. They replied "Go to the ends of your kingdom and find a fort where you will be able to defend yourself.[15] For the people you have invited are planning to attack you. They will kill you treacherously and when you are dead they will subdue all the land you have loved and your people." Then, together with his wise men, he began to look for a fort. After visiting many provinces and finding nothing, he came to the region called Gwynedd. There, as he travelled over the mountains of Eryri [Snowdon] he found a spot suitable for a fort. His wise men told him he could build the fort there [Dinas Emrys] and he would be safe from the barbarians for ever, (*Historia Brittonum*, chap. 40)

At this point Vortigern appears to have become a hunted man, wanted both by the Saxons and by his fellow countrymen. But here Nennius' narrative takes a strange turn. It would be easy enough to dismiss the episode that follows as a fragment of some lost epic or a folk tale artificially introduced into the story and say no more about it. But even if it is not history in the accepted sense it deserves some examination. For what Nennius says is that Vortigern's newly constructed fort fell in ruins that very night. His wise men then told him "Unless you find a fatherless child and kill it, so that you can scatter its blood over the citadel, you will never be able to build a fort" (*Historia Brittonum*, chap. 40). Nennius did not invent this idea of child sacrifice, for the notion that a fort would be strengthened by a child's blood is part of an extremely ancient myth. The practice of ritual sacrifice of the first born among Semitic peoples was probably attached to the same tradition.[16] It also appears in Irish literature and in a number of folk stories from all over the world. This is presumably why Nennius' account is relegated to the ranks of fable.

But if we suppose that Vortigern was unable to build exactly what he wanted at first, it is quite likely that his wise men, as distant successors of the Druids, would have suggested something of the sort. It is the rest of the story that gives more cause for thought. Apparently a fatherless child was eventually found who told Vortigern that there was a subterranean lake under the spot where he wished to build the fort. This too is feasible; it would certainly explain any subsidence under the building. But when they dug down and found the lake, the child went on to say that they should look for two snakes, one white and one red. The two snakes were duly startled out of hiding whereupon the white chased the red one away. This the child explained as Vortigern, the red snake, being chased away by the Saxons, the white snake (*Historia Brittonum*, chap. 42).

The symbolism here is quite evident. The story is obviously a fable. The snake, or dragon, was much used as a symbol both during the Dark Ages and in medieval times. British flags often portrayed dragons and chiefs were frequently given the name *penndragon*, "head of a dragon," to show their importance. Uther Pendragon is a case in point. Geoffrey of Monmouth repeats this whole expisode in his *Historia Regum Britanniae*, though he makes it purely mythological in context and accentuates the political aspects of the anecdote. Nennius, however, finishes his chapter on an even more curious note. The child begins prophesying to Vortigern.

> "And then our people will rise and bravely drive the Angles back over the sea. You, however, must leave this fort because you will not be able to build anything there. You must travel over many provinces until you find a fort that can protect you. It shall stay here." The king said to the child, "What is your name?" He replied, "Ambrosius, that is Embreis Guletic [Emrys Gwledig]!" And the king said "Of which race do you come?" He replied, "My only father is of the race of Roman consuls." And the king gave him the citadel together with all the regions of the North coast of Britain ... (*Historia Brittonum*, chap. 42)

Various comments seem called for here. Firstly a fatherless child is able to speak of his sole father, proving that he is a prophet and can see things invisible to others. Then declaring that he is of the Roman race, he suggests that there is some confrontation of political doctrines between himself as a representative of the imperial tradition and Vortigern as champion of Celtic institutions. But it turns out that the whole story is merely a hotch-potch of legends used to explain the name of Vortigern's fort, in the way that so many places are traditionally given imaginary, mythical founders. For Dinas Emrys means the Fort of Ambrosius, and if the fort had been given to the child, it would naturally take his name. In just this way, Romulus was supposed to have founded Rome, although from all the evidence, the city had acquired its name long before Romulus was first thought of. Probably the legend of the fatherless child sprang up to link Dinas Emrys with some exceptional person.

For Ambrosius was a historical character. Gildas describes Ambrosius Aurelianus as a *dux* and a *vir modestus* (chap. 25), and Bede makes him the last of the Romans and victor over the Saxons (I, 16). He certainly seems to have represented a return to Roman ideas, not so much culturally speaking as politically. For he demonstrates the imperial sense of cohesion in the face of foreign aggression and opposes the Pelagianism upheld by Vortigern. In view of the fact that Nennius describes the conflict between Ambrosius and Vortigern in later chapters of his work, it does seem strange that he should allow the British leader to give the last of the Romans areas of land in this episode.

Geoffrey of Monmouth gives the story even wider implications. His Ambrosius is the son and heir of the Emperor Constantine the Blessed, whose crown has been usurped by Vortigern. And when Vortigern asks the child who he is, he replies, "My name is Merlinus Ambrosius." Having already written his *Vita Merlini*, Geoffrey doubtless leapt at the chance of giving his magician hero an exceptional childhood. In fact, when we look closely at the character of Merlin, we find it to be an extraordinary synthesis of three ancient themes: the fatherless child who can speak (the newborn Merlin is often accredited with powers of speech), the mad prophesying poet[17] and the Wild Man of the Woods who communicates with animals. The transformation from the fatherless child Ambrosius Aurelianus into Merlinus Ambrosius (Myrddin Emrys) and then into Merlin, bard of Ambrosius (Myrddin bard of Emrys) was operated solely by Geoffrey and has no value as historical evidence. But Nennius' account can with some reservations lay claim to historical reality. After this episode, he continues:

> Meanwhile, Vortigern's son Guothemyr fought fiercely against Hengist and Horsa and all their people, and drove them back to the island called Thanet where he laid siege to them three times. He pursued them, terrorized them and beat them. The Saxons sent messengers to Germania to ask for boats and reinforcements. Then they fought the chiefs of our land again. Sometimes they won and extended their frontiers, sometimes they were beaten and driven back. (*H.B.*, chap. 43) Guorthemyr engaged four fierce battles against them. The barbarians were beaten and Guorthemyr was the victor. They hastened to their boats to flee and were drowned like women as they scrambled aboard. Soon after, Guorthemyr died. But before his death he had told his men to bury him in the port where the Saxons had put out to sea. "I command you to do this, for even if the enemy held a port elsewhere in Britain, they would never invade this one."[18] But they ignored his instructions.[19] (*H.B.*, chap. 44)

After the death of Guorthemyr, whom the Welsh authors called "the Blessed," some of the Britons appear to have followed Vortigern's lead. For the Saxons returned with reinforcements, clearly determined to conquer the whole island. It was then that the episode known as the Plot of the Long Knives occurred:

> The enemy planned to overcome Vortigern and his army by cunning. They sent messengers to sue for everlasting peace and friendship between them. Vortigern assembled his council and asked their advice. They all agreed to make peace.[20] The messengers left, then returned to arrange a meeting between the two sides. The Britons and the Saxons were to come unarmed to solemnly swear an alliance. (*H.B.*, chap. 45) But Hengist ordered his men to hide their knives under their feet. "And when I say *Eu Saxones eniminit saxas*, take your knives out of your boots and attack them. But do not kill their king. For the sake of my daughter, his wife, take him prisoner because he will be more use to us as a hostage for ransom." They promised to obey and went to the meeting. The Saxons spoke like friends and behaved with great courtesy. The men sat down so that each Saxon sat next to a Briton. Then Hengist cried out as he had said he would and the three hundred chiefs of Vortigern were all slaughtered. He alone was taken prisoner and put in

chains. To save his life and win his freedom he had to cede many regions including Essex, Sussex and Middlesex. (*H.B.*, chap. 46)

After this massacre of British chiefs, Vortigern was branded a traitor and unfit to lead. A coalition of former supporters of the Empire led by Ambrosius Aurelianus and members of the clergy roused by Saint Germanus now confronted him. The legendary attachment of Ambrosius to Constantine suggests that he came from a noble family which had enjoyed some privileged position under the Empire, and that he hoped to restore the country to the Roman system of government. This may be why the *tyranni* opposed him and clung for so long to Vortigern who was a Briton like them. As things turned out, however, they were forced to shift their allegiance. And, as Nennius puts it,

In a wretched condition, Vortigern fled to Guorthigirniaun [Radnor], the region named after him, with his wives.[21] Saint Germanus and all the British clergy followed him there ... Again Vortigern fled in shame to the citadel of Guorthigem which is in the land of the Demetae[22] near the river Tiebi. Saint Germanus followed him there also, and remained for three days and nights, fasting with his clerics. On the fourth night the whole fortress was set alight by fire from heaven ... and Vortigern perished together with all his companions. (H.B., chap. 47) Others say that when Vortigern became an outcaste and a fugitive roaming the country, it broke his heart and he died in dishonour. Others again say that the earth opened and swallowed him up the night his fortress burnt around him, for after the fire nothing of him or his companions could be found. (*H.B.*, chap. 48)

Once Vortigern had gone, Ambrosius Aurelianus, or, as the Welsh called him, Emrys Gwledig, became uncontested leader of all those Britons who wished to remain independent. In about 460 he organized the construction of a fleet to carry the Britons across the North Sea and drive back the Saxons. In 470 the island navy joined forces with a fleet of Bretons to fight for the Emperor Anthemius who was trying to restore Roman authority in Gaul. But the Western Empire was now too weak for a campaign of this kind to succeed. Even so, the Britons under Emrys Gwledig were the last people North of the Alps to prove their loyalty to the Western Emperor in so unmistakable a fashion.

In Britain itself, however, attempts to Romanize the country again met with little success. Admittedly the red dragon of the last emperors was adopted as an emblem and its appearance on the shields of British warriors led to all kinds of legends, including the story of Uther Pendragon. The only other evidence of Roman customs being re-adopted during this period lies in the fashion for giving children Latin names. Tacitus became Tegid, Caius Kai, Constantine Custennin, Gerontius Geraint, Paternus Padarn and Tribunus Tryphun, Better known in Brittany in its feminine form Tryphina. Even the name Arthur may have come from the Latin Artorius.

In the religious sphere Saint Germanus and Saint Lapus had re-established good relations between the British Church and the papacy, although the British Church still retained its own peculiarities. It was this independent attitude which later led the papacy to favour the Saxons, who as recent converts were much more obedient to orders from Rome. Besides, Saint Germanus had not altogether succeeded in extinguishing the fire of Pelagianism in Britain.

About 460 to 470 trade with the continent was resumed, with special help from the Bretons. The wealthy Britons in the West imported oil, wine and luxury goods from the Mediterranean countries. One of the biographers of Saint Germanus says that then, that is under the reign of Emrys Gwledig, Britain was a prosperous country. Bede concurs:

> When the victorious Angles had scattered and destroyed the native peoples and returned to their own dwellings, the Britons slowly began to take heart and recover their strength, emerging from the dens where they had hidden themselves, and joining in prayer that God might help them to avoid complete extermination. Their leader at this time was Ambrosius Aurelius, a modest man of Roman origin, who was the sole survivor of the catastrophe in which his royal parents had perished. Under his leadership the Britons took up arms, challenged their conquerors to battle, and with God's help inflicted a defeat on them. Thenceforward victory swung first to one side, and then to the other, until the battle of Badon Hill, when the Britons made a considerable slaughter of the invaders. This took place about forty-four years after their arrival in Britain. (Bede, 1, 16)

There is nothing to tarnish Ambrosius' golden reputation. All the evidence we have agrees that he had remarkable powers of organization. Geoffrey of Monmouth must have been aware of this when he made his Merlin divine the king's death from a star with a mass of fire in the shape of a dragon. For Merlin says "O, irreparable woe, o mourning Britons, o loss of the noblest of kings! Emrys Gwledig is dead! Hasten Uther to do battle with the enemy. You will be victor and will become king. This star, this dragon of fire, represents you."

This eulogistic obituary could almost be one of the funerary chants so common among the poetry of the 6th century Welsh bards, and clearly befits a man of great standing. Ambrosius Aurelianus probably was an important leader who enabled Britain to gather its strength for a decisive assault on the Saxons invaders. According to Bede, no side could lay claim to total victory until the battle of Mount Badon. But this battle, which halted the Saxons' advance for thirty-odd years, was fought and won not by Emrys Gwledig, but by a strange character who poses many questions. For it is here that King Arthur makes his first appearance on the British historical and legendary stage.

CHAPTER FOUR

King Arthur in History

ITHOUT trying to push the comparison too far, King Arthur has something in common with Jesus of Nazareth. For, although there is ample evidence of the actual historical existence of both men, there are no authentic documents to prove it. Pascal said that from the purely logical point of view it was no more absurd to believe in the existence of God than not to. We might make a similar comment about Arthur: logically it is no more absurd to believe that there really was a 6th-century British king with this name than to suppose that he is only a legendary character born of myth. The extent to which his name has spread and the centuries over which he has continued to fascinate men's minds make it almost inevitable that we would wish to look at him from a historical angle.

Unfortunately neither Gildas nor Bede, who provide the best documented evidence for this era, mentions Arthur. Gildas wrote his *De Excidio Britanniae* around the year 540 in Wales. But the only mention he makes of anything at all relevant to Arthur is a reference to the battle of *Mons Badonicus* which took place the year of Gildas' birth. He says that this British victory followed a war of aggression against the Britons, and led to a period of peace (*De Excidio Britanniae*, VI). But he does not say who led the victorious army at Mount Badon. But then he very rarely mentions people by name, and makes no claim to be writing a historical work. His chief concern was to expose the vices and shortcomings of his fellow countrymen. Ultimately the *De Excidio Britanniae* is little more than a vitriolic diatribe. Bede also mentions the victory at Mount Badon, but like Gildas says nothing of the British leader. Bede was in any case much more interested in ecclesiastical history and the career of Saint Germanus than in the crucial political and military events of the 6th century. Both Gildas and Bede belong to a purely ecclesiastical tradition; and while the historical Arthur was probably a Christian, he may well have fallen out with the clergy, especially the monastic clergy who laid down the law in those territories under Celtic influence. This would certainly explain why there appears to be a conspiracy of silence surrounding Arthur despite his success in halting the westward movement of the Saxons for a time.

Apart from allusions to him in Welsh poetry, there are only two documents with any historical pretensions which mention Arthur. One is the *Annales Cambriae* which were written before 956, and the other is the *Historia Brittonum* of Nennius which was compiled at about the same time. Under the date 516, the *Annales* list "the battle of Badon, in which Arthur bore the cross of our lord Jesus Christ on his shoulders for three days and three nights and the Britons were victorious."[1] It is clear from this that Arthur took part in the battle, though not whether he actually led the British forces. Later in the same work, under the year 537 there is a reference to the "Battle of Camlaan, in which Arthur and Medrawt killed each other: and there were many deaths in Britain and Ireland."[1] All we can readily glean from this is some evidence of the existence of Medrawt (Mordret) who was later to sound the death knell of the Arthurian world in the Round Table romances.

Nennius has more to say about Arthur and the battles he was supposed to have fought. The *Historia Brittanum* is actually a jumble of information from various sources assembled in apparently random fashion. But the lack of literary pretension and the disorganized nature of the work both argue in favour of some measure of authenticity. Nennius writes:

> At that time huge numbers of Saxons were invading Britain and increasing. When Hengist died, his son Octha came from North Britain to the kingdom of the Canti and founded the royal line of Kent. Then Arthur and the British kings fought the Saxons. He was their *dux bellorum* [leader in battle]. First he fought a battle at the mouth of the river called Glein [possibly Glendale in Northumberland?]. He fought four others, on the river Dubglas (Black Water) in the region of Linnuis [possibly Lennox, more likely the region of Lindsey north of Lincoln]. The sixth battle took place on the river called Bassas [Lake Bassenthwaite in Cumberland?]. The seventh was in the forest of Celidon, the *Cat Coit Celidon*.[2] The eighth was the battle of the fort of Guinnion [Binchester, Co. Durham?], in which Arthur bore the image of the Virgin on his shoulders.[3] The pagans were put to flight that day and many of them were slaughtered, thanks be to our lord Jesus Christ and the Blessed Virgin. A nineth battle took place at the City of Legions [Chester], a tenth on the banks of the river Tribuit.[4] The eleventh on a mountain called Agned or Cat Bregouin [Brougham in Westmorland]. The twelfth battle took place at Mount Badon, in which a single assault from Arthur killed 960 men and no other man took part in this massacre. And in all these battles he was victor. (*Historia Brittonum*, chap. 56)

Apart from any difficulties in pinpointing the sites of these battles, this text raised a series of questions. First of all, Arthur's status is ambiguous. Nowhere does Nennius describe him as king or *rex*. Even the word *tyrannus* used by Gildas and Bede, which like the *theyrn* or *tiern* of British means the chief of the tribe, is absent from Nennius' work. On the other hand, Arthur does fight *cum regibus brittonis*, with the British kings, and is given the title *dux*, or leader of

the army. And the added qualification *dux bellorum* shows that he had no political authority over the British kings, merely the power of a military leader. This
point is of some interest. Nennius could have used the word *imperator*, which
originally meant "general in chief," but the fact that the word had since come to
be applied to the ruler of the Empire might have led to confusion. It is hard to
say whether Arthur actually had no claim to the title *imperator* or whether his
claims were overlooked. Certainly he acquired the name *amherawdyr*, or
emperor, in two Welsh texts.

The first comes from the Black Book of Carmarthen, and is a funerary chant in
honour of Gereint, son of Erbin, prince of Devon, who stood against the Saxons
at Langport in 710 when the Devon–Cornwall peninsula was still independent.
The three relevant lines from this poem read, "At Llongborth, I saw, hewing
with steel / the brave men of Arthur / emperor and strategist of the battle." This
anachronistic reference to Arthur suggests two possibilities. Either the story of
Gereint had been integrated into the Arthurian cycle, as were the tales of Uryen
and Myrddin; and this seems likely when we look at the tale of *Gereint and Enid*.
Or else, some kind of patriotic warrior band which was working to preserve the
ancient Celtic traditions fought on under Arthur's name even in the 8th century.
Whatever the answer, Arthur is given the title emperor, but only in the military
sense.

The second reference to Arthur as *amherawdr* occurs in a medieval Welsh tale,
The Dream of Rhonabwy. Its author used very old source material to reconstruct
this episode from the early Arthurian cycle. Arthur appears throughout as
emperor. He agrees to play a strange game of chess with Owein, son of Uryen,
who owns a mysterious flock of ravens.[6] But here, too, the word *amherawdyr*
seems to be used in the sense of "chief of the armed forces."

There can be little doubt that Arthur had acquired a solid reputation as a great
warrior by the end of the 6th century. One of the oldest *Triads* of Britain tells of
the three red fighters of the island, Run son of Beli, Lleu Llaw Gyffes and
Morgan Mwynfawr, but adds "there was one who was greater than these: his
name was Arthur. Where they had marched neither grass nor any plant could
grow for one year, but where Arthur went it was seven years."[7] That Arthur was a
merciless fighter is as much part of the Arthurian myth as of the historical
character. His exceptional qualities are frequently enumerated in the *Triads*. In
many cases an additional line concerning Arthur appears to have been tagged
onto an older three-line verse to form a tetrad. Aneurin's *Gododdin* contains an
interesting description of a warrior as one who "filled the hungry black crows
on the ramparts of the city, although he was not Arthur."[8] The fact that Aneurin
was a northern bard and that the *Gododdin* lists the setbacks and heroism of the
Northern Britons, while Arthur is generally accepted as having been mainly
active in the South West shows that his reputation had travelled a considerable
distance, as the many Arthurian place names in Scotland and the North of
England would suggest.

It is clear that Arthur soon assumed the proportions of a national hero, if not
of an emperor in the later sense of the Latin word *imperator* as political and
military leader. There are various arguments in favour of the suggestion that he
was indeed the last in the line of Roman emperors in the West.

Ambrosius Aurelianus was certainly regarded as a real emperor of the Late
Empire; and as his successor, Arthur could quite naturally have assumed the
same title, even the same office. But Bede specifically states that Ambrosius was
the last of the Romans, so for him an Arthur who wore the imperial purple

would have been an interesting anomaly.

There is no doubt that the successes of Ambrosius' leadership brought a fresh impetus of Roman ideas, even if on a very superficial level. And the area generally supposed to be Arthur's main sphere of activity, that is Cornwall, Devon, Somerset and the Welsh Marches, fitted neatly within the boundaries of *Britannia Secunda*. Its capital, *Isca Silurum*, was the Caerleon on Usk where Arthur so often held court. His use of this particular town seems to suggest that he was an acknowledged successor to the Roman administrative system. The provincial structures of the Empire would not have fallen into total disuse immediately at the end of the 5th century.

It is also apparent that Arthur used cavalry against the Saxons' foot soldiers. Only the deployment of mounted troops could explain the speed with which his battles became victories, and the geographical range over which he fought. The legendary Round Table knights of the Middle Ages presumably developed from ordinary horsemen who then acquired the more sophisticated traits of Christian chivalry. But it had been the Roman administration which promoted the creation of cavalry units, not only to maintain peace within the Empire, but also to ensure swift action wherever needed along the frontiers. It is quite possible, if not probable, that Arthur led a cavalry brigade of the Roman type.

Finally there is Arthur's name. Most modern scholars agree that it comes from the Latin *Artorius*[9] and base this derivation on the existence of a *gens artoria* in Rome, and of a man named Lucius Artorius Catus who went to Brittany with the 6th legion in the middle of the 2nd century AD, and was supposed to have come from Dalmatia.[10] It is all too easy to suppose that Arthur must have belonged to some British branch of the *gens artoria*.

But this is a very simplistic way of looking at things. Latin is still regarded in the West as a kind of universal and almost magical means of explaining the existence of words. Once we trace something back to Latin roots we tend to stop there, and not to expose ourselves to any risk of contradiction by examining meanings as well as derivations. Even if we agree, for the sake of convenience, that the name Arthur is Latin in origin, the basic problem still remains.

We know that it was still customary to give children Roman names, even in Arthur's day, but it seems strange that Arthur should have retained only his family name and lost his first name and surname. Gildas refers to a character who may well be Arthur simply by his nickname *Ursus*, the bear. But we know from the names of other men which contain these roots that the Celtic words for bear were *Artu* or *Matu*. So perhaps Arthur's name has nothing to do with the *gens artoria* and is merely a Celtic cognomen.

Certainly if Arthur had come from Artorius we would expect to find the Latin form of the name used in Latin texts like the *Annales Cambriae* or the *Historia Brittonum*. And yet in both works the name appears as Arthur in the nominative case.[11] In Nennius' work the name is not even declined as all the other names are, suggesting that the author regarded it as British and therefore left it as it was. Obviously Nennius' treatment of the name sheds considerable doubt on its Latin origin.

If we return, however, to the mythological background against which his legend developed, we find equally satisfying and perhaps more penetrating explanations as to the derivation of the name. This does not mean that Arthur is only a myth. The late 19th century view of him as an ancient god whose worship the Britons resumed along with other Celtic traditions in the Dark Ages is scarcely borne out by the fact that no traces of such a god appear in pre-Arthurian Celtic mythology. The fact that many of the old pagan gods re-appeared to join him as his legend took shape does not necessarily prevent him from having been a real person. We may not be able to prove that Arthur existed, but it seems more than likely that he did. The Arthurian saga, with all its Celtic detail, was built around a historical figure who represented the spirit of patriotism and Celtic renewal prevailing in his age. So we should start by examining that historical figure.

From Nennius we hear only of those battles in which Arthur was victorious. He does not mention the final battle at Camlaan where Arthur died and which, according to the *Annales Cambriae*, was followed by a period of violent up-heaval in Britain and Ireland. Camlaan, variously dated as 537 or 541 in the *Annales Cambriae* and the Irish *Annals of Tigernach* respectively, put an end to the time of peace. After it the Saxons advanced even further to the West, forcing the Britons to fall back towards Wales, the Devon–Cornwall peninsula and the North West (from Cumberland to Dumbarton), or to emigrate altogether to Brittany.

The *Annales Cambriae* also bring Medrawt into the story. This is the earliest mention of any of the other characters who appear in the Arthurian legend, although there is nothing to specify who Medrawt was. The later romances give him the Cornish name Modret or Mordret and make him Arthur's nephew and incestuous son who seizes power while his uncle is engaged in a war on the conti-nent. But this is a much later development of the character. To discover some-thing of the original Medrawt we are forced to turn to other, less reliable docu-ments.

The *Triads* offer a few scraps of information. Here, however, Medrawt is merely a rival to Arthur and not related to him in any way. In what appears to be one of the older *Triads*, we read of three heavy raids in Britain: "The first took place when Medrawt went to Arthur's court at Kellewic in Kernyw (Cornwall): he left neither food nor drink in the court; but devoured everything; he dragged Gwenhwyfar from her throne and struck her. The second was when Arthur went to Medrawt's court: he left neither food nor drink in the court, nor in the *can-trev*."[12] A variant on this triad in the *Myvyrian Archaeology of Wales* adds that Medrawt had criminal relations with Gwenhwyfar, as the sculpture on Modena Cathedral and Chrétien's *Chevalier à la Charrette* tend to suggest.

This adds little to our knowledge of Medrawt, except that he proves a dangerous rival to Arthur, both on the political and the emotional planes, and that his court is raided by Arthur in reprisal. We can, however, identify another character in the Arthurian legend. For Gwenhwyfar is the Welsh version of the name Guinevere, and although the triad does not specifically describe her as Arthur's wife, it suggests that she probably was. It also seems likely that Medrawt's initial raid on Kelliwic was made during Arthur's absence with the intention of ransacking the place for any treasures it might contain. This would imply that Arthur was known to have lived in the South West, and more specifi-cally in Cornwall.

Another triad, which appears equally old, adds further details of the quarrel between Arthur and Medrawt. Among the three dishonourable men of Britain it lists Vortigern, for the reasons we have already discussed, and Medrawt:"when Arthur left him the government of the island of Britain to go over the sea to meet Lles, emperor of Rome." This refers to Arthur's supposed expedition against the Romans on the continent to back his refusal to pay the tribute they were demanding. "But he lost the most valiant of his warriors. When he learnt that

Arthur's army had been decimated, Medrawt turned against him. He formed an alliance with the Saxons, the Picts and the Scots to stop Arthur coming ashore. Arthur and his surviving troops returned and managed to land in Britain despite Medrawt, but was mortally wounded. After his death he was buried in the island of Avallach.''[13]

This triad is rather curious and has obviously suffered from the influence of Geoffrey of Monmouth. But it is still possible to read between the lines. The idea that the Britons owed the Romans something dates back to the time of Julius Caesar who had imposed a tribute which was never paid. But Arthur's expedition to the continent is more difficult to explain. Geoffrey of Monmouth clearly embroidered on the theme, in order that Arthur, and by inference the Anglo-Norman dynasty, should be seen trying to rebuild the Western Roman Empire by acquiring land on the continent. But this interpretation is at odds with the spirit of the *Triads*. More likely is the reading that Arthur went to help the Roman emperor as Ambrosius Aurelianus had gone to the assistance of Anthemius in 470. Even in Arthur's time the Britons regarded themselves as heirs of the Empire, and there is no reason why Arthur should not have gone to help the few groups of Gallo-Romans who were still resisting the dominance of the Franks. This is only a hypothesis, but a plausible one, nevertheless.

Whatever the reason for the expedition, this triad also makes no mention of any family connexion between Arthur and Medrawt. If anything the sense of rivalry between them is greater. It is tempting to assume that the two men formed a kind of duumvirate, in which both enjoyed equal authority and needed only to kill the other to be sure of total political, and perhaps more importantly, military control of Britain. As Arthur's co-ruler Medrawt would naturally take over full responsibility in his absence. But the fact that he did so in his own name alone constituted a breach of conduct which necessitated Arthur's return and led to the battle which killed them both.

Interestingly the triad says that Arthur was buried in the isle of Avallach (Avalon) rather than that he was taken, still living, to some mysterious island. Whether the Avallach referred to is Glastonbury remains as much open to conjecture as the identity of the two bodies found in Glastonbury in 1190. But the use of the name Avallach rather than Avalon does support Ferdinand Lot's theory that the island was called after the man who settled there.

Apart from his conflict with Medrawt and his battles against the Saxons, Arthur's life appears to have been taken up with quarrels with rival leaders and the kinds of raiding party common to all the chiefs of his time. Medrawt's looting of the court at Kelliwic, with Arthur's sacking of Medrawt's court, was probably one episode among many similar disturbances in Arthur's life. The various lives of the saints, vague and questionable as they sometimes are, confirm this impression.

Caradoc of Llancarfan wrote his *Vita Gildae* in the early 12th century, before Geoffrey on Monmouth had stressed the legality of Arthur's leadership in the *Historia Regum Britanniae*. And the Arthur of the *Vita Gildae* is a *rex rebellus*, a rebel king intent on asserting his supremacy over Britain illegally. For some unspecified reason[14] Arthur waged a merciless war against Hueil, son of Kaw of Prydyn (Scotland) and brother of Gildas. They did battle in the Lowlands of Scotland and on the shores of the Irish Sea (a geographical description which would fit either the battle of Tribuit in the region of Dumbarton, or the fight in the forest of Celidon near the source of the Clyde). Arthur won and put Hueil to death, an action uncharacteristic of the noble, benevolent and just king of a civilized society which he later became. At this point Gildas entered the story as an indignant member of Kaw's family. He returned from Ireland to protest vigorously against his brother's murder and to demand retribution. Arthur was then obliged to compensate Hueil's family according to Celtic law. For the Celts had no system of public prosecution and any grievances had to be redressed in a private arrangement between the criminal and the victim or his family. But law and custom did dictate the amount of compensation to be paid, which might be considerable if the victim was an important person.

It is somewhat surprising that Caradoc should have chosen to portray Arthur as a power-hungry and murderous schemer at a time when the Arthur of oral tradition had acquired all the hallmarks of a great and noble king. Admittedly Caradoc's image is closer to the historical figure who lived in a time of bitter factional rivalry where there was little room for the courtesies of noble society. Hueil, like Medrawt, appears to have been a rival for the leadership, whom Arthur had to curb to maintain his own authority. That Arthur is described as a rebel king suggests that he had no legal claim to the throne, which would weaken still further the argument that he belonged to a noble family of the Roman Empire.

The Life of Saint Cadoc, which was written by Lifris in about the year 1100, shows Arthur trying to wangle a herd of cattle out of the monks at the abbey of Llancarfan. Cadoc had allowed a man called Ligessauc, "a very brave chief of the Britons," to live in the monastery for seven years. Ligessauc had apparently killed three of Arthur's warriors and was being hotly pursued by the vengeful king. When Arthur learnt that his enemy had been given asylum he made a public request for justice from Cadoc and the monks. The two sides met somewhere along the river Usk. Cadoc and his monks refused to surrender Ligessauc but offered Arthur compensation instead. He then asked for a herd of cattle, but demanded that they should be half red and half white. By some miracle the monks were able to find the cattle and drove them into the ford. Arthur's warriors left their side of the bank to collect them, but when they reached them the cattle turned into clumps of fern. Furious as he was, Arthur had no choice but to recognize Ligessauc's right to asylum.

Arthur emerges from this story as a man with a lively interest in livestock. We would expect this of a Celtic king, since personal wealth and compensatory payments were usually measured in terms of cattle in Celtic countries. The Irish epic tradition is full of accounts of raids on the cattle of Cualnge, Regamma and Fraech. The Irish kings and queens made their cattle-rustling activities into full scale war against their neighbours, not unlike the heroes of American Westerns. The miraculous (for which read magical) way in which the monks change the cattle into fern is reminiscent of the trick Gwyddyon plays on Pryderi in the fourth branch of the *Mabinogion*. There Gwyddyon turns plants into horses and dogs which keep their magical form until he can exchange them for Pryderi's herd of swine and drive the swine safely out of Pryderi's reach.[15]

There is further evidence in the *Triads* of Arthur's liking for rustling. One of the three great swineherds of Britain is named as "Tristan, son of Tallwch, who looked after the pigs of March, son of Meirchyon while the swineherd took a message to Essylt. Arthur, Marchell, Kai and Bedwyr all tried, but could not take a single sow from him by trickery, violence or theft."[16] From this triad we can see that the legend of Tristan and Iseult was incorporated into the Arthurian cycle at a relatively early stage, although it was originally totally separate. And two more Arthurian characters have appeared, in the shape of Kai and Bedwyr,

Arthur's earliest and subsequently most ubiquitous followers.

In the early years of the 12th century Lifris also wrote a *Life of Saint Carannog* which has Arthur living at Dindraethou (Dunster) in Somerset. Here he has become a kind of junior partner to Cato or Cadwy, and obviously enjoys none of the absolute power the French romances gave him. According to Lifris, Saint Carannog was living in the same area, and, like most of his fellow saints, he owned a miraculous object, in this case an altar which could float on the waters of the Bristol Channel. One day the altar came ashore near Arthur who decided to keep it for himself. He tried to use it as a table but every time anybody put anything on it, the altar shook it off. Meanwhile Carannog had learnt that Arthur had taken his altar and came to ask for the holy object back. Arthur agreed on condition that in return the saint would help him kill a huge snake which was devastating the region of Carrum (Carhampton). Carannog's prayers reduced the snake to submission and a grateful Arthur returned the altar and made Carannog master of Carrum, provided he stayed in the area.

There is a very similar Breton story about Saint Efflam, whom Arthur also asks to help him against a snake. In this case, however, Arthur is not trying to exchange the saint's help for anything, and generally appears in a much more favourable light. Both stories are symbolic of Christian conversion. The snake is paganism; and as a military leader Arthur is unable to overcome it and effect a conversion by himself, but has to ask a holy man to help him. Snakes made frequent appearances in the lives of the saints and in the Celtic tradition altogether.

Arthur's willingness to turn any situation to his own advantage is also illustrated in the *Life of Saint Padarn*, written at about the same time as the *Life of Carannog*. Saint Padarn had received a precious relic from the patriarch of Jerusalem in the form of a magnificent tunic. One day a certain tyrant (*quidam tyrannus*) named Arthur came prowling around Padarn's retreat and made as if to take the tunic. But no sooner had he laid hands on the sacred object than the ground opened beneath his feet. When he called for help, Padarn found him up to his chin in the earth and said that he would only pray for his release if Arthur solemnly begged forgiveness. Arthur was forced to comply and was then freed.

From what we can see, Arthur was no plaster saint as far as the monastic tradition was concerned — far from it. He appears variously as a wicked tyrant, an opportunist, a looter of a man totally lacking in scruples. All the writers of saints' lives have something uncomplimentary to say about him: a fact which together with Gildas' and Bede's silence, suggests that Arthur had some quarrel with the clergy of his time.

It has been suggested that these particular legends are interpretations of actual events. Arthur obviously needed money to equip his cavalry for war against the Saxons and rival Britons and would presumably have taken it wherever he could find it. He may not have fleeced the monks in quite the manner described by Lifris and the other hagiographers, but he probably asked the wealthy monasteries for considerable contributions in the form of livestock or valuable objects. Historically, the throne often raised funds in this way, and was as frequently rewarded with ecclesiastical fury in the shape of excommunication or interdicts.

In the *Mirabilia* which were added to Nennius' *Historia Brittonum*, there is a reference to a curious funeral mound known as the Licat Anir because the man buried there was called Anir or Amr. Anir was supposed to have been Arthur's son whom Arthur himself killed and buried there. Unfortunately there is no other evidence to support this. The Welsh literary tradition gives Arthur a son called Llacheu who was supposed to have been accidentally killed by Kai; and some of the French romances make Medrawt Arthur's son. But that is the only mention anywhere of Arthur's falling out with one of his children and killing him. Obviously this short passage in the *Mirabilia* was based on something, but there is no knowing what. We can only assume that Arthur's reputation as a violent brute extended to include a total lack of family feeling or fatherly love.

Arthur's expeditions do not always meet with success. On one occasion, according to one of the poems in the book of Taliesin, Arthur set out with a vast number of warriors and returned with only seven.[17] One of the *Triads* lists three famous prisoners, including Mabon, son of Modron, whom Arthur rescues in *Kulwch and Olwen*, and adds "There was one more eminent than these three, who was three nights in prison at Kaer Oeth and Anoeth,[18] three nights in the prison of Gwen Pendragon and three nights in a magic prison under the stone of Echymeint: this was Arthur. In every case he was set free by the same man, Goreu, son of Kustennin his second cousin."[19]

The medieval image of Arthur as the good-natured cuckold, unsuspecting in his fidelity to Guinevere, is scarcely borne out by the earliest texts. In fact he appears to have been more of a Casanova, as ready to follow up any chances of sexual adventures as he was to rustle cattle or go looting. Folklore had it that his quarrel with Hueil sprang from rivalry over a woman, and that when Hueil wounded him in the leg Arthur disguised himself as a woman so that he could dance with his new conquest.

Of all the medieval authors only the anonymous writer of the *Lancelot in Prose* and, later, Thomas Malory allude to a false Guinevere who succeeded in seducing Arthur with very little effort. Obviously this story contains traces of an earlier reputation to which the historical Arthur was more than entitled. The *Life of Saint Cadoc* shows Arthur quite prepared to abuse poor Gladwys, Cadoc's mother, who was fleeing her father to marry the man she loved. In the event, he was stopped by a timely reminder of his duty from Kai and Bedwyr.

The *Triads* also contain references to Arthur's interest in the fair sex. According to *Triad 21*, Arthur had three wives all called Gwenhwyfar, though it is not clear whether he married them one after the other or polygamously. *Triad 22* lists three of Arthur's mistresses as Indec, Garwen and Gwyl.[20] Celtic custom permitted both married and single men to keep concubines in their own homes under a form of contract which was annually renewable on mutual agreement.

Two other triads give us some idea of where the more important of Arthur's various headquarters may have been. The fact that he in all probability came from Cornwall does not mean that his activities were confined to those areas adjacent to the Bristol Channel. *Triad 71*, from manuscript *Hengwrt 536* tells of "the three tribal seats of Britain: at Mynyw [St David's] Arthur is chief of kings, Dewi [David] chief of bishops, Maelgwn chief of ancients:[21] at Kelliwic in Kernyw [Egloshayle, near Padstow] Arthur is chief of kings, Bedwini chief of bishops,[22] Karadawc Vreichfras chief of ancients;[23] at Penryn Rionnyd [Glasgow] in the North, Arthur is chief of kings, Kendeyrn Garthwys chief of bishops, Gwrthwmwl Wledig chief of ancients."[25] and this triad is corroborated by another which states that the three main courts of Arthur were "Kaerllion on Wysg [Caerleon on Usk] in Kymry, Kelliwig in Kernwy and Penryn Rhionedd in the North".[26]

These two triads are valuable evidence; first because they confirm that Arthur's authority extended over the three most Celtic areas in Britain, the North, Wales and the Devon–Cornwall–Somerset area, and secondly because

Arthur is called "the chief of kings." This means that he was not himself a king, but in some sense higher than the kings, like a real *imperator*. Some scholars have suggested that he was given the title *Comes Britanniarum*, which was awarded to those responsible for British security under the Empire, and which would match the description chief of kings. As military leader of a coalition formed by the more important regional British chiefs, Arthur seems to be a *comes* of northern, central and southwestern Britain. He acts as leader to a confederation of tribes who are prepared to recognize his authority under specific circumstances and especially in the face of external agression from the Saxons, Picts or Irish. By the same token he acquires the right to intervene in any domestic quarrels among the Britons in order to maintain internal stability. Policing duties of this kind would certainly explain some of the battles which Nennius makes him fight.

It is possible that Arthur actually went on an expedition to Brittany. A passage in *Kulhwch and Olwen* says that he went to Llydaw (Armorica) to fetch two marvellous dogs. Any visit to Brittany would have been perfectly compatible with the strong links which have always existed between the Britons and the Bretons, and in Arthur's time these links were probably even stronger because of the large numbers of Britons who had settled or were settling in the Breton peninsula. However, Breton popular traditions concerning Arthur are few, and those Arthurian place names to be found in Brittany undoubtedly followed the much later development of the Round Table romances on the continent. Even so, the fact that the Lancelot legend, which is purely Breton in origin, slipped so easily into the Arthurian cycle seems to prove that Arthur had concrete connexions with Brittany.[28]

He almost certainly went to Ireland, if only to carry out reprisals on the Gaels for their raids on Britain. There is a specific reference to this, again in *Kulhwch and Olwen*, and also in more mythological form in the *Book of Taliesin*. Here Arthur, accompanied by his usual followers, crossed the sea in his boat Prytwen (also the name of his shield), landed in Ireland and seized the marvellous cauldron of Diwrnach the Gael.[29] He probably also acquired the sword Kaledfoulch (known as Escalibur in the French romances) on the same expedition. Arthur's band of warriors was chiefly drawn from the men of the South West, Cornwall and South Wales, and must therefore have included some Gaels, for they had established permanent settlements in these areas, notably in Dyfed. The detailed list of Arthur's courtiers in *Kulhwch and Olwen*, the oldest of the Arthurian tales, mentions several characters with the nickname *Gwyddel* (Gael); although this did not necessarily mean that the man concerned came from Ireland. He might also have earned the name by distinguished conduct in battle against the Gaels. More surprisingly, the list also includes several celebrities from the Irish tradition, such as Kynchwr, son of Ness, better known as Conchobar mac Nessa, king of Ulster, and Kubert, son of Daere, or Curoi mac Daire, not to mention Manawydan, son of Llyr, who had long been assimilated into the Welsh tradition from the Irish Mananann mac Lir.

Such details all contribute to the image of Arthur as a pan-Celtic hero, and corroborate Nennius' accounts of Arthur's battles as having taken place in widely separated parts of Britain. Local place names support this image. The name Arthur occurs in all kinds of places, but only in Scotland, Cumberland, Westmorland, the Welsh Marches, Wales itself, Somerset, Devon and Cornwall, that is in those regions which remained dominantly Celtic for some time.

Near Perth there are an Arthur's Hollow and an Arthur's Rock, near

Edinburgh an Arthur's Seat and near Dumbarton in the ancient British kingdom of Strathclyde a mountain called Ben Arthur. In a cave not far from Melrose Abbey Arthur is alleged to be sleeping an enchanted sleep. There are other caves of the same kind on the slopes of Snowdon and near Caerleon, though there the knights are sleeping until Arthur comes to wake them. Arthur's treasure is hidden near Marchlyn Mawr in Caernarvon and will dazzle anyone who happens across it. At Lake Llyn Barfog in Merioneth the visitor can still see the place where Arthur killed a monster and his horse left a hoof print on the rock. Flintshire has an Arthur's Hill, Glamorgan an Arthur's Stone, Brecon an Arthur's Chair. Between Brecon and the county of Carmarthen there is an Arthur's Bed in the mountain of Amanw. Cadbury Castle in Somerset is alleged to be Camelot, one of Arthur's homes. Glastonbury needs no further comment: Arthurian traditions haunt the place. Cornwall has an Arthur's Oven between Exeter and Bodmin which was shown to the monks of Laon at the beginning of the 12th century, and an Arthur's Kitchen, Arthur's Hall near Bodmin and Arthur's Fort at Egloshayle near Padstow (the legendary Kelliwic). Across the Channel, Brittany boasts several Arthur's Tombs and Arthur's Camps, but these names probably came over with British immigrants or, as we have said, were influenced by the French romances.

This list of names is only a small selection of the Arthurian sites in Britain, whose huge number suggests that Arthur's reputation was extensive, since it spread through the popular as well as the literary tradition. It is also clear from the passage in Aneurin's *Gododdin* already quoted that his fame spread rapidly, since his valour was to be taken as a standard by which to judge other warriors. At the turn of the 7th century, a fashion for calling children Arthur suddenly developed, when the name had hardly been used at all before then, if ever. Aedan mac Gabrain, king of Dalriada, the area colonized by the Irish Gaels on the north-west coast of Scotland gave the name Arthur to one of his sons in around 570. If a Gael used the name the prestige attached to it must have been enormous, even fifty years or so after the date on which Arthur probably disappeared.

For despite the paucity of available information about him and the legendary aura which befogs his image, the actual existence of a character named Arthur now seems almost certain. There may be no real proof, but there are too many relevant facts, too many coincidences and too many traces of a historical Arthur for us to relegate him to the realm of man-made myth.

So, as Geoffrey Ashe has done in his book *From Caesar to Arthur*, we can make informed guesses as to the main course of Arthur's career. It is obviously impossible to verify everything from historical evidence, but the documents we do have, whether they be annals, lives of saints or so-called histories, do offer points of reference and sources for interpretation and comment. Even the unmistakably legendary material has a considerable basis in reality. We should then be able to see how greatly the historical Arthur must have differed from the stereotypic image of the Arthurian romances.

Arthur was born in about 475, in South West Britain, probably in Cornwall.[30] His parents were not particularly high-born, but they were influenced to some extent by Roman attitudes and spoke both Latin and British, as did all those who had accepted the authority of Ambrosius Aurelianus. These families formed a sort of provincial petty aristocracy which replaced the imperial administration in its economic control of the country.

At the age of twenty Arthur left home to form a group of horsemen with the alleged intent of keeping law and order in Cornwall and Devon which were then plagued by brigands and refugees from the areas conquered by the Saxons. But Arthur's men were little better and established control over the area by their superior skills at raiding and foraging. As leader of this wandering band of adventurers Arthur acquired a reputation as a great warrior and attracted any number of fighting men and layabouts who were prepared to do anything for a share of the spoils. From these men Arthur drew a corps of loyal followers, with Kai and Bedwyr as his lieutenants. Kai, too, was clearly a Romanized Briton.

Arthur's fame soon spread outside Dumnonia and Somerset to Wales at about the time when ageing Emrys Gwledig was looking for a man to succeed him as commander in chief of the British armies. It was probably Emrys who brought Arthur to Caerleon on Usk, the capital of Britannia Secunda and to some extent the political capital of Celtic Britain. But a number of tribal chiefs were jealous of Arthur and wanted to get rid of him. Arthur, meanwhile, was improving his military technique. He probably arranged for the stronger and faster horses of the continent to be imported from Brittany so that he could form units of trouble-shooters which could travel to wherever they were needed. Travellers from the East had told him about Byzantine cavalry warfare and Arthur hoped to follow their example and build an Empire like theirs in the West. Scheming among the Romanized establishment brought him some allies. Indeed they had little choice, for an organized force led by an active and intelligent leader was infinitely preferable to a weak and fragmentary army when it came to resisting the Saxons. Some British chiefs even used Arthur's men as a kind of police force to sort out their own quarrels or to strengthen their position against the anticipated westward thrust of the invaders.

When Ambrosius Aurelianus died or retired, supposedly to found the monastery at Amesbury, Arthur seemed the man most likely to keep the British people together. He also declared himself defender of the Christian faith and was therefore in a position to ask for help from the expanding monastic communities which were rich in livestock and treasures. He arranged for new fortifications to be built around the old pre-Roman towns since they formed ideal strongholds from which to defend the surrounding countryside or mount offensive expeditions. Forges were then set up in the various forts for the manufacture of large quantities of weapons. The iron mines in British-held territories were systematically worked and forests cut down to provide fuel for the foundries. The Roman roads offered a ready-made means of transporting all these raw materials.

Arthur's forces began to look increasingly like a personal army, composed of regular, even professional rather than part-time soldiers. They were crack troops, experienced cavalrymen who were each bound to Arthur by a separate oath of allegiance. Although Arthur realized that political separatism made the British weak against the united Saxons, he nevertheless retained his own freedom of action, careful not to support one king rather than another, and tried to lead a confederation of tribes each led by their own *tiern*. For Arthur did not want to replace the tribal chiefs, merely to unite them for the common cause. He was the *dux bellorum* or *comes Britanniarum* officially, and nothing more. He may have had grandiose plans for Britain, but he distrusted his fellow countrymen who, like all Celtic peoples, were hostile to the idea of a central authority.

Arthur probably engaged in his first important campaign about the beginning of the 6th century. The Angles and Saxons had advanced westward in two groups along the Wash and the Humber. They hoped to meet on the West coast and effectively divide the Britons into two separate camps. Arthur foresaw the danger. He established a base at Lincoln, and moved his troops along the Roman roads to engage both wings of the Saxon army at once. Having successfully forestalled the Saxon plan and achieved relative peace in that area, he was then able to turn his attention to the South East where the enemy were beginning to move slowly westward. After several victories, he used a pause in the Saxon offensive in about 510 to lead an expedition against a Northern Briton, probably Hueil. Whatever the reasons for this war, Arthur probably saw it as a means of eliminating a dangerous rival. He was able to use his victory in the forest of Kelyddon (Celidon) to pacify the North and unite the wild frontier tribes with the rest of Celtic Britain.

It was probably at this time that Arthur assumed the characteristics of a "king," a man capable of maintaining his personal authority against the disloyal and the envious. But those chiefs and monasteries who had sided with the rebels must have suffered at his hands and they were not quick to forget. For the moment however, Hueil's death left Arthur free to resume his fight against the Saxons. When they went on the offensive again he defeated them at the battle of Guinnion (Binchester) where his role as defender of the faith was clearly marked by his use of the Virgin Mary as an emblem. It was then that fresh disturbance broke out among the Britons and Arthur was forced to fight the rebels at Chester. Suggestions that this battle was fought against the Saxons must be ruled out by the fact that Chester lay well behind the British lines. The position of Tribuit near Dumbarton suggests that Arthur's battle there may also have been against British dissidents who on this occasion had formed an alliance with the neighbouring Picts and Irish. This battle must have remained famous in the northern poetical tradition since the *Black Book of Carmarthen* contains a poem which describes it in some detail and stresses the warlike valour of Bedwyr and Kai. The battle of Mount Agned, on the other hand, was probably fought to halt a Saxon incursion towards the West.

The Saxons received a continual supply of reinforcements from the continent, and in 517 they decided to launch an all-out assault. The warriors of Kent and Sussex joined those who had settled on the banks of the Thames and together they marched westward. Arthur led the main body of his army out to meet them and won a resounding victory at Mount Badon which must have been in South West England somewhere. The whole future of Britain hung in the balance at Mount Badon. If the Saxons had succeeded in breaching the British defences they would have reached the Bristol Channel and occupied Somerset and South Wales. Independent Britain would have vanished. Whether the Britons at Mount Badon were led by Arthur or not, all historians concur that the period of truce which followed their victory there had a profound effect on the subsequent history of Great Britain. A Saxon victory would have meant that the whole island fell into Teutonic hands. As it was, the Celtic tradition remained vital and viable for long enough to influence the later development of Anglo-Saxon civilization in a lasting way.

Mount Badon also represents the zenith of Arthur's career. For twenty years after it, the war with the Saxons came to a virtual standstill. What danger they still presented seemed less imminent. The Saxon losses must have been very heavy for the invaders retreated to their base, the kingdom of Lloegr, which lay within South East England and the area immediately North of the Thames.

It was probably at this point that Arthur abandoned his role as war leader to follow a new path as a political figure. He was careful not to disband his own warrior elite, but used them to maintain law and order wherever necessary. His rivalry with Medrawt, which in all likelihood dates from this period, may well have been partly a power struggle for control of the wealth which Arthur's new position brought him. Where Medrawt came from there is no way of knowing, though we can safely assume that his quarrel with Arthur was not entirely on the level that the stories of raids and counter-raids would suggest. We should not, however, totally discount the idea that there was some emotional problem at the root of it. According to the *Vita Gildae* a minor king named Maelwas, who was one of Arthur's vassals, fell in love with Arthur's wife during a visit to his home, took her and shut her up on Glastonbury Tor. It was then that Arthur summoned his troops from Cornwall and Devon to besiege Glastonbury Tor, where Gildas brought about a reconciliation between the two sides. This story carries a ring of truth and presumably gave rise to all the legends about Gwenhwyfar's abduction by a god from the Other World.

But Medrawt was not killed like Hueil, nor banished like Maelwas. He remained just as much of a threat, and the quarrel between himself and Arthur appears to have reached a kind of stalemate until Arthur went to the continent to support the last defenders of the Empire against the Franks. Then Medrawt, whose reputation, if not his actual authority, must have been almost equal to Arthur's, openly rebelled and formed an alliance with the Picts, the Irish and the Saxons. He, too, probably had a kind of warrior militia at his service and sought to usurp Arthur's position as *dux bellorum* and political leader within British-held territory.

Then came the final confrontation. Medrawt tried to stop Arthur returning to Britain, but failed. A terrible battle was fought at Camlaan. Arthur and Medrawt were both killed. With the deaths of the only two men capable of keeping Britain free, British independence ended. The many minor, local chiefs who remained had grown accustomed to Arthur's leadership and were unable to rebuild the extraordinarily united front he had created. Once the formidable warriors who had defeated them were gone, the Saxons made use of civil conflict and lack of cohesion among the Britons to infiltrate the whole island. Britain was reduced to three pockets of Celtic civilization in Wales, Cornwall and the North.

The final curtain had descended. But Arthur had disappeared in a blaze of glory and his memory lived on. Nostalgia for his dream survived the rude awakening of Saxon conquest. And this nostalgia, which was greater than we shall ever know, gave future generations the image of an exceptional king. Arthur became the embodiment of all the conscious and subconscious desires of the Britons, their longing for revenge, their love of liberty. He came to personify the whole Celtic heritage which had lived on through the Roman Empire and the introduction of Christianity. Traditions cling to the memory and come back to life when they are needed. From the grave of a dead hero they flowed out across the whole world.

CHAPTER FIVE

The Arthurian Myth

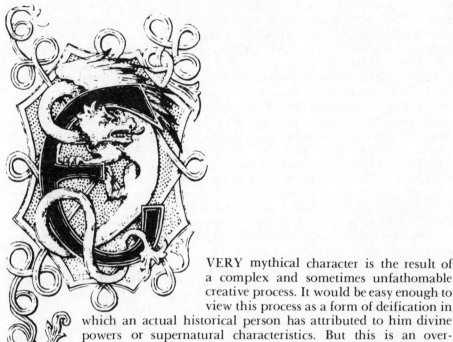

VERY mythical character is the result of a complex and sometimes unfathomable creative process. It would be easy enough to view this process as a form of deification in which an actual historical person has attributed to him divine powers or supernatural characteristics. But this is an over-simplified view of the problem and tends to underestimate the real value of myth which is to create something entirely new by taking on human form in a specific historical context. The prevailing attitudes in which-ever civilization is concerned are obviously all important. The Romans made their myth into history by bringing divine figures down to a human level. Horatius Cocles, the one-eyed hero, and Mucius Scaevola, the one-armed hero, are representations of the Indo-European gods known in Teutonic mythology as Odin and Tyr respectively. Romulus only became a god as the result of a deliberate intellectual decision to give the foundation of Rome divine sanction. The Celts and Indians, on the other hand, made their history into myth, not only by deifying their historical characters but by actually bringing myth to life within a comprehensible and meaningful historical reality.

Any examination of King Arthur as a myth must take these two different and fundamental processes into account. First there was a historical Arthur who was not a king, but the leader of a fighting force and *dux bellorum*. This Arthur soon became King Arthur and, as he did so, acquired all the trappings of many of the ancient Celtic gods whose memory had lived on through the introduction of Christianity. But the real, live Arthur, the 6th century warrior, was also an embodiment of all the hopes of his fellow countrymen. The Britons longed for a hero to deliver them from their enemies and to form the ideal kingdom to which they had aspired for centuries. The Celts had never been able to achieve this perfect world because it was not within their intellectual approach to life to do so, but the myth of a world king was common to many of them. The Gauls developed the legend of Ambigatus so fully that Livy included it in his tales of Roman history alongside other Gallic legends. Livy's Ambigatus is king of the Bituriges and apparently one of the greatest leaders in Gallic history. "During the reign of Tarquinius the Elder, the Bituriges had the greatest power of all the Celtic peoples who made up one third of Gaul. It was they who gave a king to Celtica.[1] This man, Ambigatus, excelled all others in merit, in personal fortune and in public wealth, for during his reign the harvests were so plentiful and there were so many men in Gaul that it seemed scarcely possible to govern them all" (Livy, v, 34).

The question of whether Ambigatus really existed need not concern us here. But the description of the king and his halcyon reign are wholly legendary in tone and Ambigatus himself is primarily a symbolic figure. His name is a nickname meaning "he who fights on two sides," like the Irish name Imchadh. Many of the Celtic heroes had qualificatory names of this kind. Vercingetorix, "the Great Leader of 100 battles" or "the Great King of Warriors" is an example that springs to mind. Ambigatus' subjects were the Bituriges, or "the kings of the world," so he was presumably the embodiment of the myth of a world king. The Irish later realized the same myth in the kings of Tara who were believed to govern an ideal kingdom and to bring it order and prosperity through their exceptional merits and their ability to gather the best warriors around them. So it seems more than likely that the Celts had always dreamt of establishing a single kingdom without ever accepting the conditions such a form of government would impose.

Various attempts to unite the Celtic peoples were made in Britain. When the Romans were occupying the island, Caratacus, king of the Silures, organized British resistance and persuaded other tribes to follow him, including the Ordovices from Gwynedd. But apart from the tribal confederation, his army also included dissidents of all kinds, and after some success against the Romans his final defeat in battle dealt a death blow to the coalition. Caratacus took refuge among the Brigantes, hoping that their queen, Cartismandua, would supply him with fresh troops. But she betrayed him to the Romans and he was sent to Rome as a prisoner. There he had the overwhelming audacity to ask for a hearing before the senate; and the emperor Claudius, moved by his courage and intelligence, finally set him and his family free.[2] In the Welsh tradition Caratacus became Caradawc ab Cynfelyn (Cunobelinos) and took on all the characteristics of a mythical hero, a world king. One of the *Triads* makes him one of the three courageous kings of Britain together with his father, Cynfelyn Wledig and Arthur: "They defeated all their enemies, and could not be overcome except by treachery."[3] There is an obvious link here between Caratacus, who is betrayed by Cartismandua, and Arthur who is betrayed by Medrawt. Although this particular Triad confuses him with another Caradawc, the son of Bran, the historical Caratacus who personified the myth of supreme kingship during his lifetime has obviously become one of the glorious leaders of the Celts in legend. Arthur achieved the same status after moving from Cornwall to Gwent, which Caradawc founded, to take power at Caerleon on Usk.

The Political Aspect

The Arthurian myth is largely political. In this respect it is closely related to the strange institution of supreme kingship in Ireland. There, at Tara, the symbolic centre of the island, the kingdom of Midhe (the middle) was fabricated to fit this notion of royalty, although its actual existence remains unconfirmed. Irish historians call this particular division the *Coiced*, literally "the Fifth Part," although only the four divisions of Ulster (Ulad), Connaught (Connacht), Leinster (Laigen) and Munster (Mumu) are really definable. The fifth was symbolic, an underlying mythical idea. The *Vedas* contain frequent references to the earth being divided into five parts. And Neodruidism, which first appeared in Wales in about the 14th century, laid much emphasis on there being five elements rather than the more traditional four. So, although Ireland was divided into four regions, logically speaking it required some central point, if only on a theoretical basis. In fact the choice of Tara was based on more than purely theoretical considerations. For Tara was a sacred mound, a prehistoric sanctuary of distinct spiritual importance. The Celtic ideal of supreme kingship was like Pascal's definition of "a circle having its centre everywhere and its circumference nowhere."

It is against this background that we should examine the Arthurian myth in the first instance. The historical Arthur was never a king, but merely a man above other men. Although he probably maintained his personal residence at the family seat of Kelliwic, his sphere of activities covered the whole of Britain, unlike the ordinary, local chieftains who were firmly attached to their own peoples. One of the *Triads* describes Arthur as "chief of kings" although not a king himself. The legend of Arthur as emperor and commander in chief of the Britons grew from such concepts of overall authority, and before long the emperor gave way to the king of kings, whose superior strength, generosity and skill made him supreme. In the tale of *Kulhwch and Olwen*, where Arthur is a pre-medieval monarch, he says to his companions, "We are noble men so long as others come to us, and the more gifts we distribute, the greater will be our reputation and fame and glory."[4] From this significant statement it clearly emerges that Arthur's greatness is directly dependent on others' need for him. Such a notion of kingship must date back to pre-imperial times, for the rigidity of Roman law would have made any fluctuating system of this kind impossible.

Implied in the Celtic concept of kingship is total devotion on the part of the king to his subjects. The Arthur whom the Britons remembered was the heroic defender of British independence and upholder of British rights. There are some strange ideas on this subject in the *Triads*. "Three main regions of Britain, Cymru [Wales], Lloegr [England not invaded by the Saxons], Alban [Scotland]. Each of them is entitled to the privilege of kingship, They are ruled by monarchic government and according to the law of the land as laid down in the constitution established by Prydein ab Aedd Mawr.[5] It is from the race of the Cymry [the original Britons] that comes the supreme monarchy based on the law of the land and of the nation, and conforming to the original rights and privileges. It was under the empire of this constitution that the entitlement to a king was established in each part of this island, and all royalty is subject to national law. Whence the saying, 'The country is stronger than the prince'."[6]

The extraordinary thing about this passage is that it might easily have come from John of Salisbury's *Policraticus*. The triad stresses the fact that the country, and therefore the inhabitants and their customs, are stronger than the prince. So the prince is not an autocrat, a despot or even a *tyrannus*, in the pejorative sense. His job is to maintain the ancestral traditions of the nation and the land (not necessarily one and the same). There are other comments on government in the *Triads*; and they are worth examining because, although later than some of the literature, they contain evidence of earlier attitudes and traditions not found elsewhere. The next triad says "Three mainstays of government in Britain: the law of the land, kingship and justice, according to the constitution of Prydein ab Aedd Mawr."[7] And yet another triad mentions the oppression which followed the "fury of the people and of the nation at the greed and injustice of kings. Dyfnwal Moelmud freed the country by establishing an equitable system of mutual obligation between society and society, prince and prince, country and country."[8]

In fact the prime duty of kings of the Celtic type was to maintain a balance within the miniature world formed by the kingdom. This kingdom might be no larger than a *tuath*, an Irish word meaning a large family, a large household rather than a tribe as it is usually translated. The frontiers of the *tuath* were not defined but extended as far as the king could see. Or, to put it less metaphorically, the size of the *tuath* depended on the personal merits of the leader of the community. For the *tuath* was a community formed by several *derbfhine*, or family groups. The *derbfhine* was the basic unit of Celtic society and consisted of four generations within one family, that is all the descendants of a single great-grandfather. The egalitarian structure of the *fhine*, in which all wealth was owned collectively by the community, dictated the pattern of all social systems in Britain and Ireland.

A certain number of *tuatha* were then grouped together to form a provincial kingdom, or *coiced*, which was ruled by a provincial king who owed allegiance to the *ard ri*, or high king at Tara. For a fuller understanding of the links in this social chain, it is necessary to examine the formation of early Indo-European societies. Our knowledge of these ancient institutions is based primarily on linguistic research and especially on Emile Beneveniste's valuable work *Le Vocabulaire des Institutions indo-européennes*.

The early Indo-European family was based on a narrow, if slightly surprising concept of kinship reflected in terms common to most neo-Indo-European languages. The oldest words are $*p^\circ ter$, $*mater$, $*bhrater$ and $*dhugh^\circ ter$, which correspond to the English father, mother, brother and daughter, or the Welsh *tad, modr, brawd* (plural *brodyr*) and *merch*. Logically we would expect the father-mother couple to be offset by a corresponding son-daughter couple. The appearance of the word $*bhrater$ in the quartet is due to the fact that the early words were used to denote relationships between individuals who were classified according to age and economic status, and not purely according to blood ties. The suffix *-ter* originally indicated some active function. Research has shown that the word $*p^\circ ter$ was probably used to render the idea of "the man who gives to eat," "the man who leads the group in search of wild animals," "the man who assures the survival of the group," "the huntsman-cum-leader" of the earliest societies.

The *fhine* of the Celts corresponds to the Indo-European *genos*, that is a family unit comprising several generations (like the Latin *gens*), and worshipping the memory of a common ancestor. In the beginning this unit was no more than a group of nomadic hunters. The Indo-European languages contain an exceptional number of common terms relating to the chase.

The association of several *genos* into a larger group may have been dictated by the need to widen the scope of the hunt. In any case the Indo-European peoples were all exogamous, which means that they married outside their own *genos*. So to avoid incest it would have been necessary for a minimum of three *genos* to join together. The women of *genos* A would then marry the men of *genos* B, the women of *genos* B the men of *genos* C and the women of *genos* C the men of *genos* A. The new, larger group was called a **wenos*, or a community formed by ties of blood rather than by mutual economic interest. The latter was a **weikos*, the root of the Greek word *oikonomia*. As early nomadic societies developed into sedentary or semi-sedentary communities, the whole **weikos* would settle in one place, whence the Latin word *vicus* for village.

The fact that the economy of the community now needed to be organized on a different scale produced a change in the basic relationships within the *genos*. No longer merely the physical father, the **p°ter* came to represent the *genos* as a whole in its collective ownership of property. He was the lord of the domain, the Latin *dominus*, the *potis* which the Greeks made into *despotes* and the Celts *teutates* (father of the *genos*). The original family extended to include outsiders who worked as slaves or servants for the prosperity of the *genos*. The new system was particularly in evidence in countries which the early Indo-Europeans conquered and settled, for being primarily hunters and warriors they had little time or talent for craftsmanship, but could devolve such work onto their new subjects. From historical documents, archaeological finds and the study of Irish epic, it becomes clear that the Celts followed just such an arrangement, gradually integrating the indigenous craftsmen in the lands they conquered into their own social system. The *domos* was created, together with the economic and legal intricacies which assured its proper function. And so relationships came to be defined in terms of activities. The **p°ter* kept political and religious influence for himself. The **bhratheres* were the warriors. The duties of woman and servants were purely economic. This division of society into three orders emerges clearly from the work of Georges Dumezil.

Problems of political organization produced the greatest difficulties. When several *genos* formed an association, the **p°teres* met to order the affairs of the **wenos* or **weikos*. The administration had to be flexible, since each *genos* recognized only the authority of its own **p°ter*. But, although this worked well enough in normal circumstances, the advent of conflict or war necessitated the election of a **reg-s* (Latin, *rex*) to take over responsibility for the defence of the community. The **reg-s*, literally the man who points the way, was elected from among his peers, the **p°teres*, and his authority was continually monitored and controlled by an assembly of **p°teres* like the Roman senate. His office was purely temporary and lasted only as long as the special circumstances which had made his election necessary in the first place. So, in peace time, Indo-European society tended in most cases to limit central authority to its simplest expression. This is especially true of the Celts, both in the British Isles and on the continent. But there is evidence of the same phenomenon among the Hellenes, the Indo-Aryans, the Persians and the Teutonic peoples. Only the Latins acquired a taste for firm and permanent, central government, which they then imposed on much of the world.

The fact that every Indo-European society was a magnified, if not elevated, form of the *genos* meant that most of the political activity within the Indo-European world was concentrated on defending the autonomy and individuality of the *genos*. As the basic unit of social organization, it was the mainstay of the whole structure. That is why the Celts continued their desperate efforts to safe-guard the moral and physical integrity of the *genos* even in the face of political dominance by other Indo-European peoples who had abandoned the original social structures. The Irish *fhine* was no more than a *genos* led by a **pºter* who had all the prerogatives of a king, but was only absolute master in his own *fhine*. He had then to recognize the authority of the man whom he and other petty kings elected chief of the *tuath*, which corresponded to the **wenos*/**weikos*. The preservation of the *fhine* affected the whole history of the Celts. Their refusal to accept any more than temporary control from the centre kept the various Celtic peoples apart. It gave their social structures great strength, but weakened their overall position.

This kind of social organization underlies the Arthurian story. Arthur was only the temporary leader of a federation of *fhines*, all of them intransigent on the subject of their own privileges. The *tuatha* formed by the *fhines* only accepted Arthur's authority because of an external threat to the independence of their small, respective groups. The myth of a king of kings was born of necessity and reappeared at various times embodied in men of similar appearance but diverse temperament.

Arthur's authority comes not from a legal definition of his position but from the way in which he uses it. There are traces of this peculiar concept in the French Arthurian romances. In his *Roman de Brut*, Wace says of Arthur "he excels all other princes in courtesy, prowess, valour and generosity," meaning that he is accepted because he bows to custom and does not use his office to play the dictator. His valour and generosity are essential attributes. When, in *Perlesvaux*, Arthur loses the power to give, his court disintegrates and his kingdom hangs in the balance. Only the restoration of his ability to give makes him leader of the community again. In *Érec et Énide*, Arthur says, "I am king. I must not lie, nor consent to villainy, falsehood or excess. I must safeguard reason and right. The faithful king must uphold the law, truth, justice and faith. I would never wish to be disloyal for any reason, nor do wrong either to the weakest or the strongest. I do not wish to be a cause for complaint, nor do I want the usage and custom that I must maintain by my lineage to die." In other words, Arthur must do only what is laid down by usage and custom. He is merely a symbol of tradition.

The Irish epics, which are valuable for the information they give us about the Celts' way of life, contain many references to the king's duties. Every leader, whether a tribal chieftain, the king of a province, or, indeed the high king, is bound by a series of *geisa* or incontrovertible taboos. Any transgression of these taboos may lead to destitution or even death. Conaire the Great suffered this fate.[9] Alternatively the whole kingdom may undergo adverse effects. The kingdom of the Grail, for example, became the Gaste Pays, a barren wasteland, when the Fisher-King was wounded for transgressing a *geis* and could no longer govern properly.

The duties of a king are clearly laid out in the tale of King Lugaid mac Cuind of Tara. A man who had let his sheep stray into the queen's meadow was sentenced by Lugaid to have his flocks confiscated. As he pronounced judgment one side of the house in which Lugaid was sitting collapsed and sank to the bottom of the hill. Cormac, Lugaid's adopted son, immediately declared Lugaid' judgment wanting and suggested instead that the sheep should be sheared and their fleeces given as compensation for the grass eaten, since both grass and wool would grow again. This subsidence stopped and the assembled company agreed that Cormac's proposal was fair and that he was a true prince. Lugaid continued to rule for another year, but during that time no grass grew upon the earth, no leaves on the trees and no grain in the wheat. Then the men of Ireland expelled Lugaid whose unfair judgment had brought about their misery and elected the just Cormac in his place.

The legend of Nuada and Bres contains further evidence of the requirements for kingship. When Nuada, king of the Tuatha Dé Danann, lost an arm in battle he was deemed unfit for royal office. Any physical defect was regarded as a disqualification to rule, for the king had to be in perfect physical condition to maintain harmony in his realm. The choice of successor fell upon Bres of the Fomore, who was related to the Tuatha Dé Danann. But Bres proved to be a bad king. He tended to favour the Fomore, and when the Tuatha went to eàt with him "their knives were not greased" and "their breath did not smell of ale," signs that Bres was not sufficiently generous as a host. Nor did he ever pay the poets and musicians who came to perform for him. So the Tuatha Dé Danann drove him away and restored Nuada to the throne because he had now acquired a silver arm which earned him the nickname Nuada Silver Hand.

The paradoxes inherent in Celtic notions of kingship are evident in the traditions concerning Conchobar, king of Ulster. When Fergus mac Roig was king, he wished to marry Ness, a warrior woman who had been married to the Druid Cathba. But she would not consent unless Fergus gave the crown of Ulster to her son, Conchobar, for a year. Fergus agreed, but the Ulstermen, thinking that Fergus had given the crown to Ness as a marriage settlement, decided that he had acted dishonourably and declared Conchobar king outright. Clearly Fergus was no more than a representative of the community whose contract could be terminated if his behaviour was found to be unsatisfactory. This kind of contractual arrangement foreshadows Diderot's view of monarchy in the *Encyclopédie*. For Diderot too suggests that the community should be free in cases where the king died or was impeached to form a new contract with whomever it deemed fit.

As far as the Celts were concerned, the king was merely an intermediary. In *Branwen, Daughter of Llyr*, the hero Bran, who is a giant, crosses his army over an estuary by lying between the two banks and getting his men to walk over his body. And he says "Let him who is a chief be a bridge."[10] The idea of the bridge is inherent in the king's position as upholder of tradition. He must span the gap between past and present, present and future. He also acts as intermediary between his people and the Druid, who is actually the true Celtic chief with overall authority both in the temporal, legal sphere and in the spiritual sphere of magic. The term *pontifex*, or bridge-maker, could be applied to both Bran and Arthur, though neither the legendary nor the historical king had any religious influence.

This is one of the major differences between the Celtic and the Latin peoples. The authority of the early Indo-European king was extended to include both religious and political decision making. In Rome political power soon passed into the hands of the consuls, who remained free of any magical or spiritual taboos. The religious authority of the early king passed to the *Flamen Dialis*, the high priest of Jupiter, who remained subject to all the magical taboos previously attached to the office of king. He was not allowed to leave Rome, for example, and had to perform various extremely complex rites. As far as the Romans were concerned, the state and its political officers were all-important, the priesthood merely a ceremonial body. Celtic concepts of society and social life could not have been more different. In Gaul, Britain and Ireland the Druid had pre-eminence, while the king acted merely as a go-between for the people and the Druid, and through him the gods. In Ireland, it was laid down that nobody of inferior rank was to speak in public before the king had spoken, but also that the king was to wait until his Druid had spoken. The Druid's privileges were many. He was totally free, need contribute no funds to the community, could avoid military service if he so wished and was bound by no major taboos. The king, on the other hand, was hedged round by a series of restrictions and requirements. He was not allowed to leave his house without a valid reason; he was to admit every petitioner who came to see him and make him a gift. He had also to attend his army's battles without actually fighting, for his presence was a prerequisite of victory. Obviously under these terms the real Arthur could never have been a king.

For although the Druids had gone by Arthur's time, traces of their influence remained. Sometimes their previous role was taken over by the monks. When Saint Germanus pronounced anathema on Vortigern, he might have been a Druid consigning an unwanted king to outer darkness. Arthur's quarrels with the monastic saints are proof that the Britons of his day were controlled largely by the monks. The part played by magicians, fairies, wizards and, later, by Merlin in Arthurian legend, only serves to accentuate the impotence of the king or general who lacked the support of the spiritual powers. The reason why the Arthur of the French romances has become such a pale shadow of a king is simply that he has now become a king. He leaves active combat to the other members of his court and merely waits to receive the prisoners whom they have taken in his name. This particular development of his character fits in with the way the original political theme was made into myth. Arthur has changed from the unchallenged leader who assumed power only during times of conflict into the king who upheld justice within the community at all times. The historic Arthur was a *p^oter* who ruled his own small *genos* of itinerant warriors and became a temporary king of kings when elected to that office by the *p^oteres* of all the British *genos*. But, as soon as he passed into legend, he became petrified, for mythology asked only that he should be present for great and wonderful things to happen.

As a Celtic king Arthur remained only a symbol of the community. When Kulhwch comes to ask Arthur for help, he addresses him as follows: "Hail to the chief lord of this island. May the lower couches of this house be no worse than the upper, and may my greeting apply equally to your nobles and your company and your troops, without omitting anyone. As I greeted you, properly, so may your trust and grace and glory be proper throughout the island."[11]

This form of greeting makes it clear that Arthur is identified with the whole of Britain. Interestingly, too, Kulhwch addresses him not as king, but as chief lord, and goes on to threaten him with a form of blackmail. For when Arthur tells Kulhwch to sit between two of his warriors and promises him virtually anything he wants in the form of amusement, Kulhwch becomes angry. "I did not come here," he says, "to beg for food and drink. If my request is granted I will repay it and praise you; otherwise, I will bear your shame to the farthest extent of your reputation in the four corners of the world."[12] Obviously Kulhwch stands in no particular awe of the "king." To ensure that Arthur helps him as he should, he has only to exert the same kind of pressure used by the poets and Druids of ancient Irish epic and threaten him with a "satire."

The poet Airthne, known as "the Importunate Man of Ulster" had the unpleasant habit of visiting all the Irish kings in turn and threatening them with

dire misfortune and terrible magic satires if they refused to give him what he
wanted. In the tale of the *Siege of Dun Etair*, Airthne asks the one-eyed king of
South Connaught for his only eye, the king of Munster for permission to sleep
with his wife, and the king of Leinster to hand over his wife completely, "to save
his honour." If the king refuses, not only will he be dishonoured but all the men
of Leinster with him. The king is forced to obey only to have the rapacious
Airthne remain in Leinster for a year where he gathers together 150 queens or
chieftains' wives to take back to Ulster.[13] Clearly the early kings had far less
power than the Druids and their immediate successors, the *fili*, who were poets,
musicians and formidable magicians.

Although Bres, king of the Tuatha Dé Danann, had already compromised his
position by neglecting the law of generosity, it was not until a poet had pronounced a satire against him that he finally fell. Coirpe, poet of the Tuatha Dé
Danann, came one day to ask Bres for hospitality. He was taken to a small,
narrow, dark house where there were no fire, no furniture and no bed. And there
he was given three small, dry loaves on a small plate. The following morning he
awoke feeling thoroughly disgruntled. So he stode across the court chanting
"No food—offered quickly on a plate. No cows' milk—to feed the calves. No
house for a good night's rest. No reward—for story tellers. May this treatment
now come Bres' way." "From then on Bres' affairs went from bad to worse.
Coirpe had pronounced against him the first magic curse uttered in Ireland."
And when the Tuatha Dé Danann came to make their official complaint, he
admitted that they had the right to demand his abdication and that he had no
power to refuse them.[14]

As a king, then, Arthur was subject to a whole series of taboos and requirements. His first duty was to gather around him a select few, a troop of fearless
warriors. Craftsmen were also needed to make weapons and to increase the
wealth of the community. Then there were the bards who enjoyed a privileged
position both as recorders of events and heirs of communal tradition. This
meant that admission to Arthur's house was restricted. Any newcomer had to
undergo a kind of initiation test. It had nothing to do with the initiation ceremony of the medieval knight, but demanded skills and talents on the part of the
new arrival which he had to prove.

In the Irish tale of the *Battle of Mag-Tured*, which describes the conflict
between the Tuatha Dé Danann and the Fomore, the great pan-Celtic god Lug
arrives one day at Nuada's fortress.

> At that time there were two gatekeepers at Tara. One was Gamal, son of
> Figal, the other Camall, son of Riagall. One of them who was at the gate saw
> a group of strangers approaching, led by a young warrior of handsome and
> distinguished appearance dressed like a king. The strangers told the gate-
> keeper to announce their arrival to the inhabitants of Tara. "Who are you?"
> said the gatekeeper. "This is Lug Lonnansclech (the Manyfaceted Artist),
> grandson of Diancecht through Cian, his father, grandson of Balor[15]
> through Ethne his mother. He was brought up by Taltiu, daughter of
> Magmor, king of Spain, and by Echaid the Rough, son of Dua." The gate-
> keeper spoke to Lug the Manyfaceted Artist. "What is your skill, for no one
> comes to Tara without a skill?" "To your question here is my reply. I am a
> carpenter." "We do not need you," replied the gatekeeper, "we already have a
> carpenter living here, Luchtem son of Lucachaid." "To your question, O
> gatekeeper, here is my reply. I am a smith." The gatekeeper replied, "We

already have a smith living here, Colum." "To your question, O gatekeeper, here is my reply. I am a powerful warrior." The gatekeeper replied, "We do not need you. There is already a powerful warrior living here, Ogma, son of Ethne." "To your question here is my reply. I am a harp player." "We do not need you. We already have a harp player living here, Abcan, son of Bicelmas. The men of the three gods chose him in the *sidhs*." "To your question here is my reply, I am a skilful and famous warrior." The gatekeeper replied, "We do not need you, there is already one here, Bresal Echarlam, son of Echaid Dullhand." "To your question, O gatekeeper, here is my reply. I am a poet, I am a historian." "We do not need you. We already have someone who is a poet and historian here, En son of Ethoman." "To your question here is my reply. I am a magician." "We do not need you. We already have several magicians, Druids and sorcerers with powerful spells." "To your question, here is my reply. I am a doctor." "We do not need you. Diancecht is our doctor." "To your question here is my reply. I am a cupbearer." "We do not need you. We already have nine cupbearers here." "To your question here is my reply. I am a good worker in bronze." "We do not need you. we already have a worker in bronze, Credne." "Ask the king," went on Lug, "if there is any man in his house who is skilled in all these arts. If there is such a man I will not enter Tara." So the gatekeeper went to the palace and told the king everything we have just told you. "A warrior called Lug the Manyfaceted Artist has just come to the gate," he said. "He knows all the crafts that other men do, he is an allround craftsman." "Take him the chess game of Tara," said the king, "and let him play." Lug won the game. The king was told that Lug had won. Then Nuada said "Let him in. No man like this has ever come to this fortress." The gatekeeper let Lug in. Then Lug went into the fortress and sat in the scholar's chair because he was schooled in every art."[17]

This "initiation" into the king's court underlines the sacred nature of the sovereign. Nobody can gain immediate access to the holy of holies and only those who have some skill which makes them useful to the community are allowed in. But these entry qualifications have more to do with practical ideas about how society should be organized than with vague notions of esoteric mysteries to which only the special few are to be admitted. The symbols of Arthurian myth are not the products of mysticism, but are used to preserve the main currents of Celtic thought and culture in evocative and mnemonic images. There are all too many scholars who are prepared to set themselves up as the sole correct interpreters of legends and myths which they themselves invest with superfluous and elaborate hidden meanings. Their cult of Tradition, with a capital T, is as fraudulent as the claims of the present-day Druids to be practising a Druidic religion which has been dead and buried since the first century AD. Entry to the king's court depends solely on the newcomer's potential usefulness to the community. Guests may be received with ritual, even with friendly welcome, but they will never really participate in the communal life reflected in Arthur's court.

This is the only rational explanation for the behaviour of the gatekeeper. He acts as a filter, screening the arrivals for suitable entrants. There is another reference to the gatekeeper's duties in the Welsh tale of *Owein*. "Now though it is said that there was a gatekeeper at Arthur's court, there was not: however Glewlwyt Gafaelfawr was there acting as gatekeeper, greeting guests and foreigners, beginning to honour them, telling them the customs and habits of the court and informing those who merited lodging."[18] So, although everbody is entitled to hospitality at court by law only the privileged few have the right to enter Arthur's hall. For Arthur has become the central, controlling figure of an almost ideal society, which he creates around him. This does not mean, however, that the few who gain access to Arthur's hall are there to sing his praises. That is the resident poet's job. They come specifically to serve the community or to ask for some gift which the king is obliged to give even if he does not know what it is. There is no need for them to mince their words. The king, after all, is one of them and has only acquired a temporary superiority in order to fulfil some specific purpose.

The Dream of Rhonabwy, a late compilation of older Arthurian traditions, makes this clear. Preparations are in progress for the battle of Mount Badon. King Arthur, or as he is here called the Emperor Arthur, does not seem particularly anxious to fight. So with positive insolence Karadawc Vreichvras says "You may choose to go or not to go, but I will go." To which Arthur can only reply "What you say is true. We will set out together." There is none of the refined politeness of the courtly romances here. In fact, when we look at the French romances more closely we find that there, also, Arthur's own knights are quite prepared to treat him as if he were a humble peasant. In the *Chevalier à la Charrette*, Kai is extremely rude about his king and foster brother. Even Gawain, who owes Arthur a nephew's respect if nothing else, is highly impertinent in many of the tales. It is as if insulting the king were part of a specific ritual designed to remind the monarch that the homage of his subjects is not something he should expect as a matter of course.

Insults are also directed towards Arthur through a third party. Naturally enough, any affront to one of his followers is an attack on the whole group and therefore on Arthur as its symbol. But an indirect attack on Arthur can also be made by insulting Queen Guinevere. And an affront to Guinevere is even more serious than a direct attack on the king. For it is the queen who embodies sovereignty. And without sovereignty neither Arthur nor any Celtic king would hold any authority at all. This particular facet of queenship is a vital part of any study of the Arthurian world. It also goes a long way to explaining Guinevere's ambiguous position in both the French romances and the Celtic tales. Celtic civilization was a joint product of the authoritarian, patriarchal ideas of the Indo-European Celts and the ancestral traditions of the aboriginal peoples they conquered. These traditions clearly reflect gynaecocratic tendencies which survived intact in all the Celtic tales and the Round Table romances.

The Theme of Sovereignty

One of the most important, and incidentally most neglected, of the Arthurian texts is the 14th-century English tale, *The Wedding of Sir Gawain*. Gower's 14th-century *Confessio Amantis* tells the same story, but not in an Arthurian setting, and Chaucer sets almost exactly the same adventure in an Arthurian background, but concerning a different character. There is also a 14th-century English ballad on the same subject. The kind of literary criticism required to make a separate examination of all these versions of the story, and then to synthesise our findings would take us too far from the study of Arthurian myth. But it is clear that there must have been some original, older source on which they were based, and which had precious little to do with Gawain's wedding. A reconstruction of the early story, however, will expose one of the cornerstones of Arthurian myth.

The original tale was undoubtedly part of the British oral tradition. It has the atmosphere of a folk tale and was probably one of many such stories still circulating in the British Isles and on the continent in the 14th century, although there is nothing like it in either the French Arthurian literature or the Welsh tradition. Not the least surprising thing about the tale is its actual title. The Gawain so carefully portrayed in most other Arthurian literature is definitely not the marrying kind. He is fickle and shallow in his many relationships with women. It is almost as if he were acting out the role of sun god, bringing warmth and light to all he meets. It is possible that this particular adventure was wrongly attributed to him and belongs by right to Arthur. Arthur is certainly the main protagonist. It is he who first undertakes the adventure and there is no reason, as Gaston Paris has said, why he should not finish it.

One day Arthur was hunting in the forest when he was overtaken by a man armed with a club.[19] Arthur had previously disinherited him and the stranger was seeking revenge. Although he had the unarmed king at his mercy, the man with the club agreed to spare his life on condition that he returned after a year to answer the question "What is it that women love above all else?" For long months Arthur travelled the country asking everyone he met the question and assembling a large number of different answers. When the time came he went back to the forest to look for the man with the club. But on the way he met a hideously ugly woman who said, "I know your secret. All the answers you have are wrong. I am the only one who knows what you must say, but I will not tell you unless you promise to marry me." The king hesitated, but finally agreed, presumably hoping that he could find some way of breaking his promise later. Then the woman told him "what women love above all else is sovereignty. Tell your enemy that and he will curse the woman who gave the correct reply." Arthur went on his way and found the man with the club. When none of the answers he had collected himself proved satisfactory, Arthur said "It is sovereignty." The man with the club was angry and shouted "Obviously my sister told you that. May she burn for it." But as Arthur had given the correct answer, he had to let him go. The hideous woman then reappeared and reminded Arthur of his promise. Sick at heart, Arthur returned to court with her and they were married. That evening he climbed into bed with his new wife, but immediately turned his back on her, wondering if he would survive till morning. The woman said, "At least give me a kiss, if only for politeness' sake." Arthur turned to do so and saw the most beautiful woman imaginable lying beside him. She said "You can choose to have me beautiful at night and ugly during the day, or the other way round." Arthur found the choice too difficult and left it to her. Then she said, "In that case I will be beautiful both night and day. My stepmother changed me into the horrible figure you first met by magic and I was to stay like that until the best knight in the world married me and gave me sovereignty in all things. Your courtesy has set me free."[20]

In the later versions of the story, it is Gawain whom the hideous woman wishes to marry and who helps Arthur to collect the various answers to the all-important question. But the whole adventure is sparked of by Arthur's disinheriting the man with the club; and the fact that there are folk tales on similar lines suggests that the original was actually an account of Arthur's marriage to Guinevere. None of the tales concerning her gives us a very clear picture of the queen. The *Lancelot in Prose* makes her the daughter of King Leodagan, the Welsh *Triads* tell how Arthur had three successive wives all called Gwenhwyfar. her actual name is not always the same. Gwenhwyfar is the Welsh version of the French *Guinièvre* and the English Guinevere, but Geoffrey of Monmouth calls her *Guennuera*. The sculpture on Modena Cathedral labels her *Winlogee* from the Breton *Winlogen*. In the *Romance of Yder* there is a *Guenloie* who appears to be a different character altogether, although the text is so confused that Guenloie and Guinevere may well be the same person. Finally, in the Latin tale of the *Birth of Gawain*, Arthur's wife is called *Gwendolen*.

Note that in each case the queen's name is based on the root word *gwen* which appears variously as *wen, win* or *guin,* and which, like its Gaelic equivalent *finn*, has four meanings, all extensions of the original meaning. First, it means white, and thus beautiful, since whiteness and beauty were synonymous among the Celts. Then, as beauty could be seen in golden hair, it came to mean blond. And finally, because beauty, whiteness and blond hair were all characteristics of the high-born, the word was used to mean well-bred in a generic sense for those of pure blood. (In Brittany the word was even used to mean saintly, in the Christian sense.) The Venetes, the Pays de Vannes, the Vendeans, the Vendee and the land of Gwynedd all derived their names from this root, used to indicate the idea of purity. While the Gaelic word *finn* came to be linked with *fhine*, the early *genos*, partly through phonetic similarity and partly because both words contained the concept of racial purity.

The Welsh name Gwenhwyfar literally means "white ghost, white spirit", as does the Irish Finnabair, daughter of Queen Mebdh of Connaught. So Gwenhwyfar is first and foremost the personification of beauty. She is whiteness and purity, and obviously golden-haired. But since she is linked with the *fhine*, she is also sovereignty. And it is clear from the tale of Arthur's marriage that this sovereignty may take on different forms so that its full radiance only appears to those who merit it. Before Arthur can lay permanent claim to the sovereignty embodied in Guinevere, he must first overcome his repulsion and then recognize this sovereignty by allowing Guinevere freedom of choice.

An Irish tale about the semi-legendary King Niall of the Nine Hostages is very similar:

> One day the three sons of King Eochaid Muigmdeon were hunting in a wilderness. They were very thirsty and could find no spring. Then a hideously ugly and toothless old woman appeared. She told the eldest son she would give him water if he would give her a kiss. Unable to overcome his disgust he refused. His younger brother responded in the same way. But Niall, the youngest, agreed, and as soon as his lips touched the rough skin of the old woman she turned into a beautiful girl. She then said to Niall "I am the sovereignty of Ireland. Because you dared to kiss me, you will be king of Ireland."

Clearly this tale is one of many variations on the theme of the Oedipus myth. When Niall kisses the old woman he is undergoing a kind of sexual initiation in which the mother figure opens a new world to him. The change from an ugly hag into a radiant beauty is really a change in Niall, who is seeing her through new eyes. He is like Oedipus, for whom the terrifying and monstrous sphinx disappears to become Jocasta, a mother and mistress but also a personification of the sovereignty Oedipus acquires.[21]

Not everyone, however, is qualified to perform this act of renewal. If the tired and well-worn sovereignty of former days is to become young and vital again, the youthful son must overcome both his instinctive repulsion and his rational misgivings and answer the challenge, or the riddle of the sphinx. Niall's brothers are not worthy to assume the responsibilities demanded by sovereignty, and drop out of the race. A Breton folk story, *The Queen of Prowess*, also tells of three brothers who, in this case, are on their way to marry an orphan queen. An old witch appears and asks them a question. The elder brothers find the woman so repellent that they cannot answer correctly. But the youngest gives the right reply, and it is he whom the witch enables to marry the young queen.[22] Presumably the old witch and the young queen are merely two aspects of the same woman, just as the sphinx and Jocasta are really the same person seen from different angles.

There are other heroes who are well qualified to assume sovereignty but who reject it. The Babylonian epic of *Gilgamesh* provides a memorable example of this. When Ischtar suggests that Gilgamesh become her lover, he refuses because the goddess is reputed to have turned her previous lovers into animals and he fears the same fate may befall him. So he decides to seek the supremacy she represents under a different form, and on his own terms. With his friend, Enkidou, he embarks on a search for immortality, but Enkidou dies and Gilgamesh is unsuccessful in his quest. His refusal of Ischtar had made failure a foregone conclusion. The way of solitary pride which he had chosen was bound to lead to a dead end.

Ulysses suffers a similar fate in the *Odyssey*. Having resisted the sirens' song, he refuses Circe because she might threaten his virility and turn him into an animal. His overweening male pride is totally incompatible with the concept of female domination reflected in the image of the seductive mother figure.[23] All the trials he undergoes before finally reaching home taught him nothing. For he is merely back where he started.

Seen from this point of view, the marriage of Arthur and Guinevere is a kind of sacred union. The young Arthur is marrying the sovereign goddess, Mother Britain, on whom the burden of power has taken its toll. When he breaks the spell of age, sovereignty returns to its youthful beauty.

Similarly, when Niall kisses the old woman, he is marrying Mother Ireland. The Irish hero Lugaid Laigde has an encounter with another old woman, and when she turns into a lovely girl she says:

> I will tell you gentle boy
> with me the high-kings sleep;
> I am the graceful slender girl
> the Sovereignty of Scotland and Ireland.[24]

The marriage of the king of Ireland to a woman symbolizing the country is a frequent occurrence in Gaelic tradition, and not only in the pre-historic era. The early *Prophetic Ecstasy of the Phantom* tells how King Conn of the Hundred Battles was walking on the plain of Tara when he was suddenly transported to an underground Other World. A magic mist surrounded him, a horseman appeared through the mist to take him to a fortress where a golden tree stood in front of the main house. Inside the god Lug welcomed Conn and sat him near a silver cauldron full of ale. Near the cauldron stood a beautiful girl who is made out to be the sovereignty of Ireland. She filled a silver cup with ale and offered it Conn. With every mouthful Conn drank, Lug named one of his descendants who was to succeed to the throne. Finally, Conn was taken back through the mist to the plain of Tara.[25] In this case the girl who represents sovereignty is clearly a supernatural being who lives in the Other World.

Giraldus Cambrensis records this kind of symbolic marriage in his *Topographia*. His description of the enthronement ritual still practised, or so he says, in Giraldus' own day contains obvious traces of totemism as well.

> Once the people had been assembled together in a place of this land [in this case Kenelcunnil, a town in North Ulster] a white mare was led into the middle of the crowd. Then, in full view of everybody, this person of highest rank [the king] approached the mare bestially not like a prince, but like a wild beast, not like a king, but like an outlaw, and behaved just like an animal, without shame or prudence. Immediately afterwards the mare was killed, carved up into pieces and thrown in boiling water. A bath was prepared for the king with the broth, and he sat in it while scraps of the meat were brought for him to eat and to share with the people around him. He was also washed with the broth and drank it, not with a cup or his hands, but directly with his mouth. Once this ritual had been performed his rule and authority were assured.

This strange ceremony, which makes the virtuous Giraldus shudder with horror, is almost exactly like the Indian ritual of *asvamedha*, in which the queen enters into symbolic union with a sacred stallion. For the Celts, however, it was a fertility ritual, coloured by memories of the mare-goddess whom the Welsh called Rhiannon, the Irish Macha and the Gauls Epona. The equation of sexual union with accession to the throne is evident in the legend of King Conchobar. The duties and taboos he was obliged to respect were matched by a number of privileges, though perhaps not in the sense we might understand the word. *The Birth of Conchobar* states "The Ulstermen rendered Conchobar a great honour. For every Ulsterman sent his daughter to lie with Conchobar on the first night so that he was her first husband."[26] Many people regard this custom of *jus primae noctis or the droit de cuissage* as cruel and barbarous, proof, if proof were needed, of the way in which the powerful have always abused their position. But nothing could be further from the truth. Apart from the fact that the medieval lord rarely performed more than the symbolic gesture of placing one leg in the bride's bed, the whole idea of *druit de cuissage* was that some man with superior religious or magical powers should run the risk of contact with dangerous virginal blood and spare the husband any possible ill effects. Any man who sent his bride to the king was not doing his lord a favour, but asking for his protection. And it was part of the duty of a monarch or a priest to accord it.

In the case of King Conchobar, as for many Celtic kings, giving one's daughter to the king was also a symbolic act. For the girls brought to Conchobar's bed represented Mother Ireland, and each one stood as a renewal of the king's original marriage contract with his country, a ritual affirmation of the continuation of power.

Guinevere is the embodiment of this power. Even the 12th and 13th-century romances, with their un-Celtic courtly veneer, are clear on this point. In his *Chevalier à la Charrette*, Chrétien de Troyes makes Guinevere appear highly unpleasant. She abuses her authority, is tyrannical in her demands and generally behaves like an absolute sovereign, a goddess of unlimited power. She makes her own decisions and the unfortunate Lancelot grovels at her feet, ready to act on the slightest whim of his chosen mistress. Guinevere's dictatorial attitude is generally attributed to Chrétien's desire to dramatize the theories of *fine amor*, which held that the perfect lover should faithfully execute the wishes of his Lady. But Guinevere's sovereignty should also be taken into consideration here. As the ruling and instructing force in her particular world, it is right that every man should obey her unthinkingly.

In the Irish tradition, young people are educated by women who are part sorceress, part warrior and part fairy. The hero Cú Chulainn goes to Scotland to learn the martial arts from two of these women, Scatach and Aife. Finn, king of the Fiana, is educated by terrifying-looking warrior women. In Wales too, the Welsh Peredur remains naive and awkward until the witches of Kaerloyw take him in hand. It follows quite naturally that Chrétien's Gawain should describe Guinevere as the woman "who gives instruction to all living people."

Guinevere's importance in the Arthurian world varies from tale to tale. Part from her tear-jerking affair with Lancelot, her position in the *Lancelot in Prose* is insignificant to say the least. In those 13th and 14th-century works which refer back to older traditions, however, as in the Welsh stories, she appears as the sovereign. But only Chrétien de Troyes really preserves her former character intact. Like *Peredur* and the English *Sir Percivelle*, which is closer to *Peredur* than to *Perceval*, Chrétian's *Perceval* shows Arthur's sovereignty to be no more than the executive facet of Guinevere's supremacy. When Peredur arrives at Arthur's court for the first time, he hears of a characteristic incident in which an insult has been made to the queen rather than to the king. "A chamberlain was serving Gwenhwyfar from a golden cup; the knight took this cup from her hand and poured it over her face and breast, boxed her ears severely and then said "Whoever wishes to take this cup from me and avenge this insult to Gwenhwyfar, let him follow me to the meadow." The knight was obviously trying to insult Arthur's authority through the person of the queen. The cup itself, a feminine object holding drink and thus, by analogy, a woman's breast, is a telling symbol. Certainly none of the king's companions who witness the scene mistakes its significance. But none wishes to take the risk of going to avenge the insult to Gwenhwyfar, and it is left to the ingenuous Peredur to take up the challenge.

In the tale of *Gereint and Enid*, Gwenhwyfar is insulted by Edern's servant. Gereint pursues Edern and finally wounds him in combat. He then says "I will show mercy on condition that you go to Arthur's wife, Gwenhwyfar and make good the insult ... You are not to dismount from the time of your departure until you are before Gwenhwyfar".[28] Edern arrives at court in a sorry state and publicly acknowledges his defeat. "Well," says Arthur, "Gwenhwyfar ought to show mercy, from what I hear," thereby leaving the decision to his wife. But she says "Lord, I will show such mercy as you wish, for my disgrace is as much an insult to you as is your own."[29] Obviously, if an insult to the queen rebounds on the king, the opposite must also be true. In *Gereint and Enid* sovereignty is inalienable. Gwenhwyfar is not the decorative figure of 12th and 13th-century court life, but retains her authority, even though she delegates the execution of it to her husband.

The idea that the king is powerless without the queen at his side is illustrated throughout Irish literature. It finds complete expression in the *Adventures of Art Son of Conn*. Art is banished from Ireland because his father has taken an unworthy concubine and the kingdom has become barren. He cannot return until he wins the hand of Delbchaen, daughter of Coinchend Cenfada, who lives in a mysterious island. Translated into political terms, this tale is describing how Conn, the father, has lost his sovereignty, which his son must regain in the form of Delbchaen. After a long and arduous journey Art finally reaches the house of Coinchend. Despite Coinchend's attempts to trap him, Art outwits his formidable adversary and kills her. He then returns with Delbachaen, and once sovereignty has been restored the kingdom prospers again.

The *Adventures of Art* is an interesting story in various respects. The names of the characters themselves are significant. Art mac Cuind can mean "bear, son of Dog." Delbchaen's mother is called Coinchend Cenfada, that is "head of Dog Longhead." She has the strength of a hundred men in battle and is the daughter of Conchruth (Red Head), king of the Coinchends (Heads of Dogs). The whole mythology of the tale is built on traces of totemism and bears the stamp of the supernatural, since these monsters with dogs' heads are *Cerberi*, or guardians of the Other World. Sovereignty is to be found in this Other World in the form of a fairy or goddess, the problem being to go and fetch her. But whatever trials the hero may have to endure in his quest serve to strengthen him in his resolve, so that he is finally able to overcome both the real dangers which threaten him from outside and the dangers wrought by his own imagination. He is ready to play out his part.

The fact that the woman sought by the Celtic hero stands as an embodiment of sovereignty contributes an important facet to our understanding of Arthurian myth. The Celts strongly identified woman with the sun. The sun itself was a feminine object and its beneficial rays were there to be taken and used in everyday life. The king, like the moon, derived all his warmth and light from his wife, the sun, and reflected them onto a world of darkness. Just as the Scythians had worshipped Diana as a sun-goddess, so the Celts injected solar symbolism into their mythology. Their sun-goddesses were women like the Irish Grainne, who persuaded Diarmaid to flee with her, and the Yseult of the French romances, who dragged the lunar Tristan in her glowing wake. The Etruscans worshipped a similar goddess called Turan. Her name comes from an Indo-European root meaning "to give," making the goddess the woman who gives, the *tyrannical* woman. Present-day use of the word tyrant obviously comes from a distortion of the original duties of the sun-goddess' husband, which were to give his subjects all that it was in his power to give. When the medieval clerks wrote about the British tribal chieftains or *tierns* as *tyranni*, as opposed to magistrates in the imperial tradition, they may well have been indicating something much closer to the original meaning of the word. For the duties of a king like Arthur were primarily related to the generosity which marked his position.[31]

Irish epic contains an evocative image of the tyrannical goddess in the legendary Queen Mebdh of Connaught. Her name says a great deal about her: it means "drunkenness." According to tradition she was wife to nine kings of Ireland. Indeed it was said that no man could become king until he married her. As long as King Cormac refused to sleep with her, he could not accede to the throne. She offered her body freely to those who promised to obey her, however. In the *Raid of Cualnge*, she is nominally married to Ailill, a sorry figure of a man, and she starts a war with the Ulsterman solely in order to be able to assert her superiority over her husband by owning one more bull than he does. Then she sleeps with Fergus, the former king of Ulster now exiled in Connaught, in order to win this great warrior over to her side. Ailill philosophically concludes that his wife's behaviour was a necessary expedient if she was to win the war. Mebdh, then, is a royal prostitute, a role perfectly in keeping with the capricious nature of sovereignty. For her subjects, her will is law. But because of the demands she makes on them, she is prepared to give of herself in return. In *The Drunkenness of the Ulstermen*, King Ailill remains uncommitted and would prefer to make peace with the Ulstermen. So he stays away from the battlefield, and waits to see what will happen from the shelter of his fortress. The men of Connaught are unable to overcome the Ulstermen, and Ailill remarks "What the Ulstermen have done today would make a story fit for a king. I have heard it said that there were no warriors in Ireland to equal them, but I see that the men of Connaught and Munster are merely committing treason now. Long ago the proverb said the battle cannot be won without the king there. If this battle had been fought around me, it would not have lasted long. You see I have no power over them."[32]

This passage makes the role of the Celtic king quite clear. His magical presence is required to ensure victory for his army, even though he need not fight himself and may actually be forbidden to do so. Ailill's wife can involve his people in war and he has no say in the matter, but he must attend the battle. This does not mean that all Celtic kings were quite so subordinate to their wives as Ailill. But it does show that the king's office was not an automatic passport to power. Mebdh enjoyed real supremacy, just as Guinevere did, though perhaps to a lesser extent.

Arthur, like Ailill, often gives the impression of being a puny weakling. He takes insults to himself or the queen without lifting a finger. Even when Guinevere is abducted he sits back and waits for one of his warriors to go after her. But when his companions set out on their adventures his presence is required. Sometimes he goes with them, as in *Kulhwch and Olwen*, although only as an organizer of the expedition, delegating specific tasks to those most fitted to deal with them. This picture of Arthur is much closer to a view of the old Celtic king than the later, courtly monarch who becomes increasingly inactive. The Arthur of the Round Table romances remains at court. There the heroes assemble and discuss the adventures which all take place elsewhere. When Arthur decides to send his knights on the quest for the Grail he has to stay behind to regulate the internal order of the community. Guinevere is beside him, but she is busy with her own emotional problems. She sits at the centre of the Arthurian world, weaving her own entanglements.

The whole structure of the Celtic court is like a huge chess set, a game which, incidentally, the Celts played a great deal, though possibly in a slightly different form. The Irish called it *fidchell* and the rules are taken to be common knowledge in the Irish tales. In the Welsh *Dream of Rhonabwy*, Arthur suggests that he and Owein should play chess. When Owein agrees, a red-haired servant brings the pieces, "golden men and silver board." In the Irish tale of the *Courtship of Etaine*, it is after several games of *fidchell* that the god Mider wins King Eochaid's wife, Etaine, from him and takes her off to the marvellous world of the *sidhs*. There are frequent references to magic chessboards in the romances. The hero may have to play against an invisible, fairy opponent who usually wins, much to the hero's fury. So, in *Peredur*, when the hero reached the Fortress of Marvels he found the door open and "inside he saw a chess set, and the pieces playing by themselves. The side he helped lost the game, and the other side's pieces shouted as if they were real men; this angered Peredur, so he gathered the pieces into his lap and threw the board into the lake." A black woman then appeared and reproached him for losing the Empress' chessboard, telling him to go and find it. The 14-century *Gawain and the Magic Chessboard*, which contains traces of much older traditions, has a chessboard flying in through the window of Arthur's hall. Arthur promises his kingdom to whoever will bring it to him. And Gawain goes. Among the marvels of the island of Britain is the chess set of Gwenddoleu. Once the pieces are set out, they play by themselves. The board is gold and the pieces silver.

In Peredur, the Empress values her chessboard as highly as her empire, and the same can presumably be said of Arthur in *Gawain and the Magic Chessboard*. This may be because the chessboard is a reflection of the empire, the pieces moving according to a set of rules mirrored in the way of life at the Celtic court. The knights are the active people, who leap over every obstacle to reach their goal. The bishops correspond to the Druids or *fili*. The castles stand as frontier posts; they can move because the frontiers are never really defined. The king and queen are obviously the two central figures. But there is a notable difference between them: the queen can move in virtually any direction, while the king moves one square at a time like a pawn. It is when he is surrounded that he is lost, that the game is over, for despite his limitations his presence on the board keeps his side in play, his attendance at the battle is enough. On the vast chessboard of the Arthurian world Arthur is central to the game, but it is Guinevere, the queen, who holds sovereignty and can empower her lover knights to act.

The Unfaithful Queen

Although the large majority of characters in the Arthurian epic appear to stand by basic moral values, Queen Guinevere adopts a decidedly equivocal position. The best known of her marital infidelities, with Lancelot, is only a later variation on a much older theme of flagrant adultery with several of Arthur's courtiers or with strangers, euphemistically termed abductors as if to avoid any stain on her reputation. The various Celtic traditions contain many examples of unfaithful wives apart from Guinevere, among them Iseult, Grainne, Blodeuwedd, Etaine and some less well known.

As the real sovereign Guinevere has total control and can confer a part of her sovereignty on whomever she chooses, on whichever warrior is fit to act on her behalf. It is in this way that she offers her love, and it is from this point of view that we should look at the infidelity, or rather the infidelities of the queen. Obviously she cannot confer the active role on her husband since he must stand as the stable and permanent centre of their society. It is only in the oldest writings that Arthur takes an active part in the adventures, which goes to show that he was originally a war leader rather than a king, a Celtic chief above kings. But even when Arthur is directing British resistance to the Saxons, sovereignty remains wholly Guinevere's. The traditional character who comes closest to her is Mebdh, for like Mebdh Guinevere is the royal prostitute.

In the *Chevalier à la Charrette*, there are hints of an amorous relationship between Guinevere and Kai. When Meleagant takes the queen, Kai is the first to offer to rescue her. He is, in any case, one of Arthur's two earliest followers and although the 12th-century French romances made him an unattractive braggart we can assume that there was some basis for Guinevere's name being linked with his on various occasions. The *Myvyrian Archaeology of Wales* contains a poem, incorrectly entitled "a Dialogue between Arthur and Guinevere," in which Guinevere expresses her trust in Kai as a great warrior and one capable of saving her from the clutches of Maelwas. Obviously the Kai of this poem is based more closely on the implacable Kai the Longman of *Kulhwch and Olwen*. Chrétien de Troyes, who usually remains faithful to his sources, is certainly aware of a possible relationship between Kai and the queen. In the *Chevalier à la Charrette* Kai is clearly accused of having spent the night in the queen's bed, and since he has been wounded her bloodstained sheets are taken as evidence. Although the blood stains are eventually traced back to Lancelot, Kai cannot be totally cleared of suspicion, a fact which Meleagant is only too glad to exploit against Lancelot. Lancelot, after all, was not introduced into the Arthurian cycle until quite late, and then by Chrétien de Troyes himself. It is therefore quite possible that the old sources tapped by Chrétien provided him with ancient traditions concerning Guinevere and her lovers.

The *Chevalier à la Charrette* also hints at something less than proper in the reltionship between Guinevere and Gawain. Apart from Kai and Lancelot, the only man to set off after the queen's abductor is Gawain. So, in this romance at least Gawain is in love with the queen. But a relationship between these two has wider implications in terms of the Arthurian myth.

Gawain, or Gwalchmai to give him his Celtic name, does not appear among Arthur's earliest followers. That is only to be expected, since he is the king's nephew and a member of the next generation. Arthur's two first companions, Kai and Bedwyr, are joined by Uryen, Owein, Yder, Glewlwyt Gafaelfawr, Menw the Druid and Gwrhyr Gwalstawt Ieithoed to form a body of warriors roughly the same age as the king. Their allegiance to him is strengthened by an oath, and not by the ties of blood which bind Arthur and Gwalchmai.

This does not prevent Gawain from being the most apparently active character in the Arthurian story. If there are battles to be fought, adventures to be undertaken, Gawain is sure to be there. He was almost certainly the original hero of the quest for the Grail. In Chrétien's *Perceval* the account of Gawain's adventures far outshines that of Perceval's. The sequels to *Perceval* and the Welsh *Peredur* make him the first to arrive at the Castle of Marvels, well before Peredur, who only arrives to finish the job in hand.

It is highly probable that Gawain was the ever successful heroic knight of knights at Arthur's court before the introduction of Lancelot. Most of the poems attached to the Arthurian legend are devoted to the exploits of Gawain. The fact that these adventures tend to be linked together in an apparently endless and aimless narrative chain is a function of the skilful story-teller's technique. The audience knew that the hero would win through in the end, but a series of cliff-hangers helped to keep every ear attentive. *Gawain and the Magic Chessboard* is fairly typical of such tales. It is a kind of fairy story in which Arthur's promise of his kingdom to whoever recovers the flying chessboard leads Gawain into a series of extraordinary travels. When the board disappears into the side of a mountain, Gawain follows it only to encounter a number of fearsome dragons which he kills after a terrible struggle. Once out of the mountain, he finds himself in a magnificent castle which belongs to the Marvellous King. (Here there are obvious similarities with Irish folk tales in which the hero makes his way into the world of the *sidhs*, the fairy mounds inhabited by ancient gods expelled from the earth's surface by the Gaels.) The Marvellous King promises to give Gawain the chessboard in exchange for the marvellous sword of King Amaoren. So Gawain sets off after the sword and finally manages to obtain it with the help of a fox named Roges, who turns out to be a man under a spell. Gawain brings the sword back to the Marvellous King who duly hands over the chessboard. Then Gawain returns to Arthur's court, though whether Arthur rewards him with his kingdom we are not told.[34]

Altogether, Gawain enjoys a more privileged position than Arthur's other companions. He is the son of the king's sister and therefore, according to Celtic custom, next in line to the throne. As her presumptive his relations with Guinevere are bound to be open to question. To strengthen his claims to sovereignty Absalon made public overtures to the concubines of his father David. Diane de Poitiers was mistress to both François I and Henri II. So there seems no reason why Gawain should not have been Guinevere's lover, although none of the Arthurian literature says so in so many words. If such was the case, the 12th and 13th-century romance writers would probably have tried to cover up the indelicacy of an incestuous relationship between aunt and nephew by assigning Gawain's role to Lancelot. This would certainly explain the startlingly widespread development of the romance between Lancelot and the queen.

It is clear from Celtic mythological tradition that Arthur recognized Gawain's exceptional position. When he receives Gawain at court for the first time in the *Lancelot in Prose*, he gives him his sword Escalibur to wear. This would have been a singular mark of favour and a *de facto* recognition of his nephew's right to succeed him, for Arthur was never otherwise separated from Escalibur. Moreover, when the king of Celtic tradition is deceived, as he must be in the order of things, it is often his nephew who takes his wife to bed. And this nephew must be his sister's son to accord with the ancient tradition of matrilinear affiliation in which the nephew on the sister's side had precedence over the son because succession followed the female line.

There are many examples of relationships of this kind, the best known being the story of Tristan. For Tristan is the son of King Mark's sister, whom Mark has brought up like a son with a view to Tristan's succeeding him. This sparks off a rebellion among the barons who force the king to marry so that the throne will pass to a direct descendant. Or, to put it another way, there is conflict between the supporters of matrilinear descent and the supporters of the more usual Indo-European patrilinear system. That Tristan is also the queen's lover is almost to be expected. Since Iseult represents sovereignty as Guinevere does, their relationship is an acknowledgement of Tristan's position as heir. Morality has nothing to do with it; it is a function of the Celtic social structure in which the story occurs.

In the Irish tradition the hero Cú Chulainn is King Conchobar's nephew; and although Cú Chulainn does not engage in sexual relations with any of Conchobar's wives, he is accorded special privileges not given to the other Ulster warriors. He is never officially recognized as heir to the throne, though he does act as defender of the kingdom. In the *Raid on Cualnge*, the goddess Macha has been forced to race against the king of Ulster's horses when she was about to give birth. So she lays a curse on the Ulstermen that every year they are all to be stricken by a mysterious illness resembling labour pains. Only Cu Chulainn escapes this curse, and he stands alone against the armies of the rest of Ireland, led by Queen Mebdh, until his fellow countrymen have recovered.

The legend of Finn is even closer to the story of Arthur. Finn's wife, Grainne, whom some versions call his fianceé, runs away with Diarmaid, who appears to be one of Finn's nephews. This story, which is a prototype for the Tristan legend, makes it clear that the king has an obligation to share his wife with another man because he has only a temporary claim to the sovereignty she represents.

But perhaps the closest resemblances are to be found between the story of Arthur and the legend of Math in the fourth branch of the Welsh *Mabinogion*. Math, son of Mathonwy, is king of Gwynedd in North West Wales. Strangely enough, he cannot live in peacetime unless a young virgin holds his feet in her lap, although in time of war he can rise and ride out to battle.[25] The role of the Celtic king is defined with as much precision in this tale as in Irish epic. He is a weakling, forced to remain at the centre of his kingdom, who can only leave the court under specific conditions. In fact he is trapped within a series of taboos and thereby impelled to respect an establishment which he does not rule but merely preserves for posterity.

But Math is out of the ordinary in another respect. He is one of the greatest magicians in Britain and his powers are of the ancient mythological and religious kind dating from the times of early Druidism. Math is like the early kings whose duties were both political and priestly. He is a Druid king, a shaman chief, imbued with all the traditional powers such a position entailed.

Math has a sister, Don. She does not appear in any of the Welsh tales but is generally acknowledged as the Welsh equivalent of the goddess Dana, mother of the Tuatha Dé Danann, who does not appear in any of the Irish writings either. Don's children are Arianrod (Silver Circle), a kind of goddess of the night, Amaethon, an agrarian god whose name comes from the Gallic *Ambactos* meaning labourer, Govannon, the smith god, the equivalent of the Irish Goibniu, "smith," and finally Gilvaethwy[36] and Gwyddyon. These last two appear to be Math's favourite nephews, with Gwyddyon perhaps more highly favoured. For, according to the *Triads*, Math pases on his magical knowledge to Gwyddyon as though recognizing him officially as his heir.

But then there is a bolt from the blue. Gilvaethwy falls in love with Goewin, the virgin who holds Math's feet in her lap, and he begins to waste away. So Gwyddyon works out a plan to help him. He asks Math for permission to go South to Dyfed and steal the pigs which Pryderi, king of Dyfed, has received as a gift from the king of the Other World. Math gives him leave to try. Gwyddyon and Gilvaethwy make their way into Pryderi's court by pretending that they are bards and Gwyddyon offers Pryderi various precious things which he has magicked out of plants in exchange for the pigs. Pryderi agrees to the exchange and Gwyddyon and Gilvaethwy hurry back to Gwynedd with the pigs. But when Pryderi realizes that he has been tricked he declares war on Gwynedd. And a state of war enables Math to leave Goewin and go to battle. So Gilvaethwy can then sleep with Goewin.

When Pryderi is killed and the men of Gwynedd return victorious to court, Goewin tells Math what has happened. He decides to marry her to save her good name and punishes his nephews severely by turning them into animals for three years.[37] Although both nephews are involved in the deceit, Gwyddyon as strategist and Gilvaethwy as Goewin's lover, they can almost be taken as two aspects of a single character. And this character is the sister's son, who is hoping, by raping Goewin, to set a seal on his existing claim to sovereignty through the female line. For although Goewin is not actually Math's wife, his peculiar disability being a symbol for impotence, she performs a very similar function.

One can see from this that there are various remarkable similarities between the tale of Math and the story of Arthur. Math is impotent; and apart from un-verifiable references to a son called Llacheu or Anir, Arthur appears to have no direct descendants. Certainly not through Guinevere, in any case. The *Mort du Roi Arthur* may call Mordret Arthur's son, but if so, he is the result of an in-cestuous affair between Arthur and his sister. So Arthur's sole political heir is his nephew Gawain, just as Math's heir is Gwyddyon. Like all Celtic kings, Math stands alone in the midst of his kingdom where true sovereignty is embodied in Goewin, the virgin. So when his nephew seizes power through her, Math has only his magic left to help him regain control. In the end, however, Math proves to be totally dependent on Gwyddyon, for it is he who finds a virgin to replace Goewin. Math, then, is the nominal holder of sovereignty, Gwyddyon its executor. No other Celtic legend that pre-dates the Arthurian story comes as close to the whole atmosphere we are trying to define.

Arthur's Companions

Arthur by himself is powerless. A war leader without an army behind him is just a voice crying in the wilderness. A king without the warrior elite of Britain around him is just a useless figurehead. All the different versions of the Arthur-ian legend emphasize Arthur's quality as a catalyst. Like Ailill, he need only be present at the battle to ensure victory for his forces. Obviously the sacred nature of early Celtic kingship had survived all Roman attempts to modify or destroy it. So, in order to grasp the wider mythological implications of Arthur's character, we must examine the habitual companions of his warring and adventurous life.

We can assume that Kai and Bedwyr, Arthur's two first lieutenants, were real people who rallied to him as a potential leader and who have since, like Arthur, passed into the realm of myth.

The 12th-century romances make Kai a tetchy, quarrelsome and quick-tempered braggart. This in itself would be enough to place him firmly within the Celtic tradition alongside such characters as the Irish Briciu who spends his time poisoning relationships between his contemporaries. Briciu even pays for a great feast simply to enjoy the spectacle of the Ulstermen quarrelling over who takes precedence when it comes to dishing out the choicest morsels. But the vaguely unpleasant Kai of Chrétien's works, and frankly loathsome figure in the *Lancelot in Prose* are nothing like the early character of that name. So much is clear from the Welsh poem in which he offers to defend Gwenhwyfar and another poem from the *Black Book of Carmarthen* in which Arthur sings his praises as an heroic warrior. But there is an even fuller description of this different Kai in *Kulhwch and Olwen*, a tale far more valuable for its ancient sources than is usually realized. Here Kai is not Arthur's foster brother, for whom the king might be expected to feel some affection because of their child-hood days together, but a warrior in the purest Celtic tradition with super-natural powers which place him outside any accepted category.

We are told that when he was born his father Kynyr Keinvarvawc said to his wife, "Woman, if there is anything of me in your son, his heart will always be cold; nor will there be any warmth in his hands; if he is my son, he will be stubborn; whenever he carries a burden, whether great or small, it will be visible neither from the front nor the rear; no one will brave fire and water as well as he; nor will there be any official or servant like him."[38] And later in the same tale there is a catalogue of Kai's special abilities. "He had this talent: nine days and nine nights his breath would last under water, and nine days and nine nights he could go without sleep. No doctor could cure the wound from Kai's sword. He could be as tall as the tallest tree in the forest when he pleased, while when the rain was heaviest a hand's span about what was in his hand would be dry by reason of the heat he generated; and when his companions were coldest that would be kindling for the lighting of a fire." This description would suggest that Kai is a kind of fire-god. But he has other attributes. The *Black Book of Carmarthen* says "He could drink as much as four men and fight against a hundred," and goes on "It was useless to challenge Kai in battle. His sword was never out of his hand . . . Before the kings of Emrys I saw Kai in his glory. Chief of the harrassers, he was long in anger, heavy in vengeance, terrible in his blows." There follows a list of Kai's great deeds. "The valorous Kai and Llacheu used to fight in battle even against the painful greenish boar spears. On the top of Ystavingun Kai killed nine witches. The valorous Kai went to Mona to kill lions. His shield glinted against the Cat Palu."[39] According to the *Dream of Rhonabwy* "Kai was the handsomest man in Arthur's Kingdom" and everyone rushed out to see him arrive although his skittish horse threatened to trample them underfoot. In the tale of *Owein* Arthur orders Kai to serve the mead and chops. And one of the *Triads* names him among the three diadem-wearers of Britain, together with Tristan and Hueil, although Bedwyr stands still higher.

Bedwyr and Kai are virtually inseparable. The same poem in the *Black Book* refers to the battle of Tribuit (Trywrwyd) and praises Bedwyr. "They fell by the hundred before Bedwyr on the shores of Trywrwyd . . . He was the skilful leader of a troop, for the good of the country, Bedwyr son of Bridlaw." The tale of *Kulhwch and Olwen* says that Bedwyr "never avoided any errand on which Kai went . . . and though he was one handed no three warriors on the same field could draw blood faster than he; moreover he would make one thrust with his spear and nine counter thrusts."

Apart from Kai and Bedwyr the most important of Arthur's companions is obviously Gawain, who is most fully described in the French Arthurian romances. He is out of the ordinary in one remarkable respect. "When he rose in the morning, he had the strength of a good knight; by tierce his strength had doubled, by midday quadrupled. It then returned to what it had been when he rose, and at nones it began to increase again until midnight."[40] The suggestion that this makes Gawain a solar hero, however, does not really account for the fresh increase in strength after nones. Like Kai and Bedwyr he must be imbued with magical powers.

Kulhwch and Olwen tells how Gwalchmai (Gawain) "never returned without fulfilling his errand, was moreover the best walker and rider, and was Arthur's nephew, his sister's son and his first cousin as well." The *Triads* make him one of the three inventors of Britain together with Arthur's son Llacheu. He is also one of the honey-tongued knights of Arthur's court. "They were three wise knights, so kind, friendly and eloquent in their speech that it was hard to refuse them what they wanted."[41] That is why Arthur always sends Gawain to negotiate delicate transactions. In the short Welsh *Tristan*, which belongs to a completely different tradition from the continental romances,[42] Arthur is faced with the task of reconciling Tristan and King Mark, and sends "the chief of peace, that is Gwalchmai, son of Gwyar" to see Tristan[43] Gwalchmai then chants verses designed to moderate Tristan's anger and bring him to Arthur. Tristan finally agrees to go and says "If Gwalchmai ever has a bloody task on his hands, I will do more for him than a brother would do for his brother." So Gwalchmai or Gawain is a peace-maker and an agreeable talker, a paragon of honesty and altruism. Another triad lists him among "the three men who treat their guests and strangers best."[44] All the Arthurian tales suggest that he is a lady's man, but in the most affectionate and amiable way.

The rest of Arthur's companions can be divided into two categories. First there are those who appear in the 12th and 13th-century romances and who may be pure creations of their authors. Then there are the characters found in the earlier writings, especially the Welsh tales, who tend to be completely different. Obviously there are exceptions. Yvain, or in his Welsh name, Owein, plays a fairly important part not only in Chrétien's *Chevalier au Lion*, but also in the episodic romances, where he is often included amongst Arthur's oldest companions. Owein, son of Uryen, was a real person, a Northern Briton who lived in the second half of the 6th century and was praised by the bard Taliesin as a great hero. In legend he is always made out to be the chieftain of a northern clan, but the *Dream of Rhonabwy* also gives him a flock of ravens to fight for him. The end of the tale of *Owein* tells how Owein stayed in Arthur's court as his steward until he returned "to his own land, with the 300 swords of Kynverchin (the tribe of his grandfather), and his flight of ravens, and they were victorious wherever they went." The ravens can be explained as a flock of bird-women of the kind common in folk stories. Owein's mother is supposed to have been the goddess Matrona, or Modron, whom Thomas Malory identifies with Morgan; and Modron could turn herself into a bird. This added attribute gave Owein considerable importance in the Arthurian tales. He became a sort of demigod who enjoyed the company of beings from the Other World. His father Uryen, also a historical character, remains comparatively insignificant except in the *Morte d'Arthur*. He does, though, appear in the *Quest for the Grail* under the name Urbain.

Most of the characters who appear in the *Lancelot in Prose* are recent additions to the legend. Perceval is the only one of any significance. He is the Welsh Peredur who appears very early in the Arthurian cycle in the tale which bears his name. This is quite unlike Chrétien's unfinished romance *Perceval*, its sequels or Wolfram von Eschenbach's version. He, too, was probably a historical person. And although the French romances call him Perceval the Welshman, his name "son of Evrawc" suggests that he originally came from Yorkshire, Evrawc being the British name for York.

Altogether, it is the Welsh *Triads* and the tale of *Kulhwch and Olwen* which provide most information about those of Arthur's companions who pre-dated the courtly versions of the story. These two Welsh texts contain most references to those ancestral traditions which dated back to the times of the Druids and of shamanistic magic. Edern, or Yder, is the "killer of the bear" and the "killer of giants," and has superhuman strength. His brother Gwynn has all the characteristics of a god of the Other World, like his father Nudd, or Nuada, the *deo Nodenti* of British inscriptions. Gwyn himself is supposed to be one of the guardians of hell.[45] His name means white, handsome or thoroughbred. Yder plays a fairly special part in the Arthurian tales. In Chrétien's *Érec et Énide*, as in the Welsh *Gereint*, it is he who insults the queen and is pursued by Érec or Gereint who wounds him in single combat and forces him to make amends. Gereint may also have actually existed as a 7th-century count of Cornwall whose reputation was such that he soon became incorporated into Arthurian legend.

Arthur has a guide called Kynddelic who "was no worse guide in a country he had never seen than in his own." He has an interpreter called Gwrhyr Gawlstawt Ieithoedd who "knew every tongue, including the language of animals." In *Kulhwch and Olwen*, he goes to talk with the boar Twrch Trwyth, with a blackbird, a stag, an owl, an eagle and even with a salmon. Gwrhyr is also a magician and can change his shape. He goes to talk to the boar as a bird. In this, he is very much like the shaman Druids who claimed the same kinds of supernatural powers.

There is another magician in Arthur's entourage called Menw, son of Teirgwaedd. "If they came to a pagan land, Menw could cast a spell through which they could see everyone and no one could see them." He could also render wild beasts harmless. His name means "intelligence," and according to the *Triads*, his magic is among the three greatest in Britain, alongside the magic of Math. One of the triads also lists him among the three men of magic and metamorphosis, again with Math. He is also a reincarnation of the old shaman Druid, so many of whom appear in Irish epic. The early Arthur was obviously more closely surrounded by the heirs of Celtic paganism than by men of the Church, although he did have a chaplain and bishop in Bedwini.

The remaining companions are less important, though they are all exceptional in one respect or another. Glewlwyt Gafaelfawr, Arthur's gatekeeper, was so tall and so strong that everyone fled at the sight of him. That is why he was one of the few to survive the battle of Camlaan. Another of the survivors of Camlaan was Morvran, son of Tegid and the goddess Keridwen. The tale of *Kulhwch and Olwen* tells how "No one struck him at Camlaan — because of his ugliness everyone thought he was a devil helping, for there was hair on his face like the hair of a stag." The legend of Taliesin mentions Morvran, but transfers his ugliness to his brother Afang Du (the Black Beaver) for whom Keridwen boils up the cauldron of knowledge and inspiration.[46] A third survivor of Camlaan, and another of Arthur's companions, is Sanddev Bryd Angel (with the face of a angel). He escaped because of his beauty. Everyone thought he was an angel helping.

Henbeddestyr, who name means "old footsoldier" never found a man who could keep up with him either on horseback or on foot. Henwas Adeinawc (Old Winged Servant), who participates in the battle of Trywrwyd in poem XXXI of the *Black Book of Carmarthen*, is so fast that no four-footed creature could stay with him, even for an acre, let alone anything more. "When the desire to undertake an errand for his lord came upon Sgitli Ysgawndroet (Lightfoot) he never took the road so long as he knew his way, but if there was a forest he travelled along the tree tops, and if there was a mountain he travelled on the tips of the reeds, and never did a reed bend, much less break, so light of foot was he." Tiethi Hen, the son of Gwynhan, whose lands had been submerged under the sea, also came to join Arthur.[47] "No hilt would remain attached to the blade of his knife, and for that reason he grew sick and feeble while he lived, and then he died." And then there is the knife of Osla Gyllellfawr, Osla Bigknife, who appears to have been one of Arthur's warriors for a while and then left him to become his enemy. He carried "Bronllavyn Short Broad; when Arthur and his troops came to a cresting flood. they would find a narrow spot; the knife in its sheath would be laid across the flood and that would be bridge enough for the three armies of the island of Britain and the three offshore islands with all their plunder."

The list of Arthur's companions in *Kulhwch and Olwen* is interminable. Here are a few more of them: "Sol and Gwadyn Osol and Gwadyn Oddeith (Sol could stand all day on one foot; if Gwadyn Osol stood on the highest mountain in the world, it would become a level plain under his feet; like a warm mace drawn from the forge were the bright sparks from Gwadyn Oddeith's soles when he struck something hard, and he cleared the way for Arthur in battle) . . . Sugyn son of Sugynedydd (who could suck up a sea on which there were three hundred ships until it was nothing but a dry strand; he had a red heart hidden within him) ... Klust son of Klustveinat [Ear son of Fine Ear], were he buried seven fathoms in the earth he would hear an ant stirring from its bed in the morning fifty miles away ... Gwiawn Llygat Cath [Catseye], who could cut a corner from a gnat's eye without harming the eye." Mabon son of Modron and Lleenleawg the Gael might seem less remarkable were it not for the fact that Mabon was the god Maponos of the Gauls, and that Llenleawg was supposed to have brought back Arthur's sword Kaletfoulch from an expedition to the Other World.

We can see from these amazing companions that the original story of Arthur had become a mythological legend full of the ancient gods of Celtic Druidism and of beliefs which had lasted over the centuries in the oral tradition and can still be traced in Celtic countries today. From a simple tribal chieftain, Arthur grew into the supreme god of a heteroclitic pantheon, a strange and mysterious god whose adventures have continued to stir the imaginations of men.

Similar Legends

The Arthurian epic is not an isolated phenomenon in Celtic traditions. There are other legends of Irish as well as British origin, which are very similar in content and meaning. This does not necessarily mean that the Arthurian epic was based on existing Celtic models, only that it closely resembles various mythical threads which can be followed throughout the Celtic area in the different forms which time and place gave to them. In this sense the story of Arthur stands as the post-imperial, Dark Ages version of the myth.

One of the most obvious comparisons to be made is with the *Courtship of Etaine*, a strange Gaelic legend in three different but interconnected parts. These sections are linked by the common theme of a lover from the Other World kidnapping the king's wife. Etaine is the daughter of the king of Ireland. The god Mider (probably the *deo Medru* of an inscription in the Vosges), who is lord of the mound of Bri Leith, falls in love with the girl. His foster son Oengus helps Mider win Etaine, but Mider's first wife, Fuamnach, turns into a butterfly which is absorbed by a king's wife to reappear as another girl, also called Etaine. This second Etaine then marries the high king Eochaid Aireainn. During the night the shadow of Mider comes to remind her that she was once his wife, and to sing the praises of the Other World. But Etaine will not go with Mider unless he wins her from her present husband. So Mider goes to King Eochaid and plays chess with him for Etaine. He loses and is forced to accomplish various herculean tasks for the king as his side of the bargain. They play again, but this time Mider declares that the stakes are to remain secret, and that whoever wins will be entitled to ask whatever occurs to him at the time. Mider wins and demands the king's wife. Eochaid asks for a delay and Mider agrees. But on the appointed day Eochaid closes his fortress and deploys armed guards about the place. Mider makes his way into the hall where Eochaid and Etaine are sitting with a number of warriors. When Mider asks Etaine if he has won her from her husband fairly, she replies "yes"; whereupon Mider takes her in his arms and both of them turn into swans and fly out through a hole in the roof. Eochaid tries to catch them, but fails.[48]

There is no denying the similarity between this story and the abduction of Guinevere by Meleagant. Meleagant's City of Gorre, whence no one returns, makes him like Mider a god of the Other World; and both are connected with a human queen in some mysterious way. Mider can lay claim to total possession of Etaine because he was her first husband. Meleagant lays claim to Guinevere because she represents the sovereignty of Britain. But both are motivated by the hope of achieving power. The fact that the Arthurian version of the story is repeated in the sculpture on Modena Cathedral, in the *Vita Gildae* and in the *Chevalier à la Charrette* suggests that there was a common myth relating to the abduction of the queen. What none of these three accounts tells us, however, is whether Guinevere was a willing victim. Her acknowledged infidelity with Lancelot in the later romances suggests that she may well have been capable of falling in with Meleagant's plans, though there is no proof of this. Nor is there any evidence that she actually sided with Mordret in the far more serious episode which sparked off the battle of Camlaan. Geoffrey of Monmouth hints that she did, if only for a while. But in the *Mort du Roi Arthur*, she shuts herself in a tower to escape him; and in the *Triads* Medrawt takes her by force after he has sacked the fortress of Kelliwic. Altogether, Guinevere's attitude to her suitors remains ill-defined; but if we are to compare her with Etaine and Mebdh, we can only assume that she was partly responsible for all her amorous adventures.

There are many other Irish tales which have something in common with the story of Arthur. But it is the great epic of Finn and the Fiana which resembles Arthurian legend most closely. The Fiana were a warrior band of a special kind, who actually existed at the time of the High King Cormac mac Airt, towards the end of the 2nd century. They were drawn from specific clans and acted as a kind of itinerant police force throughout Ireland, supervising the application of justice and the security of the Irish ports. They had no particular home, but would spend the winter among the local inhabitants of whichever area they happened to be in at the time, and the summer hunting in the great forests of central Ireland. As well as keeping the countryside free of brigands, they were also often employed by tribal, or even provincial kings as mercenaries. In peacetime they would work as tax collectors for a percentage of what they levied. In short, the Fiana formed an independent militia, ruled by Finn mac Cumail, who bore the title of king but was actually a kind of war leader like Arthur.

It is in this respect that a comparison between Arthur's men and the Fiana proves interesting. For, like Arthur and his companions, Finn and his horseman could use their independence to take advantage of any internal conflict by siding with one force or another, but also to levy taxes on their own account and generally act outside the law. Because of this the various provincial kings soon began to take exception to what they saw as a state within a state, and to regard the Fiana as a potentially dangerous force which threatened to disrupt the constitutional establishment.

Both Arthur and Finn also suffered from dissension within their own ranks. The stories about Medrawt and Hueil and about the war Arthur is supposed to have waged against Osla Bigknife are all evidence of strife within his warrior band. Finn had similar problems, for although he theoretically led the whole Fiana, he was in fact only chief of the clan O'Baicsne, which had an age-old quarrel with the clan Morna, also members of the Fiana. Their rivalry became more intense after the battle of Cnucha, where Finn's father Cumall was killed and the chief of the clan Morna, Aed son of Daire the Red lost an eye to become known as Goll, the one-eyed man.[49] It was a long time before the two clans became reconciled and Finn and Goll were prepared to work together again. The fact that one of Finn's important warriors is one-eyed like Arthur's lieutenant Bedwyr adds weight to the hypothesis that there is a single mythical story underlying the Irish and the Arthurian epics, and that this story concerns the three great Indo-European gods known in Teutonic mythology as Odin, Tyr and Thor.

There can be no question but that the warrior militia of the Fiana and Arthur's band of knights are identical in form and function. The knights of the Round Table did not spring directly from the concept of chivalry, but from an independent, free-wheeling warrior society like the Fiana. The medieval images of the Round Table romances, the Christian overlay and the propaganda for feudalism cloud the Arthurian story so thoroughly that it is difficult to grasp the fact that such a society actually existed. Indeed, the Fiana form a group unlike almost any other in Western history or mythology. But they do help us to view the Arthurian phenomenon within a purely Celtic context. Even though Christian writers reworked the Irish tradition, the early Fiana legends are entirely pagan in spirit, and contain traces of traditions long forgotten in Britain where contact with the continent and with Rome had pushed ancient beliefs into the background. If we are to compare the epic of the Fiana with the epic of Arthur we must find those points in common between the two which do most to bring out the authentically Celtic nature of the Arthurian story.

The episode in the Fiana cycle which appears to have most in common with Arthurian epic is the tale of *Diarmaid and Grainne.* Finn's young wife elopes with Diarmaid under a particular set of circumstances which make their affair very like the legend of Tristan and Iseult. Old Finn pursues the lovers, and after many adventures manages to recover Granne and kill Diarmaid, whom Finn regards as the guilty party although Grainne had in fact forced Diarmaid to go with her by means of a *geis.*

But there are other episodes in the Irish cycle which are strikingly similar. First there is the Boar Hunt. The *Triads, Kulhwch and Olwen*, the *Mirabilia* and Nennius' *Historia Brittonum* all refer to Arthur's pursuit of a fantastic boar. Nennius says:

> There was another marvel in the region called Buelt, a heap of stones. And one stone on the top bore the imprint of a dog's paw. When he came to hunt the pig Troynt, Cabal, who was Arthur's dog, left his paw print on the stone . . .

Compare that with this passage from the *Triads:*

> One of Koll's sows named Henwen ["the Old White"] was with young, and it had been predicted that Britain would suffer from her litter. So Arthur assembled the British army and set out to destroy her. The sow went to earth in Kernyw at Penryn Awstin and there threw herself into the sea with the great swineherd behind her. At Maes Gwenith in Gwent, she gave birth to a grain of wheat and a bee. From that day to this there has been no better land for wheat and bees than Maes Gwenith ["Field of Wheat"]. At Llonyon in Penvro [Pembroke] she gave birth to a grain of barley and a grain of wheat. The barley of Llonyon has become proverbial. At Riw-Gyverthwch, in Arvon, she gave birth to a baby wolf and a baby eagle. The wolf was given to Menwaed and the eagle to Breat, prince of the North. They would live to regret it. At Llanveir in Arvon, under Maen Du ["The Black Rock"] she bore a cat which the swineherd threw from the rocks into the sea. The children of Palu in Mona looked after it, to their sorrow. This was the Cat Palu of the three scourges of Mona . . . .[50]

There are two similar boar hunts in *Kulhwch and Olwen*. In the first Arthur is looking for the boar Iskithyrwynn Pennbeidd with his dog Kavall. But although it had been predicted that two dogs belonging to Glythwyr Lledewic would kill the boar, it was Kavall which finally did so.

The second boar hunt in *Kulhwch and Olwen* concerns Twrch Trwyth, Nennius' *porcus Troynt*. The hunt takes the form of a series of episodes apparently culled from different sources but linked by the ultimate goal of obtaining three marvellous objects which lie between the boar's ears. The boar itself is presumably a fairy being, or possibly, considering the havoc it wreaks, a devil of some kind.

The hunt is obviously a symbol for the struggle against all kinds of destructive monsters which Arthur must destroy because they threaten the proper working of society. Like Finn, Arthur is a righter of wrongs, a dragon killer in both the literal and the metaphorical senses. Both men function in a very similar way to the sheriff of the American Western, who is elected by his fellow citizens to uphold the law amongst men who find it difficult to accept. And because he is given such power over other men's lives, he runs the risk of paying for his position with his own.

The legend of Finn is also full of monster-hunting, chiefly after the boar. In *The Childhood of Finn*, the young hero goes to stay with Lochan the smith. whose daughter he has married under a kind of short-term contract. Lochan makes Finn two magical spears. And when Finn decides to leave to follow his wandering course in life, the smith says "My son, do not follow the road of the sow called Beo." This sow had devastated the whole of central Munster and the warning was justified. "But, of course, Finn found himself on Beo's road and when the sow charged him he threw his spear at her, and it pierced and killed her. Finn took the sow's head and brought it back to the smith as a wedding present for his daughter."[51] This apparently simple act is proof that Finn is destined to accomplish deeds of great brilliance, to rid the land of scourges of all kinds. The fact that his spear has been made by a smith from the Other World makes his mission divine.

In the *Hunt from the Sidh of Beautiful Women*, the clan O'Baiscne, the clan Morna and all the other clans that go to make up the Fiana assemble to go on a great hunt. While out in the field they come across a grave and one of the Fiana asks Finn who is buried there. Finn replies "That is the grave of Failbe Findmaesech, the brave chief and *fian* of my house, who was killed here by a pig, the giant boar of Formael seven years ago to this day. And the boar killed fifty of my dogs and fifty of my warriors as well that day."[51] And Finn began to improvise a funeral chant in praise of Failbe.

> They found death behind the defences
> of the wide-backed savage pig
> He slew both dogs and men
> the giant boar of Formael.
> The man who came loyally to the fight
> found the black pig with its forbidding shape.
> It threw both dogs and men to the ground,
> in a battle that scarred the land.
> He was dear to me, Failbe the Red,
> on the day when he slaughtered the strangers.
> The man who lies in the grave
> Could fight against pain and warriors.[52]

Finn then decides that they should all go after the boar the next morning. The description of what follows is one of the most beautiful passages in the Irish epic tradition.

> They rose to hunt the pig we have told of, the boar of Formael. Each *fian* warrior of Ireland positioned himself, ready to fire, waiting in the breach of danger to attack the pig. They loosed the bounding dogs with their pleasant baying and agile feet to speed across woods and forests, deserts and sloping valleys, and they made traps in the clearings and plains of the land. They startled the warlike boar from its lair and dogs, hounds and warriors all saw it. The sight of this huge boar was enough to strike terror in the heart. It was dark blue, covered in bristles, rough, horrible, earless, tailless. It had no testicles, but long fearsome tusks which jutted out of its massive head. Then dogs and warriors charged from all sides, like a whirlwind and surrounded it. The watchful beast with its red mouth made a great massacre of dogs and Fiana on the field.[53]

Whatever the Fiana do, the terrible beast floors them with its snout. And Finn has to lament the death of some of his bravest warriors. His son Oisin, his grandson Oscar and his adopted son Cailte are all there.

> When the valiant and warlike Oscar saw the warriors, dogs and men who had fallen under the pig's blows lying on the ground, a great surge of anger, and a turbulent and terrifying storm rose in the heart of the great warrior at the sight of the way the wild and fierce boar had crushed dogs, men and the great chiefs of the Fiana. And the royal warrior Oscar thought it right and honourable that he alone should avenge the evil done. Great had been the fear and dread of the armies, and great were the horror and terror of Oscar. Yet once he had seen it, he had no choice. As he approached, he carved out a passage towards the red-mouthed beast which resembled nothing so much as a snarling bear, a spectre of destruction and a heap of carnage and ruin. Like the spray from a great waterfall was each blood-red and saffron-yellow fleck of foam which came from its mouth and its jaws, biting and rough as it gnashed its teeth against the great warrior. The mane on its back bristled so that a great wild apple could have stuck on each of its rough, bristly hairs.[54] Oscar brandished his spear, hurled it straight at the pig and struck it. The spear looked as though it had pierced the animal's chest, but bounced back as though it had struck rock or horn. Oscar strode towards the beast and struck it so furiously with his sword that the weapon broke on the pig's shoulder. The boar made to attack Oscar, and he broke his shield on it and seized it by its bristling mane. The pig rose on its huge hind legs to tear at the royal warrior from above. Oscar stretched his hands over the boar and pulled the mane sharply and fiercely, so that the animal fell to the ground. Then he placed his knee on its back and gripped its mouth and jaws from behind so that the Fiana warriors could disembowel it. So the huge beast fell under Oscar's blows and the battle was done.[55]

This epic struggle against the boar is tinged with memories of totemism. The boar represents a monstrous enemy race, against which the members of the Fiana clans are fighting. Finn's clan is under the sign of the stag. In fact his real name Demne means "Buck" or "Stag." When he marries Oisin's mother, she is running from the maleficient Black Druid who turns her into a hind. And it is as a hind that she gives birth to Oisin, whose name means "Fawn." Oscar's name is equally significant: it means "The Man who Loves Deer." So it is possible that these struggles against diabolical boars are in some sense recapturing the period when the aboriginal tribes took animal names. This idea is particularly relevant to our present study, since the legend of Arthur, like the legend of Math, appears to be linked with the sign of the bear.

There is another famous boar in the Finn cycle, the boar of Ben Culbain. This boar was inextricably linked with Diarmaid, Grainne's lover. Diarmaid had been brought up by Oengus in the land of the Fairies and was foster brother to the son of Oengus' seneschal. On a visit to see him, Diarmaid's father had accidentally killed the boy and had been forced to pay compensation. Finn pronounced judgement and the seneschal turned his dead son into a boar and said "I place you under a magic spell, so that you lead Diarmaid to his death. And your own life will last no longer than this." Since that time Diarmaid had been unable to hunt boar. So when Diarmaid ran away with Grainne and Finn resolved to kill him, he placed him in a position where he had no choice but to transgress a series of *geisa* or taboos culminating in a hunt for the boar of Ben Culbain.

> The grandson of Duibhne with the red colours, was forced by Finn (alas for his treachery) to go to Ben Culbain and hunt the boar which no weapon could kill. The beast woke from its sleep to look down the valley where it could see the Fiana coming towards it from West and East. The wild boar of the *sidhs* was angry at this sight. Its tusk was longer than a spear and sharper than the Gai Bolg [the spear of the Tuatha Dé Danann]. Diarmaid, son of O'Duibhne, threw his spear at the boar and hit it, but the weapon broke against a tree. Then he drew his old sword from its scabbard and the beast died at Diarmaid's hands.[56]

But Finn then made Diarmaid measure the dead boar and the young man was pricked by the animal's poisoned bristles. Finn could have saved him by bringing him water to drink in his own hands, since this unfailing method of cure was one of Finn's special gifts. But he prevaricated, Diarmaid died and Finn's vengeance was complete. Finn had also rid the country of the wild, destructive boar. But the other Fiana reproached him fiercely for his duplicity. Like Arthur, Finn appears cruel and unjust, unscrupulous and self-interested, despite his leading role in the epics.

Apart from the story of Diarmaid and Grainne, there is Finn's adventure with Oisin's mother to be considered. One day Finn and some of the Fiana were out hunting when they saw a hind and decided to give chase. But the Fiana could not keep up with it, and finally only Finn and his two dogs "which had minds like men" were left in pursuit. The hind lay down in the grass and the dogs, instead of attacking it, started playing with it. Finn took the hind back to his fortress and that night he was amazed to find it turned into a beautiful girl. She told him that her name was Sadv and that the Black Druid had bewitched her because she rebuffed him. But the spells do not work inside Finn's fortress. So Finn marries Sadv and before long she becomes pregnant. When Finn is obliged to go away, however, the Black Druid disguises himself as Finn and stands outside the fortress calling to Sadv. She assumes he is her husband and comes out, only to fall under the spell again. Although she tries desperately to get back inside the fortress, the Druid's two dogs prevent her and she is forced to roam the woods as a hind. Although Finn, his men and his best dogs search all over Ireland they cannot find any trace of her until one day Finn's two dogs find a small boy alone in the undergrowth and appear to know him. Finn is amazed at the resemblance between the child and his unfortunate wife. So he takes the child and brings him up. When the boy can talk, he tells Finn how he was looked after by a hind in the woods', but that the hind was taken by a black man who touched her with his hand. Finn realises that the hind was Sadv and that the Black Druid has taken her for ever. He solemnly recognizes the boy as his son and gives him the name Oisin.[57]

This legend about Finn, Sadv and the Black Druid, Fir Doirche, bears a profound resemblance to the oldest Arthurian legend in which Arthur himself pursues his wife's kidnapper into the Other World. For the Black Druid's spell places Sadv firmly in the Other World, just as the spell changing Guinevere into the ugly hag Arthur first meets makes her more than an ordinary mortal. All spells of this kind are remarkably effective, whether they are applied to the characters of Irish epic or folk tales in general. They date back to the religious beliefs held at the time of the Druids and can still be observed in the various forms of shamanism practised today.

The Black Druid is just like Mider, Maelwas or Meleagant. Guinevere, under whatever name she may appear, comes from the Other World to marry the man worthy to assume the responsibilities of sovereignty. Just as the mare-goddess Rhiannon prowls round the mound of Aberth until King Pwyll follows her and asks her to marry him, so Guinevere ensures that Arthur will meet her and succeed in the initial trial of replying to the riddle. He has then to pay for her help by undergoing another trial which, for a warrior like himself, may be even more difficult. For he has to marry a woman who appears hideously ugly. But he does not hesitate to pay the price, and Guinevere, having found a man worthy to bring new life to her flagging powers of sovereignty, becomes the beautiful young woman she once was.

But the god from the Other World, the figure of the Black Druid, continues his watch from outside, waiting till the woman who still belongs to him and his world ventures out of the shelter of the fortress. Then he can reassert his rights over her, put her back under his spell or take her to his own fortress, the city of Mardoc, the kingdom of Gorre or the Citadel of Glass which only the "seers" or Druids can find in the many clearings of the Celtic forest.

A comparison of the adventures of Finn and the adventures of Arthur explains a great deal. We can see the origins of Guinevere's fairy-like quality, which she lost in the 12th and 13th-century romances but regained in some of the later romances like *Yder*, the *Marvels of Rigomer* and the *Wedding of Gawain*, which are older in spirit. Then there are her abduction by a god from the Other World, her sovereignty and her infidelities. The abduction of the queen, whether or not she consents to it, is like the theft of the flame from a primitive society unable to make fire artificially. The Roman vestals who guarded the power and sovereignty of the city in the shape of the sacred flame were, like Rhiannon, Macha and Sadv, the defenders of that fire so essential to the survival of the primitive tribe. And all these women are linked with the sun and the sun-goddess of the ancient Indo-Europeans, whom the Greeks knew as the Scythian Diana.

So we can briefly summarize the links between Finn and Arthur as follows: both marry fairy queens who represent their own supremacy, and whom they must therefore keep with them even if it means turning a blind eye to their infidelities or pursuing their abductors. Both are also hunters of supernatural monsters which are threatening the internal stability of their kingdoms. The power invested in them by their union with their fairy wives makes them the only warriors qualified to combat these menacing creatures from the Other World. They have become divine huntsmen. Finally neither Finn nor Arthur is a tribal king, but the chief of a warrior force active outside the narrow framework of the conventional kingdom. They are both war leaders, prepared to fight for their own glory or profit, or to hire out their services to tribal kings, They are both above kings, and consequently above the laws which govern the various peoples they lead into battle. So Arthur is given the title emperor and Finn the title king of the Fiana of Ireland, though neither rules over a specific area or tribe. And then there are Arthur's knights, a troop of experienced horsemen, who, like the warrior militia of the Fiana, can travel the length and breadth of the land. The legend of Finn runs along exactly the same lines as the legend of Arthur and enables us to explain it in a simple and rational way.

Arthur the God

The epic tale of Math son of Mathonwy, as he appears in the fourth branch of the Welsh *Mabinogion* also has much in common with the Arthurian story. The two epics developed side by side, from the same original myth. Each had its own central figure to match the history of the areas in which it was originally created. For just as Arthur is the hero of South West Britain and the land of Gwent, where the Silures once lived, so Math is the hero of Gwynedd, in North West Wales, the home of the Ordovices. The major difference between the two is that Math's authority extends only to the frontiers of Gwynedd, while Arthur's sphere of influence embraces virtually the whole of non-Saxon Britain.

From the legend of Math outlined earlier in this chapter, it will have become clear that Math is an impotent king, not only in the sexual sense like the Fisher King, but also politically speaking, like Ailill. In this respect it is surely right to regard these legends not as mere products of a fertile imagination, but as carefully thought out expositions of the libertarian Celtic temperament. But although the story of Math can be likened to the story of Arthur in some respects, the way sovereignty is embodied in Goewin and Guinevere for example, it is a comparison of the two central characters themselves which reveals the greatest surprises, especially when we look at their names.

Math is the son of Mathonwy, the term *math* being repeated in both names. This kind of repetition is common in the Welsh tradition, however, and it is the name Mathonwy on its own which we shall examine. According to Zimmer it corresponds to the Gaelic *Mathgamnai*, and d'Arbois de Jubainville notes that in the Irish Bible the Hebrew word *dob*, which means "bear," is rendered by the Gaelic *mathghamhuin*, literally "bear cub."[58] There was also a Gallic name *Mathugenos*, meaning "son of a bear."[59] The Gaelic word *Mathghamhuin* appears in Welsh as *Mathgamhain* as in the historical character Raghnall son of Mathgamhain, father of Gruffydd ab Cynan's foster brother, and this in turn becomes *Mathgawyn* in other documents.[60] There are obvious connexions between these various forms of the name and Mathonwy.

Then, when we look at the name Math, we find that in the poems of Taliesin he bears the nickname *Hen*, "old." W. J. Gruffydd thinks that the form *Math*

Hen came from a scribe's misreading of Mathon or Mathonwy minus the last syllable. The name Mathon belongs to a historical figure who took part in the battle of Bron yr Erw in 1075.[61] But Mathon would then be just a corruption of Mathgamhain, and in this way Math and Mathonwy become repetitions of the same name.

In Gallic the name Matugenos is formed in the same way as Artogenos, and both mean "son of the bear."[62] So, in ancient Celtic there were two words meaning bear, *matu* and *arto*, just as there were two words meaning horse, *marca* (whence the Welsh *march*) and *epo* (from an Indo-European **ekwo* which became the Latin *equus*) as in the name Eporedorix. In Welsh and modern Breton the word for bear is *arth* and *arz*, and the famous goddess with a bear in the museum of Berne, a divinity worshipped in Gallo-Roman times, is called Artio.

So Math and Arthur have something very basic in common: the name of the bear. How Arthur developed from *arth* or *Arto* may be more difficult to determine, but it must be more than coincidence. Many Celtic heroes have animal names, and as we have said, the idea that Arthur came from a Latin *Artorius* is unsatisfactory, to say the least. Then there is the passage in Gildas' work, on which Geoffrey Ashe comments in his book *From Caesar to Arthur*. Ashe notes that Gildas mentions the victory at Mount Badon without saying who led the Britons there, then adds, "His only other Arthurian allusion (or so it has been held to be) is quite incidental. When denouncing Cuneglassus, a degenerate kinglet of the 540's, he recalls that Cuneglassus was once the charioteer of a person nicknamed The Bear. Nothing is said about The Bear, but if his charioteer was of royal blood he must have been a distinguished figure, and he would seem to have flourished at the same time as Arthur. The ground for the identification is that the Celtic word for 'bear' was *arth*."

So, if Geoffrey Ashe is right, it would appear that Arthur is a nickname derived from *arth*, the bear. The theory that it comes from the Latin name *Artorius* suggests that it was a family name, but the Celtic chiefs do not appear to have used family names, rather their names followed by the word *ab* (or *mac* in Gaelic) and their father's name, as in ab Untel, son of Untel. And all Irish and Welsh genealogies follow this system of nomenclature. On the other hand, many of the first names used refer to animals in some way. Cu Chulainn means "dog of Culainn," Conchobar "Powerful Dog," like the Breton name Konomor, Finn's other name Demne means "stag," Oisin "Fawn" and Oscar "The Man who loves Deer." Art, meaning "Bear," is son of Conn, meaning "Dog." Bran means "Crow," March "Horse," Morvran "Sea Crow," Gwalchmai "Falcon of May." Math, also meaning "Bear," is son of Mathonwy, meaning "Bear Cub," and there are many others besides. Arthur must surely be a first name of this type. Nennius describes him as *mab uter, id est filius horribilis*, suggesting that he must have been a rather ugly, and certainly a violent figure. It was probably a misreading of the words *mab uter* which later gave rise to Geoffrey of Monmouth's statement that Arthur was the son of Uther Pendragon.

Obviously Arthur could be traced back to other, equally convincing etymological sources. The name *Arcturus*, for example, seems a more likely Latin candidate than *Artorius*, if it is a Latin root we are after. But in view of the fact that Arcturus derives from Arctus, the name for the Great Bear and the Little Bear, this merely brings us back to Arth, the bear. Arcturus might also, of course, be an adjective meaning "which reduces" or "the rigorous," which would suit the character perfectly.

Then there is the Indo-European root word *ar*, which means to work the land. This would make Arthur a kind of agricultural divinity, rather like the Roman Saturn, the god of the Golden Age. But although his position as guarantor of communal prosperity makes him the organizer of agriculture in one sense, Arthur's nomadic life and his adventures in the chase would seem to make him more of a divine huntsman. It would be more to the point to link Arthur with an old Sanskrit word which gave rise to *Arta* in Iranian, and which means "order." Arthur does defend the social order from the forces of chaos.

But in the last analysis, the argument that Arthur means "bear" still seems the strongest. Gildas' allusion to the eminent person nicknamed The Bear may be interpreted in various ways, but there is no reason why Geoffrey Ashe should not be right. The popular belief that Arthur is not dead but asleep and waiting for the right moment to return may well have been linked with the hibernating habits of the bear.

And of course there are the connexions between Arthur and Math, which cover more than just their names. Both have a nephew who is heir to the throne and who abducts their women. Arthur may not be a magician in quite the same way as Math, but there is a fairy-tale quality about him. He has a magic sword, Kaledfwlch, and a magic shield, Prytwen, which he can also use as a boat. Wherever he has walked the grass will not grow again for seven years. He defeats all his enemies and can only be overcome by treachery, like all the heroes and gods of ancient epic. And he has a magic cloak: "Gwenn [white] was the name of the cloak. One of its qualities was that the man who wore it could see everybody without himself being seen; he became the same colour as the cloak."[64]

The supernatural plays an important part throughout the Celtic tradition and makes its presence felt in all the Arthurian tales. But it is not just a matter of whimsical, fey creatures, rather a desanctified, popular form of ancient religion. The Celtic heroes, like the heroes of Teutonic mythology, are so closely bound up with the divine that it is impossible to tell which of them are gods made men and which men made divine. Just as Roland became transformed from a minor officer in Charlemagne's army into a kind of demigod, so Arthur and some of his companions, whose actual existence appears as real as Roland's, have passed from history into myth. Indeed the Celts had an even greater sense of myth than the Franks who celebrated Roland. They acted out their history through myth, made it reflect their subconscious or acknowledged longings in ideal kingdoms like Arthur's.

The Round Table is a later materialization of the Celtic dream. It does not appear before the 13th century and we can be sure that if a Round Table legend had existed before, then Geoffrey of Monmouth, at least, would have exploited it. Despite the symbolic meanings it later acquired, the Round Table was actually a conscious intellectual development of something very basic to the Celtic way of life in the Dark Ages. For the chief and his men would meet, sleep, warm themselves and eat round the central fire in the chief's hall. They sat or lay in a circle so that everybody could benefit from the heat.

Even the Perilous Seat can be explained in terms of a custom frequently described by the authors of classical antiquity and of Irish epic. For whenever warriors met in the chief's hall, whether for the great religious festivals or to discuss the business of the community, they would hold a kind of competition to determine which was the greatest hero present. The man claiming this title would ask for "the piece of the hero," that is the choicest cut of meat. If all those present agreed, the warrior in question was free to enjoy both his glory and his food in peace. But usually the other warriors put in counter-claims on their own behalf, and merciless battles of the kind described so vividly in the *Feast of Briciu*[65] would ensue. The Perilous Seat, then, is simply that place reserved for the greatest hero, or the man claiming the "piece of the hero," The idea that any unworthy occupant of the seat might be swallowed up by the ground is perhaps a euphemism for the death which might be awaiting him in combat with the other contenders for the title. The Christian mysticism later injected into the Perilous Seat was, like the transformation of *Peredur* from a simple story of vengeance into a Quest for the Holy Chalice, the product of the 13th-century clerical authors who altered any suitable mythical idea to suit their own religious ethic.

So Arthur changed from the war leader he became during his lifetime into a god who ruled over other gods and married a fairy queen very like the ancient sovereign sun-goddess. The trio formed by Arthur, Kai and Bedwyr also give cause for thought. Although Bedwyr, as Bedivere, has a minor role in the later romances, Kai follows his master faithfully throughout Arthurian literature; and both of them make a very early entrance into the legend. We have already discussed the possibility that Kai, Bedwyr and Arthur are developments of the three Indo-European gods known to the Teutonic peoples as Odin, Thor and Tyr. But we can also find Irish equivalents for these three figures, even if they are not quite the characters we might expect.

Bedwyr is one-armed, and although Nuada Silver Hand would appear the obvious choice as his Irish counterpart, in reality Finn is much closer. For Finn, like Bedwyr, Tyr and Mucius Scaevola, is renowned for his cunning. Ultimately it is his manipulation of the situation which rids him of Diarmaid, not his physical strength. Kai, on the other hand, is a herculean figure of almost unthinking force. He is called Kai Hir, Kai the Longman, and can clearly be matched with the Irish Cailte who overcomes the boar of Formael singlehanded.

So we are left with Arthur on the one hand and Odin, the last of the Teutonic trio, on the other. But Odin is one-eyed like Horatio Cocles, although he is a visionary, a seer, an omniscient and omnipotent god leading his warriors on their wanderings through the universe. And if we look at Irish epic, we find an equivalent figure in Aaed, Finn's rival, who is nicknamed Goll, "the One-eyed Man." Logically then Arthur should be not only a *filius horribilis* but one-eyed. Then the divine Indo-European trio would be as complete in the British tradition as it appears to be in Irish epic.

Obviously all this is mere hypotheses, but the characters of Kai and Bedwyr are so well drawn that it must surely be more than idle speculation. Although the Celts assimilated a number of the religious beliefs of the people they conquered, particularly as regards shamanism, their Druidic priesthood and the main lines of their mythology remained essentially Indo-European, So it would come as no surprise to find the three great gods of the Indo-Europeans reflected in Arthur, Kai and Bedwyr.

Be that as it may, there is no doubt that Arthur was regarded as a god by the Celts. And this is only to be expected from a people who maintained that the real and the imaginary are merely two facets of a single whole. For whether Arthur is real or imaginary, king or god, dead or asleep, generations of people have believed in him. He sleeps on, waiting to be awoken, in the minds of each one of us.[67]

CHAPTER SIX

The Early Saga of Arthur

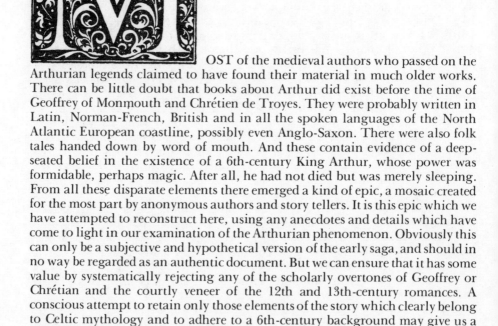

OST of the medieval authors who passed on the Arthurian legends claimed to have found their material in much older works. There can be little doubt that books about Arthur did exist before the time of Geoffrey of Monmouth and Chrétien de Troyes. They were probably written in Latin, Norman-French, British and in all the spoken languages of the North Atlantic European coastline, possibly even Anglo-Saxon. There were also folk tales handed down by word of mouth. And these contain evidence of a deep-seated belief in the existence of a 6th-century King Arthur, whose power was formidable, perhaps magic. After all, he had not died but was merely sleeping. From all these disparate elements there emerged a kind of epic, a mosaic created for the most part by anonymous authors and story tellers. It is this epic which we have attempted to reconstruct here, using any anecdotes and details which have come to light in our examination of the Arthurian phenomenon. Obviously this can only be a subjective and hypothetical version of the early saga, and should in no way be regarded as an authentic document. But we can ensure that it has some value by systematically rejecting any of the scholarly overtones of Geoffrey or Chrétian and the courtly veneer of the 12th and 13th-century romances. A conscious attempt to retain only those elements of the story which clearly belong to Celtic mythology and to adhere to a 6th-century background may give us a more vivid idea of what lay behind the Arthurian legends. For the harsh and violent life they portray is very much part of British civilization in the Dark Ages, which was totally unlike the Celtic culture of the continent, and which had inherited a wealth of ancient mythological tradition.[1]

At that time, in the fortress of Kelliwic in Kernyw, there was a lord whose name is now lost. He had a son and a daughter. The daughter was called Anna and the son Arthur because he was very ugly and looked like a bear. Two other children came, in accordance with custom, to be brought up with the lord's children. One was called Gywar, the other Kai son of Kynyr.

When Kai was born, Kynyr said to his wife "woman, if there is anything of me in your son his heart will always be cold, nor will there be any warmth in his hands; if he is my son he will be stubborn; whenever he carries a burden, whether great or small, it will be visible neither from the front nor the rear; no one will brave fire and water as well as he, nor will there be any official or servant like him." (*Kulhwch and Olwen*)

Gwyar was a handsome young man who fell in love with Anna, and she with him. But they kept their love secret and hidden from everybody. Then Anna became pregnant and gave birth to a boy. Gywar and Anna decided to entrust the baby to some passing merchants and gave them a parchment explaining the circumstances of his birth, the name they had given him and his parents' names. The merchants took the child overseas. (*De Ortu Walwani.*)

When Arthur grew up he wished to seek his fortune elsewhere. Britain had been invaded by Saxon troops who were establishing settlements all over the eastern region of the island and making frequent incursions into other areas. So Arthur decided to go and fight them, and Kai, who did not want to leave his foster brother, went with him.

Kai had this talent: nine days and nine nights his breath would last under water, and nine days and nine nights he could go without sleep. No doctor could cure the wound from Kai's sword. He could become as tall as the tallest tree in the forest when he pleased, while when the rain was heaviest, a hand's span about, what was in his hand would be dry by reason of the heat he generated, and when his compansions were coldest that would be kindling for the lighting of a fire. (*Kulhwch and Olwen*)

It was during their early battles against the Saxons that Arthur and Kai met Bedwyr son of Bedrawt who decided to join them. He was a warrior of some stature, even though he only had one arm. From that time Bedwyr felt great affection for Arthur and Kai and never avoided any errand on which Kai went. Though he was one-handed, no three warriors on the same field could draw blood faster than he; moreover he would make one thrust with his spear and nine counter-thrusts. (*Kulwch and Olwen.*)

When they were not fighting Arthur, Kai and Bedwyr had to live on whatever they could take and stay wherever they could find lodging, for such was the law in those hard times. One day they found themselves near the court of March son of Meirchiawn. March had a very beautiful wife named Essyllt who was in love with Tristan son of Tallwch, the son of March's sister. The two lovers used to meet in secret and Tristan would summon Essyllt to a meeting either by throwing wood shavings in the stream which flowed through her room, or by sending a messenger. That day Tristan had asked March's swineherd to take a message while he watched the pigs. Arthur, Kai and Bedwyr saw this as a golden opportunity to take March's pigs, for they were sure that they could distract Tristan's attention quite easily. So Arthur approached Tristan and struck up a conversation with him while Kai and Bedwyr tried to round up the pigs and drive them away. But Tristan noticed what they were doing and angrily accused

Arthur of being an accomplice. Arthur then asked Tristan to let him take some pigs and nobody would be any the wiser. Tristan refused point blank. So Arthur took Kai and Bedwyr aside and together they decided to use force. They rushed the herd and managed to drive some sows away, but just then Tristan leapt at them, sword in hand (*Triad 63*). Arthur, Kai and Bedwyr retreated; for they knew that any man who drew Tristan's blood or was himself wounded by Tristan would surely die (*The Story of Tristan*). Since that day Tristan has been numbered among the three great swineherds of Britain (*Triad 63*).

Once, when Arthur, Kai and Bedwyr had stopped on a hill top and were playing dice, a man and a young woman came to ask them for protection. The girl explained that her name was Gwladys daughter of King Brycham and that she had just eloped with Gwynnlwy, king of Glamorgan, whom she loved. But her father who had opposed the match was furious and intent on killing Gwynnlwy and bringing her home. Arthur found Gwladys very attractive and thought she would make him a fine wife; all he had to do was kill her companion and she would be his. But Kai guessed what he was thinking and said "Are you not ashamed to think such thoughts when you have always promised to help those who need protection?" Arthur realized Kai was right and assured Gwladys that he would look after her. Soon after the furious Brycham arrived, prepared to fight anybody who tried to prevent him taking his daughter home. Arthur said to him "You should realize you are not in your own territory, but on Gwynnlwy's land. You have no right over people here. Go home and leave us in peace." Brycham was forced to concede the point and reluctantly departed, threatening to take his daugther back at the first opportunity. Gwynnlwy thanked Arthur heartily for saving him, but suspicious of Arthur's intentions towards Gwladys, he immediately took her away and married her. Later Gwladys gave birth to a son, Cattawg (*Vita Cadoci*).

On another occasion Arthur came to the retreat of a saintly man named Padern. Arthur knew that Padern had received a gift from the patriarch of Jerusalem in the form of a precious tunic which Arthur wanted for himself. While Padern was asleep he rummaged round the hermitage until he found the tunic. But no sooner he laid hands on it than the earth opened beneath his feet and Arthur sank up to his chin in the ground. He could not extricate himself and had to call for help. When Padern woke and realized what had happened he told Arthur to solemnly beg for forgiveness. Arthur obeyed and the saintly man began to pray. Then the ground split further open and Arthur was able to get out. He departed ashamed of what he had done, but full of gratitude to Padern (*Vita Paderni*).

Meanwhile Arthur had formed a small troop of warriors who had come to join him, Kai and Bedwyr, for want of anything better to do. They included Edern and Gwynn the sons of Nudd, Glewlwyt Gafaelfawr, a giant of a man, Hueil son of Kaw, a lord of the North, Henwas Adeinawc who could run like the wind, Llwch Windy Hand and some others. Arthur hired out the services of his men to any king or lord who needed warriors. He had given them fast horses so that they could ride anywhere they were asked to go.

At that time a huge snake was causing havoc in the region of Carrum. The inhabitants of Carrum asked Arthur to rid the land of the monster, but he was unable to do so. Every time he and his men rushed the snake, it disappeared into a cave so they could not attack it. Arthur then went to Dindraethou to serve King Kadwy. There was a saintly man in that land who was converting the remaining pagans. His name was Carannawg and he was the grandson of Cunedda who had come from the North to live in Western Britain. Carannawg had a magic altar which could float on the waters of the sea or the Hafren. One day the altar was driven off course by currents and came ashore near Arthur. He recognized it and decided to keep it, either for his own use, or to exchange for some service later. He tried to use it as a table, but whenever anybody put anything on it, the altar shook it off. Carannawg meanwhile had learnt that Arthur had his altar and came in person to get it back. Arthur told him he would return the altar on condition that Carannawg got rid of the monstrous snake of Carrum. Carannawg agreed. His prayers rendered the snake docile and harmless, and he then ordered it to leave the people of the area in peace. Arthur returned the altar and in gratitude for the service he had done him allowed Carannawg to establish a monastery at Carrum. (*Vita Carannogi*.)

It was then that Arthur took a wife whom he loved more than any other woman. Emrys Gwledig, the last of the Roman rulers of Britain and leader of the British army at this time, had heard tell of Arthur and invited him to Kaerllion on Wysg where he had set up his headquarters. Arthur and his men arrived and Emrys gave them several jobs to do. Pleased with Arthur's achievements Emrys sang his praises to the kings who had banded together under his leadership to fight the Saxon invaders. He was an old man now and wanted to retire and found a monastery. But before leaving public office he asked the various tribal kings to accept Arthur as their supreme leader in the defence of Britain. This they did. So Arthur became chief of the British armed forces. He had heard the story of Bran son of Llyr and how, after a disastrous expedition to the island of Iwerddon, Bran had asked his companions to cut off his head and bury it at the White Hill in Llundein. Bran had said that so long as his head remained buried there, no enemy could invade Britain (*Branwen, Daughter of Llyr*). But the first thing Arthur did when elected leader of the British armies, was to exhume Bran's head from the White Hill. He did not like the idea of anyone but himself being responsible for the defence of the island (*Triad 15*).

At that time the Saxons had begun their offensives against the Britons again. A mass of them invaded the island and once there their numbers increased. Hengist, one of their most important chiefs, had died, but his son Octha brought reinforcements from Northern Britain to the kingdom of Kent to help those who had settled there. Arthur and the kings of Britain began a determined campaign to drive the Saxons back. As commander-in-chief Arthur fought a battle at the mouth of the river Glein, then four more on the river Dubglas in the region of Linnwis. A sixth battle took place on the river Bassas. On each occasion Arthur was victorious and forced the Saxons to retreat. (*Historia Brittonum*.)

During these battles Arthur picked other companions to swell his own troops. These included Taliesin, chief of the northern bards, Lleenleawg the Gael who originally came from Iwerddon but had long lived in Dyfed, and Morvran son of Tegid and Keridwen. Sgitli Light Foot who could travel along the tree tops when he was on an errand for his lord so that not so much as a blade of grass ever broke under his foot, and Tiethi Hen son of Gwynhan whose lands had been submerged under the sea and who had barely escaped himself also came to Arthur, as did Drem, son of Dremidyt, who from Kelliwic in Kernyw could see a gnat rising with the sun in Penn Blathaon in Scotland. Osla Gyflellfawr came with his magic knife. Whenever Arthur and his army arrived at a river, a torrent or an estuary, they looked for a narrow spot then threw Osla's knife over the water in its sheath, and it made a bridge strong enough for the whole army to cross. There were also Sol who could stand all day on one leg, Gwadyn Ossol who was so heavy that the highest mountain in the world became a plain under the weight of his feet, Gwadyn Odyeith who could send as many sparks flying with the soles of his feet when he struck something hard as white hot metal drawn from the forge. That is why he was always sent on ahead to clear the road of any obstacle when Arthur went on an expedition. There were also Hir Erwam and Hir Atrwm who, when they went to stay somewhere, would eat and drink all day until bedtime but still be hungry. They left their hosts neither fat food nor lean, neither salted food nor fresh, nor hot food nor cold. There was also Sugyn son of Sugynedydd who could suck up the waters of an estuary large enough for three hundred boats until their was only dry sand. He had an unquenchable thirst and a stomach of red stone. And then there were Gawfyl son of Gwestat who could droop one lip down to his navel and use the other one as a hood for his head, Gwalstawt Ieithoedd, Arthur's interpreter, who could speak any language, even that of the animals, Klus son of Kustveinat who even when buried seven fathoms under the ground could still hear an ant leaving its nest fifty miles away, Gwiawn Catseye who could take a speck out of a gnat's eye without hurting it, Bedwini who was a priest and blessed Arthur's food, Kynddelic who was Arthur's scout and knew every road both in Britain and abroad, and Menw son of Teirgwaedd who had learnt the magic arts of ancient times and could transform things and people into different shapes or cast a spell over any land (*Kulhwch and Olwen*). *With these men Arthur formed a troop of warriors unequalled in all Britain.*

At this time Cattawg had become abbot of the monastery of Llancarfan. A man named Ligessawc, one of the finest British warriors, had fought and killed one of Arthur's men. Pursued by Arthur, he had sought asylum from Cattawg at Llancarfan. Cattawg told him that he could stay in the monastery for seven years. Arthur heard this arrangement, but fear of committing sacrilege prevented him from entering the monastery and seizing his man. So he continued on his way along the river Wysg with his warriors and sent messengers to ask Cattawg to speak to him. Cattawg arrived with his monks but remained on the opposite bank. Arthur them demanded that Ligessawc should be surrendered or that some compensation be paid for the loss of the warrior he had killed. After conferring with his monks, Cattawg replied that he was unable to break his promise of asylum to Ligessawc, but would be prepared to pay some reasonable compensation. Arthur asked for a herd of cattle which were to be half white and half red. Cattawg and his monks withdrew to return soon after with the specified cattle. The monks drove the herd half way across the ford, but when Arthur's companions went in to fetch them, the cows turned into clumps of fern. Arthur was very angry but understood the point Cattawg had made and agreed to leave Ligessawc safe in the monastery for seven years, seven months and seven days. (*Vita Cadoci.*)

Arthur used often to go hunting. On one trip into the forest he came across a pack of wolves. He killed two cubs, but then a male wolf came running towards him and lay down at his feet with every appearance of feeling great affection for him. Full of compassion for him Arthur spared the animal and took it to his fortress at Kelliwic. His companions were surprised but dared say nothing, especially as the wolf followed Arthur everywhere he went, like a faithful hound. It so happened that Arthur's wife was having an affair with the court vintner and the wolf realized this. It led Arthur to the room where the lovers met and surprised them *in flagrante delicto*. Arthur was fearful in his anger. He had the vintner hung, drawn and quartered and ordered that his wife should be torn between two horses and then burnt. But he was intrigued by the behaviour of the wolf and summoned his interpreter, Gwrhyr Gwlstawt Ieithoedd to ask the animal who it really was. The wolf told them that he was once a man named Gwrgwallawn and that he had had a magic wand which could turn a man into a wolf. All one had to do was touch the victim with the wand and say "Be a wolf and take on the nature of the wolf." Gwrgwallawn's wife had been in love with a pagan king and wanted to get rid of her husband so she could marry her lover. So she had stolen the wand and managed to turn him into a wolf while he was asleep. He had then fled into the forest where he lived amongst the other wolves. He had even taken a mate and they had had two cubs. When he heard this, Arthur ordered that the wolf should be well looked after. Then he went to Gwrgwallawn's fortress to try and recover the magic wand. Gwrgwallawn's wife had married her lover and was ruling his lands after a fashion. Arthur found the wand and invited the lady to visit him at Kelliwic. When she and her accomplice arrived, Arthur had the wolf brought into the hall and touched it with the wand, saying "Be a man and assume the nature of a man." Immediately the wolf turned into a man, much to the terror of the guilty couple. Arthur made them confess their sins and ordered the pagan king to be put to death. He punished the woman by inviting her to a feast and putting before her a dish containing the head of her lover swimming in his own blood. Then he told Gwrgwallawn that he could take his wife and do whatever he wished with her. (*Arthur and Gorlagon.*[2])

At that time Gweir, son of Gweiryoedd who had come to join Arthur, had been sent to a mysterious island where there was said to be a marvellous cauldron and an insuperable sword. But Gweir had not returned and Arthur decided to go and look for him. He and his men set sail in his boat Prytwen and soon after they landed on an island somewhere in the ocean. There stood a formidable rectangular fortress said to be called Kaer Sidhi. After considerable effort Arthur and his warriors breached the walls and found Gweir chained up in a dark prison bemoaning his fate. He had been the first man ever to make his way into the city. Penn Annwfn, the lord of the city, did indeed own an extraordinary cauldron. Whoever leant over it acquired all knowledge. The bard Taliesin, who was with Arthur, decided to prove it for himself. As he inhaled the steam which rose from the cauldron he began to chant strange predictions about the future of Britain and songs about his previous incarnations. The contents of the cauldron were inexhaustible and could feed any number of men, but if a coward tried to eat from it he would find nothing. It was guarded by nine sisters who watched to see that the fire underneath it never went out. There was another girl called Modron who could transform people and objects into different shapes and could change herself into a bird. Having forced their way into the fortress, Arthur and his companions were welcomed by Penn Annwfn whom some called Diwrnach and others Pwyll. They were given a sumptuous meal. But when they had eaten and drunk their fill Arthur asked for the cauldron. Penn Annwfn refused and said that he would only give it away at the request of Odgar, king of Iwerddon, his friend and ally. At this Bedwyr rose, took the cauldron and lifted it onto the shoulders of Hygwydd, Arthur's servant whose job it was to carry his master's cauldron and light the fire under it. In the fortress there was also a precious sword called Kaledfwlch, or Hard Gash. Lleenleawg the Gael took Kaledfwlch, swung it round him and killed Penn Annwfn and all his men, although Mordron and the nine sisters were spared. Odgar, Penn Annwfn's ally, then arrived with the army of Iwerddon, invaded the island and fought a fierce battle against Arthur's men. Their position looked desperate until *Mordron showed them a path of retreat, asking as a reward that Arthur should promise to free her son Mabon*. The child had been taken away three nights after he was born, but nobody knew who had taken him nor to where. Of the three boat loads of men who had set out with Arthur only seven warriors returned, Kai, Bedwyr, Lleenleawg, Taliesin and Gweir among them. *They could not take the cauldron with them, but Arthur kept Kaledfwlch as his own sword for the rest of his life.*[3]

Some years before, Karadawg had been king of a land in the West. Although an old man, he had two small children, a boy named Meriadawg and a daughter named Orwen. Wishing to retire he had made his brother Gruffydd regent, but this unscrupulous man had Karadawg killed, whereupon his widow died of grief. The two children still stood in Gruffydd's way, but he could not bear to kill them himself and ordered his servants to take them into the forest of Arclwed and hang them. Meanwhile Ifor and his wife Morwen, who had looked after the children, followed the executioners into the forest. Together with his dog Dolffin, Ifor overtook them and set fire to all four corners of the forest, throwing meat into the flames so that the smell would attract wolves. When the wolves duly came running, Gruffydd's servants hid in the hollow of the tree from which they had hung the children by their feet. Ifor filled the tree with smoke and the executioners promised to release the children immediately. When they came out of the tree Ifor killed them both. Then having freed the children he and his wife fled with them to a cave called the Rock of Eagles. This place was so named because four eagles had nested there and looked out over the four points of the compass. Later, when Ifor and Morwen were away from the cave, chief Uryen Rheged passed by and found the girl, whom he took away with him. On the same day Kai came across the boy and took him to Arthur's fortress. When they learnt what had happened Ifor and Morwen each went their separate ways to recover the children. Morwen reached the land of Rheged on the day Uryen was to marry Orwen. She recognized Morwen and brought her to the palace. Ifor arrived at Arthur's fortress with a stag he had killed in the forest and offered it to Kai. Meriadawg, who was with Kai, recognized his foster father and shouted out his name. Then Kai took Ifor into his home and went to visit Uryen together with Ifor and Meriadawg. *At that time Arthur and Uryen were allies*. The two leaders decided to restore Meriadawg to his throne and punish Gruffydd. They raised an army and marched towards Gruffydd's land. He took shelter in a fortress on Mount Eryri. After a long siege, lack of food forced him to surrender and he was executed. Arthur and Uryen then put Meriadawg on the throne, but Meriadawg decided to follow Arthur and left Uryen to rule in his stead.[4]

It was then that Arthur heard that Henwen, one of the sows of Koll son of Kollfrewi, who was swineherd to Dallwyr Dallbern in Kernyw, was in farrow and that great trouble had been predicted for Britain from her litter. Arthur gathered a great troop of men to track down the sow, but she threw herself into the sea pursued by the great swineherd. She came ashore at Maes Gwenith in Gwent where she gave birth to a bee and a grain of wheat. Then she went on to Llonyon in Penvro where she gave birth to a grain of barley and a grain of wheat. All this had been predicted. But Arthur followed the sow as far as Riw-Gyverthwch in Arvon where she gave birth to a wolf cub and an eagle. The wolf was given to Menawedd and the eagle to Breat, a chief of the North. Both were to regret it, for the two animals destroyed their lands. Then Henwen went to Llanveir in Arvon and hid under the Black Stone. There she gave birth to a cat.

The great swineherd, who had caught up with her, threw the cat into the sea, but it was rescued by the children of Palu. They took it with them to the island of Mona and reared it, to their subsequent misfortune, for it grew up to devastate Mona and the neighbouring regions (*Triad 63*).

One of Arthur's companions was a warrior named Hueil. He was the son of Kaw of Prydyn, lord of Cwm Cawlyd who had been driven from his country by the Ffichti Gaels and had had to take refuge in the South. Hueil was proud and intractable; he refused to pay homage to any lord (*Kulhwch and Olwen*). At that time he and Arthur were wooing the same woman and decided to resolve their quarrel by single combat. Arthur was wounded in the thigh and had to admit Hueil the winner, but he made Hueil promise never to speak about what had happened and, above all, never to allude to his wound. Some months later Arthur fell in love with a woman of Ruthyn in Denbigh but he was careful to visit her incognito. On her visit, he disguised himself as a woman and arriving during some celebration he stood up to dance. But Hueil was there and recognized Arthur from his limp. He said "That would be a fine dance were it not for the thigh." Arthur said nothing, but his mind was full of murderous intent towards Hueil.[5] Later Hueil struck up an argument with one of his nephews who had also come to join Arthur and seriously wounded him. Arthur told Hueil to leave and decided to wage war on him (*Kulhwch and Olwen*). *He gathered his troops and marched towards Hueil's land*. Hueil summoned his own vassals and told them that Arthur wanted to become king of the whole island and tyrant of all Britain (*Vita Gildae* by Caradoc of Llancarfan). The two sides met in the forest of Kelyddon and a fierce battle ensued (*Historia Brittonum*). Then Arthur pursued Hueil to the shores of the Irish Sea and finally took him prisoner (*Vita Gildae*). He ordered that Hueil's head should be cut off on the stone block which has since been called Maen Hueil (*folk tale*). Kaw and his sons were angry with Arthur for having executed Hueil. One of them named Gildas returned from Ireland where he had been converting the heathen and uttered a public protest about the murder of his brother. Arthur had to recompense Kaw's family to avoid general criticism. So he patched up his quarrel with Gildas and the other sons of Kaw. (*Vita Gildae*.)

At that time Nynniaw was king of Erchyng and Pebiaw king of Glamorgan. These two arrogant men were out walking one evening under a clear and starry sky when Nynniaw remarked to Peniaw that his country was very beautiful. Pebiaw wantd to know what he was talking about and Nynniaw answered that he was referring to the sky. Pebiaw then suggested that the stars and moon were his flocks grazing on Nynniaw's land together with their shepherd. Both kings then lost their tempers and a war began (*Iolo Manuscript*).[6] It was then that Ritta the Giant took it upon himself to put an end to the injustice and oppession of the senseless kings (*Triad 132*) and managed to stop the fighting by taking both of them prisoner. He then tore off their beards and said "Here are the animals which have been grazing on my pastures. I have driven them away and they will never graze here again." (*Iolo Manuscript*.) From that time onwards Ritta had taken to fighting any king he encountered and if he won he would tear off their beards and add them to the great cloak he was making of royal beards (*Triad 131*). Since Arthur was clearly superior to all other kings, Ritta let it be known that he needed one more beard to trim his cloak and that if Arthur, as the greatest leader of the day, would cut off his own beard and send it to him, Ritta would give it pride of place on his cloak. But the giant added that should Arthur refuse this offer he intended to follow his usual practice of staking his cloak against his opponent's beard and fighting it out in single combat (*Tristan*, by Thomas).[7]

> When Arthur received the challenge he was both annoyed and aggrieved. He told the giant that he would rather fight than surrender his beard like a coward out of fear. At this, the giant came to Arthur's fortress, called him out and fought him in the lists. They launched furiously into battle and the bitter struggle which followed lasted all day. The next day Arthur overcame the giant and took both his cloak and his head. So through his bravery and his boldness he won the upper hand in the contest. (*Tristan*, by Thomas)

After this victory, Arthur went alone to hunt in the forest. As he pursued his quarry through the undergrowth, he came across a man armed with a club who threatened him. When the stranger asked if Arthur knew who he was, Arthur recognized him as a chief whose lands he had taken and realized that he was seeking retribution. Arthur was unarmed, so told the stranger that he would compensate him in some way. The man agreed to spare his life on condition that he returned after exactly one year and answered the question "What is it that women love above all else?" When Arthur had sworn to return in a year, the man went away. Throughout the next twelve months Arthur asked everyone he knew the stranger's question, hoping that one of the many different replies he received would be correct. He then returned to the forest to the place where he had met the man with the club. On the way a hideously ugly woman appeared out of a thicket and came towards him. "Stop" she said, "I know your secret, but I also knew that all the answers you have collected are wrong. If I give you the correct one you must promise to marry me." Arthur considered whether marriage to such an appalling looking woman was worth the secret. But eventually he agreed to marry her. The woman said "It is sovereignty. Tell your enemy that and he will curse the woman who told you." Arthur left her and carried on to the meeting place. When the man with the club appeared, Arthur began by giving him all the answers he had collected over the year, none of which satisfied the stranger. Finally Arthur said "It is sovereignty." The man with the club was furious. "My sister told you. May she burn for it." But Arthur had given the right answer and the stranger let him go. On his way back to his fortress the hideous woman caught up with him and reminded him of his promise. Arthur had no choice but to take her back with him and ordered preparations to be made for their wedding. Arthur's companions were astonished at his choice of wife, but the ceremony took place. That night Arthur went to bed with his bride but immediately turned his back on her. She then said "Give me one kiss at least, if only out of courtesy." Arthur turned reluctantly back to kiss her but found beside him the most beautiful woman imaginable. When he seemed surprised the woman said "You have a choice: you can either have me beautiful during the day and ugly at night, or beautiful at night and ugly during the day. I leave the decision to you." Arthur thought for a moment and then said "This is too ticklish a problem for me. I will leave the choice to you and trust in your judgement." "In that case," said the woman, "I shall be beautiful both day and night. My name is Gwenhwyfar. I had a stepmother who was jealous of my beauty and magicked me into the repulsive woman you first met. I was to stay like that until the best and bravest man in the world was willing o marry me and accord me total sovereignty. Now you have married me and made the decision mine. Your courtesy has freed me of the spell." *So Arthur had a second wife, Gwenhwyfar, the most beautiful woman in the world.*[8]

One night at Kaerllion on Wysg Arthur was in bed with Gwenhwyfar when she suddenly awoke and said to him "I dreamt that a strange man was at this moment on his way to Kaerllion and that he would prove even more valorous than you. He was to give me a golden ring and two horses he had taken in single combat." At that time Arthur used to try his strength against everyone who came to his fortress wishing to join him. So as soon as Gwenhwyfar had gone back to sleep, he rose, put on his armour and went out into the forest. He found the young man near a river in flood and challenged him. They began to fight in the middle of the ford, but the young man unsaddled Arthur and took his horse away. The faithful Kai, who had followed Arthur, also challenged the young man but fared no better than his lord. Arthur and Kai walked sheepishly back to the fortress. When Arthur returned exhausted to his room Gwenhwyfar woke and asked him how he came to be soaked through. Arthur said that he had been to drink in the spring and had fallen in the water, but this lie did not deceive Gwenhwyfar. The next day the young man arrived at Kaerllion and presented himself to Gwenhwyfar. He offered her a gold ring and two horses. Gwenhwyfar took the horses and led them to Arthur's room. He recognized them as his and Kai's and had to admit the truth. He then received the young man who told him that he had come from far away to join him. He also said that he did not know his name, but showed Arthur a parchment. Menw read it and told Arthur that the man was called Gwalchmai and that he was Arthur's nephew, son of his sister Anna and Gwyar. Arthur did not pass on the information to Gwalchmai, however, but told him that he would reveal his name when he had accomplished some notable exploit. A messenger then arrived to ask for Arthur's help. The Lady of the Castle of Maidens was being besieged by a wicked king whom she had rejected and who was seeking to avenge this slight. Arthur set off with Gwalchmai and his other companions, but they arrived at the Castle of Maidens too late, to find that the wicked king had taken the Lady away. Arthur followed only to discover that his enemy's army was large and well organized. Just when defeat seemed inevitable Gwalchmai attacked the wicked king who fled from the battle field. Gwalchmai pursued and killed him. He then returned to Arthur with the Lady of the Castle of Maidens and the head of her abductor. When they saw that their leader had been killed, the enemy forces laid down their arms and Gwalchmai was hailed as the hero of the hour. Arthur then told him his name and publicly acknowledged him to be his nephew. (*De Ortu Walwani.*)

Meanwhile Arthur still had to make good his promise to Modron that he would find her son Mabon. But Arthur's men said to him,

"Lord, go back, for you ought not to accompany the host on this sort of petty errand." "Gwrhyr Gwalstawt Ieithoedd," said Arthur, "it will be proper for you to go on this errand, for you know all tongues and can speak with some of the birds and animals. Eiddoel, it is right for you to accompany my men in seeking your cousin. Kai and Bedwyr, I hope that you will obtain whatever you seek—go on this errand on my behalf."

These men went on until they found the Ousel of Kilgwru, and Gwrhyr asked, "For God's sake, do you know anything of Mabon son of Modron, who when three nights old was stolen away from between his mother and the wall?" "When I first came here," answered the Ousel, "there was a smith's anvil. I was a young bird then, and since that time no work had been done on the anvil except by my beak every night. Today there is not so much as a nut that has not been worn away, and yet God's revenge on me if in all that time I have heard anything of the man you seek, nevertheless I will do what is right by Arthur's messengers. There is a kind of creature which God made even before me, and I will guide you to it.''

They then went to the Stag of Rhedenvre, and said "Stag of Rhedenvre, we are Arthur's messengers, and we have come to you because we know of no animal which is older. Tell us if you know anything of Mabon son of Mocron who was stolen from his mother when three nights old.'' "When I first came here," said the stag, "there was only a single antler on either side of my head, and no tree here but a single hazel oak which then grew into an oak of one hundred branches; thereafter the tree fell and today there is nothing left but a red stump. I have been here since that day and have heard nothing of the man you seek, but since you are Arthur's messengers I will guide you to an animal which God made before me.''

They came to the Owl of Kwm Kawlwyt and said, "Owl of Kwm Kawlwyt, these are messengers from Arthur. Do you know anything of Mabon son of Modron who was stolen from his mother when three nights old?'' "If I knew I would tell you. When I first came here the great valley which you see before you was wooded glen; the race of man came and destroyed it, whereupon a second forest grew up, and this forest is the third. As for me, my wings are now nothing but stumps. To this day I have heard nothing of the man you seek, but I will guide Arthur's messengers to the oldest animal in the world and the one which has travelled the most, the Eagle of Gwernabwy.''

Gwrhyr then said, "Eagle of Gwernabwy, we are messengers from Arthur who have come to ask if you know anything of Mabon son of Modron, who was stolen from his mother when three nights old.'' "I came here long ago,'' answered the eagle, "and when I first came I had a stone from the top of which I pecked at the stars every evening, and now that stone is not a hand's breadth in height. I have been here from that day to this, and I have heard nothing of the man you seek except when I made a trip to look for food at Llyw lake. There I sank my claws into a salmon expecting that it would feed me for a long time, but it drew me down into the water, so that I barely escaped. I returned with all my relatives to destroy the fish, but it sent messengers to make peace, and came itself to have fifty tridents pulled out of its back. Unless this salmon knows something of the one you seek I know of no one who might know anything. I will guide you to it.''

They came to that place and the eagle said, "Salmon of Llyn Llyw, I have come with Arthur's messengers to ask if you know anything of Mabon son of Modron, who was stolen from his mother when three nights old.'' "I will tell you as much as I know. I swim upstream on every tide until I reach Kaer Loyw, where I found such evil as I had never found before. That you may believe me let one of you ride on my shoulders.''

So Kai and Gwrhyr rode on the salmon's shoulders until they came to the prisoner's enclosure, and they heard moaning and wailing from the other side of the wall, and Gwrhyr said, "Who is crying in this stone house?''

"Alas, there is reason for this man to lament: Mabon son of Modron is here, and no one was ever so harshly imprisoned, not Lludd Silver Hand, not Greid son of Eri." "Is there any hope of securing your release through gold or silver or wordly wealth, or through battle and fighting?" "Such release as is got for me will be got by fighting." So they returned to Arthur and told him where Mabon's prison was; Arthur summoned the warriors of this island and went to Kaer Loyw where Mabon was prisoner, but Kai and Bedwyr rode on the salmon's shoulders. While Arthur's men were fighting at the fortress Kai broke through the wall of the enclosure and rescued the prisoner on his back, besides fighting with the men; then Arthur returned home, and with him Mabon, a free man. (*Kulhwch and Olwen*)

One day when Arthur was holding a meeting at Kaerllion, a horseman arrived in front of the fortress. He gave the gatekeeper a thick gold ring to guard his horse and went into the hall. Arthur was there with Gwenhwyfar and the other companions. Arthur's wife had just been given a goblet and was drinking from it, when the horseman snatched it from her hands and poured the contents over her face and breast (*Peredur*, as in the *White Book of Rhydderch*). Then he struck her and said "Whoever is daring enough to fight me for this cup and avenge the insult to Gwenhwyfar, let him follow me to the meadow where I will be waiting." Then the horseman took his horse and went to the meadow (*Peredur*, as in the *Red Book of Hergest*).

At that moment a young man called Peredur arrived. His mother had sent him to Arthur's court. The first person he encountered was Kai, who had come out of the hall because nobody had dared to take up the challenge of the unknown horseman. They all assumed that anyone audacious enough to do what he had done must be protected by magical powers from any fear of retaliation. Peredur asked Kai "Tell me, tall man, where is Arthur?" "My mother told me to come and be ordained a knight by Arthur." "Follow the knight who rode out to the meadow; take the cup and overthrow him, and take his horse and armour, and then you shall be made a knight." "Tall man, I will do that." Peredur turned his horse and made for the meadow. The horseman was expecting one of Arthur's knights, and when he saw a young man armed with two spears coming towards him he began to laugh. "Tell me," said the knight, "did you see anyone from the court following me?" "I saw no one. The tall man there told me to overthrow you and recover the cup, and to take your horse and armour for myself." Then the knight began openly laughing and told the young man to go back. But Peredur felt insulted. He aimed one of his spears at the knight which hit him in the eye. The dart left through the nape of the neck and the man fell to the ground dead. (*Peredur*.)

Meanwhile Owein son of Uryen was saying to Kai, "God knows you struck that man you sent after the knight a foul blow. He will be either overthrown or killed: if he is overthrown the knight will consider him a man of stature, and Arthur and his warriors will be eternally shamed; if he is killed they will still be shamed, and you will have sinned as well. May I lose face if I do not go and learn what has happened." Owein rode to the meadow where he found Peredur dragging the knight behind him, and so he said, "Wait, chieftain, and I will remove the armour." "This iron tunic will not come off, it is part of him." So Owein removed the armour and clothing and said, "There you are, friend, now you have a horse and armour that are better than those you had — take them gladly, and come with me to Arthur, who will make you a knight." Peredur replied "May I lose face if I go. Take this cup from me to Gwenhwyfar and tell Arthur that wherever I go I will be his man and that I will serve him to his advantage as best I can . . ." Owein then returned to the court and related to Arthur and Gwenhwyfar and the entire household what had happened. (*Peredur*)

And Peredeur set off on his marvellous adventures. He overcame seventeen knights whom he sent to Arthur's court. One day he made his way into a strange fortress where he was received by a crippled king. During the feasting he saw a procession, the meaning of which he could not understand.

He saw two lads entering the hall and then leaving for a chamber; they carried a spear of incalculable size with three streams of blood running from the socket to the floor. When everyone saw the lads coming in this way they set up a crying and a lamentation that was not easy for anyone to bear, but the man did not interrupt his conversation with Peredur — he did not explain what this meant, nor did Peredur ask him. After a short silence two girls entered bearing a large platter with a man's head covered with blood on it, and everyone set up a crying and lamentation such that it was not easy to stay in the same house. (*Peredur*)

And Peredur went on his way. He relieved a fortress which was under siege and was warmly received by a majestic and beautiful woman with a large number of followers. But after a meal she told him that he should not stay the night for there were nine witches of Kaer Loyw in the land who came every night to loot what they could and their powers were so great that no one could stop them.

"Well, I would like to stay here tonight; if trouble comes, I will do what good I can, and I will do no harm." Then they went to bed. Towards dawn Peredur heard screaming; he rose quickly and went out in his shirt and trousers, with a sword round his neck, and when he arrived he saw a hag overcoming a screaming watchman, so he took his sword and struck her on the head until her helmet and skullcap spread out like a platter. "Your mercy, Peredur, handsome son of Evrawg, and the mercy of God!" "Hag, how do you know that I am Peredur?" "It was prophesied and foretold that I would suffer harm from you, and that you would take horse and arms from me, and so you shall remain with me a while learning to ride your horse and handle your arms." "You shall have mercy upon your promise never to harm the realm of this countess." Peredur took sureties to that effect, and with the countess' permission he accompanied the hag to the hag's court, staying there for three weeks and then choosing horse and arms and setting out. (*Peredur*)

Peredur had many adventures and then returned to the countess, with whom he stayed for a long time. But one day when he was at Arthur's court among his companions, a hideous woman arrived riding on a mule. She greeted the assembled company but cursed Peredur for not fulfilling his predestined purpose. She added that whoever was to accomplish the mission should go to the Castle of Marvels. When she had gone Peredur swore that he would not spend one day in the same place until he had solved the mystery; and he left. Gwalchmai also left in a different direction, and it was he who arrived at the

Castle of Marvels first. When Peredur arrived he was told that he must avenge the man whose head he had seen borne on a platter. For the man was his cousin and had been killed by the witches of Kaer Loyw. They had also wounded the crippled king, his uncle. If he had asked the meaning of what he had witnessed on his first visit, the king would have been cured. Only Peredur, it had been prophesied, could avenge his family's ills. (Summary of *Peredur*.)

Peredur and Gwalchmai decided to send to Arthur and his retinue and ask them to come. They began to fight with the hags and one of them killed one of Arthur's men right in front of Peredur, and he ordered her to desist. She killed another man in front of him and again he ordered her to desist. But she killed a third man whereupon he drew his sword and struck her on the helmet so that helmet and armour and her head split in two. She screeched and told the other hags to flee, saying that this was Peredur, the man who had been with her learning horsemanship and who was fated to destroy them. Arthur and his men struck the hags of Kaer Loyw and killed them all, *except one*. (*Peredur*)

She was called Gorddu and was the daughter of Gorwenn, the hag from the ends of hell. She took refuge in a cave at Penn Nant Govut in the North (*Kulhwch and Olwen*).

So Arthur set out for the North and the hag's cave. On the advice of Gwynn son of Nudd and Gwythyr son of Greidyawl, Kachmwri and his brother Hygwydd were sent to fight with the hag, but as they entered the cave she sprang at them, catching Hygwydd by the hair and throwing him to the floor. Kachmwri grabbed her by the hair and pulled her away from his brother, whereupon she turned on him, and having stripped both of them of their armour and weapons drove them out yelling and screaming. Arthur was angry to see his servants half-dead, and wanted to go at the hag himself, but Gwynn and Gwythyr said "We cannot enjoy seeing you wrestle with her — send Hir Amren and Hir Eiddyl into the cave." They went, but if the first pair emerged in a bad state, these two came out even worse, so that God knows not one of the four could have left the place in any way other than being loaded on Arthur's mare Llameri. Then Arthur sprang to the cave entrance and threw his knife Karnwennan at the hag, so that it struck her down the centre and made two vats of her, and Kaw of Prydyn took the blood and kept it with him. (*Kulhwch and Olwen*.)

After this expedition Arthur gathered his companions at Kelliwic and invited the neighbouring kings to join the festivities. Maelwas, king of the Land of Summer, came and fell in love with Gwenhwyfar. Some time later Gwenhwyfar was walking in the forest when Maelwas approached her. After boasting about his own merits and the power of his horse, he was interrupted by the faithful Kai, who had arrived in the meanwhile and retorted that Maelwas' charger was no different from many others. Gwenhwyfar then declared that Kai was indeed so brave and his horse so exceptionally strong that there was none to equal him. But Maelwas managed to make Kai go away and he took Gwenhwyfar off on his horse. (Poem from the *Myvyrian Archaeology of Wales*.)

So Gwenhwyfar was held prisoner at Maelwas' fortress at Kaer Wydr. When he heard the news Arthur raised an army in Kernyw and in Dyfneint and came to

Kaer Wydr to lay siege to Maelwas' fortress. But Maelwas was well entrenched and his fortress well stocked with food and water. Arthur was helpless. The situation was resolved by Gildas son of Kaw, who was then living in a monastery near Kaer Wydr. He came to act as mediator between the two men and arranged a truce. Maelwas returned Gwenhwyfar to Arthur and Arthur solemnly promised to cease hostilities against Maelwas. Gildas then took both of them into the monastery chapel to hear mass (*Vita Gildae*).

Meanwhile the Saxons had renewed their offensive. Arthur led the British armies out against them. There was a great battle near the fortress of Gwynniawn, during which Arthur bore the image of the Virgin Mary on his shield. The Virgin interceded on the Britons' behalf and with great courage they put the Saxons to flight (*Historia Brittonum*).

When Arthur returned to Kelliwic he learnt that Owein son of Uryen had gone to look for a mysterious fountain which Kynon son of Klydno had told him about. When Kynon had poured water on the stone steps around the fountain a violent storm had broken out and devastated the surrounding area. Then, when the weather cleared, birds had begun to sing a marvellous song on a pine tree. But while Kynon was listening to the birds, a black horseman had appeared out of the blue and attacked him. Owein, having heard this story, had determined to try the same adventure, but he had been gone a long time. So Arthur decided to go to the mysterious fountain with some of his companions and find out what had happened to Owein (*Owein*, or *The Lady of the Fountain*).

> The next day Arthur set out with Kynon as his guide . . . *After several days* they came to the green tree, where they saw the fountain and the bowl and the stone. Kai went to Arthur and said, "Lord, I know the meaning of all this, and I ask permission to throw the water on the stone and undertake the first adventure which follows." Arthur consented and Kai threw the bowlful of water on the stone. Immediately there came thunder and a shower the like of which they had never heard nor seen, and the shower killed many of the servants who had accompanied Arthur. After that the sky brightened, and when they looked at the tree there was not a leaf on it. The birds alighted on the tree, and they were certain they had never heard songs like those the birds sang. Then they saw a knight on a pure black horse, dressed in pure black brocade and approaching boldly. Kai went against him and they jousted, and it was not long before Kai was thrown to the ground . . . Thereafter each man in Arthur's retinue went to joust with the knight, and all were thrown until there remained only Arthur and Gwalchmai. Then Arthur armed himself to joust, but Gwalchmai said, "Alas, lord, let me go out first." Arthur consented and Gwalchmai rode out to face the knight. Finally the knight gave Gwalchmai such a blow that his helmet turned on his face: the knight recognized him. (*Owein* or *The Lady of the Fountain*)

Then the knight took off his own helmet and Gwalchmai saw that it was Owein. Arthur and all his companions were very pleased. Owein explained what had happened. His adventures had followed the same course as Kynon's.

But when the black knight attacked him, Owein had mortally wounded him and then followed him back to his fortress where he had been taken prisoner. A servant named Luned whom he knew and had helped on a previous occasion hid him carefully away. But he had fallen in love with the Black Knight's widow and with Luned's help had married her. So, he had taken over the Black Knight's duties as guardian of the fountain, for every intruder who unleashed the storm caused great devastation and misery for the local inhabitants. Owein invited Arthur and all his companions into his fortress where they feasted for three nights and three days. When Arthur was preparing to take his leave, he asked the Lady of the Fountain to let Owein accompany him for a while since he needed to have such a skilful man with him. The Lady agreed and Owein left with Arthur and his men (*Owein* or *The Lady of the Fountain*).

When he returned to Kelliwic, Arthur learnt that his erstwhile companion Osla Gyllellfawr had made an alliance with some of the kings and chiefs of the Saxons and was preparing to do battle with Arthur and the loyal Britons. Arthur decided to anticipate him. He assembled as many warriors as he could and approached Kaerllion from the North in order to surprise Osla before he had had time to finish his preparations. He made camp on the banks of the Hafren. A servant spread a cloak before Arthur. This cloak was magic in the sense that anyone who wore it could see everyone but not be seen himself. Arthur sat on the cloak with Owein son of Uryen in front of him. Arthur asked Owein if he would like to play chess. When Owein agreed, a servant brought them the board and pieces (*The Dream of Rhonabwy*).

Owein and Arthur began to play, and they were deep into the game when from a white red-topped pavilion . . . came a young man with curly yellow hair . . . He came to where the emperor and Owein were playing chess and greeted Owein. The latter wondered that the lad had greeted him and not Arthur, but Arthur read his thoughts and said, "Do not wonder that the lad greeted you just now, for he greeted me earlier, and besides, his message is for you." The lad said to Owein, "Lord, is it with your permission that the emperor's young lads and servants are harassing and molesting your ravens? If not, then have the emperor forbid it." "Lord, do you hear what the page is saying?" said Owein, "If you please, call your men off my ravens." "Your move," said Arthur, whereupon the page returned to his pavilion.

They finished their game and started another, and towards the middle of that game they saw a ruddy young man with curly auburn hair . . . coming out of a pavilion of pure yellow . . . He approached the chess players and greeted Owein . . . "Lord, is it with your permission that the emperor's pages are stabbing your ravens, killing some and wounding others?" asked the page. "If it is not, ask him to call them off." Owein said "Lord, if you please, call off your men," but Arthur answered only "Your move," and the page returned to his pavilion.

They finished their game and began another, and as they were making the first move they saw far off . . . a page with bright yellow hair . . . Violently angry he galloped towards the chess players and they perceived his anger; he greeted Owein and told him how the noblest ravens had been killed, and those that were not dead had been molested and wounded so badly there was not one that could lift its wings an inch off the ground. "Lord, call off your men," said Owein. "If you please, play on," said Arthur. Then Owein told the page, "Go, and where you see the fiercest fighting raise the standard, and let God's will be done."

The page went off to where the fighting was going badly for the ravens; he raised the standard, and at that the ravens rose, full of anger and violence and joy as well, to let the wind into their wings and to cast off fatigue. Having recovered strength and the will to fight they swooped down in anger and joy on the men who had earlier inflicted wounds and injuries and losses upon them. Some carried off heads, some eyes, some ears, some arms, and as they rose into the air their fluttering and gleeful cawing set up a great din, while another such commotion was raised by the men who were being pecked and stabbed and even killed.[9] While playing chess Arthur and Owein were amazed to hear such a noise, and as they looked round they saw a rider on a dapple-grey horse . . . This rider approached the chess players and they saw that he was tired and angry; he greeted Arthur and said that the ravens were killing the squires and pages, whereupon Arthur looked at Owein and said "Call off your ravens." Owein replied, "Your move, lord." They played on; the page returned to the battle and the ravens were no more called off than before.

When they had played a while they heard a great uproar and the screams of men and the cawing of strong ravens carrying the men up into the air and pulling them apart and letting the pieces fall to the ground. From this commotion came a rider on a pale white horse . . . This page greeted the emperor and said, "Lord, your pages and squires have been killed, and the sons of the nobles of Britain, too, so that from now on it will not be easy to defend this island." "Owein, call off your ravens," said Arthur. "Your move, lord," said Owein.

They finished their game and began another, and as they were finishing that game they heard a great uproar and the screaming of men, and then the cawing of ravens and the flapping of their wings and their dropping undented armour and pieces of men and horses to the ground. After that came a rider on a handsome black high-headed horse . . . This rider approached Arthur angrily and said that the ravens had killed his retinue and the sons of the nobles of this island, and asked him to have Owein call the ravens off. Arthur asked Owein to do so, and he squeezed the gold men on the board until they were nothing but dust; then Owein ordered Gwres son of Rheged to lower the banner, and when this was done there was peace on both sides. (*The Dream of Rhonabwy.*)

It was then that twenty-four men came from Osla Gyllellfawr to ask Arthur for a truce of one month and two weeks. Arthur rose and went to seek advice. (*The Dream of Rhonabwy.*) *But everyone was of the opinion that they should do battle with Osla straight away.* So followed the battle of the City of the Legions, and Arthur was the victor (*Historia Brittonum*). Owein, who had stayed at Arthur's court until then, wished to leave. He returned to his own land with the three hundred swords of Kynvarch and his flight of ravens, and they were victorious wherever they went (*Owein* or *The Lady of the Fountain*).

A short time before, Kreiddylat daughter of Llud Llaw Ereint had gone to Gwythyr son of Greidyawlm but before he could sleep with her Gwynn son of Nudd came and carried her off by force. Gwythyr collected an army and went to fight Gwynn, but Gwynn conquered . . . When Arthur heard of this he went into the North and called on Gwynn and freed the nobles from prison and peace was made between Gwynn and Gwythyr: Kreiddylat was left in the house of her father undisturbed by either side, and every May Day the two men would fight, and the one who conquered on the Judgment Day would keep the girl. (*Kulhwch and Olwen*)

It was then that Arthur fought a great battle against the Picts and their allies on the banks of the river Trywyrwyd (poem XXXI, *The Black Book of Camarthen*). Mabon son of Modron, Henwas Adeiniawc, Llwch Llawynnawg, Kai and Bedwyr distinguished themselves at this battle and slaughtered many of the enemy (*ibid.*).

During Arthur's absence, however, a giant named Karadawg had carried Gwenhwyfar off to the fortress of King Mardawg, who had long loved her and was now keeping her in the Painful Tower. As soon as he heard about it Arthur hastened to lay siege to the Painful Tower, together with Kai, Bedwyr, Gwalchmai and Edern son of Nudd. But the tower was well defended and as the giant Karadawg was defending the entrance with great daring and energy, Arthur was unable to get in. A woman whom Karadawg had abducted on a previous occasion and who was also held prisoner in the tower came to Gwalchmai and gave him a sword. This weapon was the only one which could kill Karadawg and clear the entrance to the fortress. Gwalchmai took it and thrust it through Karadawg's body. So Arthur and his companions were able to gain entry to the Painful Tower and resue Gwenhwyfar who returned with them to Kelliwic (the romance of *Durmart*, and the sculpture at Modena).

Soon after Kulhwch the young son of Kilydd, who had been sent to Arthur by his father, arrived at Kelliwic. At first Glewlwyt Gafaelfawr who was gatekeeper that day refused to let him into Arthur's hall. But he finally reached Arthur and greeted him. The king told him to sit down among his warriors where he would be given food and drink. But Kulhwch was angry. He had not come to eat and drink, but to ask Arthur something (*Kulhwch and Olwen*).

"Chieftain," said Arthur, "even though you do not stay, you shall have the request that head and tongue name, as far as the wind dries, as far as the rain wets, as far as the sun rises, as far as the sea stretches, as far as the earth extends, excepting only my ship, my mantle, my sword Kaledfwlch, my spear Rongomyant, my shield Gwyneb Gwrthucher, my knife Karnwenhan and my wife Gwenhwyfar. In God's truth name what you want and you shall have it gladly." "I want my hair trimmed."[10] And Arthur took a gold comb and silver-handled scissors and combed the lad's hair. (*Kulhwch and Olwen*)

Kulhwch told Arthur who he was and asked for Olwen daughter of Yspaddaden Penkawr, invoking her in the name of all those present. Arthur ordered that the young man should be given what he wanted and sent men to look for Olwen. Kai and Bedwyr found her, but they also discovered that Yspaddaden Penkawr did not wish to part with his daughter, for he had been told that he would die on the day that she married. He threw three spears at Kulhwch intending to kill him. But each time one of Arthur's warriors caught the spear and threw it back at Yspaddaden, wounding him badly. Finally Yspaddaden told Kulhwch to bring him various marvellous objects which were virtually impossible to obtain. But with the help of Arthur and his companions, Kulhwch brought them all back and won the woman he loved. Then Goeu son of Kustennin killed Yspaddaden Penkawr and cut off his head (*Kulhwch and Olwen*)

One of Arthur's warriors was a man named Drutwas son of Tryphun. His wife, a fairy woman, had given him three marvellous birds which could understand the language of men and carry out their master's orders. He took them into battle where the birds performed wonders against the enemy. But Drutwas had become so proud that one day he challenged Arthur's right to lead the army on the grounds that he, Drutwas, was as capable. Arthur replied by suggesting that they should measure their strength in single combat. But at the appointed time Drutwas sent his birds instead and told them to kill the first man who appeared. Drutwas' sister, who had long been in love with Arthur, knew about Drutwas' treachery. She invited Arthur to come and see her, and kept him with her for long after the time arranged for the fight. Meanwhile, anxious to know what had happened, Drutwas went to the appointed spot only to be torn to shreds by his own birds (*Iolo Manuscripts*, p. 188).

Following renewed aggression from the Saxons, Arthur fought the battle of Bregwyn at Mount Agned (*Historia Brittonum*). *The Saxons were defeated and Arthur was free to turn his attention elsewhere.*

For a monstrous boar was causing havoc in Britain and the adjacent islands. It was called Twrch Trwyth and was said to be a man who had been changed into an animal as a punishment for his sins. The men of Britain asked Arthur to hunt the boar. Nobody could kill it, so the story went, *but it could be rendered harmless* by removing the comb, the razor and the shears it wore among the bristles on its head (*Kulhwch and Olwen*).

Arthur and his men returned to Kelliwic in Kernyw, and from there Menw son of Teirgwaedd was sent to see if the treasures were between the ears of Twrch Trwyth, lest Arthur be shamed by going there to fight, and not finding the treasures. Twrch was there, however, and he had destroyed a third of Ireland. Menw went after the treasure and found them in Esgeir Oervel; he changed himself into a bird and alighted on the lair and tried to seize one of them, but he got only bristle. Moreover Twrch rose boldly and stirred so that some of the poison overtook Menw who thereafter was never completely without injury.

Then Arthur collected all the warriors that were in Britain and the three off-shore islands, in France, Brittany, Normandy and the Land of Summer, along with selected dogs and renowned horses, and that entire army went to Ireland; at their coming there was fear and trembling in that island. When Arthur landed, the saints of Ireland came to him seeking protection, and when he granted them that, they gave him their blessing. The men of Ireland also came, bringing a gift of food. After that Arthur went to Esgeir Oervel where Twrch Trwyth and his seven young pigs were; from all sides dogs were unleashed at Twrch and the Irish fought with him all day until evening, and at that he destroyed a fifth part of Ireland. The next day Arthur's troops fought with him, but except for the harm they suffered they got nothing; the third day Arthur himself fought with Twrch, nine days and nine nights, and killed nothing more than one piglet. His men asked him about the meaning of the pig and Arthur said, "He was a king, but because of his sins God turned him into a pig." After that Arthur sent Gwrhyr Gwalstawt Ieithoedd to try to talk with Twrch. In the form of a bird Gwrhyr alighted on the lair of Twrch and the seven young pigs and said, "for the sake of Him who put this shape upon you, if you can speak, I ask one of you to come and talk with

Arthur." Grugyn Gwrych Ereint (like silver wings were all his bristles, and the path he took through forest or plain could be told by the way the bristles glittered) answered, "For the sake of Him who put this form upon us, we will neither say nor do anything for Arthur. God did us injury enough making pigs out of us without your coming to fight us." "I can tell you that Arthur will fight you for the comb and razor and shears that lie between the ears of Twrch Trwyth." "Until you take his life, you will not get the treasures. Tomorrow we will start out for Arthur's country, and once there we will do the greatest possible damage." Then the pigs made for the sea and swam towards Kymry; Arthur and his troops and horses and dogs boarded Prytwen and at once saw the swine and Twrch Trwyth landing at Porth Kleis in Dyfed. Arthur reached Mynyw that evening, and the next day he was told that Twrch had already passed through; they overtook him killing the cattle of Kynnwas Kwrr y Vagyl, after he had killed the men and beasts in Deu Gleddyf prior to Arthur's arrival. Twrch Trwyth then set out for Presseleu, and Arthur went after him with all the forces in the world, and sent his men into the hunt . . . and Bedwyr with Arthur's dog Kavall at his side, and Arthur deployed his men along the banks of the Nyfer. . . . But Twrch made from Glynn Nyfer and went as far as Kwm Kerwyn where he stood at bay and killed four of Arthur's champions . . . and having killed these men Twrch stood at bay a second time in the same place and killed Gwadre son of Arthur . . . and he himself was wounded.

The next morning at daybreak some of Arthur's men overtook Twrch and the boar killed the three servants of Glewlwyt Gafaelfawr, so that God knows Glewlwyt had no servant to hunt with him except Llaesgenym who was of no use to anyone. Twrch killed many other men of the country as well, including Gwlydyn Saer, Arthur's master builder, before Arthur overtook him at Pelumyawc where Twrch killed Madawc son of Teithyon . . . From there he went to Aber Tywi, where he stood at bay and killed Kynlas son of Kynan . . . and then he went to Glynn Ystu and both men and dogs lost his trail. Arthur summoned Gwynn son of Nudd and asked if he knew anything of Twrch Trwyth but Gwynn did not, so all the houndsmen went out to hunt the pigs, as far as Dyffrynn Llychwr, where Grugyn Gwallt Ereint and Llwyddawc Gofynnyat attacked so that only one man escaped with his life. Then Arthur and his troops came to where Grugyn and Llwyddawc were, and all the dogs brought for that purpose were unleashed. With the shouting and barking that followed Twrch Trwyth (who had not seen them all since they crossed the Irish Sea) came up to help, and men and dogs attacked him; he made his way to Mynydd Amanw and there one of the piglets was killed. They went at each other life and death, first the piglet Twrch Lawin was killed and then Gwys. Twrch then went to Llwch Ewin and Arthur overtook him, but he killed . . . many men and dogs. From there they went to Llwch Tawy but Grugyn Gwallt Ereint separated from them and made for Din Tywi, and after that for Keredigiawn; he was followed by Trchmyr and many others, and when he reached Garth Grugyn he was killed, but not before killing Ruddfyw Rys and many others. Llwyddawc Gofynniat went on to Ystrad Yw where the men of Brittany met him. He killed Hirpeissawc king of Brittany . . . and was himself killed.

Then Twrch Trwyth passed between Tawy and Euyas whereupon Arthur summoned the men of Kernyw and Dyfneint to meet him at the mouth of the Hafren and there he said to the warriors of this island, "Twrch Trwyth has killed a number of my men. By the courage of man he shall not go into Kernyw while I am alive, nor will I pursue him further, rather I will pit my life against his. You men may do as you wish." On Arthur's advice a troop of horsemen were sent out, along with the dogs of this island; they went as far as Euyas and turned Twrch back towards the Hafren, and there the battle-tested warriors of this island met him and drove him into the river by force. Mabon son of Modron mounted on Gwynn Mygdwnn the horse of Gweddw, went into the river with him, as did Goreu son of Kustennin and Menw son of Teirgwaedd, between Llyn Lliwan and Aber Gwy. Then Arthur and the champions of Britain joined the fight . . . they closed in and grasped Twrch's feet and dunked him in the river until the currents rolled over him. On one side Mabon son of Modron spurred on his steed and seized the shears. Before they could get the comb, however, Twrch found his feet, and when he reached land neither dog nor man nor horse could stay with him as he made for Kernyw. For all the harm they came to in seeking the treasures, they came to worse trying to save two men from drowning . . .

After that Arthur and his men overtook Twrch in Kernyw. The harm they had come to already was nothing compared to what they suffered in seeking the comb, but though they went from one disaster to another, the comb was finally obtained. Twrch was hunted out of Kernyw and driven into the sea, and from then on it is not known where he went . . . Arthur himself went to Kelliwic to bathe and rest. (*Kulhwch and Olwen*)

As Kai and Bedwyr were sitting on Pumlummon, on Karn Gwylathyr, in the greatest wind in the world, they looked round and saw a great smoke blowing towards the south far away, and not being blown by the wind, and Kai said, "By my companion's hand, that is the fire of a warrior." They made for the smoke and approached and saw from a distance Dillus Varvawc singeing a wild boar. He was the greatest warrior who ever avoided Arthur. Bedwyr asked Kai, "Do you recognize him?" "I do — that is Dillus Varvawc. No leash in the world will hold Drutwyn the pup of Greit son of Eeri save one of the man you see before you, nor will that avail us unless it is plucked with wooden tweezers while he is still alive, for if he is dead it will be brittle. "What is your plan?" asked Bedwyr. "We will let him eat his fill of meat, and after that he will fall asleep," said Kai, and while Dillus was stuffing himself they were making wooden tweezers. When Kai was certain that Dillus was asleep he made the biggest pit in the world and then struck him an infinitely powerful blow; they pressed him down into the pit until his beard had been entirely plucked out with the wooden tweezers, and then they killed him outright. From there the two made for Kelliwic in Kernyw, taking with them the leash from the beard of Dillus Varvawc and giving it to Arthur, and Arthur sang this song:

> Kai made a leash
> From the beard of Dillus son of Eurei:
> If Dillus were alive he would kill you.

Kai became so angry that the warriors of this island could barely make peace

between him and Arthur; nevertheless Kai would have nothing to do with
Arthur from then on, not when the latter was wanting in strength or when
his men were being killed. (*Kulhwch and Olwen*)

One day when Arthur when talking to Gwenhwyfar, he asked her what she
would do if he were to disappear. Gwenhwyfar tried to avoid giving a direct
answer, but Arthur persisted and merely rephrased the question. "If I went, you
would be forced to take a man to protect you. Which of my companions would
you choose?" There was a long silence until finally Gwenhwyfar said, "I would
choose Edern son of Nudd." From that day onwards Arthur was consumed with
jealousy for Edern and planned how he might kill him. Some time later he set off
on an adventure with Kai, Bedwyr, Edern and some other men. Gwenhwyfar
had told them she would reward whoever brought her the magic knife
belonging to two fearsome giants who lived in the forest of Malvern near Kaer
Lloyw. When Arthur and his men reached the forest of Malvern they sent Kai to
spy out the land. He found that the stakes forming the palisade round the giants'
fortress were covered with severed heads and, reluctant to go any further, he hid.
When Kai did not return Arthur told Edern to go and see what had happened.
Edern boldly made his way into the fortress. There he heard a noise coming from
the hall and, on going to see what it was, found the two giants roasting a boar.
After a terrible battle he managed to kill them and sat down by the fire to rest and
warm himself in peace. Arthur had heard the battle raging in the hall but
prevented his companions from interfering. When the noise stopped, he made
his way cautiously into the fortress and was amazed to find Edern safe and well.
Kai meanwhile had come out of hiding and was very jealous of Edern's success
in obtaining the knife. Arthur decided to spend the night in the fortress. During
the night Edern was thirsty and Kai offered to fetch him some water. But Kai
went to a well which he knew to be poisoned and when Edern drank the water he
fell into a deep sleep. The next day Arthur and his men assumed that he was dead
and left him in the fortress when they went. Soon after, the two sons of the king
of Iwerddon arrived and found Edern lying unconscious. Being wise in the art of
medicine they saw that he had been poisoned and cured him with the magic
herbs they carried with them. Edern told them what had happened and, leaving
him to recover fully, they set out to find Arthur at Kelliwic. There they met
Gwalchmai and told him what they know about Kai's treachery. Gwalchmai
was furious and publicly accused Kai of having tried to poison Edern. Arthur
had no choice but to condemn Kai to death. Then Edern arrived completely
recovered, asked that Kai's life should be spared and gave Gwenhwyfar the
giants' knife. (The last part of the *Roman d'Yder*.)

Soon after, Arthur had to contend with the fiercest of the Saxon offensives.
They had formed an alliance with the Picts and the Irish pirates and mustered a
formidable army. Arthur summoned all the kings and armies of Britain and
advanced against the enemy. The battle took place at Kaer Vaddon. Arthur
himself killed 960 men on that day and the battle went to the Britons. The
Saxons left the Britons in peace for a long time after that, for they had suffered
such losses that they could no longer hope to take the whole island. (Gildas and
Historia Brittonum.)

Arthur had had three sons. One of them named Gwadre had been killed by
Twrch Trwyth. *One day when Arthur was on an expedition to the North he
encountered a strange horseman with whom he fought.* Only when Arthur had
killed him did he realize that his opponent was his son Amr. That is why there is

a burial mound near a spring known as Llycad Amr. His father had buried Amr there under the great slabs of stone. Miraculously the mound is never the same length no matter how often one measures it. Sometimes it is six feet long, sometimes nine, sometimes twelve (*Historia Brittonum*).

But Arthur had a third son named Llacheu. He was a proud warrior who had fought alongside Kai and Bedwyr, notably at the battle of Trywrwyd (poem XXXI, in the *Black Book of Carmarthen*). He was one of three men in Britain — he, Riwallawn Gorse Hair and Gwalchmai son of Gwyar — who could invent new things (*Triad 27*). Everytime he killed any enemy he would go to sleep on the corpse of his victim. One day Llacheu had just killed a fearsome giant called Llogrin who roamed the forest of Lloegr and was sleeping on his corpse when Kai passed by and saw them there. He became obsessed by jealousy of Llacheu, who was as valorous a warrior as he, and of Arthur who tended to be over-sarcastic towards him. So he killed Llacheu in cold blood and buried him in a stone coffin. Then he cut Llogrin's head off and bore it to Arthur on his saddle to demonstrate his bravery. And Arthur believed that Kai had killed the giant (*Perlesvaux*).

That day a messenger came from the Lady of Pympfyddeilen. She was a young orphan who was being besieged in her fortress by one of her cousins who wanted to take her lands. He had offered to settle the matter by single combat between himself and a champion of her choice. She wanted Arthur to fight for her. So Arthur agreed and prepared to go. Gwalchmai offered to be his squire, but Arthur asked him to remain with Gwenhwyfar and said that he would go alone. As he was mounting his horse, he looked down to see Gwalchmai holding the stirrup and began to laugh. Gwenhwyfar was shocked, but Arthur said, "I have good cause to laugh. First I am the best chief in the world, and then the best knight in the world is holding my stirrup for me." Arthur's wife said nothing, and when he asked her why she hesitated, then answered, "If you want the honest truth, there are other knights as good as Gwalchmai." This angered Arthur. He told Gwenhwyfar to prove her statement or she would lose her head. He would have grabbed her by the hair so angry was he if Gwalchmai had not stopped him. Gwalchmai promised Gwenhwyfar that he would put an end to their quarrel. But Arthur would have none of it and agreed only to delay his judgment until he returned. Gwenhwyfar then promised to justify her words on condition that Arthur took another of his men with him. So Arthur took Bedwyr as his squire. They hastened to the fortress of Pympfyddeilen and arrived on the day the fight was to take place. The Lady of Pympfyddeilen organized great banquets and feasting to celebrate Arthur's victory. He then returned to Kelliwic and admitted to Gwenhwyfar that there was indeed another knight just as good as Gwalchmai. And Arthur was glad that he had gathered round him the best warriors and most skilful knights in the world (*Les Merveilles de Rigomer*, second part).

When Arthur assembled his men, it was always for some important festival which would be celebrated with great bouts of drinking and merry making. In the midst of one such celebration a giant dressed all in green came into Arthur's hall holding an axe. He challenged each of the companions to cut off his head with the axe on condition that the knight in question should then go to the Green Chapel in the giant's northern land after a year and submit to the same form of execution. This challenge was greeted by total silence. In view of the size and obvious self-assurance of the unknown man none dared answer him. Arthur rose and indignantly declared that he would accept. The green giant knelt before him, Arthur took the axe, whirled it around his head and brought it down on the victim's neck. But to everyone's amazement the green giant picked up his head and, holding it in his hand, reminded Arthur of their meeting in one year. Then he left the hall and nobody knew where he went. Months passed and Arthur travelled northwards to honour his promise. After a difficult journey he was given shelter in a fortress. The following morning his host told him that he was going hunting and would leave him alone with his lovely young wife. He felt that he could trust Arthur, but in the evening when he returned they would exchange whatever they had acquired during the day. As soon as her lord had gone the young woman approached Arthur and made every effort to seduce him. Arthur was conscious of his agreement with her husband and stood firm. So that evening he had nothing to give his host in exchange for the game he had caught. The next day the agreement was renewed, but Arthur proved less strong minded than the day before and allowed the woman to give him several kisses which he faithfully passed on to her husband at the end of the day. The third day the woman tried a different form of temptation. She offered him a belt which she claimed was magic and would keep the wearer safe from death or injury. Arthur would obviously have had to give the belt to his host that evening, but when he thought of the horrible death in store for him if the green giant went through with his threat, he decided to keep it for himself. He promised the woman that he would say nothing to her husband in case he was angry that she had given him such a present, and when the man returned that evening Arthur offered nothing in exchange for the venison he brought. The next day Arthur thanked his hosts and journeyed on across wild and desert country to the Green Chapel where the green giant was waiting for him. Arthur said nothing, but knelt to receive the fatal blow. When the giant raised his axe Arthur could not help trembling, whereupon the giant mocked him, saying that he had not trembled in similar circumstances. Arthur held still but the giant let his axe fall without even touching Arthur's neck. Again he raised the axe and let it fall in the same way. The third time the axe grazed Arthur's neck. Then the giant said, "Do you not recognize me? I have been your host for the past three days. I have put you to the test. The first two blows did not touch you. That is your reward for two days of total loyalty. The wound I have given you is punishment for the lie you told me on the third day when you hid the belt you had been given. But as you are obviously a brave man and kept your promise of a year ago, I shall absolve you of your debt to me and let you go." So Arthur returned from the North safe and sound and went back to his fortress of Kelliwic (*The Green Knight*).[11]

But Arthur's courage and valour were not universally admired. Many wished him harm. Many envied him his victories and his power over other kings. Some tricked him into captivity. So it was that Arthur spent three days and three nights in prison at Kaer Oeth and Anoeth (*Triad 56*). This prison had been built by Manawydan son of Llyr and Karadawg son of Bran from the bones of Roman soldiers killed in battle. The bones had been mixed with lime to make a huge round house, fitted with various cells including underground dungeons for traitors (*Iolo Manuscripts*, p. 193). Arthur also spent three nights in prison when Gwen Pendragon caught him, and another three nights in prison under the spell of Llech Echymeint. On all three occasions he was rescued by the same man, Goeu son of Kustennin who came to his aid (*Triad 56*).

Some men used Arthur's absence to their own advantage. One such man, named Medrawt, who was also a war leader and had formed his own troop of warriors, hated Arthur and was obsessed with the idea of taking his place as chief of the kings of Britain. While Arthur was away Medrawt raided the fortress of

Kelliwic leaving neither food nor drink in the whole place. He also dragged Gwenhwyfar from her throne and struck her. He then sexually assaulted her. When Arthur heard of it he gathered his best warriors together and hastened to Medrawt's fortress. There he looted and pillaged, leaving neither food nor drink in the whole place. He then despoiled the surrounding countryside. So the mutual hatred between Arthur and Medrawt grew (*Triad 19*).[12]

Meanwhile, over the sea the men of Brittany were under pressure from their neighbours, who were trying to impose heavy tributes on them. They sent messengers to ask Arthur for help, which he could hardly refuse since large contingents of men from Brittany had come to swell his own forces on several previous occasions. So he took his crack troops over the sea.

Once he had arrived in Brittany he learnt that a dragon was devastating the area. It was a strange and monstrous beast with a man's head, a snake's body and a fish's tail. This creature had gone to earth in a cave at the bottom of a cliff which was said to lead to hell. At dawn the dragon would emerge from the cave, roam round the beach and breathe flames and smoke over the surrounding area until the whole place reeked of sulphur.

Every Christmas Eve it demanded a human victim who had to be of royal blood, and all babies who died before being baptized were also handed over to it.

Arthur tried a score of times to rid the country of this monster, but each time he and his men were forced to flee, urging their horses until they appeared to take flight. At that time there was a saintly hermit called Efflam living in the region. He was Arthur's first cousin. One day when Arthur was hunting he met the hermit, recognized him and fell on his neck, saying "What neither I nor my men have been able to do, you can surely do, for you are a man of God. I pray you, free us of this dragon." "Very well," said Efflam, "take me to its lair." But when they reached the cave it was empty. The dragon had scented Efflam's approach and had hidden in another hole. "We must get it out of there," said Efflam. And he turned to one of Arthur's men and said "Take off your clothes and give them to me." He tore the clothes into pieces and then stood in front of the cave and shouted "Oh snake, if you are really a wizard, make me some new clothes from these rags." This challenge intrigued the dragon. It stuck its nose out, breathed on the rags and they immediately turned into a new suit. But as the dragon was doing this, Efflam made the sign of the cross in the air above it and said "From now on, you belong to me."

"That is true, you have trapped me. But you have not heard the last of me." Efflam, Arthur and his men had to drag the monster along the strand. It was exhausting work and Arthur and his men felt as though their arms were breaking and their throats were on fire. They told Efflam that they would die of thirst without something to drink.

It was then that Efflam made a fountain of pure water flow from the sand. Arthur and his men drank carefully from the spring and a supernatural strength flooded through their veins. They were then able to pull the dragon quite easily to Roc'h Ru where they chained it up for ever. (*Folk tale*).[13]

Then Arthur marched further into Brittany, ridding the land of all foreign invaders as he went. He made camp in the forest of Huelgoat. Finally he advanced through the great forest which covers the whole of central Brittany, and which some call Broceliande. He fought determinedly against any enemies sent to meet him, and won every battle. But he lost the bravest of his warriors (Triad 10) and unfortunately the best of them, including Kai, Bedwyr, Gwalchmai and Edern. When he learnt that Arthur's army had been weakened,

Medrawt saw that the time had come to take his place. He abducted Gwenhwyfar, with the intention of marrying her. Then he formed an alliance with the Picts, the Gaels and the Saxons, with all those who wished Arthur harm. He amassed a formidable army to defend the island shores from Arthur. Arthur decided to go and fight Medrawt. He managed to land in Britain with the remnants of his army only to find Medrawt advancing to meet him. The battle of Camlaan followed. There Arthur killed Medrawt, but was mortally wounded himself (Triad 10). Apart from Gilvaethwy son of Don, there were only three survivors of the battle of Camlaan, Morvran son of Tegid, Sannddev Bryd Angel and Glewlwyt Gafaelfawr. Morvran was saved by his hideous appearance, everyone thought he was a devil and kept out his way. Sannddev was saved by his beauty; no one would strike him because they throught he was an angel. While Glelwyt was so huge and so strong that the enemy fled before him (Triad 96).

Arthur did not die, however. He left the battle field with Gilvaethwy son of Don. He stood on the shore, unbuckled his sword, drew it from its scabbard and looked at it for a long time, saying "Ah, Kaledfwlch, my good and magnificent sword, the best in this country, you are going to lose your master. where will you find another man who can make such good use of you as I have?" Then Arthur said to Gilvaethwy, "Go up that hill. There you will find a lake and you will throw my sword into the water, for I do not wish it to pass into unworthy hands." "Lord," said Gilvaethwy, "I will obey you, but I would rather you gave it to me, if it pleased you." "No," said Arthur, "for you would not make good use of it."

Gilvaethwy climbed the hill and when he reached the lake took the sword out of the scabbard and looked at it. Then he took his own sword and threw it into the lake, hid Kaledfwlch in the reeds and returned to Arthur. "Lord," he said, "I have done as you asked. I have thrown the sword into the lake." Arthur asked, "What did you see?" "Lord, I saw nothing out of the ordinary." "Then you have lied to me. Go back and throw my sword into the lake." Gilvaethwy went back to the lake, took the sword out of its scabbard and began to lament over it. It seemed to him a terrible shame that such a fine weapon should be lost for ever. So he took the scabbard and threw that into the lake, hid Kaledfwlch under a tree and returned to Arthur. He told Arthur he had done as he wished, and again Arthur asked "What did you see?" "Lord, I saw only what you would expect me to see." "Ah, you still have not thrown in my sword. Go back and do as I say, then you will see that there are to be great marvels accompanying the disappearance of this sword." Gilvaethwy went back to where he had hidden the sword, took it and threw it out as far as he could into the deepest part of the lake. Just before the sword hit the surface a hand rose from the water, seized the sword by the hilt and brandished it three times before disappearing under the water again. Gilvaethwy waited there for a long time to see if anything else would happen. And when nothing occurred he went back to Arthur and told him what he had seen. "God!" said Arthur, "I thought my end had come." He remained deep in thought until finally he told Gilvaethwy to leave. Gilvaethwy protested, but Arthur insisted. So Gilvaethwy left Arthur, his eyes full of tears (from the Mort du Roi Arthur).

And nobody knew what happened to Arthur. Some say he was taken to the isle of Avallach by Modron, and that he is waiting there until the time comes to resume his leadership of the British armies. Others say that he lies sleeping in a cave somewhere in a mountain until a messenger comes to wake him with the news that his time has come again. But the more sceptical say that he is really dead, and that they have seen his tomb in Glastonbury Abbey.

PART THREE

Waiting for Arthur

CHAPTER SEVEN

The Specific Qualities of the Celts

ELTIC civilization was entirely paradoxical. It.
spread its net from Ireland to Galtaia in the Anatolian Plateau, and throughout
this area there was a remarkable unity of language, religion and attitudes,
allowing for regional variations. And yet, historically speaking, the Celtic
domain was fragmented into myriads of smaller divisions. It is impossible to
talk of a Celtic kingdom, even less an empire. The territories in which the Celts
lived had no real frontiers and no central governing body. The political
vocabulary of the present day is out of place in their impossible realm,[1] eroded as
it was by its own internal contradictions and by the external pressure of other
civilizations with other conceptions of the order of things.

The Arthurian epic is a reflection of this paradox. Arthur appears to live in a
unified society. The classic, if artificial image of the Round Table with its lack
of precedence among the seated knights is significant. Replaced in its original
context of a gathering round the central hearth in the chieftain's house, the
assembly of knights takes on a distinctly symbolic character. It becomes the
organization of the universe around the fire, whether it be a real fire, a sacred
flame, a cosmic star or the kind of feminine sun represented by Guinevere, the
nucleus and guardian of society. But around this central axis, everything
diverges, disperses. The knights leave on their individual adventures and
quarrel amongst themselves. Arthur is not a king but a convener of kings, a chief
above other chiefs, but with no legal authority. His society is composed of
members of different clans and nations who join temporarily together. And,
because he has no one residence, his court moves with him around the country,
from the North to the South West.

The impression given in the Arthurian romances that there is something

stable and permanent behind Arthur's court is an illusion. Our examination of
the Arthurian myth has already demonstrated its fragility. The centre would
only hold in times of external aggression and was liable to fall apart at the first
outbreak of internal conflict over questions of precedence or self-interest. The
knights' oath of allegiance to Arthur often appears little more than a sham. Even
Kai and Bedwyr, Arthur's earliest followers, are more interested in personal
fame than the prestige of Arthur. Kai may seem unswerving in his devotion, but
he often proves capable of sacrificing everything to save his own good name. So,
the fellowship of the Round Table, which is portrayed as a model of unity, is
actually an assorted band of experienced adventurers. The same paradox is
evident in Arthur's court as in Celtic civilization as a whole. There is an almost
continual swing between the centre, even in its fictitious form, and the world
outside as represented by the knights' adventures, the expression of dreams of
decentralization.

It is this paradox which is supposed to have dealt the death blow to Celtic
civilization. But in fact it did not die, it was only overshadowed by the restrictive
administration of foreign invaders. Gaul may have changed under the Roman
occupation, but the Gauls never became Romans. Britain under the Roman
Empire may have enjoyed a new unity of purpose, but once the empire had
done, all the Celtic tendencies to decentralization floated back to the surface.
The country began to drift its way through the Dark Ages, but, as if to
compensate for the apparent lack of national unity, the Celtic spirit reasserted
itself more explicitly than ever before. For the spirit of the Celts is part and
parcel of the contradictions which shape their civilization, the almost
institutionalized opposition to any ideal of a monolithic administrative
structure. This being so, it is important that we attempt to define Celtic society
and to evaluate its offices, customs and practices.

Roman Society and Celtic Society

Since the Celts were Indo-Europeans, it is perhaps most sensible to compare
Celtic society with Roman society, that being the Indo-European society with
which most of us are familiar. We should, however, remember that Roman
society as we know it, is not purely Indo-European, since the Italian people who
settled in the peninsula which took their name adopted many of the traditions of
the indigenous inhabitants. Neither does Roman society present a homogenous
whole. Like any other living society it evolved over the centuries under various
kinds of pressure. So we shall confine our examination to the earliest Roman
social structures, which have been so well described by Georges Dumezil in his
work on ancient Roman religion.[2]

The essential difference between Roman and Celtic society lies in the ways in
which they grew and developed. Roman civilization was shaped solely
according to the wishes of the Latins, who started by forming an autocracy, then
a defensive establishment continually on its guard against potentially
dangerous neighbouring states,[3] and finally an expansionist, imperialist state.
Even in the final stage, Rome, the *urbs* and *civitas*, remained the centre from
which the empire grew like the circular ripples following a raindrop falling into
a pond. So Roman civilization was the civilization of the Latin people. It owed
its spread across the Italian peninsula and then over the whole Mediterranean
world to force of arms and the strength of its legal organization.

Apart from the great religious sanctuaries of central Gaul, Celtic society has no such focal point. Neither did it have the disciplined authority of a single people converting others to its own form of law. In this respect the civilization of the Celts was more like that of the Greeks, who formed a number of rival cities, all with their own history, their periods of greatness and decline. No one Celtic people ever really dominated the others, except for very short periods.[4] There was no Celtic state in the Latin sense of the word, no ripples flowing from a single, central *urbs*, rather a series of isolated circles of varying importance and size, each developing independently on parallel lines.

The differences between Roman and Celtic society and the ways in which they developed are clearly evident in their social institutions. Here they diverged from an original Indo-European basis, often taking those diametrically opposite directions determined by their separate conceptions of social life and the rules which should govern it.

In Rome the ancient *rex* was both a spiritual and a secular leader, the mediator between the human and the divine. The semi-legendary Numa Pompilius was a model of this kind of legislator, who interpreted divine will for his citizens. But Numa Pompilius is also supposed to have created a special body of men whose duties were to be solely sacred in nature. These *flamines*, whose name corresponds to the Indian word Brahmins, were concerned with the administration of the *res sacrae*. And of them, the *flamen Dialis*, whose life was dedicated to the cult of Jupiter, was by far the most important. The process by which he acquired some of the religious attributes of the *rex* was a fairly complex one.

When the Romans dispensed with the office of king and freed themselves from Etruscan domination, the powers of the ancient *rex* were delegated to other officials. Civil, secular and military authority passed first to a *judex* and then, as political leanings became more republican, to two annually elected consuls. But all religious matters were dealt with by priests. The old *rex* had been able to seek support and advice in religious matters from the *Pontifex maximus*, and once the *rex* had gone, the *Pontifex* naturally felt entitled to some of the king's authority. But there were other priests equally qualified to assume the king's administration of the *res sacrae*, and the *Pontifex* came some way down the hierarchy. According to Festus, "The *rex* is regarded as the greatest of these priests, then comes the *flamen Dialis*, after him the *Martialis*, fourth the *Quirinalis*, fifth the *Pontifex maximus* . . . the *rex* because he is the most power-ful, the *Dialis* because he is the priest of the universe, called *dium*, the *Martialis* because Mars is the father of the founder of Rome, the *Quirinalis* because Quirinus was called from Cures to be associated with the Roman empire, the *Pontifex maximus* because he is the judge and arbiter of things human and divine."

The *rex* referred to above is the republican *rex sacrorum*, that is the man who presided over sacrifices, an office of some importance in a society where every religious ceremony took the form of a sacrifice. As the position of *rex sacrorum* gradually became outmoded, the *flamen Dialis* and the *Pontifex maximus* grew more important. Curiously enough, the *Pontifex* assumed greater political authority, until he became responsible for organizing the whole religious life of the Romans. This explains why Caesar and the emperors who succeeded him felt it necessary to take over the title themselves.

The *flamen Dialis*, on the other hand, became less influential, although as priest to the great god Jupiter and inheritor of the mystical duties of the *rex* he was theoretically the most important of the priests. But as Rome developed, the life of the community passed increasingly into the control of the laity. The consuls had no religious authority, and the fact that even the *Pontifex* became a kind of master of ceremonies meant that his office also passed into lay hands before long. The consuls and the *Pontifex* had specific areas of responsibility, but were subject to no other behavioural taboos than those imposed by their duties. The *flamen Dialis*, on the other hand, was bound by all the taboos which had previously paralysed the ancient *rex* and which also limited the conduct of the Celtic kings.

The *flamen Dialis* was not to leave Rome for any reason whatever, since it was considered essential that he remain in actual physical contact with Roman soil. He even had the feet of his bed covered with a thin layer of mud, and was supposed to sleep in it at least one night in every three. He was only to remove his top clothes inside a building, so that he never bared his skin to the sky. Nor was he ever to take off the apex of his cap, which was his badge of office. If his wife heard thunder or saw lightening, she was *feriata* until she had appeased the gods. The *flamen* himself had to avoid all contact with death, whether with dead people or with uncooked meat. His whole life appears to have been bound up with the god of the sky, and his duty as a priest was to ensure that Jupiter looked kindly upon the Roman soil. He lived with his office, day in and day out. He did, however, enjoy one considerable privilege, for unlike the other citizens of Rome, he was not obliged to respect any oath. As if to underline this right, his clothes and cap contained no knots, and he could wear only hollow or open-work rings. Nor need he uphold the judgment of others. In fact, any fettered man who managed to make his way into the *flamen's* house had to be set free, and his bonds be carried up to the roof and thrown into the street. Similarly anyone who had been condemned to be whipped could throw himself at the feet of the *flamen* and would be saved a beating that day.

Celtic kings were bound by similar restrictions and obligations. The Irish epics furnish a great deal of information about the role of the monarch in Ireland. Although the obligations of the Celtic king varied from one country to another, they were all centred on the idea of permanent authority and on the privileged relations which the king enjoyed with the mysterious domain of the gods.

But the Celtic king appears singularly weak when compared to the Latin *rex*, or even the later Roman consul. He was hemmed in by a vast number of taboos, some of which denied him any freedom of action whatever. The fact that he was chosen from the warrior class by his peers, under the supervision of the Druids, for his physical and moral qualities, made him dependent on those who had elected him. Although his duties often demanded that he involve himself in religious matters, he was not a priest and remained subordinate to the Druids who had ultimate authority. So the king appears as little more than an upholder of public order, and a mediator between his Druid and his people.

For, unlike the *flamen Dialis* and the other Roman priests, whose influence was slowly eroded, the Druid was the driving force behind the communal life of the Celts, on both the sacred and secular levels. The Druid could make or break the king. He took precedence over the king at public ceremonies and had the right to speak before he did. He controlled policy making, presided over trials, supervised contracts, organized political alliances or treaties of friendship with other peoples, and often made decisions about military strategy during wartime. Although exempt from military service he could fight if he wished. Even his purely religious duties gave the Druid considerable power over men's minds. He could declare somebody an outlaw, or worse, condemn him to eternal damnation. And as a doctor and "wizard" he retained a kind of physical hold on the whole community. So, in Celtic countries, where society was essentially theocratic in its leanings, power remained in the hands of the priestly caste, while in Rome, where political tendencies were more democratic, power passed totally to the laity.

The Roman maxim "divide and rule" appears to have been applied as much to the religious area as to any other. There were an astonishing number of priests, but they had none of the corporate identity of the secular powers. So, although they continued to enjoy great prestige, their isolation prevented their having any real influence on Roman politics. Among the Celts, the Druid reigned supreme. There were no other priests, and the Druids formed a highly structured, hierarchical body. This explains why the priestly class maintained its singular importance. In Ireland, their influence lasted even after the advent of Christianity. For the *fili*, the spiritual heirs of both the Druids and the bards, aligned themselves with the new religion and managed to sway both religious and political decision-making. In Britain, the Druids disappeared comparatively early and, although the bards continued some of the more intellectual elements of Druidism, the Druidic priests had no obvious successors. But in those areas where the Celts remained independent, the monks and, more especially, the episcopal abbots remained highly influential figures. In Gaul, on the other hand, the breakdown of Druidic power came much earlier even than in Britain. According to Caesar and the classical writers the Gauls themselves began to reject their governmental structure of king and Druid. During the first century BC, most of the Gallic tribes discarded the monarchy in favour of a system of magistrates who were elected for a fixed period. The Druids continued to uphold the religious traditions and to enjoy a certain amount of prestige, but they surrendered their influence in public affairs to the *equites* or warrior class. This explains why Gaul found it easier to adjust to the new ways of the Roman Empire. Once the *equites* had been accorded Roman citizenship, the total Romanization of Gaul became almost inevitable. The *equites'* aristocratic regime, which divided the population into two categories, noble and plebeian, resulted from a shift in economic thinking. Notions of communal property were gradually replaced by the more Roman ideas of private ownership and entitlement to land. It may well be that this new system was merely a reflection of the existing state of affairs in Gaul. For agriculture was developing at a great rate on the continent, while the British and Irish continued their semi-nomadic, pastoral way of life.

The kind of economic development observable in Gaul from the first century BC did not affect Britain until much later, and hardly affected Ireland at all until the Anglo-Norman conquest of the island. The difference between the island Celts, with their loyalty to the ancient ideals of open, communal society, and the continental Celts, with their increasing emphasis on individualism, may be due also to the influence of the Romans or of the non-Celtic indigenous peoples of Gaul. For although the Gauls' concept of State remained equally ill-defined, they realized that land meant wealth, whether in terms of agricultural output or mining. And once the *equites* became land conscious they were able to use their skill as warriors to seize everything of value and reduce the rest of the population to a state of servitude or outright slavery. The king was powerless to stop them, while the Druids, whose political authority had functioned reasonably well within an egalitarian and integrated community, found their power diminishing as society divided along the vertical plane.

Nevertheless the Celts of Gaul, Britain and Ireland continued to think and organize their lives along very different lines from the Romans. Roman democracy was a hollow façade covering what was actually an aristocracy. The governmental structure of the empire was merely an extension of the early Indo-European system whereby power was limited to one tribe, or a group of three *genos*. This tribe had assumed authority over all others and ruled the community of the *viri*, or, as they were called within the *civitas*, the *quirites*. The *civitas*, or state, was originally almost synonymous with the *urbs*, or town; but then, as centralization appeared more necessary, it came to be linked with the town of all towns, Rome. Urbanization among the Celts was virtually non-existent. What Gallic towns there were, were all built in the immediate vicinity of Greek or Roman settlements and in imitation of them. Entremont, near Aix-en-Provence, for example, looks more like a fortress than an ordinary town, and the Salluvii, who lived there before the Roman conquest, are classified as Celto-Ligurians, people of mixed origins whose culture and politics were Gallic but whose technical skills and general attitudes came from the indigenous peoples. According to the authors of classical antiquity, the Gallic towns were all fortresses which provided a temporary haven for the peasants in times of danger and a permanent home for the warriors and the craftsmen who made their weapons. *Bibracte*, or Mont Beuvray, the capital of the Heduens, and Alesia are typical in this respect. In Britain, the towns so carefully constructed by the Romans were abandoned after they left for a life on the land or in well-defended fortresses.

The Roman religion, too, was clearly centred in Rome. The early Roman gods were local divinities, and although they later came to be confused with the gods of the Greeks, and other peoples, they remained essentially Roman and urban. The principal temples stood within the *pomarium*, that is within the city limits of early Rome, and were built not only to last but also to provide a focal point for the Roman people as they set out to conquer Europe. The religion of the Celts could not have been more different. A number of gods are classified as pan-Celtic because there is evidence that they were worshipped both in Ireland and in Gaul, but there were also vast numbers of local gods, by no means necessarily Celtic, throughout the various countries occupied by the Celts. Apart from very rare exceptions, the Celts built no temples, but preferred to worship in the *nemeton*[5] or sacred grove, which was regarded as a piece of heaven on earth. And, apart from the religious sites of pre-Celtic tradition, like the sanctuary at Stonehenge and the prehistoric sanctuary at Tara, places of worship were not necessarily fixed. There is no reason to suppose that the sanctuaries inside the Celtic fortresses were any more important than the temporary sanctuaries scattered here and there over forest and countryside. The way in which religious sites were dispersed continued into the Christian Era, as we can see from the development of Celtic abbeys as isolated and autonomous spiritual centres.

The fact that in Rome one tribe assumed authority over the others, within the precise and limited framework of the urban state, suggests that the Romans were a sedentary people. The Celts, however, hovered continually between a nomadic and a settled existence. This is evident even in first-century-BC Gaul. There the tribes were established in specific regions, but their frontiers were not clearly delineated, and they appear to have migrated, either totally or partially, from place to place. There were Boii both in Bohemia and south of the Gironde, where they gave their name to the Teste de Buch. The Parisi and the Atrebates, who were established in the area of Arras, also settled in Britain. The Cornovi, who originally lived in eastern Wales and central England, are later found in Cornwall, the Kernyw which bears their name; while the movement of peoples in Ireland refutes any suggestion that the Celts had become purely sedentary people.

Roman agriculture and craftsmanship rested on a well-rooted, established existence. The boundaries of the state were fixed and marked by frontier stones. There was even a god named Terminus who presided over the fixing of frontiers, and these frontiers were regarded as static, even if they had to be moved after wars of conquest. The role of the priests known as the *Fetiales* is also significant. They would cross the frontiers into enemy territory and call upon the gods of Rome to witness their solemn declaration of a state of war. When the empire grew so large that such ritual became a physical impossibility, the custom continued in a more symbolic form, with the *Fetiales* marking out a piece of land to be regarded as enemy territory and pronouncing their sacred formulae there. The early Roman state was an *urbs* which cast its net over a vast area to form the *civitas*, all of whose inhabitants were to be regarded as its citizens. So there developed a very precise notion of the fatherland, which gave rise to the well documented patriotism of the early Romans.

For the Celts the idea of the fatherland was related solely to the idea of common racial origin. Under threat of total conquest, as in the final phases of the Gallic Wars, or during the Arthurian period, this abstract notion might become more concrete, but such cases were exceptions. An identical culture, an identical language and an identical religion provided fellow-feeling enough for the Celts: they needed no more. Since their frontiers fluctuated they would only bother to defend them if neighbouring peoples became too troublesome in their attacks. There was nothing to mark their boundaries, which in any case usually coincided with the geographical walls provided by rivers, seas, mountain ranges and the great forests. These last formed a kind of no-man's-land like the area of early medieval Brittany which legend turned into the forest of Broceliande.[6] Within their respective societies, the Romans and the Celts also differed in their methods of delineating property. The Romans had an acute sense of private ownership, the Celts little or none. Until the 12th-century, the Irish maintained their system of communal land on which the collectively owned flocks of the *fhine* were sent to graze.[7]

In Rome the authority formerly in the hands of the ancient *genos*, and then of the tribe, passed to one man, the head of the family. He had total control over the members of his family or *genos*, and as one *genos* became predominant, his sphere of influence extended to cover the whole tribe. This *pater familias* was a reflection of his totally male-dominated society, in which the exclusive ownership of land and animals gave rise to strong feelings of individualism. Among the Celts, the chief of the *fhine* or tribe was only a representative of the community and owned neither land nor animals nor people in his own name. His job was to maintain a balance within the community and when he acted it was in the name of the whole social body which had given him a mandate to do so. The early *genos* survived as the Romans *gens* because the memory of former days was deliberately kept alive. The mortal superiority derived from the standing of one's forebears, which enabled the head of the *gens* to claim pre-eminence over other men less fortunate in their ancestors, led to a glorification of lineage and even, if needs be, to the invention of noble antecedents. Even when the plebeians began to infiltrate political life and were given military or civic responsibilities under the empire, the ancient *gentes* continued to enjoy great prestige. They were the *liberi*, the only men publicly acknowledged as the first free citizens of Rome. It was the *gens* which formed the basic unit of non-egalitarian Roman society. The fact that the *fhine* stood as the basic unit of Celtic society might lead us to suppose that the early Indo-European *genos* had developed along similar lines in both cases. But there were in fact many differences. The Celtic community was united in its purpose and the *fhine* was not so obviously defined in patriarchal terms. Succession was often matrilineal, from mother to son, from maternal uncle to nephew. And the chief of the *fhine* was not necessarily a *pater familias* of the Latin type, since he was elected by the members of the *fhine*, the upholders of tradition. Finally, all the Celts, whether they divided their societies into *fhines* or tribes, inherited some of the totemism of the non-Indo-Europeans, probably from the aboriginal peoples they conquered. So clans grew up, united by both the memory of common ancestors and by a kind of blood brotherhood. We have an example of this in the warrior clan of the Red Branch in Ulster which formed around King Conchobar, or in any of those collections of individuals who sought to create new social groupings outside the family circle and therefore chose to accept the authority of a chief and live in brotherhood together. This is the only plausible explanation for the traces of totemism evident throughout the area dominated by the Celts. In Gaul, it emerged mainly as symbolic representations of animals and plants, but the tendency to totemism was much more pronounced and explicit in Britain, and positively blatant in Ireland. We have already discussed the connexions between the dog and Conchobar together with his nephew Cú Chulainn, between the stag and Finn (Demne), his son Oisin and his grandson Oscar, between the horse and King March, and between the bear and King Arthur. A more detailed study of these non Indo-European totemistic leanings would undoubtedly furnish a key to a number of the peculiarities of Celtic society that differentiate it from other Indo-European societies. But it would require great discernment, for although the early magico-religious structures behind totemism passed into Druidism, they are difficult to sift from the scraps of evidence we have relating to this field.[8]

As far as we can tell from Irish customs, the creation of the Celtic *tuath* or tribe[9] followed a total agreement on the part of the chiefs of the *fhine*, rather than any attempt at domination by one *fhine*. Since the king of the *tuath* was elected from among the members of a royal *fhine*, all active members of the community had to give their assent. And as the king of the *tuath* was himself bound by personal allegiance to a higher king, who was bound in the same way to a provincial king, a hierarchy was created, but a hierarchy within which every man kept his independence. The whole system worked as a kind of confederation based on mutual trust. So much is evident from the practice of giving hostages. The inferior king gave hostages to his lord and received from him a sum of money or a certain amount of livestock as a token of his dependence. This sort of *cheptel* contract appeared in Britain and Ireland and must have developed throughout Celtic territory in early times. The inferior king was then obliged to pay an annual tribute and to supply and equip a certain number of warriors for military service. In return, the lord was to help his vassal whenever he needed it, whether as a result of personal quarrels or intertribal conflict. But this system of mutual obligation affected only the two kings involved. The community as a whole remained the ultimate proprietor of its lands and master of its own fate. So, in theory, the members of even the smallest social group were in no way subject to the authority of a king of higher rank.

It is very hard for minds like ours conditioned by Latin thought to grasp ideas like these. How can kings be bound to one another without their allegiance involving the members of the communities they represent? But it is these ideas which make Celtic society so paradoxical, and which laid it open to the aggressive thrust of the centralized Roman powers. From the strictly Latin point of view shared by most of our contemporaries the Celtic system is unworkable.

Nevertheless it did work, and for a long time. In Ireland, where its very purity of application made it appear weaker, the system lasted until Henry II assumed the title of *ard ri*, or high king, and exploited the *status quo* there to colonize the island. The Celtic system only became unviable when confronted by other systems which demanded other methods and were based on totally different intellectual or philosophical criteria.

No Roman could have fully understood the Celtic concept of kingship. The Celtic monarch appears so powerless. The Druids acted as a kind of senate, creating legislation and upholding both spiritual and secular tradition. Real authority was vested in the community. The king remained a symbolic figure. And yet the number of taboos and obligations to which he was subject prove that the Celts attached great importance to his office. Apart from having to attend battles, he also presided over the grand assemblies of the community. These gatherings were usually held in a sacred place, on a burial mound for example. So it was that the general assemblies of the Irish provinces were held at Tara, the home of the high king, which had become a sanctuary because of the prehistoric burial mound there. And on a smaller scale, each province, *tuath* or tribe would hold their meetings in the same way throughout Ireland, Britain and Gaul.

These meetings were intended to provide a forum for all the different members of the community. An Irish text says that any Ulsterman who did not come to the Samain meeting (on November 1) at Emain Macha would die. So there was a sacred obligation to attend, and anyone who chose not to go was dishonoured on both a religious and a national level. Apart from enabling people to form friendships and discuss their private affairs, these gatherings also performed the function of a parliament where decisions affecting the whole community could be taken. In this respect they were not unlike the democratic assemblies of early Rome where the limited number of citizens made direct access a feasibility. The Celtic assembly also doubled as a kind of judicial hearing at which any man could ask for justice. The king was not expected to overstep his rights. In Ireland there was a special judge, the *brithem rig*, who could intervene whenever the king infringed the customs of the community. This judge could also hear family disputes within the *tuath*, but only at the specific request of the two parties concerned, for there was no system of public prosecution. The principle underlying this system was that the two sides should be able to choose whichever qualified judge they wanted. Nothing could be further from the rigidity of the Roman judicial system.

In Roman society there were three classes of citizen which corresponded to the accepted Indo-European tripartition. First there was the royal and priestly class, protected by Jupiter, then the class of the *equites* or patricians, who were originally warriors and became the great land owners, protected by Mars, and lastly there was the plebeian class of agricultural workers and craftsmen protected by Quirinus, a deity frequently confused with Romulus. The *servi* or slaves remained outside the class system. They might be prisoners of war or convicted debtors, and were the property of the *pater familias*. Then there were the freemen who worked as servants and dependants of the head of a *gens*. They were counted among the members of the *gens* but not as members of any of the three social classes.

As one might expect, these three classes also existed in Celtic society, with various differences however. The king and the Druids occupied the highest position in the hierarchy and formed a separate class although they were originally drawn from among the warrior noblemen (Irish *flaithi*) who made up the second class. On an equal footing with the warriors were the *aes dana*, or "men of art," the poets, historians, doctors and master craftsmen. The third class was composed of the free men who worked the earth and bred the livestock, paying their taxes in kind to the king as representative of the community. These free men (Irish *grad fene*) formed a considerable proportion of the population, but cannot strictly be compared to the Roman plebeians. The free man was usually a *cele*, which meant that he served a nobleman or *celsine*. The *cele* would offer the *celsine* a specific quantity of goods and unpaid labour in return for live-stock to graze on his land and limited protection against unprovoked assault from more powerful neighbours.

The Celtic second class differs totally from the Roman patrician class in that it includes craftsmen and intellectuals or artists, proof that these men were highly esteemed members of the community. The early Roman poets were slaves, usually Greeks, and even teachers were only more privileged servants. The Celts, on the other hand, regarded their cultural traditions as extremely important and placed skill in fighting on a level with intellectual or technical ability. So although the Romans and the Celts must have lived within very similar social structures to start with, their societies moved in completely different directions. The course of development followed by the Celts had much to do with the influence of those non-Indo-European peoples whom they conquered and integrated into their own society. For the indigenous peoples tended to be the artists and craftsmen.

Those men outside the social hierarchy belonged to two groups as in Rome, but there the comparison ends. First there were the dependants, probably originally native peoples, who could be divided into two categories: free men and servants. The master would give his dependant a number of livestock in return for agricultural produce or gifts. But whatever his supposed status the dependant was free to sever relations with his master by annulling their contract, an option open to either side in certain circumstances. There is evidence of this system at work and throughout the Celtic area, especially in Gaul, where it appears to have the power and prosperity of the noble class.

Although slavery was common practice in Rome and increased as the wars of conquest brought new captives, it appears to have been less prevalent among the Celts. That they had slaves there can be no doubt. They had words for them, *mug* in the masculine and *cumal* in the feminine. But the Romans tended to treat their slaves like beasts of burden, whereas the Celts were more considerate and do not appear to have kept so many of them. The Celts had respect for human life and individual freedom.

They also regulated their society according to a set of well defined customs. These cannot be termed laws, since the word itself implies written legislation and writing did not exist among the Celts. They preferred to adhere to the oral method, in which tradition could be kept continually vital and evolving as they sought to adapt it to suit the circumstances. It is this which distinguishes the pragmatism of the Celts from the immovable juridicature of the Romans. Roman written law had all the force of modern statutes. And as the Roman state became politically stable and well defined, the *jus privatus* and the *jus publicus* began to run on separate lines. Among the Celts there was no distinction between the two. Since the basic social unit was the *fhine*, a community, and not the individual, private and public law were one and the same.

The Celts believed that the gods, like the community, were indifferent to the justice or injustice of individual human acts. It was up to men themselves to sort out their problems and obtain justice and satisfaction. There were effectively two means of redressing wrongs. We have already discussed the obligation on the part of the master or overlord to intervene on behalf of his weaker dependant and thus enforce the preservation of his traditional rights. But the Celts also used the oath as an arm of the law. This was not a simple declaration of intent but something much more serious which could involve either an individual or the whole community. Since this oath was generally uttered in public and in the presence of a Druid with the gods being called upon to witness, it went beyond the secular domain. In this respect it was as awe-inspiring and incontrovertible as the oaths which the ancient Greeks made before the gods of Hades. When Gallic ambassadors came to form an alliance with Alexander the Great in 336 BC they rectified their treaty by swearing a solemn oath involving the elements. "If we do not keep to our promises, may the heavens fall on us and crush us, and may the earth open up and swallow us, may the sea swell up and drown us." This has been rather insultingly and crassly interpreted as evidence that the Gauls lived in constant terror of the sky falling on their heads. But the reports of Alexander's conversation with the Gauls make it clear that they regarded their oath very seriously indeed. For when he asked them whom or what they feared the most, undoubtedly hoping that they would answer it was he, they simply replied, "The sky falling on our heads." Obviously they were far more concerned to respect their oath, and conscious of the burden it imposed on them than they were frightened of even so powerful a man as Alexander. There are many examples of oaths of this kind in Irish epic. On each occasion the man uttering the oath calls on the forces of nature, thus acknowledging that any failure to keep his promise will make him an outcast in the eyes not only of his own community but of the natural world and of the gods who are above every-day life.

When King Conchobar has been told that enemies are looting the land and killing the men of Ulster, in the *Raid of Cualnge*, he utters a solemn oath in the form of a sacramental formula. "The sky is above us, the earth beneath us, the sea surrounds us. If the sky does not fall with its shower of stars upon the earth where we live, if the earth does not shake and break open, if the sea of blue-grey solitudes does not come over the long-haired forehead of life, I will be victorious in fights and battles, and bring back the cattle to the cowshed and the women to the house." (*Book of Leinster*, p. 91.)

A legend about the supreme king of Ireland, Loegaire, a 5th-century contemporary of St Patrick, tells how he promised not to claim tribute from his vassal kings and gave the sun and the moon, the water and the air, the day and the night, the sea and the earth to pledge his words. But he went back on his oath and it is said that the earth swallowed him up, the sun burnt him, and the wind suffocated him. The perjurer had to die, for there was no place for him in the land of the living.

This explains the importance of the legal oath. It laid hands on every aspect of

Celtic social life, taking on various forms more closely allied to magic than to the calculated and rational logic of the Roman judicial system. In a sense we might call Celtic civilization magical and Roman civilization logical. Any man accused of murder by the victim's relatives could defend himself with an oath, since perjury would be unthinkable in the part religious, part magical aura pertaining to the oath. Indeed all the judicial problems arising in daily life could be dealt with in this way.

In any organized society the marriage contract tends to be given special attention. And for the Celts and the Romans, whose social structures were based on exogamic relationships, marriage might be regarded as especially significant since it lay at the basis of the all important family unit. In Rome the marriage ceremony was momentous enough to require the protection of the *flamen Dialis*, but it was also a legal contract creating a new couple as the bride became part of her husband's family. In ancient Rome marriage was a remarkably stable institution. It was not until much later, when morality became more lax and Greek ideas began to penetrate Roman society that divorce became possible. For the most part, however, marriage was a permanent contract, as solid and inviolable as Rome itself.

A Celtic marriage was also a contract made before gods and men, but of a much more temporary nature, with no pretensions to perpetuity, and this despite the fact that polygamy was also practised. Unlike the Roman bride the Celtic wife continued to belong to her own family, and divorce was relatively easy to obtain on various grounds, including mutual consent. The Romans tolerated the practice of concubinage although it was formally forbidden by law, but a married Celt could keep one or more concubines in his home always provided his wife agreed. And the concubine was also protected by a kind of short-term marriage contract which guaranteed her financial security and independence. After a year she would then be free unless she formed a new contract for the following year.

Celtic women, generally speaking, enjoyed a far more liberated position in society than their Teutonic or Roman counterparts. A Roman wife remained a minor within her husband's family, with no right to her own property, while a Celtic married woman had full adult status and could acquire or own property of her own so that her independence was assured. In Rome all decisions relating to family affairs were taken by the husband alone. This also happened among the Celts, but only if the wife had no property of her own. When both partners had an equal fortune, the wife's advice and consent had to be sought in all things. And if the woman owned more than her husband she was regarded as the head of the household and could settle any family matter without her husband's consent. It was also possible for women to claim the throne, either by birth or as the late king's widow. We know that there were reigning queens like Boudicca and Cartismuanda in Britain, and Irish epic contains examples of such female sovereigns, including the paradigm of queenliness, Medbh. All this would seem to suggest that the Celts had diverged from the patriarchal attitudes of their Indo-European forebears.

And yet the women of ancient Rome appear to have had a slightly higher status than their descendants. We find evidence of this in the legend of Acca Larentina and in the institution of the Vestals, priestesses whose duty it was to watch over the sacred flame of Vesta in her unique circular temple. The high regard in which they were held by the king, and later by the consuls, suggests that they may have been involved in major decisions concerning affairs of state.

But we know very little about them, although the semi-legendary Numa Pompilius is traditionally accredited with their inauguration; and it would be wrong to jump to conclusions about their real position in Roman society. It is however possible to compare the Vestals with the Celtic warrior women, later described as witches, who were responsible for the sexual initiation and general education of young people, more especially in the fields of magic and warfare. There is no record of this strange sisterhood in the historical documents relating to the period, but traces of it exist in Irish and Welsh epic, notably in the *Education of Cú Chulainn*, the *Childhood of Finn*[10] and *Peredur.*[11]

It is possible that the role of women in Celtic society was conditioned by external influences. Certainly there were memories of distant times when the native peoples colonized by the Celts had lived in a more gynaecocratic society. These peoples may also have been responsible for the strange system of adoption or fosterage practised by the Celts. Whereas an adopted child in Rome would sever all relations with his natural family, the adopted child in Celtic society belonged by law to both families. So while the child was bound to come to the assistance of his adoptive father and was regarded by other members of the family as one of them, he was still a member of his natural family and had to respect his obligations towards them also. In Rome, moreover, the process of adoption involved nobody but the adopter and the adopted, the two families remaining entirely separate. Among the Celts both families were totally involved and the system of fosterage came to give society in general a cohesion on the horizontal plane which its lack of allegiance on the vertical scale tended to deny it. For the emotional bonds formed in this way humanized other social relationships which might otherwise have remained purely legalistic. The customs of fosterage continued in Ireland even during the Anglo-Norman occupation when it became fasionable to send one's sons or daughters to be fostered by some unrelated person who was known to be highly skilled in a specific area. The children brought up together in this way acquired a new sense of brotherhood of the kind so vividly portrayed between Kai and Arthur in the Arthurian romances. One of the most tragic episodes in Irish epic occurs in the *Raid of Cualnge*, when Cú Chulainn has to fight his foster brother Ferdead. Ferdead is killed and the victorious Cú Chulainn bewails the unhappy fate of his brother.

It is also interesting to compare the Roman dictator with the Celtic war leader. If the fatherland of republican Rome was threatened in any way the normal form of government was suspended and the magistrates entrusted the care of the nation to a dictator. This man was given total control for six months so that he could do whatever was necessary to lead the army to victory. The office of dictator was a temporary and extraordinary institution. There was nothing like it among the various Celtic peoples. At times of conflict one man would come forward and offer to organize the defence of the country into a confederation. We have various examples of this. Vercingetorix was not a king, but took it upon himself to unite his countrymen and drive the Romans out of Gallic territory. The Briton Cassivellaunus tried to raise a coalition against the Roman legions The British queen Boudicca attempted to do the same, and there are further examples in Irish history. The historical Arthur, the *dux bellorum* can only really be viewed in these terms, as the last hope of the Celtic peoples. But the motley crew of chieftains who followed Arthur's lead were a far cry from the Roman dictator. There is an undeniable impression that the Celts preferred not to entrust too much authority to any one man, in case they compromised their own civil liberties to pay for his services against the enemy. There was a libertarian spirit among the Celts which remained with them throughout their history and which shines through their epic traditions.

Roman military organization altogether differed from that of the Celts. Indeed it might be more accurate in the Celts' case to call it "unorganization." The Romans had a well developed sense of warfare and military technique, of discipline and respect for the military hierarchy. History and epic have left an equally vivid impression of the Celts as a disordered mass of warriors rushing headlong into battle without any forward planning and any real "esprit de corps." This did not prevent them winning many of their battles and inspiring terror in their enemies. The campaign of 387 BC which culminated in the fall of Allia and the capture of Rome by the Gauls makes this clear enough.[12] All the classical historians agree that the Gauls were excellent fighters of exceptional courage, but they had none of the scientific approach to battle strategy of the Romans. And what emerges from the *Gallic Wars* is their lack of unity in the face of the implacable organization of Caesar's legions. This would certainly explain how so few legions managed to hold the Gauls even when they rose behind Vercingetorix apparently intent on driving out the Romans once and for all. The Celtic form of warfare probably worked perfectly well within the Celtic area, but it was helpless against the crushing weight of the Roman military machine.

All these differences come down to a basic opposition between the singular logic and philosophical ideas of the Celts and the rational thought of the Romans, an opposition which manifested itself on every level. The Romans realized this when they outlawed the Druids, not because they opposed other religions in general, but because Druidism represented a whole system of thought incompatible with Latin rationalism. The Celts had diverged from the Indo-European mould just as much in religious practice as in any other facet of daily life. The Romans gradually abandoned mythology in favour of an increasingly complicated and political ritual; while the Celts discarded ritual in favour of an increasingly rich and complex mythology. Similarly in the legal sphere, the Roman *lex* is the *jus* or ancient sacred law rendered fixed and secular by written, immutable legislation. The Celts also had a sacred *jus* which governed interpersonal relations and every kind of contract. Their law, however, was embodied not in stone inscriptions but in customs and usage, constantly maintained by tradition and fed by fresh contributions from each passing generation.

The importance they attached to mythology goes a long way to explaining the mentality of the Celts as compared to their Roman neighbours. In Rome myth was made into history to conform with the logical Latin temperament. Among the Celts history was made into myth. In this sense, the Celts were closer to the Indians who lived on the far side of the Indo-European world.

As Georges Dumezil has pointed out,

> The Romans thought *historically*, the Indians [and Celts] *in fables*. People of every land tell their stories about some moment in the past. For the Roman audience this moment had to be in the relatively recent past and belong to a recognizable time and place. The story had to be about men, not imaginary beings, and had to stick as closely as possible to the conflicts and events of everyday life. The Indians [and Celts] had different tastes. They delighted in great distances, long periods of time and wide open spaces. They liked digressions and vagueness, and larger than life monsters. They were greedy

for marvels of all kinds. The Romans thought *in national terms*, the Indians [and Celts] *in cosmic terms*. The Romans only took any interest in a story if it had some connection with Rome. Their tales had to be episodes of Roman history, used to explain the origins of some facet of urban organization, the dos and don'ts of acceptable conduct, local government or prejudice. [The Indians and Celts] on the other hand . . . were not interested in shortlived national dominions. They reserved their concern for the origins, vicissitudes and rhythms of the Universe rather than for the trials and tribulations of humanity. The Romans thought *along practical lines*, the Indians [and Celts] *philosophically*. The Romans made no speculations about past, present or future. They acted only in full awareness of the aims and means of their actions, and never sought to understand or imagine anything more. The Indians [and Celts] lived in a world of ideas and contemplation, conscious of the fallibility and the possible dangers inherent in any action, aware of their own longings and of existence itself. The Romans thought *politically*, the Indians [and Celts] *in ethical terms*. Since Rome was the most conspicuous thing within reach of their perceptions, the life of Rome a continual problem and even religion no more than one aspect of public administration, everything the Romans thought about and did was governed by the *res publica*. Their duties, their rules and consequently the tales which make up the fount of Roman wisdom all incline towards politics, institutions and procedure, towards the casuistry of the consul or the censor or the tribune. Every Indian [or Celt] from the highest class to the lowest saw his first duty as being to the gods, or to the great ideas which could be put on a par with the gods. As their social order only held firm when it conformed to the general laws governing the world, the organization of society was merely a secondary science, deduced from greater truths, rather than an art directly induced from the examination of its constituent parts. Finally, the Romans thought *in judicial terms*, the Indians [and Celts] *mystically*. The Romans arrived at the concept of the individual very early in their history and used it, together with notions of autonomy, security and personal dignity to construct the *jus*, their ideal of human relationships. The gods were only called upon to act as witnesses or guarantors. India [and the Celtic world], on the other hand, grew increasingly convinced that individuals are no more than deceptive appearances and that ultimately there is only the One. They believed, therefore, that true relationships between men and men or between men and other beings should be concerned with participation and permeation, rather than opposition and negotiation. So, however earthbound the matter in hand, the senior partner in all dealings remained the great invisible one with whom the visible partners joined and intermingled.[13]

Not all Romans believed in life after death, and those who did saw the world beyond the grave as a pale and ethereal reflection of life on earth. For the Celts, as Lucan writes in the Pharsalia, "death is only the middle of a long life." This belief in the existence of another world, a short distance away from ours, where humans continue to live a similar life, is an important contributory factor to the psychological balance of the Celts. Both the Latin writers and the British and Irish traditions furnish evidence that the Celts believed the soul to be immortal, and this would certainly explain the ease with which they adapted to Christianity. For them, the other world was not a totally invisible place, a dark and sinister underground, but a close, adjacent, familiar spot rather like the Castle of the Grail which only the receptive eye can see. It was not hostile because there were times when it became accessible to everyone; and in any case death held no fear for the Celts since they expected to find all their usual friends and enemies in the after life. Celtic legend teems with journeys to the resting place of the gods and the dead which, according to all accounts, is a marvellous paradise, an orchard where the fruit is ripe all year round, where death and old age are unknown. This explains the serenity and inner tranquility of the Celts. They are always ready to sound the depths of human life, to imagine the kind of world they might find if they were to open their eyes on the shores of another life. Unlike Roman civilization, Celtic civilization is totally unmaterialistic, but paradoxically it is also totally amoral. Celtic society had a basic faith in man and tended to overlook those minor sins which the strict formalism of the Romans would have inevitably attributed to every man. It is clearly a civilization of magic as opposed to the Roman civilization of logic, but above all, it is a civilization of mystical contact between the beings of the other world and the men of the living.

Finally there is the climatic difference to be taken into account. Roman civilization developed in a Mediterranean environment where everything is very distinct, bright and well delineated, where light and dark form a sharp and total contrast. It follows that the civilizations of the Mediterranean basin were affected by Manicheism or, at the very least, by a marked tendency to dualism. In a climate where only dark and light exist, choices become reduced to two alternatives, and two alone. Having inherited these Mediterranean ideas, Latin civilization could only allow of absolute principles with absolute value, even if these values were restrictive and cut out all possibility of exploring the realms of dream and intuition which are not based on absolute criteria.

The Celts' answer to Roman logic is their sense of analogy. Their whole system of thought is different and ultimately this difference can be laid at the door of their geographical environment. The Celts were Nordic peoples, living in landscapes of delicate nuances and blurring mists, grappling with the boundless sea which they thought marked the end of the inhabited world and a passage to the land of night and the dead. Living conditions were extremely harsh. Life was a constant struggle against the unfriendly elements. Given these conditions, it becomes as clear to us as it was to the Baronne de Staël and the other early Romantics that differences between peoples are a function of their different responses to their natural environment. Climate even dictates habitat. Urbanization was possible, even essential in Mediterranean countries, where people congregated around water sources and sought to protect themselves from the heat. It was far less vital in the temperate humidity of the northern lands where water never became scarce and where settlements would be built wherever the livestock which formed the basic wealth of the Celts could be free to roam across good grazing land.

Roman society started life inside a fortified town where a continual state of defensiveness eventually led to aggression, in a country of small valleys and a hot dry climate. Celtic society developed within vast panoramas and misty horizons, where small bodies of people grouped together to rear animals and only used their fortresses when seriously threatened. The ideals of the Celts and the Romans were as different as the motives which drove the farmers and the cattlemen of the American Far West to their bitter fighting. The farmers wanted to fence in the land and to shelter behind rigorously enforced laws. The cattlemen on the other hand wanted to be able to graze their herds across the wide open spaces, unrestricted by any form of enclosure, and to be free of any law specifically designed to hinder rather than help them. The Romans were the farmers, the Celts the cattlemen. As Gaul slowly changed from a pastoral to an agricultural way of life, the Gauls and the Romans grew much closer together, until it became possible for Gaul to be colonized and assimilated into the empire.

The Contribution of the Celts

It has all too often been said that the Celts organized their society in an unworkable manner, and that this was the main reason for their progressive elimination from the political map of Europe. Nothing could be more wrong. Some people would have us believe that the Roman system is the only one which can possibly endure. But it all depends on one's viewpoint. Obviously it is hard for people educated in the present classical tradition to countenance the apparent disorder of Celtic society; but by taking a step back and ridding our minds of the oppressive weight of our Greco-Roman heritage, it is possible to look at our forefathers' extraordinary social system in a completely different light.

There is one point which must be made at the outset. Celtic civilization did not simply die, as so many others did, from degeneracy within. The Roman Empire, in particular, declined because its heterogeneous populations were influenced by various other cultures, including that of the "barbarians," which gradually penetrated the frontiers of the Roman World. Celtic civilization died in the stranglehold of other societies of a different kind which conquered it by military force. The Romans put down Gallic society by decimating the intellectual elite of Gaul. The Anglo-Normans overcame Ireland by simply colonizing the island. The Saxons overcame the Britons by brutal repression and assimilation. Brittany, which remained an object of contention between the Anglo-Normans and the Capetians for so long, was finally subdued after a military defeat at St Aubin du Cormier at the end of the 15th century, and allowed itself to be annexed to the French crown. In none of these countries, however, did the death blow come from inside. Ireland's ancient and singular system kept it perfectly intact and viable until the 12th century. Wales maintained its own customs until the 13th century, and some of them survive to this day within the federal framework of the United Kingdom. Brittany survived as a nation until the 16th century. History has shown that the social system of the Celts was workable, stable and enduring. Once we look at it more closely we find that it was a specific and highly efficacious system. Far from being disorganized and anarchic, Celtic society was well ordered, but in a way which had nothing to do with the logical Roman system.

To understand what made Celtic society so idiosyncratic we have to go back to the dialectical argument, to its inherent paradoxes and contradictions. The need for unity, which is so often stated and reasserted in the epic texts, is offset by an almost deliberate longing to remain dispersed and independent. And while the need for unity works along a vertical line, the desire for independence functions along the horizontal. The social system realized by the Irish managed to reconcile these two contradictory ideas. Since the basic social unit was the *fhine* or *derbfhine*, the family to four generations, and exogamy meant marrying outside one's own family, a minimum of three *fhines* were needed to form a *tuath*. The *tuath* therefore included three heads of family, or **p°teres*, who, in response to the need for unity would agree that one of them should take precedence and become elected king of the *tuath*. This king, however, represented only the common interests of the *tuath*, while the head of each *fhine* continued to be responsible for his own particular family group. This meant that the king of the *tuath* played an outward looking role, and the heads of *fhines* (including the king) concerned themselves with the internal affairs of each family.

Above the king of the *tuath* there was a higher king or overlord, whose superior authority came from the larger numbers of livestock or warriors at his disposal as the representative of his community. He too was head of a *fhine* which had joined several other *fhines* to create a new and much larger body, and it was the increased size of his community alone which gave him his superiority. The bonds of allegiance between the tribal kings and the suzerain king were personal and did not bind even the tribal communities, let alone the community of the *fhines* from which they came. So *tuath* and *fhine* remained independent sovereign bodies as far as their domestic affairs were concerned.

Of higher rank again was the provincial king, the head of a social body of considerable size, not unlike a city in the original sense of the word. The provincial king was also chief of a *fhine*, which had been joined by others to form a separate *tuath*. And as the bonds of allegiance between the suzerain king and the provincial king were also personal, the vassal communities were again guaranteed total autonomy. A similar system persisted when Ireland later introduced the office of *ard ri* or high king. This monarch lived in Tara, the mythical and religious centre of the island, and was elected by the provincial kings either from among their own number or from the members of a royal *derbfhine*. He was therefore himself the chief of a *fhine* and the allegiance of his vassal kings was also a personal matter. So the Irish had a vertical hierarchy, uniting the kingdom of Ireland in a kind of theoretical feudalism, with the high king responsible for the future of the whole island. But in fact the powers of the *ard ri* were extremely limited and confined to the area of moral responsibility. He was necessary for the balance of the kingdom, but unless the whole community of Ireland were threatened, had no real command, since the kings of the *tuatha* or the chiefs of the *fhine* took care of internal current affairs. For outside the hierarchy political and social life was organized on a horizontal plane within the communities of the *fhine* or *tuath*, however small. As independent bodies they alone were able to take the decisions necessary to deal with their particular set of circumstances. It was this pragmatic approach which the Anglo-Saxons inherited, in part at least.

There is obviously a real danger in this kind of society that the various small communities will start quarrelling amongst themselves. And there is evidence that conflicts of this kind did arise, and even blew up into full-scale war. But social strife on this level is not a phenomenon confined to Celtic society. And it was then that the suzerain kings could intervene as the traditional upholders of social stability. A king whose moral authority was not great enough to ensure this stability was judged incapable and usually replaced or forcibly removed if he refused to resign.

In any case the ties formed by marriage and fosterage made for a considerable sense of unity. One *fhine* probably thought twice about making war on another when there were relatives or friends involved. In such cases they would seek the judgment of an overlord, a judge or a Druid. The Druids, too, brought separate communities together, since they belonged to a single nation-wide institution. There is evidence that they exercised their political authority to forward negotiations between opposing factions. In fact, the Druids were often the real masters of the situation. But the king remained the centre of political and social life, nevertheless, and was nominally at least mediator for the community.

The tale of the *Birth of Conchobar* sheds some light on the life and customs of a provincial king. We have already mentioned the "great honour" bestowed on Conchobar by the Ulstermen, which he was to repay by deflowering every virgin in Ulster. This, however, was more of a sacred duty than a privilege. Conchobar never "made false judgments," for the king was meant to personify justice. Any king who did make a false judgment was removed. The Irish epic also states that "there was no more powerful champion on earth," meaning that the king had to be strong and physically unmarred. The legend of Nuada, who was dethroned because he had lost an arm in battle is significant in this respect. But as the symbol of the province he governed, the king "was never exposed to danger. The champions, the men of war and the brave heroes stood before him in battle and fighting, so that he should be safe." This suggests quite distinctly that his presence was vital, but that it was not necessary for him to fight. During peace time, every Ulsterman "offered him a night of hospitality, and he slept with his wife that night." Indeed, it is specifically stated that this meant every free man in Ulster, whether noble, craftsman, warrior, poet or ordinary servant. Obviously Conchobar transcended all social distinctions. In his house there were 365 free men to serve him, but these men took it in turns, so that there was only one man on duty at a time. Conchobar distributed great quantities of food to his serving men, and himself served them at the great feast of Samain to demonstrate that he was no more than a warrior like any other.

There were many other people living in the royal household and the adjoining houses at Emain Macha, his fortress: "three times fifty rooms and three couples in each room." Conchobar himself had a majestic chamber befitting a great king "on the threshold of the house." It was richly decorated with "plaques of bronze all round it, and silver bars and golden birds on these plaques, with gems of precious stones as the eyes in their heads. There was a silver wand above Conchobar and golden apples over him to instruct the assembly, and when he struck them or raised his voice, the people fell silent and so still were they out of respect for him that one could have heard a pin drop." (*Ogam*, xi, 64-5) There is no doubt that the Celts held the royal office in high regard and that the wealth and splendour of the king were considered symbolic of the wealth and prosperity of the whole country.

But esteem for the king was subject to one major reservation. The people would only respect him for as long as he merited their respect, and he would only merit their respect for as long as the affairs of the kingdom prospered and factional interests were suppressed. In the *Drunkenness of the Ulstermen*, the important nobles of Ulster are visiting Conchobar's house when a quarrel breaks out among them. They ignore the presence of the king, and as the Druid Senche who acts as judge has already dealt with some previous problem, the situation becomes very unpleasant. "The Ulstermen rose fiercely with their weapons since Senche no longer dared intervene. They were so quarrelsome that Conchobar had to leave them in the royal palace" (*Ogam*, xii, 495). Even a king as powerful as Conchobar did not have authority enough to appease his angry warriors.

So we can see why political development in Gaul led relatively early to the elimination of kings in favour of *vergobrets* or annually elected magistrates. The *vergobret* was a noble, one of the *equites*, but paradoxically he appears to have had more real power than the king, even though his office had none of the sacred nature attached to the throne. Legally he had total control over his own subjects, but none outside the land he governed. For here too the principle of independence for each social body was respected. This obviously did not prevent *vergobrets* from forming alliances with rulers of the same or superior rank. The fact that the Veneti were able to build a confederation of Armorican peoples shows that under specific circumstances the *tuatha* were capable of uniting in a common interest.

The Gallic move towards an aristocratic system was doubtless due to a conscious wish on the part of the land-owning *equites* to take a larger part in public life, and to the Gauls' excessive love of speech making. The classical authors make several allusions to their love of oratory. The Celts were known as great talkers, drinkers and brawlers. Strabo even mentions one of the rules pertaining the Gallic assemblies: "If one man were rowdily to interrupt the speaker or cause some disturbance, the *lictor*, or public officer, went sword in hand and threatened him into silence. If the interruptions continued, the *lictor* repeated his command two or three times and finally went to the offender and cut a large piece off his cloak, so that he could no longer wear it" (*Strabo*, IV, 4, 3).

But the aristocratic system of Gaul was a comparatively late development. "A couple of generations before Caesar," writes Albert Grenier, "the Gallic peoples had kings, and even in his day there were still some kings, particularly among the Belgians. There might be two men reigning together. Ambiorix, for example, shared the throne of the Eburones with Catuvolcus . . . In some cities Caesar tried to re-establish the throne for his own use. He mentions a person of high birth among the Carnutes of Orleans, whose ancestors had practised hereditary kingship. Caesar made him king; but three years later this king was assassinated and the throne abolished again. The father of Vercingetorix was killed in similar fashion by the Averni for trying to reinstitute the throne of his forefathers for his own use."[14] The Gauls, and more especially the Gallic nobility, appear to have distrusted kings, presumably because the existence of a king was more likely to favour the plebeians than themselves.

In Ireland, however, tribal monarchy survived until the Anglo-Norman conquest, and when the Roman administration left Britain a similar system reappeared there and lasted till the Plantagenets seized Wales. But, as we have said, it was not an authoritarian, absolute monarchy. On the contrary. Caesar says that Ambiorix, joint king of the Eburones, had told him that the multitude had as much power over him as he had over the multitude. This comment could equally well be applied to all the kings of the Celtic world. Neither can it be called a constitutional monarchy, for true sovereignty belonged by right to the community and was apparently considered inalienable. In fact, Celtic monarchy was concerned to maintain a balance of power. And it is this which makes the system so remarkable. From the very beginning the Celts seem to have dreaded more than anything else the idea that one man should have exclusive authority over other men. It is this same dread which has made various peoples at various times rebel against dictatorship. And behind it lies the libertarian spirit which for the Celts flourished within their community-oriented society where the freedom and independence of the individual was guaranteed by the privileges accorded to the *fhine* or *tuath*.

Distrust of the king is also evident in relation to war. Theoretically, of course, the king was supreme leader of all the warriors of the tribe or province. But Strabo says that each Gallic army elected its own leader, which suggests that there was no permanent general and that the king did not lead his men into battle. During the Gallic Wars, there was a great deal of discussion before the majority of the Gauls elected Vercingetorix their leader. When the Gauls invaded Italy and captured Rome, Brennus, their leader, was not a king, but head of the army. And although the Welsh and Irish epics insist that the king be present at battle, they lay far greater emphasis on the valour and prowess of the heroes or champions, who are more like generals than the king. Conchobar may be a powerful monarch, but the chief warrior of Ulster is his nephew Cú Chulainn. After describing the king's warriors, and particularly the hero Conall Cernach, the *Birth of Conchobar* continues "And besides, there was the famous boy against whom all the men of Ireland fought, that is Cú Chulainn, son of Sualtam . . . Fierce and vigorous were the exploits of the young lad. It was dangerous to be near him when he was angry. His feet and ankles curled . . . Every hair on his head stood up as pointed as a hawthorn prickle and he had a drop of blood on each hair. One of his eyes sank into his head and the other stuck out as far as a fist. He recognized neither his loved ones nor his friends. He could strike an equally strong blow both behind and before him. He was as well versed in the art of war as any man in Ireland, and he also knew what he had learned from Scatach."[15] Cú Chulainn emerges from this account as the symbol of the warrior, the awe-inspiring, exceptional and invincible leader of the Ulster army, who is capable of defending his land against the united armies of the other provinces single handed.[16]

Cú Chulainn is the champion of champions, a sure road to victory. And as such he is the obvious choice as a war leader. But his sphere of influence remains limited to the province of Ulster. He is the archetypal warrior of the Ulstermen, but not of the Irish. Arthur, on the other hand, is the champion of all the British peoples.

Caesar records a similar tendency on the part of an exceptional warrior to go beyond the bounds of the tribe in his account of the Aeduan Dumnorix, who proved a subtle political strategist as well as a bold military leader. He established links with other tribes and married the daughter of the Helvetian Orgetorix in order to form an alliance with a powerful nation and a leader as cunning as himself. He was "a man of boundless daring, extremely popular with the masses on account of his liberality, and an ardent revolutionary. For many years he had bought at a cheap price the right of collecting the river-tolls and other taxes of the Aedui, because when he made a bid at the auction not a soul dared bid against him. In this way he had made a fortune and amassed large resources to expend in bribery. He maintained at his own expense a considerable force of cavalry, which he kept in attendance on him, and his power was not confined to his own country, but extended over the neighbouring tribes. To increase it he had arranged a marriage for his mother with a nobleman of very great influence among the Bituriges; his own wife was a Helvetian, and he had married his half-sister and other female relations to members of other tribes" (*Gallic Wars*, I, 18, 3).

There is an obvious comparison to be made between Dumnorix and Arthur. The Aeduan's liberality is matched by the legendary Arthur's generosity, which is one of his most essential attributes. But the historic Arthur must surely have been equally generous towards some of his countrymen. They would never otherwise have agreed to cede him so much power. The way Dumnorix amassed his fortune can be compared to the looting activities of the historic Arthur which are recorded in British hagiography. And finally there is the force of cavalry which Dumnorix kept in attendance upon him. This private army must be a historical precedent for Arthur's faithful band of warriors. The legends of Arthur and his knights and of Finn and the Fiana are a development of Caesar's account of Dumnorix. Celtic society must have allowed private militias of this kind to be formed, so that they could be called upon to fight over a wide area if needed. Strictly speaking they were illegal since the king was theoretically head of the army of his *tuath* or province, and no more powerful leader than he was admissible. But these supranational warrior bands solved the basic Celtic contradiction between the need for unity and the desire to remain separate, by ensuring the independence of each *tuath* or province.

The Celts must have been very relieved to find that a warrior troop, however illegal, was prepared to take over the defence of their land in return for the customary right to billet its men and keep any spoils of war. It should not be forgotten, however, that Dumnorix, Arthur and Finn were something more than mercenaries. Their horsemen felt that they were serving all their fellow countrymen and protecting them not only against the enemies of their own *tuath* but against threats to the confederation of *tuatha*. This form of patriotism, if such it can be called, sprang from a recognition of common origins, a common civilization and common interests. In that respect it is more accurate to speak of Irish, British or Gallic "nationalism," though not perhaps in the sense that the supporters of regional autonomy now give the word. Celtic nationalism was not the aggressive, empire-building impulse of the 13th-century Arthurian romances, but a desire to maintain the *status quo,* and resist any form of oppression or foreign invasion which threatened the harmony of a basically peace-loving society.

The Celts' desire for peace is evident in the care taken over methods of settling various inter-community disputes. War was a last resort when all other procedural possibilities had been exhausted. Any quarrel was investigated on a private level between the plaintiff and the defendant, there being no form of public prosecution. As a general rule both parties agreed to go before a judge whose ruling on the case was accepted by both sides. The oath played an important part in all such disputes, as we have seen. But there were various other means of seeking justice, from the satirical curses uttered by a Druid or a *file*, to a plaintiff's fasting in front of the defendant's house. Fines, determined by tradition, could be imposed on the guilty party and taken as reparation for the injury or damage suffered. There is evidence in the Arthurian saga, as in all the Welsh and Irish texts, that automatic compensation was paid for loss, either in money or in goods, which were usually measured in terms of the value of live-stock or of a female slave. Interestingly, an affront to the victim's honour was regarded as the most serious of crimes, and compensation for it was compulsory.

There was also an obligation to tend victims who were sick or wounded. In Early Ireland, the offender was obliged to provide for the cure of his victim. Nine days after the wound is inflicted, a leech pronounces his verdict. If he says that the patient will recover, the defendant must take him into his house, or to the house of a kinsman, and provide for him till he recovers . . . Besides a basic ration of two loaves a day and an unspecified quantity of fresh meat, to which every patient is entitled, a member of the "noble grade" receives honey, garlic and especially celery for its peculiar virtue as a remedy, salt meat every day from New Year's Eve till Lent, and twice a week from Easter to the end of summer. A member of the "freeman grades" gets salt meat only on Sundays until Lent, and not at all after Easter. Celery is prescribed for all.

The prescriptions as to lodging are quite exacting. Fools, lunatics and enemies are not to be admitted. No games are played. Children are not to be beaten, nor may there be any fighting. There is to be no barking of dogs nor grunting of pigs. The patient is not to be awakened suddenly, and people may not talk across him as he lies in bed. There must be no shouting or screaming . . . And finally the defendant must find a substitue to do the patient's work during his absence.[17]

Celtic society is often accused of being barbaric and anarchic, but details of this kind show just how much care was taken over the righting of wrongs.

Obviously within the constricted world of the *fhine* or the *tuath* every one knew every one else, and knew them for what they were worth. So the kind of theoretical and abstract institutions created for large anonymous masses of people were out of the question. What characterizes Celtic society is its infinite flexibility. Nothing is decided until all the relevant facts have been examined, so that the most fitting solution to any problem can be applied. This prevailing principle enables traditions which have proved their worth by bending to circumstances to stay alive. It is never enough to preach brotherhood between the members of a community. Fellow feeling cannot be ordained; it has to be lived and experienced on a daily level, in the way that the system of fosterage made possible. The Celts understood this perfectly and the fact that social institutions of this kind kept Celtic society viable and alive. Just as the warrior militia inspired and led by Arthur adds another dimension to the usual hierarchy in which the king leads the army, so fosterage adds another dimension to the normal family relationships created by marriages contracted according to exogamic principles.

The part played by the *fili* in Ireland and the bards in Britain is also interesting. Even during the area of active proselytizing Christianity, they formed a kind of artistic aristocracy which was integrated into the nobility. Although they had obligations towards the king and the members of the community in which they lived, they also enjoyed exaggerated privileges, proof that they occupied a considerable position in the social hierarchy. Indeed, no past civilization has ever accorded its cultural elite such prestige. "At the time I received existence," writes the bard Taliesin, "the people lived in dignity, and the bards were highly favoured" (*Cad Goddeu*). Celtic society was awake to the importance of intellectual pursuits. The authors of classical antiquity all concur that the Druids were great philosophers and that the Celts generally speaking had a well developed taste for hypothetical argument. The Druids and bards served a long apprenticeship, for they had to know everything about Celtic tradition in order to be able to pass it on to the next generation. Intellectually, the Celtic world is closer to the present day than to the Greek or Roman. As Albert Grenier says, "It in fact preserves many of the forgotten traditions of the ancient Greco-Roman world, which coexist with the Celts' own original attempts to keep a viable society going in a huge and fertile land. This explains why Gallic civilization sometimes seems incoherent."[18] But these ancient traditions never become routine. Over the ages many innovations of an intellectual, religious, artistic or technical nature were integrated into the existing customs and brought them a new life and maturity. Celtic society was never closed in on itself; on the contrary, it remained continually open to progress and renewal.

It could also rise like a phoenix from its own ashes. In Arthur's time there was a conscious attempt to bring about a cultural renaissance throughout the territory held by the Britons. Under the superficial layer of Romanization lay a well-rooted tradition waiting to produce new fruit. The fact that the Anglo-Saxons choked the young shoots of the renaissance was hardly the Britons' fault. Wales and some parts of South West England still show the effects of their Celtic history; Ireland has become a Celtic country again after many centuries of colonization, and Brittany is the largest area in the modern world where the Celtic language is still in current usage. The various movements existing in modern Celtic countries have all sprung from an attempt to rediscover their original culture. The most attractive thing about the ancient Celtic system is its insistence on autonomy, even at the lowest level, and its consequent resistance to any form of blind, centripetal force. The Celts thought of society as an agglomerate of interpersonal and intercommunal relationships, aimed at achieving a social organization which was not self-restrictive. This meant that the foundations of society had to control their own sovereignty. The monarchy was only conceived as a means of resolving the internal conflicts inherent in all fragmentary societies, and of defending the whole community against aggression or threats from other communities.

Within the Celtic social system internal or external conflict appears inevitable. But such conflict is far from disruptive; rather it strengthens existing relationships. For opposition between members of a community or between one community and another ultimately tests the efficacy of whatever feelings of interdependence there are. Dialectically speaking, Celtic society would not have existed without its inherent conflict. As evidence of strife became manifest, a cohesive force developed to counteract it, impelling the community as a whole to seek a way out of its difficulties. There is much evidence of the Celtic willingness to find unity in diversity throughout the literature and art of the Celtic peoples. And this bias is still observable in a large part of European civilization today, particularly among the Anglo-Saxons, who inherited much of the wisdom of their predecessors in Britain.

Celtic society does not rely on absolute rules and regulations, but on traditions which can be adapted to suit the circumstances. Just as the poetry of the Irish and Welsh rejected precision in favour of nuances of tone and meaning, so, in a sense, did the Celts avoid taking any definitive stand on political or social issues. They refused to sacrifice the wealth of interpretative possibilities to the rigidity of an established system. Theirs was a relative society.

The early Celts did not use the indefinite article, but learned it from societies of Latin origin, anxious to impose their legalistic attitudes. For the indefinite article smacks of the judicial process in which something can be alluded to without actually being named or judged. The Celt makes judgments. He judges that society should respond to his need for personal freedom. He judges himself in terms of society, and society judges him as it judges itself in terms of the individual. In this way a chain of relationships is created far stronger than any theoretical structure laboriously put together to satisfy the demands of Aristotelian logic.

Anything is possible in a society which rejects the principle of absolute dualism. The need to use one's imagination transforms individuals as it does society. Analogy allows one to grasp the subtlest nuances of reality. Truth becomes no more than a dialectical moment of thought and cannot be applied as an absolute criterion to anyone or anything. In Ireland and Wales, wealth was measured in heads of livestock, but never in land. And although the fact that the Latin word *pecunia*, meaning money, was derived from *pecus*, a herd of animals, suggests that the early Romans used a similar system to the Celts, later societies of the Roman type always evaluated property in territorial terms. The essential difference between the Celts and Romans is related to what we nowadays call the quality of life. In actual fact land is a poor guide to prosperity, since its potential productivity varies from area to area, depending on the terrain and the climatic conditions. Obviously the fortune of a *fhine* could be assessed far more effectively by a head count of the livestock it could feed on its land. The end product is what matters, and quality is more important than quantity when it comes to grazing land.[19] There is an enormous gap between the kind of society which looks for the efficacious, but is prepared to approach each new situation with an open mind, and a technocratic, injurious modern society in which everything is mapped out in advance and worked out on paper by highly-educated bureaucrats with scant contact with the living, relative qualities of nature. In this sense, Celtic society, which protects individual freedom within the community and looks at the quality of life pragmatically rather than in terms of what it theoretically should be, is a far cry from our productivity-conscious and convoluted society.

We have said that Celtic society was one large paradox. That is true. But this paradox was its motive force. Social organization of the Celtic type, whether in Gaul, Ireland or Britain, has demonstrated its viability. The Celts' specific approach found its own form of expression in a continual confrontation between contradictory elements. For the fact that the two opposing forces met within a firmly based social group meant that they imposed their own solution.

CHAPTER EIGHT

Arthur's Legacy

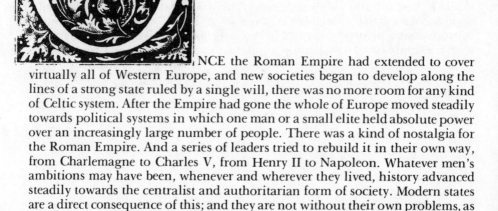

NCE the Roman Empire had extended to cover virtually all of Western Europe, and new societies began to develop along the lines of a strong state ruled by a single will, there was no more room for any kind of Celtic system. After the Empire had gone the whole of Europe moved steadily towards political systems in which one man or a small elite held absolute power over an increasingly large number of people. There was a kind of nostalgia for the Roman Empire. And a series of leaders tried to rebuild it in their own way, from Charlemagne to Charles V, from Henry II to Napoleon. Whatever men's ambitions may have been, whenever and wherever they lived, history advanced steadily towards the centralist and authoritarian form of society. Modern states are a direct consequence of this; and they are not without their own problems, as we can see from the breakdown of many traditional social structures today.

And yet even when centralist tendencies were at their strongest, odd attempts were made to promote counter ideologies. Usually no more than timid and tentative, these glimpses of light in the darkness nevertheless demonstrated that different ways of thinking had not entirely disappeared. It would perhaps be overstating the case to claim that the Magna Carta was a product of the Celtic mind. But it is nonetheless true that this great charter, which formed the basis of English constitutional monarchy, halted the advance towards absolutism, if only in England. Moreover the Magna Carta would seem to have been influenced by John of Salisbury's *Policraticus* which, as we have seen, was relatively close to Celtic notions of kingship. The teaching of St Thomas Aquinas also tried to temper the autocratic tendencies of kings. His formula, *a Deo per populum* put the king in his rightful place as intermediary between divine will and the will of the people. Thomism, however, was more concerned to limit royal authority so that the established Church could play a stronger part in secular affairs.

Where Celtic ideas manifested themselves most obviously, if sporadically, was among the works of writers who appear to have had less immediate connexion with politics. Here they appear as utopian ideals, or as fictions which can be read at deeper levels. Such is the case with the work of Rabelais, particularly *Gargantua* which, though supposedly contrasting the good kingdom of Grandgousier and the wicked kingdom of Picrochole, actually teaches us a lesson in political ethics.

Rabelais condemns the aggressive spirit of conquest by caricature. The irrational Picrochole has let his position go to his head and abuses his authority to further his own boundless ambition. As a contrast there is the wise and balanced ruler, Grandgousier, who "after supper warms his arse by the large, bright fire, while chestnuts spit and hiss, and writes on the hearth stone with a burnt stick used to poke the fire, regaling his wife and family with tales of long ago" (*Gargantua*, chap. XXVIII).

Unlike Picrochole, Grandgousier dislikes war, defensive or not, and is reluctant to use force. He only agrees to do so in the end because he is conscious of the duties of his regal office. "I can see that the time has come when I must take the harness on my poor, weak shoulders, and the spear and club in my trembling hand, so that I can save and protect my poor subjects. It is only right, for their labours keep me, the sweat of their brows feeds me, my children and my family" (*Gargantua*, chap. XXVIII). The king has an obligation towards his subjects and a kind of tacit contract with them. The people agree to pay the expense of keeping the king, not for display, nor to fulfil a divine law, but because the king will then come to their aid when needs be. Any further theorizing by Rabelais on the nature of kingship must have rung false, for in his day royal authority was hardly questioned at all except by the Protestants on religious grounds. But the character of Grandgousier speaks for itself. It proves that despite his education in Greco-Latin humanism, Rabelais was equally sensitive to the great Gallic traditions which he so often used in his work. His ideal king is undoubtedly Celtic rather than Latin.

An anti-authoritarian streak, however unconscious it may have been, is even more noticeable in the work of Cyrano de Bergerac, who wrote at a time when absolute monarchy was nearing its peak in France. His poetic fiction *Les Etats et Empires du Soleil* is a curious work which runs counter to the official attitudes of the day. Cyrano tells how he visited the kingdom of the birds and, seeing an eagle approaching, made to rise "as he assumed it was the king." But the magpie which was acting as the author's guide and friend dissuaded him:

Did you think that great eagle was our sovereign? That is just what you men would believe. Because you allow yourselves to be ordered about by the largest, strongest and cruellest of your companions, you stupidly apply your own experience to everything else and assume that the eagle must rule us. But our politics are quite different. We choose as our king only the weakest, gentlest and most peace-loving of our number. We change our king every six months and we make sure that he is peace-loving so as to avoid war, the channel of all injustice. The government meets every week, and everybody has a chance to speak his piece and make complaints about the king. If there are just three birds dissatisfied with his rule, he is dethroned and another election is held. Throughout the day of the assembly our king sits on top of a great cypress on the edge of a lake, his feet and wings bound. All the birds pass before him one after another; and if one of them knows him to be guilty of the ultimate crime, he can throw him in the water. But the accuser must justify his action immediately afterwards, or he too is condemned to a wretched death.

The political theories of Cyrano de Bergerac are clearly expressed in this passage. For him the king is simply a representative of the people. And he is responsible to all people, not just a majority, since a single bird can kill him if he has a valid reason, and three birds can dethrone him by declaring him incapable. This is much more like direct democracy than enlightened monarchy. Every member of the society gathers at the assembly and if the king is elected by a majority, he is still only a single individual who holds as much power as the majority. Cyrano's system, which goes far beyond the bounds of traditional monarchy or even parliamentary democracy, can be justified by the fact that the king, as the Celts had intended, was required only to maintain the social balance. Once he was no longer able to do so, society had no further use for him and could simply remove him.

This emphasis on the power of the community and respect for the individual member of the group is reminiscent of Celtic ideas about society and the paradox which arises from equal importance being accorded to both the individual and the group. Furthermore, the king of the birds is chosen from among the weakest and therefore has no real power except inasmuch as he coordinates the various social functions. In this respect he can be compared to the Irish king, who was placed under various taboos. When Conaire the Great was chosen King of Tara, there were two primary *geisa* laid on him. He was not to appease any argument between two of his servants (in other words, he had to ensure that there were no quarrels at all); and there was to be no theft committed during his reign (in other words he was to make sure that there was no injustice or inequality between the members of the community). As long as Conaire respected these *geisa*, his kingdom prospered in harmonious balance. But no sooner had he transgressed one taboo than he transgressed them all. The balance was shattered, the kingdom fell apart and the king died.[1] Whatever else we may say about the work of Cyrano de Bergerac it does reveal that marginal current characteristic of an ancient Celtic tradition which lived on in the unconscious as a nostalgic memory of what has passed but might yet come again.

However, the reign of Louis XIV was hardly conducive to this kind of thinking. Although Pascal did not question the monarchy as such, he did believe in relativity in all things. And he was forced to the bitter conclusion that "not being able to make justice strong we have made strength just." This is a condemnation of authority as a usurpation of civil rights. Pascal also wrote that "equity is entirely a matter of custom, for the simple reason that custom is received: that is the mystical basis of its authority. Whoever reduces it to its basic principle destroys it." There is real perception behind these comments.

It was in the intellectual melting pot of the 18th century that certain tendencies closer to the Celtic ideal were to become manifest. And these tendencies led, when they were realized, to very different ends from those originally envisaged. Montesquieu also demonstrated remarkable awareness in his nostalgia for an aristocratic conception of power which exposes the French style of absolute monarchy as despotic. Montesquieu, however, was an enthusiastic disciple of the English philosophers and supported the idea of constitutional monarchy in which the king's activities were restricted by law. And his perceptivity is best expressed in his theory of climates. Although most of the propositions contained in the *Esprit des Lois* are only a definition of the ways and means by which a Roman-type society functions, the "theorie des Climats" appears singularly revolutionary. We can be sure, in any case, that Montesquieu did not realize the full implications of what he had written. His supposedly scientific observations about the different character traits recognizable in different peoples might raise a smile now; but there can be no doubt about his meaning when he wrote "If there is indeed a great difference between the intellectual outlook and emotional life of peoples living in different climates, the laws affecting them should be relative and differentiated to suit them" (*L'Esprit des Lois*, IV, chap. 1).

Nobody appears to have argued against this principle during the 18th century, but it never developed beyond the theoretical level. There was no change of policy, either then or later, basically because Montesquieu's justification of social differentiation went against the grain. Both the old systems of government and the new systems which developed in their wake stuck to centralist policies with all their emphasis on the universal application of law. The French Revolution used liberty and equality as excuses to destroy the last vestiges of regional tradition to survive under the old regime. After all, privileges had to go, and although the equality proclaimed from the rooftops actually applied only to the few, the specific requirements of the various French regions had to go too. The concept of a united state of France, already latent under the monarchy, reached its glorious climax in the Jacobin revolution. The fatherland became a justification for every act, good or bad, and joined communities of diverse origins together to form an artificial and aggressive whole.

It is fashionable in would-be revolutionary circles to enthuse over Robespierre and, more especially, Saint-Just, those saintly but unfortunate victims of the Thermidor reactionaries. Perhaps the time has come to cock a snook at these two plaster saints. Their almost sinister appeal to the masses came from the way they chanted violence and patriotism in the name of a liberty too abstract to be perceived. In fact they dug the grave of the revolution. After them the middle class were able to emerge victorious from the disturbances and turn all the revolutionary principles to their own advantage. Robespierre and Saint-Just paved the way for Bonaparte, that ambitious petty bourgeois with a complex about his height, who expressed himself in a taste for military uniforms and the bloody stench of the battlefield. And all this came about because Robespierre and Saint-Just tried to apply the *Social Contract* without understanding either its real meaning or its real scope.

Rousseau wrote his *Contrat social* as a "citizen of Geneva," that is a member of a community limited in its physical area and in the size of its population. It is therefore patently absurd to try to apply the *Social Contract* to communtities as large as France or any other country. And yet most modern states have developed from a misinterpretation of the *Social Contract*, including the socialist countries. Lenin himself said "We should never ignore the fact that basically we have taken over the old political machine of the tsar and the bourgeoisie." Modern societies are only modified forms of older societies in which the middle classes have acquired more power. A few of the more obvious points of the *Social Contract* have been applied in a superficial way, but outside their original context they have become meaningless.

The influence of Rousseau's political and social theories should never be underestimated, and to discover their origins we have to look at the man himself. Uncomfortable in the society of his day, he extended the difficulties he encountered in his immediate environment to cover the whole framework of the time. He took refuge in nature, but it was a natural world carefully organized according to his own plans, a small, closed microcosm in which he felt safe in the warmth of real human solidarity. It was this warmth, which he lacked during childhood, that Rousseau sought to discover in an ideal universe, an ideal society, in a state close to nature.

The *Social Contract* is no more than a vision of a utopia which is impracticable here and now but desirable on the theoretical level. What makes it pertinent to the human condition is the fact that it is based on instinctive arguments which match the potentially natural elements of the human temperament. From these basic intuitions he constructs a mathematical problem: "to find a form of association which will defend and protect with the whole common force the person and goods of each associate, and in which each, while uniting himself with all, may still obey himself alone and remain as free as before" (*Social Contract*, 1, chap. 6). The solution to this problem is simple enough, but it required some thought. The Celts, however, had reached the same conclusion long before the 18th century, without any scholarly socio-political calculations. The community rather than the individual had to become the basic unit of social life.

As a social animal, man cannot live outside some form of society which establishes his humanity. In fact his association with other people and the fact that he can reason are the only two real indicators of humanity. But since society can only be formed by men, it must necessarily be directed towards the development of man and towards his freedom to exercise his reason. These are the arguments which Rousseau uses to define a communal society as that social body "in which each of us puts his person and all his power in common under the supreme direction of the general will, and, in our corporate capacity, we receive each member as an indivisible part of the whole." (*Social Contract*, 1, chap. 6.) This is a return to the concept of a tribe as a social body in which all the members fuse into a single, collective identity.

It is then that the notion of sovereignty becomes an issue. According to Rousseau, the sovereign cannot be an individual, but must be the general will. In other words, decisions must be taken by the whole body and not just by one of its members. It is this that leads Rousseau to support a system of direct democracy without representation. The sovereign can only be represented by himself. His power of sovereignty is therefore inalienable and consequently indivisible. Any divisions of power tend to weaken it and to give authority to men who might use it in ways which go against the wishes of the community as a whole. So, logically, Rousseau has to demand unified powers.

It is in this area that confusions may arise. A literal application of Rousseau's ideas to a political framework unlike his original conception of society, led to the notion of a single, indivisible French Republic, a scarcely justifiable notion in view of the representative parliament and the separation of powers in France. And so the French state, instead of becoming a truly fraternal community, has acquired an authoritarian and technocratic administrative structure, its rules and regulations an attack on personal freedom. The modern state is an octopus, extending its tentacles in all directions. It organizes everybody's life and dictates the extent to which each citizen should participate in communal life. As a result sovereign power is usurped by a rigid machine which can be manipulated by capitalist interests, whether self-declared or not.

Rousseau never intended his ideal type of society for large numbers of people. He himself said so, although his self-avowed disciples have carefully overlooked the fact. "As nature has set bounds to the stature of a well-made man, and, outside those limits, makes nothing but giants or dwarfs, similarly, for the constitution of a State to be at its best, it is possible to fix limits that will make it neither too large for good government, nor too small for self-maintenance. In every body politic there is a maximum strength which it cannot exceed and which it only loses by increasing in size. Every extension of the social tie means its relaxation; and, generally speaking, a small State is stronger in proportion than a great one." (*Social Contract*, II, chap. 9.)

He could hardly have been more explicit. But Rousseau is always very careful to support his arguments and he goes on to analyse the reasons behind his choice of a restricted social body. "First, long distances make administration more difficult, just as a weight becomes heavier at the end of a long lever. Administration therefore becomes more and more burdensome as the distance grows greater." He then gives examples of the various administrative levels of government and comes to the conclusion that "so far from being better governed by all these different orders, they are worse governed than if there were only a single authority over them [the subjects]" (*Social Contract*, II, chap. 9). But this is in no way an apology for a single, centralist authority. Rousseau adds "not only has the government less vigour and promptitude for securing the observance of laws, preventing nuisances, correcting abuses and guarding against seditious undertakings begun in distant places; the people has less affection for its rulers, whom it never sees, for its country, which to its eyes seems like the world, and for its fellow citizens, most of whom are unknown to it." This passage is reminiscent of the world Kafka created in *The Great Wall of China*, a very prophetic work in view of what is happening in the great centralist states of today. Rousseau also takes up Montesquieu's ideas about the influence of climate. "The same laws cannot suit so many diverse provinces with different customs, situated in the most various climates, and incapable of enduring a uniform government." History in the 20th century furnishes several examples which suggests that Rousseau was right. We have only to look at the problems in former colonies, where the colonists have withdrawn in disastrous circumstances, leaving European type constitutions as a farewell present. The total unsuitability of these forms of government as far as the mentality and customs of the indigenous peoples are concerned often means that the emerging states have more difficulties to contend with than they had under colonial rule.

Rousseau condemns the universal application of law as contrary to the natural tendencies of different peoples, thereby pronouncing judgment on what the French Revolution was later to do to the various ethnic groups which made up the kingdom of France, both under the Jacobin regime of Robespierre and Saint-Just, and under the Napoleonic Empire. In an ideal world, every group of people could and should have their own laws, their own government, their own social organization. That is the only way to ensure that the nation is strong and its citizens will value and help one another. The kingdom of France in Rousseau's day was structured roughly along these lines. Each province had been allowed to keep its own peculiarities and privileges. There were even regions like Burgundy and Brittany which were known as "pays d'état" and had independent parliaments. Law and customs varied in different parts of the country. Weights and measures were different. The language of Flanders was not the same as the language of the Mediterranean coast. Altogether, 17th and 18th-century France was more like those modern states based on a feudal system, such as the United States of America.

This did not mean, however, that Rousseau was able to reconcile the French society of his time with his own principles. Apart from the fact that the sovereign was not the whole social body but one man with totalitarian powers, it was clear to Rousseau that such variety within one kingdom was bound to lead to total confusion. He also looks at the other side of the coin. "Different laws lead only to trouble and confusion among peoples which, living under the same rulers and in constant communication one with another, intermingle and intermarry, and, coming under the sway of new customs, never know if they can call their very patrimony their own."

If we confine our options to the Latin models used by present-day states, there would seem to be no solution to the problem, since both centralist and federal governments tend to produce strife and discontent. But Rousseau found an answer in terms of this dialectical opposition. For him, neither form of government would do. It was necessary to find a third system, as yet undefined, which would take both centralist and federal concepts into account. It is hard to imagine anything which comes closer to this ideal than the Celtic system. We have the independence of the separate *tuatha* on the one hand and the dependence on a personal level between the chiefs of *tuatha* on the other. What Rousseau was contemplating, however, was miniature states or nations, with a single identity, communal property and interests, a specific tradition and laws to match the temperament of the citizens and local climatic or economic conditions.

His sole stipulation concerning this small state was that it should be potentially self-sufficient. Obviously any community which could not provide for itself by domestic production or trade with other communities would soon fall a prey to richer or more enterprising peoples. Rousseau gives a solemn warning against the aggresive face of some states "so constituted that the necessity of making conquests entered into their very constitution, and that, in order to maintain themselves, they were forced to expand ceaselessly." His use of the past tense is evidence that Rousseau was thinking of the Romans and developing Montesquieu's ideas. It is hard to imagine what he would have said had he lived to see the expansionism of Bonaparte, the colonialism of 19th-century Western powers and the violence of Nazi Germany.

So there emerges from the *Social Contract* the idea of a small state whose economic potential and particular temperament make it independent from others. The *Social Contract* is still quoted by supporters of centralist policies. But it would make a far better manifesto for the present claimants of regional autonomy, especially since it puts forward all the basic ideas necessary for avoiding totalitarianism of any kind. Sovereignty being the unalienable property of the people as a whole, the government consists only of non-political magistrates elected to supervise the running of community affairs. It is a form of government like the Celtic monarchy, which does no more than maintain the balance, thereby guaranteeing equality and personal freedom within the socio-cultural community.

This interpretation of Rousseau's thesis is supported by the more symbolic miniature world he creates in *La Nouvelle Héloise*. Here it is the small, enclosed, agrarian realm of Julie, the mistress of all hearts, which conveys

Rousseau's innermost dreams. He can only feel at ease in a microcosm created by the voluntary commitment of its members to a common task, where every person has an opportunity to profit from the labour and emotional warmth of his fellows. We should not overlook the sentimental and emotional aspect of Rousseau's perfect society, for it lies at the heart of the problem raised by the relationship-cum-opposition between the individual and society. The first requirement of the individual is that he should actively enjoy his position inside society, just as the first duty of society is to guarantee the physical and spiritual well-being of all its members. The community which then emerges depends not only on formally recognized and therefore objective laws, but on emotional factors which are purely subjective.

Left-wing intellectuals and Rousseau's middle-class disciples have betrayed him by ignoring the man and omitting to take any account of the spiritual and emotional background against which his work was conceived. After the Jacobins, attempts were made to mould the population to suit the kind of ideal society prophesied by Rousseau, whereas his idea had always been to mould an ideal society to suit the population, not forgetting the emotional elements which play just as important a part in personal relationships as objective concepts of interdependence. Rousseau's *Social Contract* was read completely the wrong way round, and we can say, as Marx did of Hegel, that once we have put him back in his rightful place, his principles will lead to something worth-while.

Rousseau marks the resurgence of a current of thought which had lain hidden during centuries of Roman logical formalism. In fact, it had retained all its old vigour, but had remained in the realms of the utopian and the imaginary. This current gave rise to various movements during the Romantic era; but none of them had much contact with reality because the stereotypic images formed by education and habit left no room for anything else and anything outside the mainstream tended to be regarded as hysterical or deviant. Altogether the 19th century proved disappointing. The middle classes rose to new heights. So, too, did the powers of colonialism and centralism which were as blindly self-interested as they were intolerant. The European Romantics, liberal as they were, felt little desire to reshuffle the cards in the game between revolutionary and reactionary forces. To a greater or lesser extent they allowed themselves to be carried along in the tide of their own eloquence and sentimental lyricism. It was then that the great figure of Charles Fourier appeared. His contemporaries thought him insane, although he is now regarded with the seriousness to which he is entitled.

Without digressing into the finer details, it is possible to state that Fourier's bold and non-conformist ideas have much in common with some of the main points which have come to light in our study of Celtic society. He was possibly the first man to understand that the social conditions of his time could only be changed if the whole notion of work was redefined. Fourier began with the revolutionary principle that work should be a pleasure and not a burden. Such an idea might be regarded as no more than wishful thinking, a new form of paternalism perhaps, or a confidence trick like the motto "work through joy" so widely used by the Fascist and Nazi regimes. But Fourier's argument is validated by the stress he lays on what psychoanalysis was later to call the "pleasure principle." For Fourier, this meant that the lost sense of community had to be restored to labour, so that even the most unpleasant and thankless tasks could bring their own sense of satisfaction in the knowledge that they were being performed for the good of others. If people were also to change their jobs from time to time so that no groups were being exploited and sacrificed for the majority, work could prove as satisfying to the individual as it is profitable to the community. Obviously certain tasks have to be done, to ensure the survival and development of the group. But if the division of labour prompted by specialization were to become less rigid, as happens in "primitive" societies, each man would be able to assume temporary responsibility for some area of work which he enjoys but which is not usually regarded as his particular province. The worker would then become free to develop and blossom because his labours would be dictated not by some objective and external legislation but by his own instinctive and emotional desire for pleasure. In the *Phalanstère*, as Fourier called his imaginary community, the desire for solidarity of effort would lead to freedom from the almost institutionalised solidarity demanded by the capitalist industrial system. The very geography of the *Phalanstère*, with its dwellings, its places of work, worship and culture, its canteens and meeting halls, shows Fourier's intentions of simplifying the life of the group as much as possible, so as to take the sting out of the inevitable drudgery involved in certain tasks and make sure that the burden falls on the community rather than the individual. The *Phalanstère* is the ideal place where society becomes transmuted. It is Rousseau's closed world, the tribal environment within which a self-sufficient community can remain independent and ensure justice for all.

Fourier lays great emphasis on the importance of the group's emotional life. Long before the discoveries of psychoanalysis he was putting forward the idea that the *passions*, by which he meant everything connected with our emotions, have a determining effect on human behaviour, both in one to one relationships and in the relationships between the individual and the community. As far as Fourier was concerned, all the primary passions are gifts of God, and therefore infinitely respectable and good. It is only when these passions are obstructed that they become what we choose to call bad. "Any obstructed passion gives rise to its own counter-passion which is as maleficent as the natural passion would have been beneficient." If we replace the word "obstructed" by the word "repressed" this statement could quite easily have been written by Freud. In the *Nouveau Monde amoureux*, Fourier gives an example of what he means, which his early followers found rather offensive. He describes a princess of Moscow who was torturing a slave by "pricking her with pins." But if someone "had suggested the idea of lesbianism" to this princess, "the two women would have become passionate lovers." However, either the idea never occurred to the princess, or if it did she repressed it as sinful; and so she "was subverted by the counter-passion" and persecuted the woman with whom she could have been so happy. "Her fury was the greater because the obstruction was born of prejudice which, by hiding from the lady the true object of her passion, left her no freedom to seek an ideal."

If we extend this remark to the political and social spheres, it becomes clear that people cannot fulfil their potential, nor society function properly if individual passions are thwarted in some way or another. Fourier was obviously a libertarian. His virtue lay in the way he kicked against the kind of closed morality which prevents people from showing their emotions for the good of the community. It is this form of morality, designed to control social relations and avoid disorder, that becomes a constrictive, negative force and paradoxically creates disorder itself. By realizing this, Fourier came down on the side of Celtic society, which relied on men's ability to discriminate themselves, rather than intimidation as a means of influencing public morals.

Fourier was clearly seeking to form an ideal world like Eden before the Fall where man made no distinction between good and evil. As far as he was concerned, nothing but good could come from God. Evil was therefore the creation of man, who flies in the face of the good because he is not able to achieve it. These ideas have little to do with orthodox Christianity, but they do free man of the burden of dualism and allow him to make those decisions which religion and ethics have previously controlled. Fourier is tackling the question of personality. Alienated by repressive social systems, man has no hope of recovering his true personality until he can overcome the conflict between instinct and reason, which conflict Fourier defines as one of the root causes of social disaffection. Only instinct, however, is natural. Reason is an invention, highly convenient for those whom Fourier calls "moralists" and holds responsible for all evil. The moralist demands that we repress our natural instinct, which is to do no harm to others, and that instead we consciously sacrifice ourselves for our neighbour. We could argue that the end product would be the same in both cases, but it is scarcely possible to keep the peace on a public level by demanding that each person maintains a private war within himself. If conflict cannot be checked within the individual (and according to Fourier, it never is), then there is no hope of arresting conflict between individuals. Morality is "camouflaged violence," a "utopia," "the dream of good without any efficacious means of achieving it." If we try to live by morality alone, we will torture, alienate and finally destroy ourselves. It is a path which leads only to despair for the man who would be totally moral and to hypocritical success for the man who assumes only the trappings of morality. But instinct and passion cannot be destroyed: they are part of our nature, and must be satisfied so that individual satisfaction will lead to communal satisfaction. Instinct then acts in the same way as reason. It can look at itself and take whichever direction is likely to prove most suitable and beneficial for both the individual and the group.

Fourier's sytem of what he calls "religious and social science" contains the outlines of an extremely subtle dialectic. The basis of everything is contradiction. The pitiless stuggle between opposing interests it taken to be competitiveness but is actually a product of the very primitive law of the jungle. And yet these internal contradictions within society will ultimately resolve themselves. "In nature extremes exist side by side; it is its excessive vices that lead civilization to ruin." Fourier is here prophesying the fall of economic liberalism, otherwise known as capitalism in its most hypocritical form. But his analysis goes beyond the economic contradictions of society. He explores the battle of the sexes, in which woman as the victim of society retaliates with lies and infidelities. He examines the conflict between parent and child and between the generations which, in a civilized regime, are motivated by entirely different passions. But Fourier's great contribution was his examination of the emotional as well as the economic alienation of civilized man, his realization that the creation of a new society depends on a solution to the emotional conflicts which deny man his humanity. He therefore describes the organization of the *Phalanstère* in great detail. He suggests that there should be an *organigramme* to keep the *Phalanstère* functioning properly. In this and various other respects he seems somewhat out of touch with reality. But it is nonetheless true that ideally speaking Fourier understood the necessity of radically changing inter-personal relationships within any future society and of basing future social patterns on the needs and tendencies of man. In this respect Fourier is a humanist above all else, but a humanist who has grasped two fundamental realities. First there are the human passions which reflect the inclinations of mankind. And then there is the repressive but inevitable social structure which curbs these passions. Somehow it should be possible to reconcile the two in a "harmonian" system.

It is in this area that Fourier's ideas are totally revolutionary. His "harmonian" system cannot be a development of the existing state, since the state is too vast, its institutions potentially too anonymous and inhuman. Nor can it be a development of the family, since the family, especially in industrialized societies, is far too restricted a social unit, in which conflict is almost a certainty. In any case the family has neither the resources nor the scope to protect its members against serious misfortune. According to Fourier, therefore, the answer lies in a Phalange, a social unit of medium size, ideally containing about 1,600 people. This number will allow for diversity of labour and for the various combinations of basic passions which go to form a kind of hierarchy within the group.

Ingenuous and utopian as it may seem, this system is logical. It allows each person to satisfy his or her own desires, whether or not they would be regarded as abnormal or eccentric in an industrialized, repressive society. Fourier examines almost every sphere of human activity, be it eroticism, the arts or dress. He even invents something called *Gastrosophy*, which is a form of gastronomy linked to dietetics. His overwhelming aim is that man should be able to develop and expand, free from any alienating forces. In the *Phalanstère*, "pleasure becomes the business of the state and the specific goal of social policy making."

Despite a certain amount of financial assistance, attempts actually to organize *Phalanstères* failed miserably. But rather than blame Fourier and his disciples for this, we should look to the reactionary society in which these experiments took place. Even today, virtually all attempts to set up communes in various parts of the world have gone the same way. Social experiments of this kind cannot hope to succeed until there is a radical revolution in the attitudes, morality and laws which govern society.

The need which Fourier and Rousseau saw for a medium-sized social group, larger than a family but smaller than the organically structured Latin state of the Western world, was again highlighted by the Paris Commune. This was an attempt to combine direct democracy with communal living on a small scale. The word "Commune", however, needs some clarification. As Marx says in *The Civil War in France*, it had nothing to do with the medieval commune which lay behind the rise of the middle classes and consequently the development of the modern state. On the contrary "it shattered the power of the state . . . The Constitution of the Commune was supposed to give back to the social body all those powers previously absorbed by the parasitical state which fed on society and paralysed it."

Imperfect as it was, the Commune obviously represented a worse threat to the French bourgeoisie than any other it had known. The middle classes felt that their very foundations had been shaken and retaliated accordingly with an army from Versailles. If the state were to be undermined, then so too would the privileges hitherto reserved for themselves. Marx was well aware of this when he analysed the Communard phenomenon, and applied some of his observations there to his own system. The Commune should not be "a parliamentary organism, but an active body which is both executive and legislative." Officials, magistrates and judges should be "elected, responsible and replaceable." There should be no regular army, but worker militias. Education should be free of all ecclesiastical and state control. And, finally, "the commune system should be adopted even by the smallest rural hamlet."

The fragmentary nature of this system was totally foreign to the centralism of the 19th century. Leaving aside any ideas of the dictatorship of the proletariat, it reflected much of the old spirit of the Celtic legislators of earlier centuries. Its chief advantage lay in the way it removed the shackles of bureaucratic tyranny and restored to each member of society that sense of responsibility which had been lacking since the state assumed the running of the administrative and socio-political machine. Obviously there is no knowing exactly what would have happened if the communal system had survived in Paris and extended through-out the country. Marx claims that it would have been the springboard for a new life in France. But that is by no means certain, for the people were not ready to accept the changes demanded of them. It appears more likely, in fact, that the forces of the establishment would eventually have tamed the revolutionary fervour and sucked the life blood from it. Nevertheless, on a purely theoretical level, Marx was surely right to view the Commune as a result of the struggle between the producing and the acquiring classes, and as the most adequate form of government to allow the economic emancipation of labour. "The Commune ought therefore to act as an instrument in undermining the economic bases which lead to the creation of classes and thus to the domination of one class by another. Once labour has been emancipated every man becomes a worker and productive work ceases to be the attribute of one class alone."

Certain aspects of Marxism can be compared to those ideas which had flourished on the fringes of society throughout the centuries. And both are linked, if only by their respective aims, to Celtic society. All reveal the same leaning towards a classless society in which every member of the social body is a worker. Within the Celtic tribe each person had his or her own position and duties to perform. Since property belonged to the group as a whole, each person was also the owner of the sum of communal goods and contributed to them in a not inconsiderable way by improving the level of community life. The materialist view of history gives collective society as new focus; sociologically, only individual people and their relationships exist. Society as a general entity cannot exist without the individuals who form it. There is a fundamental difference here between totalitarian docrines, which consign whole sections of the population to an inferior class and make them the slave of society, and Marxism, which tends to be confused with totalitarianism by people who are badly informed or blinded by anticommunist propaganda. And this difference makes it possible to appreciate the Marxist attempt to understand the inter-personal social relationships which lie at the foundation of every social structure. For, ultimately, it would seem to be a mistake to assume that tribal society is wholly directed towards some abstract body. A deeper examination of "primitive" societies reveals that the tribe is merely a structure which enables individuals with the same rights to find their own fulfilment in the company of others. We must put an end once and for all to the idea of society's being all powerful. It can only be an abstract concept. The idea that there is some kind of collective being with a soul of its own has been fabricated by well-meaning sociologists who claimed to be scientific but were actually metaphysicians indulging in wild guesswork. In the name of Society, with a capital S, some or all of the characteristics of existing social structures have been elevated to the ranks of absolute truth. But the characteristics of a specific social group are always relative, dictated as they are by their historical era and by economic or geographical factors. They shift and evolve, they cannot be enmeshed in the net of the absolute.

Once we have understood all this, it becomes much easier to perceive the influences which moulded a social body like that of the Celts which remained flexible in its structures and in the kinds of interpersonal relationships it expected of its members. Marxist analysis allows us to come to grips with concrete phenomena which can be measured and assessed. The way 20th-century man looks at Celtic society is too often clouded by cultural fetishes. It makes no sense, for example, to analyse Celtic civilization, with its undefined frontiers and its total adaptability, solely in terms of contemporary Western civilization, which has slowly evolved from Roman rigidity into capitalist paralysis.

The Celts deliberately inclined towards a classless society. They held out for as long as possible against Roman ideas, refusing to accept the division of labour and the aggressive centralism which allowed one privileged class to prevail by cultivating abstract notions of the fatherland, its defence and enrichment, its tendency to classify. But the Celts carried no weight outside their own sphere of influence. And before long the whole of Europe was swamped by the assertive structures of Roman society. Indeed this stranglehold has continued to the present day, even in the self-professed socialist states. And, as a result, we tend to think that no material or moral advancement is possible without systems of the Roman type. The aggressive face of such systems manifests itself in expansionism, colonialism and in the class struggle between the majority and their middle-class rulers. And yet Roman structures only continue to influence Western attitudes because we continue so blindly to believe in them. They have no independent reality. In this respect even those who profess to follow the doctrines of dialectical materialism are as guilty as anyone else. There are now large numbers of pseudo-Marxists all busy condemning each other as revisionists, imperialist lackeys, or what you will, and all falling into the worst ideological trap of all, which is to hail as absolute what can only be relative. They forget, as Gérard Mendel put it, that "socialism must itself come up with a new political solution, progressively but speedily predetermining the ultimate influences on the economy, and taking the realization and development of social relationships as its starting point. This means that the aim of society should be pleasure in social relationships and thence a new birth for mankind. Account must be taken of those needs which are hidden, forbidden and perverted in daily life. Work must be concrete, not abstract; and on a wider level, the person who accomplishes the act must regain appropriate control of the social powers inherent in that act in every aspect of his life."[2] Marx's work is an invitation to create and invent new kinds of social relationships, like those which Fourier anticipated in his *Phalanstère*, those which Rousseau dreamed of in his solitary enjoyment of freely structured nature, and those which the Celts tried to achieve through their original trains of thought.

So far this challenge has not been met. Marxism like all other doctrines tells us what ought to be done. Like the Latin future infinitive, it is a *facturum* leading to a *futurum*.[3] But what makes Marxism superior to all the doctrines which preceded it, is its use of a form of argument which enables man to go beyond his human condition. The dialectical reasoning so widely practised by the Celts and the pre-Socratic Greeks is the most revolutionary means we have of freeing ourselves from the apparent contradictions of life. It also provides us with a powerful counter-argument to the pervasive forces of scientific determinism.

Only the suggestion that reality is a perpetual shift between two fundamentally opposite poles allows us to shake off the restrictions of preformed ideas, of "what goes without saying," and to wipe the mental slate clean of all those ideological fetishes which have burdened mankind since societies began to develop along Latin lines.

When we look at the present situation in industrialized countries, or in countries which are little more than satellites of the multinational industries, we are forced to recognize the signs of a civilization in decline. Firstly, the liberial economy is burning its boats in the shape of its energy resources. Despite efforts to plaster over the cracks, the end seems inevitable sooner or later. Then, there is a growing awareness that some part of every worker's real wage is being hived off, either into the profits demanded by the capitalist system, or into direct or indirect taxation imposed by the government. There has also been a widespread upsurge in the influence of the pleasure principle. People are realizing that labour brings little or none of the satisfaction they might have expected from it. And there has been a sudden outburst of eroticism, which capitalism has turned into a consumer product and exploited as pornography. Finally, and equally paradoxically, there is a movement against the unifying and centralist tendencies manifest in the world today. Supra-national institutions look for uniformity on every level, material, political, economic, religious or cultural. But these tendencies are being challenged by new aims: the breakdown of traditional state structures, the rediscovery of ethnic differences. In other words, there is an increasing number of regionalist movements.

The bankruptcy of the capitalist system is easy enough to understand. Continued expansion into new markets and the growth of production are pushing the system to a point of no return. Business concerns are obliged to increase their productivity in order to justify their investments and repay the loans necessary to make the investments in the first place. But profits can be adversely affected by a number of factors: fluctuations in demand on a vast scale, overproduction, continual improvements in the conditions of the workers, the cost of social services. And when business is at risk the state intervenes, either to avoid the kinds of social discord which are bound to lead to stoppages, or to bail out the share-holding and managerial classes. Industry becomes nationalized or subsidized. The state buys at a loss. But whatever the operation, it is public funds which are used. And now a crack appears in the structure, for state capitalism is replacing private capitalism. The barons of industy have lost control, they must bow to the man who pays the piper. The way is then open to collectivization of the means of production, even if the citizens whose taxes are actually paying for the state schemes are not consulted about the decisions involved. Forward-planning becomes vital, both to protect industry and to organize the distribution of its products. So the term "liberal economy" becomes meaningless. Ultimately economic life is controlled by the state; and a time will come when the free enterprise system of Western capitalism has nothing to differentiate it from the state capitalism of the socialist countries.

As the work force becomes aware that it is being fleeced of part of the fruit of its labours and fails to find the satisfaction it seeks in its work, it grows increasingly frustrated. This sense of frustration is evident at every level of professional life in the Western world, and manifests itself in strikes, absenteeism and claims for improved working conditions. Young people, above all, are rejecting those forms of work which they consider pointless, dehumanizing and uninteresting. Even though it is on its last legs, capitalism is still trying to reverse the current of ideas by brandishing its own form of morality, but no one believes in it any more. It is too late. And the consequent upheavals affect almost every aspect of human life.

These troubles were already latent during the period of classical capitalist society which lasted until the Second World War, but they were contained by a rigidity in moral attitudes. In former days everything which did not conform was automatically condemned as impermissible or abnormal. The perversions of repressive societies betray basic tendencies in mankind which somehow manage to find their way to the surface. In psychoanalytical terms, perversion of whatever kind is an attempt on the part of the son in us to destroy the father once and for all. More generally, it is a struggle for freedom against the social and moral taboos which the ruling classes use and abuse in order to check the impulses of their subjects. In this sense the present expression of sexual liberation in industrialized societies is the result of centuries of repression of those psycho-emotional tendencies previously only evident in the form of perversions. As soon as morals become more lax, eroticism increases and pornography is tolerated, perversions come out into the open and, whether it will or no, society enters a stage of permissiveness on the road to total freedom. Here, too, private capitalism takes a last ditch stand against the forces of rebellion by taking over the expression of eroticism and sensuality. It uses advertising to increase production and consumption, but controls and corrupts basic human tendencies in the process. And it manufactures pornography as a safety-valve against the most explosive of those tendencies.

These sociological phenomena are a sign of the times. Until now sexuality has been little more than a vacuum. Instead of involving the whole body, and so satisfying the total man, whatever he is doing, the libido has been repressed and concentrated on one part of the body which is in itself regarded as shameful.[4] And so sexuality becomes functional. The extensive spread of eroticism and pornography is only the beginning of the liberated process. Not until we grow weary of the "liberated" images before us and see them for the exploitation they are, will we be able to free the libido from its present exclusive connexion with the human sex organs and apply it to every human activity, including work. Only in this way can we hope to achieve a revolution.

However, the libido will never be free unless men and women regain full use of their potential and full responsibility for their means of production. This is impossible in industrialized societies, because the environment is becoming increasingly artificial, anonymous and inhuman. By alienating the emotions, the bureaucratic state suppresses the libido. For the libido is as much concerned with psychology as it is with biology. If both mind and body are one in their responses to life, the libido becomes free to express itself.

The other basic movement of our time is the shift away from excessive centralism and uniformity. There is a growing reaction against large supranational bodies of people and the standardization of life along lines traced by the American materialist civilization. Men and women are now harking back to their origins, demanding new social structures which will allow for variation and enable people to live close to nature in societies ruled by human warmth rather than by legal obligation. Ethnic groups which had nearly disappeared altogether, have now come to the fore again. In the United States, the Indian problem is being restated, with all the old violence. In Europe, several historic regions are beginning to claim greater economic and cultural autonomy, if not total independence. Many of these regions laid the foundations of our modern European states, only to be supplanted by them. Their prerogatives have since been usurped by the creation of an economically and politically united Europe. But people are starting to remember just how important the provinces once were. The kingdom of France was built on the province of Ile de France, which eventually imposed its language, its expansionist politics and its dynasty on the whole French hexagon. The Basque country is now recognized by its historic name Euskadi and is seen to be split between the two centralist states of France and Spain. It is realized that the Flemish people in Northern France are brothers of the Belgium Flemings. People remember that Burgundy and Brittany were very rich and powerful nations in the 15th century, and that Germany is a mosaic of small provinces artificially joined together by the king of Prussia. We are being reminded that the United Kingdom is composed of several lands, all essentially different racially and culturally, the only link between Northern Ireland, Scotland, Wales and England being the crown, itself a subject of controversy.

This important phenomenon is a rude awakening on the part of ethnic groups which have been repressed and ridiculed over centuries of abusive centralism. Their emphasis on the right of the individual to use the vernacular or language of his ancestors as well as the language of common parlance in his country is more significant than it might at first appear. For these languages are symbolic of a whole new awareness and play a decisive part in the rediscovery of cultures once despised and ignored. Cultural claims are cries of protest from ancient societies which do not wish to die and which want to play their part in a modern world. Their past need not be a burden. If they can adapt it to suit the present and the future, it can become a new source of energy.[5] Economic and political claims have an explosive effect on routine and indifference and force us to face the problem of minority groups head on.

The reason why this problem is becoming so important is that it reflects very profound human tendencies. The only hope of solving it lies in some original social structure which can allow both for the large economic and political entities like Europe, and for much smaller social groups in which it is possible to express the natural passions Fourier spoke of and to develop new relationships based on something other than the abstract concept of citizenship in one of the great centralist states.

It is in this area that we might learn something from the example of the Celts. Since the new movements of the present day belong to that spirit of non-conformism which dates from Celtic times, any return to our origins ought surely to include an examination of those ancient systems which were stifled before they could prove their viability.

We have already said that the Celtic system worked perfectly in its own context, and that it only fell before the power-seeking of the Romans who organized their society in a different way and were convinced of their superiority. If we are to create a new Europe, the idea that one social group is superior must go, so that there is room for a system which separates ethnic groups on a horizontal plane. They should not have to suffer the imposition of any arbitrary form of government which bears no relation to their physical or emotional needs. It seems far more natural that Europe should be divided into ethnic groups rather than into nations. For the nation still carries overtones of the fatherland, of the aggressive and competitive state.

The Celtic social pattern encourages us to value the intellectual and emotional imperatives of a specific group. It also raises the whole question of nature, which they used in a rational way to further the interests of the individual rather than those of a privileged class which could exploit their natural resources. There is a real problem here. For the survival of mankind depends in some sort on our abusing nature. Every civilization has marked a struggle between man and the forces of nature. In any case, industrialized society exists and there is no turning the clock back. If we were to abandon the industrial techniques now used in the exploitation of nature for the simpler agrarian existence of long ago, we would undoubtedly perish. The fact that there are still dreamers enough to preach that particular solution only demonstrates the strength of feeling that society must do something to curb the damage it is doing, or humanity will face total disaster.

The time has therefore come to revise our attitudes and realize the vital necessity of organizing social and economic relationships in a new way. We have first to resolve the opposition between nature and cultivation by creating a new harmony between them, and then to attempt the same thing in the political, cultural and emotional spheres. If we examine these oppositions in dialectical terms and reject the Aristotelian method of problem-solving which industrial civilizations tend to turn to at all times, the solution will present itself. In this way we might look forward to the creation of a more flexible system and to the formation of medium-sized and self-sufficient communities in which both specific circumstances and individual needs can be taken into account.

We have to define man according to his context. "The basis of human essence in any given society," according to Gérard Mendel, "is . . . the sum total of the social conditions in which *homo sapiens* lives. The secret of mankind is the sum total of social relationships."[6] It is therefore a matter of urgency that we institute social relationships which will satisfy man and make him a whole person once more. The Celts tried to do this, despite pressure from agressive outsiders and the restrictions of a reality which only served to stimulate their imaginative faculty still further. They have left us a message of balance and harmony, of the man who is fully responsible for his actions and fully conscious of his almost boundless potential. The Celts have been accused of being over-imaginative and of inventing their history. If that is so, it surely proves that imagination is capable of transporting life to a higher plane where nothing is impossible.

It is in this respect that the study of Celtic society in all its diverse manifestations, its literature, even the Arthurian epic, takes on its total significance. It forces us to reflect on the very nature of the human personality and on the potential role of our powers of creation in the formulation of a new society based on a human scale.

The Celts achieved the impossible. They based their society on small, independent but potentially self-sufficient groups, and at the same time integrated them into a larger whole which bore the mark of a single civilization with its own language and religion, its own peculiar logic, its own method of thinking and forms of self expression, its own flexible way of life. Even if we cannot reasonably hope to return to the pastoral or agrarian community of the Irish *tuath*, it should be possible to imagine an equivalent social group within the partly agricultural and partly industrial civilization of today.

Having established our ultimate aim, our first task must be to mould minds capable of understanding and assimilating it. Education has a large part to play here. It should be drawing on the experiences of those who have tried to form new communities in various parts of the world. At the moment it is merely stagnating in a single Greco-Latin pattern under constant review by the intellectual and industrial middle classes who have every interest in maintaining the *status quo* to their own exclusive advantage. A more open mind would be bound to lead to a greater appreciation of the facts concerning a wide range of such experiences, to an awareness of various possible solutions to our problems, and so to wider freedom. Any conclusions we may come to in this way must obviously remain open to modification. But the Celts' capacity for leaving their options open provides a useful example to anyone who truly seeks to better the human condition.

For the Celts, the frontiers of a country stretched as far as the king could see. This is surely a symbol. As the pivot of his social group, the king cast his eyes towards the horizon and so delineated the area in which the community was to live. There seems no reason why we should not try the same experiment on a local level, as the theoreticians of the Commune thought to do. A group of people who know each other and live in continual contact with each other is more stable and alive than a group in which anonymity and lack of knowledge lead to disinterest and indifference. To ensure that every individual feels concerned in the community, there must be links forged by common economic, intellectual and emotional interests. Without this collective spirit, the administration of the community would become so much of a habit that unconcern and negligence would be bound to follow.

The appeals to patriotism which have held modern states together through thick and thin in the past are now obsolete cliches used only by politicians and men nostalgic for the war. The word fatherland has no meaning. This being the case, it would seem eminently sensible to return to a much narrower concept of the community where the members of the group could feel they really belonged to a classless society, and where factional interests could be balanced on a horizontal plane. This does not mean a policy of regionalization on the part of central government. This kind of fragmentation is no more viable than any other form of organized decentralization. We have to change the course of history. The tide of men's affairs should be flowing not from a single, central point, but from a large number of central points all prepared to contribute their own particular gifts to a cohesive whole of limited power. For the authority of the whole must be maintained to some extent. Just as the Celts formed temporary confederations, it is possible to envisage larger political bodies which would take over control in certain areas in order to suit the government to the circumstances and then redelegate authority as the occasion demanded.

The present-day state is an ailing structure dragging everything after it in its headlong path to oblivion. While the system allows power to belong exclusively to one privileged class, whether it be the capitalist bourgeoisie or the new elite of computer-mad technocrats who deal only in numbers, there can be no respect for the principles of democracy. Western democracy has become a parody. It allows the state to turn despot, to act, decide and plan on our behalf, and what is worse, when we consider the influence of the mass media, to think for us as well.

The future path of history leads inevitably towards diversity in unity. To be free, society has no choice but to follow this route. For all other roads lead only to new forms of absolute and dictatorial government. In spite of the pressure of the centralist political machines, there is an increasing awareness of this at every level of society, even among the traditional class enemies of the capitalist system. We can no longer compare any aspect of the present with the past. Western civilization has reached a crisis point where the opposition between different systems can only give rise to a new formula for social structures.

The Celtic heritage has something positive to bring to this new formulation of society and of the society relationships which give it its shape. The Celts have taught us that it is possible to establish independent social groups separated from each other on the horizontal plane and to provide for temporary links between them when the immediate interests of the more extended group demand it. As each of these groups would be in a position to deal with its own problems, there would be an improvement in the overall management and economy of the community. And as continual modifications could be made to weak or inefficient structures so that they were relevant to the circumstances, both the smaller and the greater social group would benefit from a flexibility in social strategy.

It is in this sense that the Arthurian epic, whether it be really historical or mythically real, provides food for thought. For the Arthurian world is an ideal in which the unity of an extensive nation and the diversity of many very particular social groups are combined. It matters little whether it was a medieval dream or not; it is up to us to bring it to life.

The Breton tradition contains frequent references to Arthur's sword which the Britons of Britain and Brittany were supposed to have split between them before they separated to their own sides of the Channel for ever. And they kept the two halves to remind them of the heroic days when unity was maintained through diversity. It is said that one day men will manage to solder the two ends of the blade together, much as Perceval did his own sword with the help of Trebuchet the smith. Symbolically this tradition could be interpreted on a much wider level. The two halves of the blade are the two irreconcilable concepts of classical logic, unity and diversity. And the Breton belief that only Arthur has the power to brandish the two halves of the sword and bring them together again is reflected in the way we wait for the new type of society we have been promised.

Arthur lies sleeping somewhere. Perhaps he is in a marvellous island where apple trees produce ripe fruit all year round. Perhaps he is lying in a dark cave among his treasures. He is waiting for someone to wake him and tell him that his time has come again. The world is on the brink of a major upheaval. The times of darkness are done. For centuries we have been waiting for Arthur. We have given him the title of king because according to the Celts the king maintains the balance of the world, his presence is required before anything can happen. We have made him the symbol of an ideal society such as was promised us by the prophets and the poets. One day their predictions must come true. It is our right and our duty to waken King Arthur.

Notes

Introduction

[1]I have attempted to define the way popular tradition lives on in different forms in my work *La Tradition celtique en Bretagne armoricaine* (Payot: Paris, 1975), pp. 291-330.

[2]A characteristic example of these tendencies is furnished by a conference held in June 1975 in Paris about James Joyce. Here it became clear that French critics were prepared to examine Joyce's work in total isolation from the historical, economic and cultural context in which it was written. As professor Leonard Feldman of the University of New York pointed out at the time, Joyce's works demand access to a huge system of Anglo-Saxon and Irish cultural cross-references on the part of the reader. To suggest that the title of *Finnegan's Wake* can be divided into FIN and NEGANS, as some French critics did, completely ignores the central myth of the eternal return which would enable the Anglo-Saxon critic to divide Finnegan into FINN and AGAIN. The same shortcomings tend to afflict those modern historians who apply the structuralist approach to the exclusion of any other.

[3]In the conclusion added to the second edition of my *Épopée celtique en Bretagne* (Payot; Paris, 1975), I quoted the Welsh tale of Peredur in which black and white sheep change colour each time they cross the river. I applied this same argument to language in an article for a collection entitled *La Civilisation surréaliste*, ed. Vincent Bounoure (Payot: Paris, 1976).

[4]I developed this idea in *La Tradition celtique en Bretagne armoricaine* (Payot: Paris, 1975), pp. 291-309, and in the above mentioned work *La Civilisation surréaliste* where I applied the argument to language and its power as a revolutionary weapon.

[5]I used this approach to trace the image of women among the Celtic peoples in *Women of the Celts* (Gordon & Cremonesi: London, 1975).

PART I. King Arthur in the Medieval World

Chapter 1. Arthurian Literature

[1]For a detailed résumé of *Brut of the Kings*, see Markale, *L'Épopée celtique en Bretagne*, 2nd ed. pp. 231-60.

[2]*Gereint and Enid* is translated into English in *The Mabinogion*, Penguin Classics. For a commentary on the work see Markale, *L'Épopée celtique en Bretagne*, pp. 152-65. *Érec et Énide* raises various questions which have never been satisfactorily answered. It seems strange that Yder, normally portrayed as one of the best of Arthur's knights, should have the role of the aggressor, though his traditional love for Guinevere might have made him jealous of Érec. Then there is the rather obscure character of Énide. Rachel Bromich suggests that her name derives from *Gwenyd*, the goddess of the Venetes, which is based on the word *gwen* (Irish *finn*) meaning white and fair. She supports her argument by suggesting that the name Érec (or Warog) is typical of the land of the Venetes (*Études celtiques*, IX, 2). But the fact that Erec becomes Gereint in the Welsh version (from the Latin Gerontius) which is a name typical of Cornwall makes it appear more likely that Énide has come from *Gwynedd*, the name of the land of the Ordovices in North Wales; especially as Gereint is mentioned by several Welsh poets. But Rachel Bromwich does follow her suggestion with some interesting comments about the Hunt for the White Stag which leads to the marriage of Érec and Énide. It is possible that this adventure harks back to ancient Celtic traditions concerning the sovereignty of women, so that Érec becomes king by marrying the goddess who embodies sovereign authority. In the Irish tradition Finn, whose real name is *Demne*, or buck, marries a woman changed into a doe by a Druid and has a son *Oisin*, or fawn. Many of the Celtic epic cycles contain clear traces of a much earlier totemism. The cycle of Leinster is linked to the worship of the stag, the Ulster cycle to that of the dog (*Cú Chulainn* means Dog of Culainn and *Conchobar* Powerful Dog), the Tristan cycle to that of the horse (March meaning horse), the Arthurian cycle to that of the bear (through *art*, bear), and so on.
[3]Transl. by René Louis (Livre de Poche, 1972), pp. 77-82.
[4]For comments on the Breton origins of the Lancelot legend see Markale, *La Tradition celtique en Bretagne armoricaine* pp. 109-32.
[5]J. Marx, *Nouvelles recherches sur la littérature arthurienne*, p. 266.
[6]*Ibid.* p. 265. See also *Histoire littéraire de la France*, xxx, 146-51.
[7]R. S. Loomis, *Arthurian Legend in Medieval Art*, pp. 32-6 and figs. 4 and 6.
[8]*The Mabinogion* (Penguin Classics), p. 140.
[9]J. Markale, *Women of the Celts*, pp. 111ff.
[10]Yvain (Owein) and his father Uryen belong to the saga of the northern Britons who formed the kingdom of Strathclyde which bordered onto Pictish lands. This saga was then artificially tacked onto the Arthurian cycle. Note that here Arthur is holding court at Carlisle, in the kingdom of Strathclyde.
[11]This actually exists in the forest of Paimpont in central Brittany. See Nora Chadwick, *Early Brittany*, pp. 292-354 and J. Markale *L'Épopée celtique en Bretagne*, pp. 168-9, also *Women of the Celts*, p. 133. The fountain at Barenton had been a sacred spot since earliest antiquity, its name deriving from *Bel-Nemeton*, the sacred clearing of the sun god Belenos. It is curious that the northern Britons should be taking part in an adventure set in Brittany.
[12]At this point in the narrative Luned and Gawain have a conversation which clearly reveals the solar nature of Gawain and the lunar nature of Luned. The fact that Gawain's strength was traditionally supposed to increase until midday and then slowly dwindle again, and that Luned's name is obviously associated with the French *lune*, or moon, would seem to support this. But the Welsh name Luned comes from *llun* or image, whereas Laudine comes from the Welsh *lleaud*, or moon.
[13]Kynvarch is Owein's grandfather, and the three hundred swords of Kynverchin were northern Britons who probably came to serve the Briton chiefs who had taken refuge in Wales. The "flight of ravens" is an allusion to the fact that Owein's mother was a fairy and could turn herself into a bird. Owein and Uryen were historical characters from the 6th century celebrated by Taliesin and in the poems attributed to the bard Llywarch-Hen. See Markale, *Les Grands bardes gallois*, pp. 42-5, 85-90 and 91-2.
[14]For a detailed examination of the Tristan legend see Markale, *Women of the Cults*, the chapter entitled Iswult.
[15]For the various versions of the Tristan legend see G. Bianciotto, *Les Poèmes de Tristan et Iseut* (Nouveaux Classiques Larousse).
[16]For these two texts, see Markale, *La Tradition celtique en Bretagne armoricaine*, pp. 62-9 and 52-9.
[17]G. Paris, *Romania*, VIII, 45.
[18]This character is the same as the Breri supposed to have inspired Thomas' *Tristan*. Giraldus Cambrensis also speaks of Bledhericus, the "famosus ... fabulator," who was supposed to have settled at the court of Poitiers and been responsible for much of the spread of old British legends on the continent. On this subject see J. Loth, *Les Mabinogion*, I, 72-5.
[19]See in particular the *Saga de Yann*, pp. 148-68 and the *Saga de Koadalan*, pp. 149-85 in Markale, *La Tradition celtique en Bretagne armoricaine*.
[20]In *The Fate of the Children of Tuiren*, the children of Tuiren have to bring back three apples from the garden of the Hesperides, a pigskin which can cure any illness, a magic spear which is burning

hot, a chariot faster than the wind, seven magic pigs which can be slaughtered in the evening and will be reborn the next morning, a dog which will scare off any wild beast, a magic brooch and three shouts made on a hill, all in order to expiate the murder of Lug's father by their own father.

[21] Wolfram's *Parzifal* has been translated into English by E. H. Zeydel (1951).

[22] The only complete edition is Oskar Sommer's *Vulgate-Lancelot*, 1907, though *La Quête du Saint-Graal* has been edited by Albert Pauphilet and *La Mort du roi Arthur* by Jean Frappier.

[23] This episode has much in common with the rituals of choosing and enthroning a king practised in Ireland. The stone is obviously a lech, a kind of menhir dating from the Celtic rather than the mega-lithic period. The sword belongs to the Other World and returns there when Arthur dies. In fact the French version is wrong. For as Thomas Malory tells it in his *Morte d'Arthur*, Arthur acquires Escali-bur much later from the Lady of the Lake.

[24] The theme of the boaster is common in folk tales. and Kai is given this characteristic in all the French Arthurian texts, though not in the earlier Welsh legends.

[25] The French makes Escalibur a Hebrew name, though it in fact comes from a British word meaning Hard-Sharp. In the Irish tradition there is a sword *Caladbolg*, whose name means the same thing and which is one of the magical objects brought to Ireland by the Tuatha Dé Danann.

[26] Loth is the father of Gawain, Gahieret, Agravain and Guerrehes. His wife was daughter of Hoel of Tintagel and Arthur's half-sister. Their youngest child was actually Arthur's, and grew up to be the Mordret who usurped his uncle and incestuous father's throne. Urien is Owein's father, Ydier (probably Edern or Yder) was in fact king of the land north of the Humber according to the Welsh, while Caradoc of the Short Arms, a British and Breton hero, should be Caradoc of the Long Arms; his name has been wrongly translated from Karadawc *Vreichbras*.

[27] In other traditional tales Guinevere (Welsh *Gwenhwyfar*, or white spirit) is the daughter of Kadwr, count of Cornwall.

[28] The geography of the *Lancelot in Prose* is rather confused. It seems more likely that the forest men-tioned here is not in Brittany, but the forest of Kelyddon (Caledonia) where the bard Myrddin took shelter after the battle of Arderyd.

[29] Vivienne is also known as Niniane, or Ninue (Thomas Malory). Niniane is a Pictish name which would support the idea of Merlin being in the forest of Kelyddon. But the same character plays an important part in the story of the Breton Lancelot. The accounts of how she eventually traps Merlin vary. Thomas Malory has her trap him under a rock.

[30] Morgan must be Arthur's half sister, though it is not said whether she is the daughter of Uther Pen-dragon or of Ygerne. In the older texts she is known as the daughter of Avallach, though she is scarcely mentioned in the Welsh tradition except as Modron, mother of Owein and Mabon. She does have an Irish equivalent in Morrigane, a kind of erotic and martial goddess who can change herself into a raven.

[31] Historically speaking there was a struggle between the Bretons and the Franks, first the Mero-vingians, then the Carolingians. See my introduction to the "early saga of Lancelot" in *La Tradi-tion celtique en Bretagne armoricaine*.

[32] These temporary fits of insanity occur frequently among the heroes of Celtic legend, and especially to Lancelot. In this respect he is very like the Irish hero Cú Chulainn who is given to the same sort of extremes of behaviour and who has much in common with Lancelot besides.

[33] The Celtic tales contain many references to islands where all those who go ashore begin laughing, weeping or dancing and are unable to return home. See the *Voyage of Maelduin* Markale, *L'Epopée celtique d'Irlande*, pp. 196-202.

[34] Details from Thomas Malory *Morte d'Arthur*, XIII, 2.

[35] Arthur's blindness towards his wife's infidelity and his unqualified admiration for Lancelot are among the most curious aspects of the *Lancelot in Prose*.

[36] Trial by combat was common practice in the 12th and 13th centuries and is frequently mentioned in the Arthurian romances. The king as judge cannot defend his own wife.

[37] It is likely that in the earlier versions of the legend Gawain was one of Guinevere's lovers. Chrétien certainly suggests that he had formed some kind of ideal and impossible love for her.

[38] In every epic there is someone who survives the final battle to tell the tale. This text also mentions Bliobleheri, the *famosus fabulator*, as being among the last of Lancelot's companions.

[39] This suggests a Celtic fortress which was made up of single-storey houses, rather than a medieval fortified castle.

[40] There is an obvious connexion between Brunissen and the Welsh goddess Rhiannon whose birds wake the dead and put the living to sleep and make their listeners lose all sense of time.

[41] Vivienne, the Lady of the Lake, here known as Ninue, is Arthur's guardian in the *Morte d'Arthur*. It is she who gives him Escalibur.

[42] In the *Historia Regum Britanniae*, Geoffrey tells how, when Brutus had settled in the country which bears his name, he held great feasts but was attacked by a group of giants. The Britons

managed to kill all the giants except one, Goemagog, who was finally beaten by the hero Cornineus, founder of Cornwall.

Chapter 2. The Political Background

[1]Erich Köhler, *L'Aventure chevaleresque*, 2nd ed. (Gallimard: Paris, 1974), p. 26.

[2]Ferdinand Lot, *Nouvelles études sur la provenance du cycle arthurien*, in *Romania*, XXVII, 57-571. In this valuable article Lot is actually seeking to prove that Geoffrey used authentic legends and forged documents for his *Historia*, not that he invented it all himself. Gautier and, more especially, Caradoc contributed a great deal to the popularity of Arthurian traditions.

[3]See Ferdinand Lot in the article mentioned above. Also Gordon Hall Gerould, *King Arthur and Politics* in *Speculum*, II (1927), followed by notes on the same subject by R. S. Loomis, and Loomis, *Geoffrey of Monmouth and Arthurian Origin*, in *Speculum*, III (1928).

[4]The king was limited in his actions by a system of *geisa* or taboos. See J. Markale, *L'Épopée celtique d'Irlande*, p. 177.

[5]The adverb *individually* does not really translate the Latin *singulariter*. What John means is that once the normal legal framework has been destroyed, each of the members of the *populus* is individually but separately concerned in any action undertaken by one person or a group of people. The *universitas* cannot oppose the tyrant who does not recognize it.

[6]For further reading on John of Salisbury, see John Dickinson's study in *Speculum*, I (1926), pp. 308ff.

[7]I have attempted to examine the important question of gynaecocratic tendencies in Celtic society in *Women of the Celts*.

[8]In my conclusion to *La Tradition celtique en Bretagne armoricaine*, I have tried to show the immanence of myth as compared to the permanence of the legends in which they take their intelligible form.

[9]My italics. This is important evidence since it was written by a contemporary chronicler. It shows that British singers frequented Henry II's court and that Henry himself was anxious to find the body of Arthur and put an end to the myth of Arthur's return so that he could himself claim to be Arthur's legitimate heir. During his reign there were rebellions in Celtically dominated areas not inconnected with the myth of Arthur's return, and the fact that Henry could point to a British singer as the source for his information about Arthur's return meant that he would avoid accusations of political bias in thus quashing all hopes of a new Celtic resurgence based on Arthur.

[10]Henry's good relations with Glastonbury were already evident in the way he had financed the reconstruction of the monastery after a fire in 1184. So the monks had every interest in finding what Henry told them to find. His successors must have been a sad disappointment to the monks. Richard the Lionheart was too busy fighting crusades and quarrelling with Philip Augustus to show his gratitude to them, while John deliberately disregarded them.

[11]The position of this tomb was discovered in 1931, in front of the main altar, and is marked in the ruins today. The tomb itself had been destroyed during the Reformation and the bones thrown away.

[12]All the chroniclers stress that they used *written* sources, although no mention is made of what language they were written in. Any documents of this period must, however, have been in Latin.

[13]Some of this story matches what we know about the history of the period. During the Dark Ages there was a shift in population from the North to Wales and Cornwall. The Celtic tribes who had been moved to the North by the Romans to guard the frontier with Scotland returned to North Wales. In fact much of what is regarded as Welsh literature can actually be attributed to the Northern Britons. Cunedda is certainly a historic character, mentioned by Nennius as having moved southwards around the end of the 4th century. Tradition makes him the grandfather of a Welsh king who died in 547, which would suggest that Cunedda actually lived around the middle of the 5th century. Glasteing would then have made his journey after the first period of Saxon invasions.

[14]The Latin word for apple was actually *mala*, but by the Middle Ages the word *poma* (Latin for fruits) had superseded the original term. *Mala* came from the same Indo-European root as the British *aval*.

[15]We do not know where William found his material for this story, but Avalloc is mentioned in some of the romances as being Morgan's father and we know that Morgan was supposed to have ruled over the Isle of Avalon.

[16]Translated from the text quoted by Ferdinand Lot, *Romania* XXVII, pp. 529-30.

[17]J. Loth, *Les Mabinogion*, II, 344.

[18]*Romania*, XXVII, 532.

[19]Some manuscripts add "Glasimpere nan-Gaedel," that is "the Glastonbury of the Gaels" (Whitley Stokes, *Three Irish Glossaries*, p. XLVIII).

[20]Quoted by Ferdinand Lot, *Romania*, XXVII, 533.

[21]See, for example, the romance *Escoufle*, where Jean Renart writes "May no serf ever come to your courts to be your bailiff, for a man who makes a villein master is shameful and base. Villein! how could a villein be honest and kind." (v, 1616ff.)

[22]I have developed my ideas about the original Guinevere in the chapter on Iseult in *Women of the Celts*, and those on the original Lancelot in *La Tradition celtique en Bretagne armoricaine*.

[23]The Quest for the Holy Grail is a perfect example of the kind of distortion demanded by the knightly class and the Church. The strength of the original pagan themes sometimes overcomes the Christian veneer, so that the work remains a strange jumble of traditions. In fact the values which the authors were trying to uphold are eventually turned on their head. The quest itself takes the knights away from the communal cohesion of the court and eventually many of them are killed, but by each other. There are also continual, hardly veiled references to sex. Lancelot fails in the quest because of his adultery with the queen, while Perceval who is tempted by the devil in the form of a woman is said to punish himself by wounding himself in the thigh (actually a euphemism for castration, as practised by various pagan priests).

[24]The medieval Roman Catholic Church played a very negative role in all areas of life. It was during the time when the Arthurian romances were written that the Inquisition came into being. The Church also sold Ireland and its people to Henry II, changed the original message of Christian peace into exhortations to fight for Christ and preached to the laity a chastity never practised by all its priests. It was a strong political force and affected the whole cultural heritage of the West by discarding anything which did not match its dogma.

PART II. King Arthur in the Celtic World

Chapter 3. Britain in the Dark Ages

[1]Nora K. Chadwick, *The Celtic Realms* (1967), p. 31.

[2]Macsen Wledig is the hero of a Welsh tale in which he comes to Britain to marry a girl he has seen in a dream. In fact there was a certain amount of confusion between Maxentius and the usurper Constantine. But the legend is characteristic of what was happening in Britain around the year 400.

[3]Procopius, *The War against the Vandals*, I, chap. 2.

[4]Geoffrey Ashe, *From Caesar to Arthur*.

[5]Discussions about the historical accuracy of Gildas' work still persist. Recent research suggests that the work can be divided into two parts. The first chapter and the end of the work after chapter 27 would appear to be the work of Gildas himself, and the intervening chapters on early British history the work of some anonymous author writing at the end of the 8th or beginning of the 9th centuries. This does not necessarily mean that the central chapters have no basis in reality. See A. W. Wade-Evans, *Welsh Christian Origins* (Oxford, 1934), and *The Emergence of England and Wales* (Cambridge, 1959), also Rev. Paul Grosjean, *La Tradition manuscrite du "De Excidio" attribué à Gilda*, in *Analecta Bollandiana*, LXXV (1957).

[6]The original parts of the *Historia Brittonum* are supposed to have been written in South Wales from the end of the 6th to the end of the 8th centuries. It was solely concerned with the history of the Britons and used material from Gildas, Frankish genealogies, the legend of Saint Germanus and various other sources. A later writer added fables about the Trojan origins of the British race which can now be seen in the manuscript at Chartres. Then in about 800 Nennius is supposed to have taken the early work and added details about the Picts and Scots, royal genealogies of the 7th century and information about the kings of Strathclyde. Nennius, who wrote in North Wales, was obviously influenced by the Irish, since there are many allusions to Gaelic tradition in those parts of the work attributed to him. See *Revue celtique*, xv, 195ff., also *Nennius Vindicatus* by Zimmer, and *Nennius et l'Historia Brittonum* by Ferdinand Lot (Paris, 1934).

[7]This was a patent anachronism. Uryen and Owein lived in the second half of the 6th century while Arthur flourished in the first half of that century. Similarly Myrddin probably lived at the end of the 6th century, while Geoffrey gives his birth date as during the time of Vortigern, around 450.

[8]See J. Markale, *L'Épopée celtique en Bretagne*, pp. 81-93.

[9]See J. Markale, *Les Grands Bardes gallois* (Paris, 1956). In a preface to the later edition of 1976 I have expounded on the influence of the Northern poets on Welsh literature.

[10]The fortress-cum-sanctuary of Maiden Castle near Dorchester is the focal point of John Cowper Powys' novel of that name. This fascinating work is concerned with ancient Celtic festivals, and I have discussed it in some detail in my study on *Powys and Celticism, Granit*, no. 1 (Paris, 1973).

[11]For the peculiarities of Celtic Christianity, see the chapter on this subject in my *Les Celtes*. See also Olivier Loyer, *Les Chrétientés celtiques* (Paris, 1956), and L. Gougaud's basic work *Les Chrétientés celtiques* (Paris, 1911), transl. into English as *Christianity in Celtic Lands* (1932).

[12]"When they reached his house they saw an old pitch-black hall with a straight front and smoke enough coming from it. Inside they saw a bumpy pitted floor: where there were bumps a man could scarcely stand, so slimy was the floor with cow dung and urine, and where there were holes a man might sink to his instep in the mixture of water and urine, and it was all strewn with holly stems whose tips the cattle had been eating. When they reached the forecourt they found a dusty threadbare floor and an old hag before the fire at one end, and when she was cold she would throw a lapful of chaff onto the fire, so that it was not easy for any man to put up with the smoke that entered his nostrils. At the other end they saw a yellow ox-skin, and lucky the man who was privileged to sleep on that" (*The Dream of Rhonabwy*, transl. Jeffrey Gantz, Penguin).

[13]As in some peasant houses to this day, the earth floor was made of a mixture of straw and clay. But rye straw was spread over this to keep out the damp.

[14]This passage is rather confused. The Ambrosius referred to is Ambrosius Aurelianus, the leader of Romanized British resistance to the Saxons. But since Nennius specifically states that Ambrosius was not involved in this particular conflict, we must assume that Vortigern was being opposed by other champions of the imperial way of life.

[16]Although the Druids had officially disappeared by Vortigern's time, their influence remained, and we can assume that these wise men were in some sense the inheritors of the Druidic tradition. Their advice certainly matches what we know to have happened at the time, for former fortresses were being re-used as defensive posts.

[16]See J. Markale, *L'Épopée celtique en Bretagne*, pp. 109-10.

[17]This theme developed from the historic bard Myrddin, a Northern Briton who went mad after the battle of Arderyd in the 6th centuries and fled to the woods to compose his poetry. But this figure lived a century after Vortigern.

[18]There was a firm belief that the burial of a hero in a strategic position would keep the enemy at bay. The Welsh hero Bran was buried at the White Hill in London for the same reason.

[19]The *Triads* say otherwise. Guorthemyr, according to them, was indeed buried in the place he had chosen but was later exhumed by Gwrtheyrn Gwrtheneu (Vortigern). The same triad says that Arthur did the same thing with Bran's head because he wanted to be sole defender of the island. (*Triad 15*, J. Loth, *Mabinogion*, II, 241)

[20]There is another contradiction here between the suggestion that Vortigern had the support of all the Britons and the fact that he was opposed by the supporters of Ambrosius. But even if we accept Nennius' view that Vortigern was indeed the supreme leader, he was still a king in the Celtic fashion and had to seek the agreement of all the tribal chiefs.

[21]Vortigern was supposed to have married Hengist's daughter and his own daughter, and thereby roused the wrath of Saint Germanus.

[22]Dyfed in South West Wales. This would suggest that Vortigern had replaced the Irish dynastics there.

Chapter 4. King Arthur in History

[1]J. Loth, *Mabinogion*, II, 372.

[2]The fight of the forest of Kelyddon. This forest was well known as the *Silva Caledonia*. The battle may have taken place at the place where both the Tweed and the Clyde have their sources. It was certainly a battle against the Britons.

[3]Or "on his shield." Nennius' work is probably a Latin translation of a British original to judge by some of the syntactical structures. It would seem more likely that as an active participant in battle Arthur would have worn the emblem of the Virgin on his shield.

[4]Or Trywrywyd, as one of the oldest poems in the *Black Book of Carmarthen* suggests. This is not far from Dumbarton on the Firth of Forth and was probably a battle against the Picts, unless the rebellious Britons were active in this area at this time.

[5]There are several possible sites for the battle of Mount Badon, including Badbury, near Swindon, Badbury Hill near Faringdon and Badbury Rings near Blandford. Unfortunately the word *Bad* is a Saxon name and not British at all. The British *Din Badon* would have turned into *Baddanburg* in English. But there may have been some confusion and it is possible that the word Badbury, formerly Baddan-Byrg came from a corruption of *Badon*.

[6]See J. Markale, *L'Épopée celtique en Bretagne*, pp. 210-15.

[7]J. Loth, *Mabinogion*, II, 254.

[8]*The Gododdin*, v.v. 1241-2, in Ifor Williams' edition.

[9]Kenneth Jackson, in Loomis, *Arthurian Literature in the Middle Ages*, p. 2.

[10]A. G. Brodeur, *Arthur dux bellorum* (University of California, publications in English), III, 7, pp. 237-84

[11]As I write this, I have before my eyes a facsimile of one of the manuscripts of the *Historia*

Brittonum. It is quite legible and there can be no cause for confusion. Hengist's name is mentioned in an ablative absolute construction where it is properly declined (*mortuo Hengisto*), but Arthur's name, although used in a construction where it should be in the genitive case, remains *Arthur* and not *Arthuri.*

[12] J. Loth, *Mabinogion,* II, 247-48. A *cantrev* was an administrative area of one hundred inhabitants as in the Norman *shire.*

[13] J. Loth, *Mabinogion,* II, 236-7.

[14] A Welsh folk story adds further detail here (Jones, *Welsh Bards,* p.22). Apparently Arthur and Hueil were pursuing the same woman. They fought over her and Arthur was wounded in the thigh. Arthur forbade Hueil to speak of his injury, but remained slightly lame. Later Arthur fell in love with another woman and went to see her, disguised as a woman. When he stood up to dance with her, Hueil, who was present, recognized him and made some remark about his wound. Arthur, furious, put Hueil to death.

[15] See *Math Son of Mathonwy* in the *Mabinogion,* transl. Gantz, also Markale, *L'Épopée celtique en Bretagne,* p. 62.

[16] J. Loth, *Mabinogion,* II, 270-2.

[17] This is the poem entitled *The Spoils of the Abyss.* See J. Markale, *Les Grands bardes gallois,* pp. 83-5 (first edition).

[18] This was a prison made by Manawyddan ab Llyr with the bones of Roman enemies killed in combat. See J. Markale, *L'Épopée celtique en Bretagne,* p. 266.

[19] J. Loth, *Mabinogion,* II, 267-8.

[20] J. Loth, *Mabinogion,* II, 250.

[21] This was Maelgwyn Gwynedd, king of North West Wales in the second half of the 6th century. He was a historical character recorded by Gildas and Nennius as Maglocunus. He also came into the legend of Taliesin in which the bard fights against the bards of the king of Gwynedd. See J. Markale, *L'Épopée celtique en Bretagne,* pp. 94-108.

[22] Dewi was a kind of chaplain to Arthur, and followed him wherever he went, even into battle.

[23] Karadawc Great Arm who was mistranslated as Caradoc Short Arm in the French romances. He was the hero of various adventures in Brittany as well as Britain, though Ferdinand Lot has shown that he originated in Britain.

[24] Kendeyrn is the Welsh form of the name Kentigern. This saint founded the bishopric of Glasgow in Strathclyde. Following a war between the northern chieftains he came to Wales to establish a new bishopric at Saint-Asaph in Flintshire, or Powys. When the northern chieftain Rydderch Hael had defeated all his enemies he recalled Kentigern, who left Saint-Asaph to one of his disciples and returned to Glasgow.

[25] J. Loth *Mabinogion,* II, 277-9.

[26] *Ibid.* p. 285.

[27] J. Loth, *Mabinogion,* I, 333.

[28] See J. Markale, *La Tradition celtique en Bretagne armoricaine,* pp. 109-18. The Lancelot tradition was totally independent and was not incorporated into the Arthurian story until the time of Chrétien de Troyes. Even Geoffrey of Monmouth makes no mention of it, though he does refer to Arthur and Hoel of Brittany mounting a joint expedition into Gallic territory. There are also Bretons among the lists of Arthur's warriors given in *Kulhwch and Olwen* and the *Dream of Rhonabwy.*

[29] J. Loth, *Mabinogion,* II, 334-5.

[30] Geoffrey of Monmouth must have been aware of the oral tradition that Arthur was born in Cornwall, since he places Arthur's birth at Tintagel.

Chapter 5. The Arthurian Myth

[1] Celtica was the area between the Garonne and the Marne, which under the Roman Empire became the province of Lyons with subdivisions at Bourges and Tours.

[2] See J. Markale, *Les Celtes,* pp. 232-5.

[3] J. Loth, *Mabinogion,* II, 307-8.

[4] *The Mabinogion,* transl. Gantz, p. 139.

[5] Prydein ab Aedd Mawr was the mythical ancestor of the Britons. The name Prydein (Britain) was used to denote the whole of Great Britain except Scotland which was given the name Prydyn. These two words came from an old Celtic *Cruithni* (the British P corresponding to the Gaelic Q), the name used for the Picts. *Cruithni* came from *cruth,* meaning "shape," indicating that the Picts painted their bodies with the shapes of animals.

Among the Greek authors Britain was called *Pretannia.* Interestingly in this triad Prydein is called son of Aedd Mawr, and Aed is a Gaelic name frequently found in Ireland.

[6] *Triad 105*, J. Loth, *Mabinogion*, II, 294-5.

[7] J. Loth, *Mabinogion*, II, 295.

[8] *Triad 114*, J. Loth, *Mabinogion*, II, 303. According to the 10th-century genealogies, Dyfnwal Moelmud (Dunvallo the Bald Mute) was descended from a northern chieftain. He was said to have been a great legislator and to have established a system of measurements still in use at the time of Howell Dda.

[9] J. Markale, *L'Épopée celtique d'Irlande*, pp. 171-84.

[10] *The Mabinogion*, transl. Gantz, p. 76.

[11] *The Mabinogion*, transl. Gantz, p. 139.

[12] *Ibid.*

[13] J. Markale, *L'Épopée celtique d'Irlande*, pp. 61-4.

[14] D'Arbois de Jubainville, *L'Épopée celtique en Irlande*, pp. 414-15.

[15] Balor, one of the chiefs of the Fomore, was a cyclops, whose single eye could destroy everything he looked at. A stake or a trident had to be used to prize his eyelid open. Yspaddaden Penkawr in *Kulhwch and Olwen* had similar characteristics. Lug is both a Fomore and a Tuatha Dé Dannan, since his father is a Tuatha and his mother the daughter of Balor. Later in the story Lug kills his grandfather by hitting him in the eye with a stone from a sling.

[16] The game of chess, which the Irish called *fidchell*, appears to have been regarded very highly by the Celts, and especially by the Irish. It is generally supposed to have originated in India.

[17] D'Arbois de Jubainville, *L'Épopée celtique en Irlande*, pp. 418-21.

[18] *The Mabinogion*, transl. Gantz, p. 193.

[19] There is a man with a club in Irish epic named Dagda, whose name means "The Good God." In the tale of the *Battle of Mag-Tured* he is the goddess Morrigane's lover and appears to be a powerful, greedy giant of a man. As a chief of the Tuatha Dé Danann who were expelled from Ireland by the Gaels, he may well have something in common with the character in this tale.

[20] *Historie littéraire de la France*, XXX, 97-101. A 12th-century Breton lay, *Le Lai du Lecheur*, contains a rather obscene version of the same story. A group of lords and ladies are asked to reply to the question "What do men like best about women?" Among a variety of different answers comes the response "The cunt, because every woman, whether she is beautiful or ugly, retains supremacy over a man with her cunt."

[21] See my comments on this in *La Tradition celtique en Bretagne armoricaine*, pp. 309-19.

[22] J. Markale, *La Tradition celtique en Bretagne armoricaine*, pp. 41-6.

[23] This may mean that the *Odyssey* has been influenced by Semitic ideas. This kind of fear of women is characteristic of Semitic peoples, and although the Indo-Europeans were patriarchal in their leanings, the status of women, especially in their mythology, was higher than the *Odyssey* suggests. Ulysses' refusal of Circe is on a level with Gilgamesh's refusal of Ischtar, while the true Greek tradition is best exemplified by Oedipus, who accepts his sexual initiation, his punishment being for the incest he has committed.

[24] Quoted by M. Dillon, *The Celtic Realms*, p. 86.

[25] *Ibid.* p. 150.

[26] *Ogam*, XI, 60.

[27] *The Mabinogion*, transl. Gantz, p. 221.

[28] *Ibid.* p. 267.

[29] *Ibid.* p. 271.

[30] J. Markale, *L'Épopée celtique d'Irlande*, pp. 184-91.

[31] For commentary on the sun-goddess see J. Markale, *Women of the Celts*, the chapter entitled Iseult or the Lady of the Orchard.

[32] *Ogam*, XIII, p. 357.

[33] *The Mabinogion*, transl. Gantz, p. 254.

[34] *Un Roman néerlandais du cycle d'Arthur*, in *Revue des traditions populaires*, XXXI (1916), pp. 164-70. This tale is compared with a number of European folk stories.

[35] I have expanded on the strange duties of the virgin foot-stool in *Women of the Celts*.

[36] Gilvaethwy appears under the name Girflet or Giflet, son of Do, in the *Lancelot in Prose*, and in *La Mort du Roi Arthur* where he is told to throw the king's sword into the lake.

[37] Math son of Mathonwy, in *The Mabinogion* transl. Gantz. See also J. Markale, *L'Epopée celtique en Bretagne*, pp. 59-67.

[38] All the quotations from *Kulhwch and Olwen*, *The Dream of Rhonabwy* and the tale of *Owein* in the section which follows are taken from *The Mabinogion*, transl. Gantz.

[39] All the quotations from this poem are taken from the *Black Book of Carmarthen*, XXXI.

[40] J. Boulenger, *Les Romans de la Table Ronde*, p. 35.

[41]J. Loth, *Mabinogion*, ii, 289.

[42]See J. Markale, *L'Épopée celtique en Bretagne*, pp. 215-22.

[43]*Revue celtique*, xxxiv.

[44]J. Loth, *Mabinogion*, ii, 291.

[45]The legend of Saint Collen who gave his name to Llangollen in Denbighshire and Langolen in Finistère, includes a significant anecdote about Gwynn. Collen, who was abbot of Glastonbury, heard of the wealth of Gwynn, son of Nudd, king of Annfwn (the Other World), and assumed that he must be a devil. Gwynn therefore invited Collen to visit him and entertained him with great splendour. But Collen sprinkled holy water on Gwynn and his followers and they disappeared.

[46]J. Markale, *L'Épopée celtique en Bretagne*, p. 95.

[47]Another instance of the legend of the submerged town, Is, which tends to change location according to which version of the legend one reads. The Isles of Scilly were also said to have been attached to Cornwall at one time.

[48]J. Markale, *L'Épopée celtique d'Irlande*, pp. 43-55.

[49]*Ibid.* p. 141.

[50]J. Loth, *Mabinogion*, ii, 271-2.

[51]*Revue celtique*, v, 200. See J. Markale, *L'Épopée celtique d'Irlande*, pp. 144-5.

[52]MS. Egerton 1782, G. Dottin, *L'Épopée irlandaise*, p. 175.

[53]G. Dottin, *L'Épopée irlandaise*, p. 181.

[54]This description is a cliché in Gaelic literature, though it is usually applied to a wild man whose hair is hard and bristling, and sometimes to Cú Chulainn when he is full of warlike fury. We can compare it with the description of Fer Caille (the Man of the Woods) in the *Destruction of the House of Da Derga:* "His hair was stiff and frizzled. You could have emptied a bag full of wild apples over his head and not one would have fallen to the ground, but stuck instead to his hair." (J. Markale, *L'Épopée celtique d'Irlande*, p. 179)

[55]G. Dottin, *L'Épopée irlandaise*, pp. 182-3.

[56]The Book of Lismore, *Revue celtique*, xxxiii, 175. Sec J. Markale, *L'Épopée celtique d'Irlande*, p. 163.

[57]R. Chauvire, *Contes Ossianiques*, pp. 102-6.

[58]D'Arbois de Jubainville, *Les Druides et les dieux celtiques à formes d'animaux*, p. 150, concerning ii Samuel, xvii, 8.

[59]G. Dottin, *La Langue gauloise*, p. 93.

[60]For all matters relating to Math's name, see W. J. Gruffydd, *Math vab Mathonwy*, pp. 168-72.

[61]"Lewis ap Guern verch Morgan ab Risart a John ab Ywel ab Mathon" according to an old genealogy, (*Cymru*, i, p. 332).

[62]G. Dottin, *La Langue gauloise*, p. 93. In modern Welsh it would be Arthien and in Gaelic Artigan.

[63]Cuneglassus, under his Welsh name Cynlas ab Cynan, appears in Arthurian legend. He takes part in the hunt for Twrch Trwyth and is killed by the boar.

[64]J. Loth, *Mabinogion*, i, 364. The Irish hero Oengus mac Oc, one of the Tuatha Dé Danann, possesses a similar cloak. See J. Markale, *L'Épopée celtique d'Irlande*, p. 47 and p. 159.

[65]J. Markale, *L'Épopée celtique d'Irlande*, pp. 108-14.

[66]As I have shown in *L'Épopée celtique en Bretagne*, pp. 208-9, and in *Women of the Celts*.

[67]It may seem surprising that I should have ommitted the two Welsh tales *Kulhwch and Olwen* and *Peredur* from this analysis, especially as they are among the oldest Arthurian stories. But I have examined them in some detail in *L'Épopée celtique en Bretagne*, pp. 137-52, and 182-209. In the following chapter, which is an attempt to reconstruct the original myth of Arthur, I have had cause to quote several times from these two works.

Chapter 6. The Early Saga Of Arthur

[1]Because the material for this reconstruction has been drawn from so many different sources, I have differentiated the various sections in the following way: those passages in ordinary type are résumés or adaptations of existing manuscripts; the indented paragraphs are direct quotations and the passages in italics are suggested links between the various episodes. I have stuck to Welsh nomenclature as being the oldest.

[2]*Arthur and Gorlagon* is a 14th-century Latin text which appears to be a translation of a Welsh work. It is published by G. L. Kittredge, *Studies and Notes in Philosophy and Literature*, viii (Harvard University: Boston, 1903). Kittredge suggests that the name of the hero may mean wolf man or werwolf.

[3]This episode was suggested by poem xxx in the *Book of Taliesin*, which is entitled *Preiddieu Annwfn* (the Spoils of the Abyss) and by the tale of the cauldron of Diwrnach the Gael in *Kulhwch and Olwen*. The idea of Modron's marvellous island was borrowed from the Vita Merlini.

[4]*Historia Meriadoci*, an early 13th-century Latin text dedicated to Robert de Thorigny abbot of Mont-Saint-Michel (J. Douglas Bruce, *Hesperia* Gottingen, 1913). References to Rheged and Gwynned make it clear that this tale came from North Britain.

[5]Folk tale, Jones, *Welsh Bards*, p. 22.

[6]*Iolo Manuscripts*, p. 118. These are folk tales dating from earliest times.

[7]The fact that the author refers on several occasions to Breri, the *famous fabulator Bledhericus*, suggests that this work is drawn from Welsh sources.

[8]This episode was suggested by the *Wedding of Gawain*, an anonymous 14th-century ballad, Gower's *Confessio Amantis*, and one of Chaucer's tales.

[9]Owein's flock of ravens remain something of a mystery, although there was a legend that Morgan could turn into a bird, and the Irish tradition has Morrigan and her two sisters, Bodbh and Macha, who often appear as ravens. There is also an episode in the *Lancelot in Prose* where Urbain (or Uryen, Owein's father) appears as the defender of a ford who is protected by a flock of ravens and who tells Lancelot that one of the birds is his lady's sister.

[10]It appears to have been customary among the Celts, and more particularly among the Britons, to have a young man's hair cut for the first time by someone of rank.

[11]In this 14th-century English work, Gawain is the hero of the adventure. But in similar works the same adventure is attributed to Karadawc or even Lancelot, and it is definitely reminiscent of Cú Chulainn's exploits in the *Feast of Briciu*. So, since the legend obviously belongs to a very old Celtic tradition, there is no reason why Arthur should not become the hero instead.

[12]The old Welsh tradition contains no references at all to any kind of family relationship between Arthur and Medrawt. Their rivalry, which was probably based on historical reality, is solely concerned with the leadership of the armed forces.

[13]Breton folk tale collected by Anatole Le Braz, *Annales de Bretagne*, xi (1895-1896), p. 193.

PART III. Waiting for Arthur

Chapter 7. The Specific Qualities of the Celts

[1]It was in this sense that I gave the title *L'Impossible Royaume d'Irlande* to a series of broadcasts for the O.R.T.F. in 1971, in an attempt to convey the paradox of constant dreams of a unity never achieved.

[2]Georges Dumezil, *La Religion romaine archaique*, 2nd amended ed. (Payot: Paris, 1974).

[3]The war between the Romans and the Sabines appears to be a historical myth of the war of the Ases and the Vanes and should therefore be approached with some reservations. Indeed the greater part of early Roman history is a historic account of mythical events.

[4]For example, the Bituriges tried to form a confederation under them; the Aedui and the Arveroni held economic control of other states and the Veneti led an Armorican federation based on shipping.

[5]The word *nemeton* contains the root *nem* which gave rise to the Breton *neñv* meaning the heavens, in the sense of the Other World rather than the sky.

[6]See J. Markale, *Broceliande ou la forêt bretonne, Cahiers du Pays de Baud* no. 1, 1971.

[7]The *fhine* took various forms depending on the groups of relatives involved. The *Gelfhine* or "family of the hand" included father, son, grandson, great grandson and great great grandson. The *Derbfhine* included both the direct line and the uncle, first cousin and first cousin's son. The *Iarfhine* included the direct line for three generations and the great uncle, his son and grandson. The *Indfhine* included the direct line for three generations, the great great uncle, his son and grandson. All these kinsmen were *agnats*, but only the members of the *Gelfhine* and the *Derbfhine* were strictly speaking family. There was also a curious institution called the *Glas fhine*. When a foreigner with no relatives in Ireland married a woman, his offspring were included in his wife's family which was given the name *Glas fhine*, or "blue family" because he had come over the blue sea. It was then said that the marriage belonged to the husband but the goods to the wife. Whatever form it took, the *fhine* created a state of permanent solidarity among its members. The whole *fhine* was responsible for any crime committed by one of its members and for whatever compensation had to be paid. Within the *fhine*, murder was forbidden, and property collectively owned. Any decisions affecting the *fhine* had to be taken by all the members although the chief could be given a mandate to take whatever steps

were necessary for the daily running of the group. That is why the chief gradually assumed a political, judicial and military role both within his immediate family and in the wider context of the *tuath*. This system was also in operation in Gaul and in Arthurian Britain. The goods of the family were called the *baile* in Gaelic, a word which passed into French as *bailliage* and can also be seen in the practice of *bail*. The Welsh family was called a *teulu*, a word which survived into the Middle Ages in the form of *penteulu*, the steward of the royal household. *Teulu*, which came from the word *teu* or *ty* meaning house, literally means "host of the house."

[8]The word clan is a Gaelic term used by ethnologists to denote a pseudo-familial system in operation in so-called primitive societies. Smaller than a tribe, the clan is based on descent from a common ancestor and not on the political and territorial considerations which affect the tribe. From a legal point of view, the clan is characterized by solidarity in the seeking of vengeance and by the fact that murder within the clan is forbidden. Land is communally owned, and the clan totem brings religious unity. Unlike the well-defined totemism of the American Indian and the Eskimo, however, the Celtic version appears to consist mainly in the animal names given to semi-legendary chiefs and heroes. The clan was based on blood brotherhood which meant not only blood relationships but relationships formed with strangers by taking a blood oath and drinking each other's blood. Sexual relationships between members of the clan are forbidden. But here any comparison between the Celtic clan and the clans seen outside Europe ends. The basic social unit of the Celts remained the family as defined by the *fhine*, and the Gaelic word clan came to be used for descendants, as in the clan Morna and the clan Goll in the epic of Leinster.

[9]In the sense that it formed a group of several families, the *tuath* can best be compared with the tribe. In Wales where peoples tended to be more settled in one place, a social body of this kind was called a *cantrev*, or "one hundred dwellings" from the prefix *treb-* found in the Breton names Trebeurden, Trehorenteuc used to denote the extent of a parish. In Gaul the nearest equivalent of the *tuath* in Gallo-Roman times was the group of people known as *Pagi*, a *pagus* being a number of families settled in one place with an elected leader. The members of the *tuath*, *cantrev* or *pagus* were therefore supposedly members of one extended family, living in one place and looking after one herd. They may also have had their own divinities apart from the gods of the Druids which were supranational. As agriculture developed, the criterion of kindred probably gave way to territorial considerations when it came to defining the *tuath*.

[10]J. Markale, *L'Épopée celtique d'Irlande*, pp. 88-95 and 141-2.

[11]J. Markale, *op. cit.*, pp. 195-6.

[12]See the chapter in my *Les Celtes* on Rome and the Celtic epic, pp. 65-90.

[13]G. Dumezil, *La Religion romaine archaique*, pp. 129-30. See also Dumezil, *Horace et les Curiaces*, pp. 65-8 where he discusses similar connexions and differences between the Romans and the Celts. There is nothing to add to Dumezil's comparison of the two civilizations, except perhaps to point out that, unlike the Indians, the Celts did not believe in a universal soul but in the value of individual life within the community.

[14]Albert Grenier, *Les Gaulois*, 2nd ed. (Payot: Paris, 1970), p. 158.

[15]*Ogam*, XI, 63, Scatach is the Scots warrior woman who taught Cú Chulainn the art of war.

[16]See the exploits of Cú Chulainn in "the Cú Chulainn cycle," the third part of my *L'Épopée celtique d'Irlande*, pp. 75-137.

[17]Myles Dillon, *The Celtic Realms*, pp. 101-2.

[18]A. Grenier, *Les Gaulois*, pp. 182-3.

[19]In certain parts of France, like le Velay, the value of farms is still measured in cattle rather than the extent of land.

Chapter 8. Arthur's Legacy

[1]J. Markale, *L'Épopée celtique d'Irlande*, pp. 171-84.

[2]Gérard Mendel, *Pour une autre société*, (Payot: Paris, 1975), p. 147.

[3]To my everlasting shame, I am forced to use Latin words here, since saying that the factor leads to the future means nothing in English.

[4]G. Mendel, *Pour une autre société*, pp. 100-1.

[5]See Pierre-Jakez Helias' excellent book *Le Cheval d'orgueil, mémoires d'un Breton du pays bigouden* (Plon: Paris, 1975). This work makes no claims, nor does it express any regrets, but it provides a remarkable account of peasant life with all its advantages and its inconveniences in a part of France which is little known.

[6]G. Mendel, *Pour une autre societe*, pp. 100-1.

Select Bibliography

Arbois de Jubainville, H. d', *Cours de littérature celtique*, 12 vols. Paris, 1883-1902
Ashe, G. *From Caesar to Arthur*, London, 1960
Ashe, G. *The Quest for Arthur's Britain*, London, 1973
Baring-Gould, S. and Fisher, J. *Lives of the British Saints*, 7 vols. London, 1957-1966
Barber, R. W. *Arthur of Albion*, London-New York, 1961
Bromwich, R. *The Early Culture of North-west Europe*, Cambridge, 1950
Bromwich, R. *Trioedd Ynys Prydein*, Cardiff, 1961
Bruce, J. D. *The Evolution of Arthurian Romance*, 1958
Chadwick, N. K. *Celtic Britain*, London, 1964
Chambers, E. K. *Arthur of Britain*, New York, 1964
Collingwood, F. G. and Myres, J. *Roman Britain*, Oxford, 1936
Collingwood, F. G. and Wright, R. *The Roman Inscriptions of Britain*, 1965
Dillon, M. *The Cycle of the Kings*, Oxford, 1946
Dillon, M. and Chadwick, N. *The Celtic Realms*, 1967
Dottin, G. *L'Épopée irlandaise*, Paris, 1931
Faral, E. *La Legende arthurienne*, 3 vols. Paris, 1929
Frappier, J. *Études sur Yvain*, Paris, 1969
Frappier, J. *Études sur la mort, le Roi Arthur*, Paris, 1936
Frazer, J. *Les Origines magiques de la Royauté*, Paris, 1920
Frazer, J. *Le Totémisme*, Paris, 1938
Gantz, J. (transl.) *The Mabinogion*, 1976
Grenier, A. *Les Gaulois*, Paris, 1970
Gruffydd, W. J. *Math ab Mathonwy*, Cardiff, 1928
Harvey, J. *The Plantagenets*, London, 1948
Hubert, H. *Les Celtes*, 2 vol. Paris, 1932
Jackson, K. H. *Language and History in Early Britain*, Edinburgh, 1953
Jackson, K. H. *The Oldest Irish Tradition*, Cambridge, 1964
Jaffray, R. *King Arthur and the Holy Grail*, 1928
Jones, J. M. *Taliesin*, 1918
Jones, W. L. *King Arthur in History and Legend*, 1911

Joyce, P. W. *Old Celtic Romances*, London, 1914
Jullian, C. *Histoire de la Gaule*, 8 vols. Paris, 1908-1926
Kohler, E. *L'Aventure chevaleresque*, Paris, 1974
Leroux, F. *Les Druides*, Paris, 1961
Lindsay, J. *Arthur and His Times*, 1966
Loomis, R. S. *Wales and Arthurian Legend*, Cardiff, 1956
Loomis, R. S. *Celtic Myth in Arthurian Romances*, 1927
Loomis, R. S. *Arthurian Literature in the Middle Ages*, Oxford, 1959
Lot, F. *Études sur le Lancelot en Prose*, Paris, 1918
Lot, F. *Nennius et l'Historia Brittonum*, Paris, 1934
Loth, J. *L'Emigration bretonne en Armorique*, Paris, 1883
Loth, J. *Contribution a l'étude des romans de la Table Ronde*, Paris, 1912
Loth, J. *Les Mabinogion*, 2 vols. Paris, 1913
MacNeill, E. *Celtic Ireland*, Dublin, 1921
Marx, J. *La Légende arthurienne et le Graal*, Paris, 1952
Marx, J. *Nouvelles recherches sur la littérature arthurienne*, Paris, 1970
Markale, J. *Les Celtes et la Civilisation celtique*, Paris, 1969
Markale, J. *L'Épopée celtique d'Irlande*, Paris, 1971
Markale, J. *L'Épopée celtique en Bretagne*, Paris, 1971, 1975
Markale, J. *Women of the Celts*, London, 1975
Markale, J. *La Tradition celtique en Bretagne armoricaine*, Paris, 1975
Meyer, K. *The Voyage of Bran*, Dublin, 1895-1897
Meyer, K. *Fianaigecht*, Dublin, 1901
Newstead, H. *Bran the Blessed in Arthurian Romance*, 1939
O'Curry, E. *On the Manners and Customs of the Ancient Irish*, 1873
O'Grady, S. *Silva Gadelica*, 2 vols. London, 1892.
Paris, P. *Les Romans de la Table Ronde*, Paris, 1868-1877
Rhŷs, J. *Celtic Britain*, London, 1904
Rhŷs, J. *Studies in the Arthurian Legend*, 1891
Rhŷs, J. *Celtic Folklore*, Oxford, 1901
Skene, W. F. *The Four Ancient Books of Wales*, 2 vols. Edinburgh, 1868
Vries, J. de, *Keltische Religion*, Stuttgart, 1961
Weston, J. *The Legend of Gawain*, London, 1897
Weston, J. *The Legend of Sir Lancelot du Lac*, London, 1901
Weston, J. *The Legend of Sir Perceval*, London, 1906
Weston, J. *From Ritual to Romance*, London, 1920
Williams, I. *Lectures on Early Welsh Poetry*, Dublin, 1944
Williams, I. *Canu Aneirin*, Cardiff, 1938
Williams, I. *Canu Llywarch-Hen*, Cardiff, 1935
Williams, I. *Canu Taliesin*, Cardiff, 1960
Zumthor, P. *Le Prophète Merlin*, Lausanne, 1943

Periodicals: *Revue celtique, Études celtiques, Annales de Bretagne, Ogam, Eriu, Bulletin of the Board of Celtic Studies, Speculum, Romania, Revue des Traditions Populaires, Bulletin bibliographique de la Société arthurienne internationale.*

Index

Alternative names are indicated by the symbol '@' (alias); 's / o' and 'd / o' are used to indicate son of, and daughter of. Where it cannot be established that variants of a name clearly refer to one and the same person, (e.g. Padern and Padarn), both names have been variously indexed. In cases where an alternative name is given (e.g. Guinevere and Gwenhwyvar), readers should also consult the entry given as the alternative for further page references.
The letter-by-letter system of alphabetization has been adopted.

Absalon, 131
Accolon, 45-6
Adam of Domerham, 66, 67
a Deo per Populum, 56, 202
Adultery, 129-33
Adventures of Art, Son of Conn, 31-2, 127
Aed s / o Daire the Red, 138, 147
Aeduan peoples, 197
Aes Dana, 186
Afang Du, 136
Agravadain, 35
Agravain, 40-1, 72
Agricola, 78
Ailill, King, 127-8
Airthne, 118-19
Alain, 33
Alexander, the Great, 14, 187
Amangon, King, 31
Amaoren, King, 131
Ambigatus (Livy), 112
Ambiorix, 196
Ambrosius, the orphan, 90, 93-4

Ambrosius Aurelianus (@ Emrys
    Gwledig), 95-6, 99-100, 108, 151
Ambrosius Aurelius, 96
Amaethon, 132
Amfortas, King, 32
Amr s / o Arthur (@ Anir), 104-5, 133, 169-70
Analogy, Celtic sense of, 192, 200
Anir (@ Amr) s / o Arthur, 104-5, 133, 169-70
Annals of Cambria, 66, 98, 100, 101
Annals of Tigernach, 66, 101
Annals of Waverly, 67
Antonius Pius, 79
Antor, 35
ar, significance of word, 146
Arcturus, significance of name, 145-6
Ard ri, title of, 185, 194
Arianrod, 132
Art s / o Conn, 127
Arthur:
    and the dragon, 172
    and the green giant, 170-1
    as a God, 144-7

battles in which involved, 98, 151
children of, 104-5, 169-70
companions of, 133-7
country wide use of name for places, 106-7
death of, 40-2, 173
derivation of name, 95, 100-1, 144-6
'discovery' of body of, 64-9
first appearance of, 96
historical accounts of, 97-109
in prison, 171
invasion of Europe by, 101-2, 106, 172
legacy of, 202-20
marries Guinevere, 35
mistresses of, 105
principal seats of government of, 105
retrieves the sword Escalibur, 35
similarities with Finn, 143-4
titles of, discussed, 98-9, 105-6
tour of Ireland by, 106
Arthur and Gorlagon, 153
Arthur of Albion (Barber), 53, 65
Arthur I, King of Brittany, 63
Arthurian cults:
  chivalry, 70-4
  legend, 23, 81-2
  myth, 111-47:
    introduction, 111-12
    Arthur's companions, 133-7
    Arthur, the God, 144-7
    political aspects, 113-21
    similar legends, 137-44
    theme of sovereignty, 121-9
    unfaithful queen, 129-33
Arthur of Britain (a French romance), 26
Artogenos, 145
Ashe, Geoffrey, 66, 107, 145
Asvamedha ritual, 125
Atrebates tribe, 183
Aue, Hartmann von, 25
Augustine, St, 55
Avallach, *see* Isle of Avalon
Avalon, *see* Isle of Avalon
Aventure Chevaleresque, L', (Köhler), 49, 58, 59, 71
Averni tribe, 196

Badon Hill, battle of, 97-8, 109, 121, 145
Ban, King of Benoic, 35-6
Barbarossa, Frederick, 53
Barber, Richard, 53, 65
Bath, 80
Battle of Mag-Tured, 119
Battles fought by Arthur, 98, 151
Baudemagu, King (@Bran of the Plain), 25-6
Bayeux, 63
Bear, significance of the, 144-5, 184
Bede, Adam, 82, 90-2, 96, 97
Bedier, Joseph, 52
Bedivere (@Bedwyr), 29, 33
Bedwini, 136
Bedwyr s/o Bridlaw (@Bedivere), 84, 103, 105,

109, 130, 133-4, 138, 147, 149-54, 165, 168-72
Ben Culbain, boar of, 142
Benoist, Jean-Marie, 15
Bernard of Ventadour, 62
Béroul, 28-9
Birth of Conchobar, 195, 197
Birth of Gawain, 123
Bituriges peoples, 112, 197
Black Book of Carmarthen, 109, 133-6, 165, 170
Black Druid (Fir Doirche), 27, 142-3
Blaise, 33-4
Blanchefleur, 30
Blathnait (Blodeuwedd), 26, 129
Bleheri, 44, 63
Blihis Bliheris, 31
Blodeuwedd (@Blathnait), 26, 129
Boar, hunt of the wild, 68-9, 139-42, 166-8
Bodmin, 53
Bodr s/o Odin, 53
Bohort, King of Gaunes, 35-6
Bohort s/o Bohort, 36-42, 72
Boii tribe, 182
Book of Armagh, The, 69
Book of Lancelot, 36
Book of Leinster, 187
Boudicca, Queen, 78, 188, 189
Bran de Lis, 31
Brangore, King, 38
Bran of the Plain (@Baudemagu), 26
Bran s/o Llyr, 151
Branwen, Daughter of Llyr, 117, 151
Breat, Chief, 154
Brennus, 197
Bres, King of Tuatha dé Danann, 117, 119
Briciu, 133, 147
Bridge of the Sword, 25
Bridget, St (of Ireland), 68
Bridge Under The Water, 25
Brigantes, 78, 79, 112
Brien de la Gastine, 44
Britain:
  Celtic, 80-9
  Roman, 78-80
  the new kings of, 90-6
Britannia (Camden), 66
Britannia Prima, 79
Britannia Secunda, 79, 100, 108
Brithem Rig, 185
Brittany, British emigration to, 91
Broceliande Forest, 28
Bron, the Fisher King, 33-4 *see also* Fisher King
Brun of Morrois, 26
Brunissen, 44
Brycham, King, 150
Burmaltus (@Burmald), 27

Cadbury, *see* Camaalot
Cad Goddeu, 199
Cadoc, St, 103
Caen, 63
Caerlion, *see* Carlion

Caesar, Julius, 77
Cailte, 141
Caledvwlch, the sword, 27
Calogrenant, 28
Camall s/o Riagall, 119
Camaalot, 36, 38-9, 87, 107
Camille, the enchantress, 37
Camlaan, battle of, 41, 53, 98, 101, 110, 136, 173
Canterbury, 80
Capitalism, 215-16
Caracalla, 79
Cardawc ab Cynfelyn, see Caratacus
Caradawc s/o Bran, 112
Caradoc of Llancarvan, 26, 37, 49, 50, 51, 102, 103
Carannawg, 150-1
Carannog, St, 104
Caratacus, King 78, 112
Cardigan, 24
Carduel (Carlisle), 27-8, 30, 34, 36, 43, 80
Carhays, Cornwall, 35
Carlion, 30, 35, 100, 108, 112, 151, 157, 159, 163
Carlisle (Carduel), 27, 28, 30, 34, 36, 43, 80
Carmelide, 37
Carnutes, 196
Carnwennan, the knife, 27
Carodus Biebras, 35
Carrum, 150-1
Cartismandua, Queen, 78, 112, 188
Cas mac Glais, 69
Cassivellaunus, 77,189
Castle Dore, 87
Castle of Maidens, 157
Castle of Marvels, 160-1
Cathba, the Druid, 117
Cattawg, 150, 152
Cattle rustling, 103
Catuvolcus, 196
Cavalry, Arthur's use of, 100, 108
Cele, 186
Celsine, 186
Celtic Britain, 80-9
Celtic Myth (Loomis), 26
Celts, specific qualities of, 177-201: Roman and Celtic Societies compared, 178-93
   Contribution of the Celts, 193-201
Chadwick, Nora, 81, 83
Chanson de Guillaume, 52
Chanson de Roland, 17-18, 52
Chansons de Geste, 49, 52-3, 67, 71
Charlemagne, 81, 202
Charles V, King of France, 202
Chasse, La, au Blanc Porc, 29
Chaucer, 121
Che, see Kai
Cheptel Contracts, 85-6, 184
Chessboards, 128-9, 130-1, 163, 164
Chester, 79, 109
Chevalier, Le, a la Charrette, see Lancelot (or Le Chevalier etc.)
Childhood of Finn, The, 140, 189
Child sacrifice, 92-3

Chrétien de Troyes, 23-32, 48, 52, 63, 126, 130
Chronicum Anglicanum (Ralph of Cogge-shall), 66
Civil War in France, The (Marx), 212
Classlessness of the Celts, 214
Claudas of the Waste Land, 36
Cligès ou la Fausse Morte (Chrétien), 25
Cnucha, battle of, 138
Coiced period, 113
Coirpe, 119
Colchester, 79
Commius the Atrebatian, 77
Commune de Paris, 212-13
Compensation, Celtic view on, 198
Conaire the Great, 116, 204
Conchobar mac Nessa, King (of Ulster), 106, 117, 125, 184, 187, 195, 197
Concubinage, 188
Confessio Amantis (Gower), 121
Conn, 32, 124-5, 127
Conquest of Gaul, The (tr. Handford), 77
Constance, wife of Geoffrey Plantagenet, 63
Continuations, 31
Corbenic (the Grail Castle), 31, 34, 38-9
Coritani tribe, 79
Cormac mac Airt, High King, 138
Cormac s/o Lugaid, 116-17, 127
Cornovi tribe, 79, 183
Courtly love, concept of, 24, 58-61
Courtship of Etaine, 128, 137
Crone, Die (a German romance), 26
Cú Chulainn, 26, 87, 126, 131, 184, 189, 197
Culture, Celtic, 199-200
Cuneglassus, King, 145
Cunneda, 68-9, 82, 150
Curoi, God of the Other World, 26-7
Cynfelyn Wledig, 112
Cyrano de Bergerac, 203-4

Dalourous Guard, Castle of, 36-7
Damas, 45-6
d'Arbois de Jubainville, 144
Dark Ages, beginning of, 80-90
David, St (of Wales), 68
De Antiquitate Glastoniensis Ecclesiae (William of Malmesbury), 68
Death of King Arthur, The, 40, 72
De Civitate Dei (St Augustine), 55
De Excidio Britanniae (Gildas), 82, 91, 97
Democracy, 219
De Ortu Walwani, 149, 157
Derbfhine, 114, 193-4
Diane de Poitiers, 131
Diarmaid and Grainne, 139
Diarmaid s/o O'Duibhne, 127, 132, 142, 147
Diderot, 55, 117
Didot-Perceval, 33-4
Dillus Varvawc, 168
Dinas Emrys, 92-3
Dinas Powys, 87, 89
Dindraethou, 150

Diodorus, 14
Divorce, 188
d'Oberg, Eilhart, 28
Dobunni tribe, 79
Dodinel, 38
Dolorous Tower, 37
Domina, concept of, 58, 60
Don d/o Mathonwy, 132
Dover, 80
Dream of Rhonabwy, The, 99, 121, 128, 135, 163-4
Droit de Cuissage, practice of, 125
Druids, 27, 54, 56, 68, 78, 84, 117-18, 132, 136, 180-1, 190, 195
Drunkenness of Ulstermen, The, 128, 195
Drutwas s/o Tryphun, 166
Dumezil, Georges, 115, 178, 190
Dumnorix, 197-8
Durmart the Welshman, 26

Eagle of Gwernabwy, 158
Early Brittany (Chadwick), 83
Eastbourne, 68
Eburones tribe, 196
Edern (@Yder), 24, 126, 135
Edern s/o Nudd, 52, 84, 150, 165, 169, 172
Education of Cú Chulainn, 189
Edward I, King of England, 56, 67
Edward II, King of England, 51
Edward III, King of England, 67
Edward the Confessor, 51
Efflam, St, 104
Efflam, the Hermit, 172
Eiddoel, 157
Elaine, 35, 38-9
Eleanor of Aquitaine, 47, 48, 53, 61, 62, 63, 73
Elucidation, 31
Emrys Gwledig (@Ambrosius Aurelianus), 95-6, 108, 151
Engels, 15-16
Enkidon, 124
Eochaid Aireainn, King, 137
Eochaid Muigmdeon, King, 123
Eporedorix, 145
Érec et Énide (Chrétien), 23-5, 58, 116, 135
Escalibur, 35, 41, 46, 67, 106, 131 *see also* Kaledfoulch
Esprit des Lois, L', (Montesquieu), 205
Essyllt, 149
Etaine, wife of Eochaid Aireainn, 26, 128, 129
Etaine, wife of Mider, 26, 137, 138
Etats et Empires du Soleil, The (Cyrano), 203
Evallack, King (@Nascien), 34
Exeter, 80

Failbe, 140
Fal, stone of, 34
Falerin, 26
Fate of the Children of Tuiren, The, 32
Feast of Briciu, 43, 147

Fenice, Queen, 26
Fergus mac Roig, King, 117
Festus, 179
Fetiales, 183
Fhine, 114, 116, 183-4, 193-6
Fiana warriors, 138-42, 198
Fidchell, 128
Fili, 199
Fine amor, 24, 58, 59, 61, 62
Finn, King of the Fiana, 27, 126, 131, 138-44, 147, 184, 198
Finn mac Cumail, 138
Finnabair d/o (Queen) Mebdh, 123
Fir Doirche, *see* Black Druid
Fisher King, 30-4, 38-43, 116
Flaithi, 186
Flamen Dialis, 179-80
Flamines, 179
Flavia Caesariensis, 79
Florence (Italy), 26
Formael, the boar, 140-1, 147
Forts, Celtic, 87-9
Fostering, 189, 194, 199
Fourier, Charles, 209-14
Fourth Continuation, 32
François I, King, 131
Frolle, Duke, 35, 39
From Caesar to Arthur (Ashe), 107, 145
Fuamnach, 137

Galahad, 38-40, 72
Galehaut, Lord of the Far Isles, 37-8
Galessin, Duke of Clarence, 37
Gallic Wars, 197
Galvagnus (@ Gawain), 27
Galvariun (@ Gauvarien), 27
Gamal s/o Figal, 119
Gargantua, the giant, 46, 47, 203
Gargantua, 203
Gasozein, 26
Gautier de Montbeliard, 32
Gautier of Oxford, 49-51
Gauvarien (@ Galvarian), 27
Gawain (@ Galvagnus; Gwalchmai), 24-46, 58, 72-3, 122, 130-4, 157, 160-2, 165, 169-72
Gawain and the Magic Chessboard, 129, 130
Geisa, 116
Generalship, 196-7
Genos, 114-18, 183-4
Geoffrey, Seneschal of France, 62
Geoffrey of Monmouth, 23, 45, 49-51, 60, 63, 93-6, 102, 138, 146
Geoffrey Plantagenet, 63, 73
Gerbet de Montreuil, 32
Geraint s/o Erbin, 99
Gereint and Enid, 25, 99, 126, 135
Germanus, St (of Auxerre), 85, 90, 95-6, 118
Gildas, 26-7, 68, 82, 84, 90-1, 97, 103, 110, 155, 162, 169
Gilgamesh, 124
Gilvaethwy s/o Don, 24, 132, 173

Giraldus Cambrensis, 62-7, 125
Girflet (@ Gilvaethwy), 24
Girflet s/o Do, 41-2
Glasteing, 68-9
Glastonbury Abbey (Urbs Vitrae), 26, 32, 42, 43, 64-9
Glewlwyt Gafaelfawr, 120, 130, 136, 150, 165, 167, 173
Gloucester, 79, 84
Gododdin (Aneurin), 83, 99, 107
Goeu s/o Kustennin, 165, 171
Goewin, 132-3
Gog and Magog, 46
Goll, 138, 147
Gorddu d/o Gorwena, 161
Goreu s/o Kustennin, 105
Gorre, Kingdom of, 25-6, 137, 143
Gottfried of Strasburg, 28
Grad Fene, 186
Graelent-Meur, 29
Grail, 31-6, 39, 43
Grainne, 127, 129, 131-2, 142
Grandgousier, 203
Great Wall of China, The (Kafka), 207
Green Knight, The, 171
Grenier, Albert, 196, 199
Gronw Pebyr, 26
Gruffydd, 154
Gruffydd, W.J., 144
Grugyn Gwrych Ereint, 167
Guenloie (@ Guinevere), 123
Guennuera (@ Guinevere), 123
Guennevar (@ Guinevere), 27
Guerrehes, 41
Guigomar, 24, 69
Guinevere, Queen (@ Guennevar; Gwenhwyvar; Guennuera; Guenloie; Gwendolen; Winlogee), 24-29, 35-44, 58-61, 73, 101, 121, 123, 125-6, 128-9, 138, 143
    for other references see Gwenhwyvar
Guinnion, battle of, 109
Guorthemir s/o Vortigern, 92, 94
Gurgalan, King, 42
Guyomard, 36
Gwadre s/o Arthur, 167, 169
Gwalchmai, *see* Gawain
Gweir s/o Gweiryoedd, 153-4
Gwen, meaning of, 123
Gwendolen (@ Guinevere), 123
Gwenhwyvar (@ Guinevere), 27, 101, 123, 126, 156-62, 165, 169-73
    for other references see Guinevere
Gwen Pendragon, 171
Gwladys d/o Brycham, 150
Gwrgwallawn, 153
Gwrhyr Gwalstawt Ieithoed, 130, 135, 153, 157-8 166
Gwrthevyr, 92
Gwrtheyrn Gwrteneu (@ Vortigern), 82
Gwyddel, origin of the nickname, 106
Gwyddyon, the magician, 24, 132, 134
Gwynn, s/o Nudd, 52, 84, 135, 150, 161, 164, 167

Gwynnlwy, King of Glamorgan, 150
Gwythyr s/o Greidyawlm, 161, 164
Gywar, 149

Hades, the god, 26
Hadrian, Emperor, 79
Hadwita of Gloucester, 67
Hector, 38-41
Hegel, 19, 209
Henbeddestyr, 136
Hengist, 90-1, 94, 151
Henry II, King of England, 49-51, 54, 57, 61-4, 131, 185, 202
Henry III, King of England, 56
Henry de Sully, Prior of Bermondsey, 66
Henry of Huntingdon, 50
Henwas Adeinawc, 136, 150, 165
Henwen (a sow), 154-5
Herodotus, 14
Hiruath, King, 69
Histoire de Merlin (Robert de Boron), 32-3
Historia Brittonum (Nennius), 69, 82, 83, 84, 90, 92, 93, 98, 100, 139, 151, 162, 164, 166, 169, 170
Historia Regnum Britanniae (also known as *Prophecies of Merlin* (Geoffrey of Monmouth), 17, 23, 29, 50, 61, 93
History of the English Church and People, The (Bede), 82, 91
Hoel, 35
Honorius, Emperor, 81
Horsa, 90-1, 94
Hueil s/o Kaw, 102-5, 109, 138, 150, 155
Hunt from the Sidh of Beautiful Women, The, 140
Hygwydd, 161

Iceni tribe, 78
Ifor, 154
Iliad, 18
Indo-European languages, 114-16
Infidelity, 129-33
Infirmity, Celtic attitude towards the plight of, 198-9
Inis Avallon, 65
Inis Gutrin, 65
Iolo Manuscripts, 155, 166, 171
Irish, emigration of, 80-1, 90-1
Isabel of Angoulême, 67
Isabella, Queen (of England), 51
Ischtar, 124
Isdermus (@ Yder), 27
Iseult, 129
Isle of Avalon, 34, 41, 65-6, 68, 102, 173
Ivanhoe (Scott), 51

Jauffre, 44
Jesus of Nazareth, 14, 97
Jocasta, 124
John, King of England, 63-4, 67

John of Salisbury, 54-64
Joseph (Robert de Boron), 32
Joseph of Arimathea, 32, 34, 42
Josephus, 34
Jus primae noctis, practice of, 125

Kachmwri, 161
Kadwy, King, 150
Kaer Gutrin, 88
Kaerlion, *see* Carlion
Kaer Loyw, witches of, 160-1
Kai (@ Che), 24-38, 43, 58, 84, 103, 105, 109, 121,
    129-34, 147, 149-50, 154, 157-62, 165, 168-72
Kai s/o Kynyr, 149
Kaledfoulch, Arthur's sword, 106, 146, 153-4,
    165, 173
    see also Escalibur
Kamlann, *see* Camlann
Karadawe Vreichvras, 121
Karadawg, King, 154
Karadawg, the giant, 165
Karnwennan, Arthur's knife, 161
Kentigern, St, 83, 84
Keridwen, the goddess, 136, 151
Kernyw peoples, 183
Kingship:
    discussed, 113-21
    John of Salisbury on, 54-64
Knights, the age of chivalry and, 70-4
Knights Templar, 71
Köhler, Erich, 49, 58, 59, 71
Koll s/o Kollfrewi, 154
Konan IV of Brittany, 63
Kore, 26
Kreiddylat d/o Llud Llaw Ereint, 164-5
Kropotkin, 55
Kulhwch and Olwen, 27, 32, 69, 89, 106, 113,
    118, 128, 130, 133-6, 139, 140, 149, 152, 155,
    159, 161, 165-9
Kundry, 32
Kynddelic, 135
Kynon s/o Klydno, 162
Kynyr Keinvarvawc, 133

Lady of the Lake, *see* Vivienne
Lai de Lanval (Marie de France), 29
Lai de Tyrolet, 29, 32
Lancelot, 35-43, 58-9, 72-3, 130-1
Lancelot du Lac, 25-6
Lancelot du Lac (Bresson), 59
Lancelot en Prose, see Lancelot in Prose
Lancelot in Prose (or *Corpus Lancelot-Grail*),
    34, 42, 44, 45, 48, 52, 73, 105, 123, 126, 131,
    133, 135
Lancelot (or *Le Chavalier à la Charrette*), 25-7,
    58, 61, 101, 121, 126, 129, 130, 138
Lanzelet (Zatzikhoven), 26
Laudine, 28
Laws of the Celts, 186-7
Leenleawg, the Gael, 151, 154

Leodagan, King, 35
Levi-Strauss, Claude, 13
Libido, 216
Life after death, 191-2
Life of Saint Caronnog (Lifris), 104
Life of Saint Cadoc, The (Lifris), 103, 105
Life of St Padarn, 104, 150
Lifris, 103, 104, 105
Ligessauc, Chief, 103, 152
Lincoln, Alexander, Bp of, 50
Lincoln, city of, 79, 109
Lionel, 36-42, 72
Llacheu s/o Arthur, 105, 133, 134, 170
Lleu Llaw Gyffes, 26
Llogrin, the giant, 170
Llwch Llawynnawg, 165
Llywelyn ap Gruffydd, 67
Loegaire, King of All Ireland, 187
London, 35, 80
Loomis, R.S., 26
Lore, Queen of Cardigan, 45
Lot, Ferdinand, 69, 102
Loth of Orkney, 35
Louis VII, King of France, 61-2
Louis the Pious, 9
Lucan, 191
Lug, the Celtic god, 119-20, 125
Lugaid Laigde, 124
Lugaid mac Cuind, King of Tara, 116-17
Luned, 28, 162

Mabon, *see* Mobon
Macsen Wledig (@ Maxentius), 81
Madruc (@ Malduc), 26
Maelgwyn Guynedd, King, 82-3
Maelwas (@ Maheloas), 24, 26-7, 110, 130, 161,
    162
Magna Carta, 56-7, 202
Maheloas (@ Maelwas), 24, 26, 27
Maiden Castle, 84, 87
Maiden of Escalot, 40
Maiden of the Mule, 60
Malduc (@ Madruc), 26
Malehout, the Lady of, 37
Malory, Thomas, 29, 42, 45, 105, 135
Mananann, the god, 84
March s/o Meirchiawn, 149, 184
Mardawg, King, 165
Mardoc, City of, 27, 143
Marie de Champagne, 63
Marie de France, 29
Marriage contracts, 188
Marvellous King, The, 130-1
Marvels of Rigomer, The, 143, 170
Marx Est Mort (Benoist), 15
Marxism, 10-11, 16, 18, 209, 212-15
Mary, the Virgin, cult of, 60, 109, 162
Materialism and Empiriocriticism (Lenin), 15
Math s/o Mathonwy, 132-3, 136, 144-6
Mathgamnai, 144
Mathgawyn, 144

Mathghamhuin, 144
Mathilda, Queen, 53
Mathugenos, 144
Matrona, the goddess, 135
Matugenos, 145
Maxentius (@ Macsen Wledig), 81
Maxima Caesariensis, 79
Mebdh, Queen of Connaught, 127-9, 131, 138, 188
Medrawt, *see* Mordret
Meleagant, 25-6, 38, 60, 129-30, 137-8
Melusine, 67
Menawedd, 154
Mendel, Gérard, 214, 218
Menw s/o Teirgwaedd, 130, 136, 157, 166, 168
Meriadawg s/o Karadawg, 154
Meriadeuc, 44-5
Merlin, Myrddin, 50, 83
Merlin, the wizard, 32-6, 46, 83, 94, 96
Merlin, 57
Merlinus Ambrosius (@ Myrddin Emrys), 94
Merveilles de Rigomer, Les, 143, 170
Messiah, the myth of, 14
Mider, King of the Other World, 26-7, 137
Migration of British southwards, 83
Military Organization, Celtic, 190
Minstrel of Rheims, 62
Mirabilia, 104-5, 139
Mobon, s/o Modron, 154, 157-9, 165, 168
Modena Cathedral, 27, 51, 101, 123, 138, 165
Modron, 153-4, 157-9, 173
        see also Matrona
Monarchy, 196-7, 202-5
        see also Kingship
Mons Badonicus, battle of, 97-8, 109, 121, 145
Montesquieu, 55, 71, 204, 207-8
Morality, Fourier on, 211
Mordrain, King (@ Seraphe), 34
Mordret, 26, 33, 41-2, 53, 59-60, 98, 101-2, 105, 110, 112, 133, 138, 171-3
Morgan la Fée, 24, 34, 36-41, 45-6, 65,135
Morna tribe, 138
Mort du Roi Arthur, 59-60, 133, 138, 173
Morte d'Arthur (Malory), 29, 42, 45, 135
Morvran s/o Tegid, 136, 151, 173
Morwen, 154
Municipium, 80
Myrddin, the bard, 83
Myrddin Emrys (@ Merlinus Ambrosius), 94
Myths, research into, 13-14
Myvyian Archaeology of Wales, 101, 130, 161

Nantes, 24-5
Napoleon, 202
Nascien (@ Evallach), 34
Nennius, 82-3, 90-5, 98-100, 101, 139
Neodruidism, 113
Ness, 117
Newcastle, 80
Niall, King of the Nine Hostages, 123-4
Ninian, St, 84

Nodens, the god Nuada, 84, 117, 147
Noumena, Kant's theory of, 14
Nouveau Monde Amoureux (Fourier), 210
Nouvelle Héloise, La (Rousseau), 208
Nuada, King of De Danann, 84, 117, 147
Numa Pompilius, 179, 189
Nwirin (Aneurin), 84
Nynniaw, King, 155

Oath of fealty, 54, 58, 187-8
O'Baicsne tribe, 138, 140
Octha s/o Hengist, 98, 151
Odgar, King, 153
Odin, 147
Oedipus myth, 123-4
Oengus, 137, 142
Ogam, 195
Oisin, 27, 141-3, 184
Olwen d/o Yspaddaden Penkawr, 165
Oratory, 196
Ordovices, 78, 112, 144
Orgetorix, 197
Orwen d/o Karadawg, 154
Oscar, 141-2, 184
Osla Gyllellfawr (Big Knife), 136, 138, 151, 163-4
Otadini tribe, 79, 82-3
Ousel of Kilgwru, 157-8
Owein s/o Uryen, 83, 99, 128, 130, 159, 162-4
        see also Yvain
Owein (or *Lady of the Fountain*), 28, 120, 135, 162-4
Owl of Kwm Kawlwyt, 158

Padarn, St, 104
Padern, 150
Painful Tower, 165
Paris, Gaston, 52, 122
Paris Commune, 212-13
Parisi tribe, 79, 183
Parmenides, 15-16
Parzifal (Eschenbach), 32
Pascal, 12, 204
Passion in human nature, 210
Patrick, St (of Ireland), 68, 69
Patriotism, 197-8, 219
Pausanius, 14
Pebiaw, King, 155
Pelagianism, doctrine of, 85, 95
Pelagius, 68
Pelles, the Fisher King, 38
        see also Fisher King
Penalties, 198
Penn Annwfn, 153
Pensée, La (Althusser), 16
Perceval, 33-4, 39-42, 135
Perceval (or *Le Conte du Graal*), (Chrétien), 29-32, 60, 126, 130, 135
Peredur, 32, 43, 126, 128-30, 135, 159-61, 189
Peredux, 32

Perilous Bridge, 42
Perilous Seat, 33, 39-40, 146-7
Perlesvaux, 42-3, 116, 170
Persephone, 26
Phalanstère, 210-14
Pharsalia (Lucan), 191
Philip Augustus (of Brittany), 63
Picrochole, 203
Picts, 78-81, 90-1
Plantagenets, 49-54
Plot of the Long Knives, 94-5
Poitiers, 63
Policraticus (John of Salisbury), 54-9, 202
Political and Social structures, 113-16
Polygamy, 188
Pontifex, position of, 179-80
Populus versus Universitas, 55-9
Pour Marx (Althusser), 16
Prasugatus, King, 78
Procopius, 81
Prophecies of Merlin, see Historia Regnum
       Britanniae
Prophetic Ecstacy of the Phantom, 124
Proserpine, 26
Pryderi, King, 132
Prytwen (a magic shield), 146
Prytwen (Arthur's ship), 153, 167
Pwyll, King, 143
Pympfyddeilen, 170

Queen of Prowess, The, 124
Queenship, significance of, 121
       see also Kingship; Monarchy;
       Sovereignty
Quest for Arthur's Britain, The, (Ashe), 66-7
Quest for the Holy Grail, 39-42, 72, 135

Rabelais, 46-7, 203
Raid of Cualnge, 127, 131, 187, 189
Ralph of Coggeshall, 66
Raymond of Toulouse, 62
Reclus, Elisée, 55
Regni tribe, 78
Rex, position of, discussed, 179-80
Rhiannon, the mare-goddess, 143
Rhongomynyad, the spear, 27
Richard I, King of England, 56, 63, 66
Richmond, Count of, 51
Rion, the giant, 35-6
Ritta, the giant, 155-6
Robert, Count of Gloucester, 49-50
Robert de Boron, 32
Robespierre, 205, 207
Rochester, 80
Roland, 146
Roman Britain, 78-80
Romance of Durmart, 165
Romance of Jauffre, 44
Romance of Yder, 123, 169
Roman du Brut (tr. Wace), 23, 116

Round Table, fellowship of, 177-8
Rousseau, 55, 205-9, 214
Royaume de Gorre, 88

Sadv, 27, 142-3
Sagremor, 30, 33, 35, 38
St Albans, 80, 84
Saint-Just, 205, 207
Saint-Simon, 9
Saladin, Sultan, 62
Salmon of Llyn Llyw, 158
Sanddev Bryd Angel, 136, 173
Saxons, invasion by, 81, 90-1
Scott, Sir Walter, 51
Senche, the Druid, 195
Septimus Severus, 79
Seraphe, King (@ Mordrain), 34
Sexuality, 216
Sgitli Ysgawndroet, 136, 151
Siege of Dun Etair, 119
Silures, 78, 79, 112, 144
Sir Gawain and the Green Knight, 43
Sir Percivelle, 126
Slavery, 186
Social Contract (Rousseau), 205-9
Souls, City of, 42-3
Sovereignty discussed, 121-9, 156, 206
       see also Kingship, Monarchy;
              Queenship
Stag of Rhedenvre, 158
Stephen of Blois, 53, 63
Stonehenge, 182
Story of Merlin, The, 34
Story of Morgan and Arthur, The (Malory), 45
Strabo, 196, 197
Structural Anthropology (Lévi-Strauss), 13
Studies in Early British History (Chadwick),
       83

Taliesin, 151, 153-4, 199
Tancredi, King of Sicily, 67
Tara, 34, 113, 182, 185
Taulat de Ruginon, 44
Teutonic Knights, 71
Thanet, 90, 94
Theodosius, 81
Thomas, 28-9
Thomas Aquinas, St, 202
Thor, 147
Tiern, office of, 85-6
Tiethi Hen s/o Gwynhan, 136
Tintagel, 34, 43, 87
Topographia (Giraldus), 125
Tower of Glass, 65
Triads, 99, 101-3, 105, 113-14, 132, 134, 139
Trinovantes tribe, 79
Tristan s/o Tallwch, 149, 150
Tristan (Thomas), 156
Tristan and Iseult, 28-9, 58, 103, 131, 139
Tuatha, 114, 116, 184-5, 194, 196, 198, 208

242

Tuatha dé Danann, 117, 119, 132
Turlin, Heinrich von dem, 26
Turning Castle, 43
Twrch Trwyth, a boar, 166-8
Tyranny, John of Salisbury on, 57
Tyrolet, 29
Tyrr, 147
Tyrranus discussed, 82, 90, 95, 127

Unfaithfulness discussed, 129-33
Universitas versus Populus, 55-9
Urbain, *see* Uryen
Urbs Vitrea (Glastonbury), 27, 88
    see also Glastonbuty
Urien of Gorre, 35
Uryen, King, 28, 45, 46, 83, 130, 135
Uryen Rheged, Chief, 154
Uther Pendragon, 34-5, 145

Vedas, 113
Veneti rebellion, 77
Venta Silurnum, 79
Vercingetorix, 112, 189, 197
Vergobrets, 196
Vita Cadoci, 150, 152
Vita Carannogi, 151
Vita Gildae (Caradoc), 26, 102, 110, 138, 155, 168
Vita Merlini (Geoffrey of Monmouth), 45, 50, 94
Vita Paderni, 104, 150
Vivienne (The Lady of the Lake), 36-9, 46, 60
Vocabulaire de Institutions Indo-Européenes (Beneviste), 114
Volusenus, 77
Vortigern, Chief (@ Gwrtheyrn Gwrteneu), 34, 81-2, 85, 90-5, 118

Wace, Robert, 23
Wealth, how measured, 201
Wedding of Sir Gawain, The, 121, 122, 143
Weikos, 115-16
White Stag, custom of the, 24, 58
William the Conqueror, 51
William of Malmesbury, 50, 68
William of Tyre, 62
Winchester, 40, 80
Winlogee (@ Guinevere), 27, 123
    see also Guinevere
Women:
    place of in politics, 60-2
    situation of Celtic, 188-9
Work, attitude towards, 209-10
Wynebgwrthucher, the shield, 27

Yder (@ Edern; Isdermus), 24, 27, 37, 130
Yder, 143
Ydier of Cornwall, 35
Ygern, 34-5
Ynisgutrin, 68
York, 79
Yseult, 127
Yspaddaden Penkawr, 165
Yvain, s/o Uryen, 28, 35, 37, 38, 46, 135
    see also Owein
Yvain (Chrétien), 28
Yvain (or *Chevalier au Lion*) (Chrétien) 27, 28, 135

Zatzikhoven, Ulrich von, 26
Zimmer, 144